The PMI Guide to
BUSINESS ANALYSIS

Library of Congress Cataloging-in-Publication Data

Names: Project Management Institute, issuing body.
Title: The PMI guide to business analysis.
Description: Newtown Square, Pennsylvania : Project Management Institute,
    Inc., [2017] | Includes bibliographical references and index.
Identifiers: LCCN 2017052118 (print) | LCCN 2017054419 (ebook) | ISBN
    9781628254730 (ePub) | ISBN 9781628254747 (kindle) | ISBN 9781628254754
    (Web PDF) | ISBN 9781628251982 (pbk. : alk. paper)
Subjects: LCSH: Project management. | Business planning. | Decision making.
Classification: LCC HD69.P75 (ebook) | LCC HD69.P75 P5828 2017 (print) | DDC
    658.4/04--dc23
LC record available at https://lccn.loc.gov/2017052118

ISBN: 978-1-62825-198-2

Published by:
    Project Management Institute, Inc.
    14 Campus Boulevard
    Newtown Square, Pennsylvania 19073-3299 USA
    Phone: +1 610-356-4600
    Fax: +1 610-482-9971
    Email: customercare@pmi.org
    Website: www.PMI.org

To place a Trade Order or for pricing information, please contact Independent Publishers Group:
    Independent Publishers Group
    Order Department
    814 North Franklin Street
    Chicago, IL 60610 USA
    Phone: +1 800-888-4741
    Fax: +1 312-337-5985
    Email: orders@ipgbook.com (For orders only)

For all other inquiries, please contact the PMI Book Service Center.
    PMI Book Service Center
    P.O. Box 932683, Atlanta, GA 31193-2683 USA
    Phone: 1-866-276-4764 (within the U.S. or Canada) or +1-770-280-4129 (globally)
    Fax: +1-770-280-4113
    Email: info@bookorders.pmi.org

10 9 8 7 6 5 4 3 2

NOTICE

The Project Management Institute, Inc. (PMI) standards and guideline publications, of which the document contained herein is one, are developed through a voluntary consensus standards development process. This process brings together volunteers and/or seeks out the views of persons who have an interest in the topic covered by this publication. While PMI administers the process and establishes rules to promote fairness in the development of consensus, it does not write the document and it does not independently test, evaluate, or verify the accuracy or completeness of any information or the soundness of any judgments contained in its standards and guideline publications.

PMI disclaims liability for any personal injury, property or other damages of any nature whatsoever, whether special, indirect, consequential or compensatory, directly or indirectly resulting from the publication, use of application, or reliance on this document. PMI disclaims and makes no guaranty or warranty, expressed or implied, as to the accuracy or completeness of any information published herein, and disclaims and makes no warranty that the information in this document will fulfill any of your particular purposes or needs. PMI does not undertake to guarantee the performance of any individual manufacturer or seller's products or services by virtue of this standard or guide.

In publishing and making this document available, PMI is not undertaking to render professional or other services for or on behalf of any person or entity, nor is PMI undertaking to perform any duty owed by any person or entity to someone else. Anyone using this document should rely on his or her own independent judgment or, as appropriate, seek the advice of a competent professional in determining the exercise of reasonable care in any given circumstances. Information and other standards on the topic covered by this publication may be available from other sources, which the user may wish to consult for additional views or information not covered by this publication.

PMI has no power, nor does it undertake to police or enforce compliance with the contents of this document. PMI does not certify, test, or inspect products, designs, or installations for safety or health purposes. Any certification or other statement of compliance with any health or safety-related information in this document shall not be attributable to PMI and is solely the responsibility of the certifier or maker of the statement.

TABLE OF CONTENTS

LIST OF TABLES AND FIGURES

PART 2. THE STANDARD FOR BUSINESS ANALYSIS

PART 3. APPENDIXES, GLOSSARY, AND INDEX

PREFACE

The *PMI Guide to Business Analysis (*Includes *The Standard for Business Analysis)* joins PMI's suite of foundational, consensus-based standards. *The Standard for Business Analysis*, accredited by American National Standards Institute (ANSI), is considered to be the preeminent standard for business analysis. The standard and guide exemplify PMI's continuing commitment to support organizations and portfolio, program, and project professionals by delivering a defined body of knowledge and standard in business analysis.

PMI views business analysis as an essential capability that cascades across and throughout portfolio, program, and project management. As such, the *PMI Guide to Business Analysis* is aligned to *A Guide to the Project Management Body of Knowledge (PMBOK® Guide)*; *The Standard for Program Management*; *The Standard for Portfolio Management*; *Organizational Project Management Maturity Model (OPM3®)* and the *Agile Practice Guide*. *Business Analysis for Practitioners: A Practice Guide* is a complement to this standard.

A standard is not a methodology because it does not prescribe the order, procedures, and rules. Hence the business analysis standard provides a framework of suggested Process Groups, corresponding processes, Knowledge Areas, inputs, and outputs. Those familiar with the *PMBOK® Guide* will benefit from the mapping tables located in the Process Group introductions within the standard to compare project management processes to business analysis processes to understand how business analysis is used to support successful project management.

The guide expands on the framework in the standard and, in addition, provides practices, tools, and techniques for anyone committed to understanding and performing business analysis responsibilities at the highest level. Organizations and practitioners can tailor the processes and practices contained herein to meet specific organizational needs and goals.

One of the difficulties in developing a standard is to make it easy to understand, usable, and applicable to the multitude of conditions that may exist on any given portfolio, program, or project. This standard and guide were developed to be adaptable to any condition and flexible through the use of common language and tailoring tables. The language ensures content does not side with one industry, one specialty, or one project size (e.g., it does not apply only to large IT projects), focuses on the role of business analysis and not the job title, and explains how each process may vary depending on whether an adaptive, predictive, or hybrid delivery approach is used.

The Standard for Business Analysis mirrors a similar structure to *The Standard for Project Management* utilizing process groups and processes to describe the work. It discusses business analysis work via 35 processes distributed across six Business Analysis Process Groups including:

◆ Defining and Aligning

◆ Initiating

◆ Planning

◆ Executing

◆ Monitoring and Controlling

◆ Releasing

The guide provides guidance on how to effectively apply business analysis processes and practices to drive better business outcomes regardless of the industry, project size, or project type. It provides business analysis guidance for any delivery method including predictive (waterfall) and adaptive (agile). *The PMI Guide to Business Analysis* includes these six Knowledge Areas:

◆ Needs Assessment

◆ Stakeholder Engagement

◆ Elicitation

◆ Analysis

◆ Traceability and Monitoring

◆ Solution Evaluation

The *PMI Guide to Business Analysis* defines what the work of business analysis is, why it is important, and concepts related to business analysis that can be applied consistently across all project life cycles, project types, and industries to deliver successful business outcomes. It describes over 40 skills and over 100 techniques needed to effectively perform business analysis processes and highlights collaboration points between business analysis and other roles alongside which business analysts typically need to work. The glossary also includes 500 commonly used terms in business analysis. To receive the most value from the guide, PMI recommends its use in conjunction with *Business Analysis for Practitioners: A Practice Guide.* Where the guide describes the "what", the practice guide describes the "how to." For example, the guide describes what technique can be used while the practice guide describes how to perform the technique.

The *PMI Guide to Business Analysis (*Includes *The Standard for Business Analysis)* was developed by leading experts for practitioners in the field. As full consensus standards, the guide and standard were subjected to PMI's rigorous development process, including a subject matter expert review and a public exposure review, where practitioners commented and submitted changes for consideration by the core committee. All comments and requests for change were considered and many were incorporated into the publication providing added value. Some comments were deferred for future iterations of the guide. As such, PMI encourages practitioners to continue to provide feedback for future editions. PMI standards are required to be updated on a routine basis and the core committee is appreciative of any and all feedback from users of the guide.

Part 1

The PMI Guide to Business Analysis

1

INTRODUCTION

1.1 OVERVIEW AND PURPOSE OF THIS GUIDE

The PMI Guide to Business Analysis, referred to here as the guide, is intended to serve the needs of organizations and business analysis professionals by providing practical knowledge and good practices needed to contribute to portfolio, program, project, and product success and support the delivery of high-quality solutions. This guide is intended to enable business analysis to be effectively performed regardless of the project life cycle, whether a predictive, iterative, adaptive, or hybrid approach is used, and provide guidance for business analysis regardless of the job title of the individual performing it. This guide:

- ◆ Defines what the work of business analysis is and why it is important;

- ◆ Describes the competencies, processes, tools, and techniques needed to effectively perform business analysis tasks and activities;

- ◆ Defines concepts related to business analysis that can be applied consistently across all product and project life cycles, product types, and industries to deliver successful business outcomes within portfolios, programs, and projects;

- ◆ Highlights collaboration points between those who perform business analysis activities and other roles that business analysts typically need to work with collaboratively; and

- ◆ Provides and promotes a common business analysis vocabulary for organizations and business analysis professionals.

According to *PMI's Pulse of the Profession® In-Depth Report: Requirements Management: A Core Competency for Project and Program Success* [1],[1] 47% of unsuccessful projects fail to meet original goals due to poor requirements management. In the 2017 *Pulse Report: Success Rates Rise—Transforming the High Cost of Low Performance* [2], 39% of failed projects identify inaccurate requirements gathering as a primary cause of failure. Research continues to validate that when organizations do not embrace business analysis and overlook the importance of establishing effective processes to perform it, there is a direct impact to their ability to perform effectively on projects. Those organizations that demonstrate maturity in business analysis practices are 55% more successful in implementing strategy and are much more likely to achieve the expected value from the investments made on programs and projects. These are just a few of the statistics obtained from recent PMI research proving the value of business analysis.

---

[1] The numbers in brackets refer to the list of references at the end of this guide.

Currently organizations are interested in understanding how best to:

◆ Strategically leverage business analysis to ensure that investments are allocated to the highest-value initiatives;

◆ Adequately invest so that product teams have the resources they need to properly identify and solve the right problems; and

◆ Deliver solutions that provide measurable business value and meet stakeholder expectations.

Such trends are driving the need for additional skilled business analysis professionals globally.

PMI research has also shown that improved business analysis skills and practices can significantly impact the success of an organization, including providing a competitive advantage in the marketplace. In this research, business analysis was identified as a contributor to gaining a competitive advantage over the past five years by 81% of the business analysts who stated they work in an organization where business analysis practices are considered highly mature [2]. In addition to skills development and process maturity, organizations are also taking steps to champion an improved and stronger integration of business analysis with project management, recognizing the contributions of each role in ensuring project success.

Business analysis professionals from every level of experience and competency, regardless of where they report functionally, require a business analysis standard that can be universally applied in any size organization, industry, or region of the world. Business analysis professionals need a standard that recognizes generally accepted good practices to support the practice of business analysis efficiently, effectively, and consistently to deliver solutions that provide the most value.

This guide identifies business analysis practices that are generally recognized as good practice. These terms are defined as follows:

◆ **Generally recognized.** *Generally recognized* means the knowledge and practices described are applicable to most portfolios, programs, and projects most of the time, and there is consensus about their value and usefulness.

◆ **Good practice.** *Good practice* means there is general agreement that the application of the knowledge, skills, tools, and techniques when performing business analysis contributes to the successful delivery of the expected business values and results across portfolios, programs, and projects. *Good practice* does not mean that the knowledge described should always be applied uniformly to all portfolios, programs, or projects; the business analysis professional, working with stakeholders and the product team, determines what is appropriate for given situations.

This guide is different from a methodology. A methodology is a system of practices, techniques, procedures, and rules used by those who work within a discipline. The guide, on the other hand, is a foundation upon which organizations can build methodologies, policies, procedures, rules, tools, and techniques needed to practice business analysis effectively. This guide aligns the global community on what comprises the business analysis profession and aims to help organizations realize improvements in business analysis capabilities by ensuring that business analysis is commonly defined and understood.

1.1.1 THE NEED FOR THIS GUIDE

As organizations strive to meet market demands, the expectation is to deliver better solutions in a faster and less expensive manner. Recent PMI research identified business analysis as a key competency to help organizations achieve this goal. *The Standard for Business Analysis* and the *PMI Guide to Business Analysis* are intended to assist organizations and individuals in understanding the business analysis discipline as a basis for attaining mature and effective business analysis processes.

1.1.2 INTENDED AUDIENCE FOR THIS GUIDE

This guide is intended for anyone who performs business analysis activities, regardless of job title or percentage of time spent performing business analysis. This guide is also intended for anyone who works with someone who performs business analysis, for example, those who perform portfolio, program, or project management; the information presented here supports better collaboration among roles. This guide can be used by organizations and project teams to understand what constitutes good business analysis practice and can serve as a framework to provide a common business analysis language and structure by which practices can be further understood with regard to the value and purpose each provides.

1.1.3 THE VALUE OF BUSINESS ANALYSIS

Organizations with highly mature business analysis practices believe that business analysis has a tangible impact on their organization's success and provides a competitive advantage [3]. Research confirmed that a significantly larger percentage of highly mature organizations rank themselves well above average against their peer organizations with regard to:

◆ Ability to implement strategy,

◆ Organizational agility,

◆ Management of projects, and

◆ Overall financial performance [3].

With strong research validating business analysis as a key competency, organizations that follow mature business analysis practices will deliver better results and do so more efficiently and effectively than peer organizations with immature practices [3].

PMI's Pulse of the Profession® In-Depth Report: Requirements Management: A Core Competency for Project and Program Success [1] reports that organizations can focus more attention on the following three critical areas to improve the effectiveness of their business analysis capabilities:

◆ **People.** By putting in place the necessary human resources who can properly apply business analysis to recommend solutions to the problems or opportunities addressed by the portfolios, programs, and projects, and at the same time, recognizing and developing the skills needed to perform this important role.

◆ **Processes.** By establishing and standardizing processes at the portfolio, program, and project levels, so consistent application of good business analysis can occur across initiatives within an organization.

◆ **Culture.** By creating a sense of urgency at the top so that executive management and sponsors fully value the practice of business analysis as a critical competency of portfolios, programs, and projects, and provide the appropriate support and commitment needed to excel throughout the organization.

Those responsible for performing business analysis can work collaboratively with members of their organization to determine and apply the appropriate level of generally recognized good business analysis practices for different situations and needs. The effort to determine and apply the appropriate business analysis processes, tools, techniques, and other items, including the life cycle(s) being employed, is referred to as *tailoring*. Refer to Section 1.3.4 for more information on how business analysis practices may be tailored to address the specific needs of the organization.

Business analysis can be performed when creating or enhancing a product, solving a problem, or seeking to understand stakeholder needs. The value of business analysis spans many industries and types of projects. For instance:

◆ In the financial industry, business analysis can be used to create or modify financial products that meet customer needs;

◆ In the health-care industry, business analysis can be used to minimize wait times from entrance to first diagnosis;

◆ On construction projects, business analysis can be used to define the requirements of a new building for use as the basis for the scope of work;

◆ Governments use business analysis to analyze situations and determine the best solutions to improve issues such as poverty, economic crises, and environmental issues;

◆ In manufacturing, business analysis can be applied to optimize assembly-line processes; and

◆ On IT projects, business analysis is performed to translate the business requirements into stakeholder and system requirements to provide clear guidance to designers and developers on what to build.

There are many uncertainties that affect business outcomes, such as whether consumers will purchase a product when it is built, whether existing infrastructure will support future growth rates, uncertainties over having sufficient staff to support customer demands, or the many unknowns that could result in a product being broken when used in unconventional ways that were not considered during product design. Effective business analysis enables individuals, groups, and public and private organizations to achieve better business outcomes. Effective business analysis helps:

◆ Address business needs;

◆ Manage risk and reduce rework;

◆ Minimize product defects, recalls, lawsuits, and reduction in consumer confidence; and

◆ Achieve stakeholder satisfaction.

These items are further discussed in Sections 1.1.3.1 through 1.1.3.4.

1.1.3.1 ADDRESSING BUSINESS NEEDS

Organizations are often tempted to provide solutions before fully understanding a situation. Business analysis enables the organization to identify and fix the root causes of problems instead of repeatedly addressing symptoms as they occur. Good business analysis hinges on conducting a needs assessment and recommending a solution based on the specifics of the problem space, including, but not limited to, understanding the business and enterprise architectures. Business analysis assists in detecting new opportunities that are essential for the growth and perhaps even the survival of an organization. Exploiting opportunities is imperative to secure a competitive advantage in the marketplace. Business analysis helps organizations obtain business value when addressing business needs.

1.1.3.2 MANAGING RISK AND REDUCING REWORK

What constitutes sufficient business analysis is dependent on the risk appetite of the organization and the level of confidence required before the organization is comfortable proceeding with its initiatives. The decision to proceed without performing sufficient business analysis and accepting a higher level of uncertainty is often the result of undervaluing business analysis activities. Although business analysis requires considerable time and resources, if overlooked, it can result in insufficiently understood requirements, missed stakeholder expectations, and frustration on the part of the project team and other key stakeholders. These issues can lead to much rework and many requests for change. It may seem counterintuitive, but taking the time to conduct business analysis actually saves time, reduces costs, and minimizes risk exposure in the long run.

1.1.3.3 EFFECTS OF PRODUCT DEFECTS

When insufficient time is allocated to business analysis activities, gaps in requirements can arise. Missing and misunderstood requirements can lead to product defects. Product defects uncovered within the confines of the project result in rework, but if these product defects are uncovered once a product is released to the consumer, the results are exponentially worse. Product defects in production may result in product recalls, lawsuits, reduction in consumer confidence, or harm to end users.

1.1.3.4 STAKEHOLDER SATISFACTION

Creating products to address the needs of the business and delivering those products on time and within budget while minimizing potential threats to the organization results in increased stakeholder satisfaction. Looking at how accepting stakeholders are of the end product or how willing the stakeholder is to pay for the solution once it is built can provide an overall indication of true stakeholder satisfaction. The application of good business analysis practices can result in the product or solution being accepted early on and fully adopted once implemented or released, and achieving high levels of stakeholder satisfaction.

1.1.4 UNDERSTANDING ROLE BOUNDARIES

The business analyst role is often misunderstood and underutilized and often commonly confused with other roles within the organization. The role of the business analyst is often confused with that of a project manager, because of a perceived overlap; however they both serve in critical leadership roles on programs and projects [3]. Another complicating factor is that many people who perform business analysis have different titles across various industries and sometimes even within the same organization. Similarly, many organizations create business analysis positions but use the position as a "catch-all," asking business analysts to perform activities outside of what is common responsibility for the discipline, such as performing testing activities or administrative tasks.

To ensure successful role collaboration, it is imperative to understand the role boundaries between critical resources engaged in work on portfolios, programs, and projects. The research indicated that organizations that achieve a high level of collaboration between project managers and business analysts are able to deliver more successfully on projects [3]. This research should serve as encouragement to establish an organizational culture that embraces collaboration between these roles. When an individual is tasked with performing more than one role, such as a business analyst and project manager hybrid, this individual will have the added responsibility of distinguishing between different and sometimes competing priorities, tasks, and methods involved in each role.

Section 3 further explores role boundaries by looking at the position of the business analyst within the organizational structure and presenting a comprehensive list of the skills often demonstrated by those who perform business analysis.

1.1.5 *THE STANDARD FOR BUSINESS ANALYSIS*

The Standard for Business Analysis [4], referred to here as the standard, is a foundational reference for the practice of business analysis and PMI's business analysis professional development programs. The standard identifies the processes that are considered good business analysis practices on most portfolios, programs, and projects most of the time. The standard identifies the inputs and outputs that are usually associated with those processes. One or more methodologies may be used to implement the business analysis processes outlined in this standard.

1.1.6 USING THE STANDARD IN CONJUNCTION WITH OTHER PMI PRODUCTS

The Standard for Business Analysis complements PMI's other foundational standards by identifying and discussing the alignment between business analysis and portfolio, program, and project management. The other foundational standards are:

◆ *A Guide to the Project Management Body of Knowledge (PMBOK® Guide)* [5],

◆ *The Standard for Program Management* [6],

◆ *The Standard for Portfolio Management* [7], and

◆ *The Standard for Organizational Project Management* [8].

The Standard for Business Analysis and the *PMI Guide to Business Analysis* can be used in conjunction with *Business Analysis for Practitioners: A Practice Guide* [9]. While the guide and standard define the business analysis processes and concepts that are generally recognized as good practice, *Business Analysis for Practitioners: A Practice Guide* provides practical knowledge about how to apply business analysis tools and techniques to develop and manage requirements to perform the work. For example, the guide will help determine which tools and techniques may be used to perform each business analysis process and the *Business Analysis for Practitioners: A Practice Guide* may be consulted for examples and information on how to use the tool or perform the technique.

1.1.7 COMMON VOCABULARY

This section describes common vocabulary necessary for working in and understanding the discipline of business analysis.

1.1.7.1 BUSINESS ANALYSIS

Business analysis is the application of knowledge, skills, tools, and techniques to:

◆ Determine problems and opportunities;

◆ Identify business needs and recommend viable solutions to meet those needs and support strategic decision making;

◆ Elicit, analyze, specify, communicate, and manage requirements and other product information; and

◆ Define benefits and approaches for measuring and realizing value, and analyzing those results.

In short, business analysis is the set of activities performed to support the delivery of solutions that align to business objectives and provide continuous value to the organization.

Business analysis is performed through the application of a set of processes that are defined and explored in this guide. The sum of all the processes within this guide provides a thorough definition and knowledge of business analysis.

Business analysis is conducted in support of solution development, through portfolios, programs, and projects, as well as ongoing operational activities, such as monitoring, modeling, and forecasting. The practices defined within this guide apply wherever business analysis is conducted.

1.1.7.2 BUSINESS ANALYST

Business analysis may be performed by any individual regardless of the person's job title. In this guide, the person(s) who performs business analysis processes will be referred to as a business analyst. The term is being used in the broad sense and represents all the roles that are responsible for performing business analysis activities across industries or within organizations, regardless of whether the work is performed to support portfolios, programs, or projects. Many portfolios, programs, and projects require a team of individuals to perform business analysis, and in these scenarios, the term *business analyst* will also be applied.

Section 3 elaborates on the role of the business analyst and presents job titles often used to identify those who perform business analysis.

1.1.7.3 PRODUCT

A product is an artifact that is produced, is quantifiable, and can be either an end item in itself or a component item. Products are also referred to as materials or goods. A product can be tangible or intangible—for example, an organizational structure, a process, or a service. A service is the performance of duties or work for another party. Products are created or updated as parts of solutions to address business needs; therefore, they provide business value.

1.1.7.4 PRODUCT REQUIREMENTS

A requirement is defined as a condition or capability that is required to be present in a product, service, or result to satisfy a business need. This guide uses the term *product requirement* to describe the types of requirements that are part of the business analysis effort. Product requirements are the primary focus of this guide, and the term *requirement* without a qualifier is used to specify all product requirement types.

A product requirement represents something that can be met by a solution and addresses a need of a business, person, or group of people. A product requirement should be independent of the design of the solution that addresses it. Product requirements are specified to clarify and communicate a business need or required capability. Whether they are expressed as requirement statements, use cases, user stories, backlog items, or visual models, a clear understanding of product requirements is essential for developing solutions that meet the business needs. Sometimes requirements are unstated because stakeholders are unaware of what is really needed until they are using a solution or viewing a prototype. Although unstated, these needs are still requirements. This highlights the importance of using a variety of elicitation techniques to draw forth sufficient information to develop the solution, reducing the likelihood that stakeholders have expectations that have not been verbalized.

This guide uses the term *product requirement* in the broad sense; therefore, when performing the work of requirements elicitation, specification, or requirements management, one may choose to indicate the type of requirement to be able to communicate whether the product requirement represents a need of the business, an aspect of the solution, or a product requirement for a particular stakeholder group. To provide clarity and context, product requirements are often categorized by type.

The following product requirement types are discussed in this guide:

◆ **Business requirement.** Describes the higher-level needs of the organization such as business issues or opportunities, reasons why an initiative has been undertaken, and measurable representations of goals the business is seeking to achieve. Business requirements are used to provide context and direction for any solution so that the solution addresses the business need. Business requirements are typically defined before a portfolio component, program, or project has been initiated, as they represent the reason why the portfolio component, program, or project has been undertaken or why the product should be created or modified. Business requirements are often used to define the success criteria for the portfolio component, program, or project. An organization may have multiple business requirements. All other remaining product requirement types—such as stakeholder, solution, and transition requirements—are typically defined within the context of a project.

◆ **Stakeholder requirement.** Describes the needs of a stakeholder, where the term *stakeholder* refers to an individual, group, or organization that may affect, be affected by, or perceive itself to be affected by a decision, activity, or outcome of a portfolio, program, or project. Examples of stakeholders include customers, users, regulators, suppliers, and partners, as well as internal business roles.

◆ **Solution requirement.** Describes the features, functions, and characteristics of a product that will meet the business and stakeholder requirements. Solution requirements are further grouped into functional and nonfunctional requirements as follows:

  ■ *Functional requirement.* Describes the behaviors of the product. Examples of types of functional requirements include actions, processes, and interactions that the product should perform. The data and rules needed to support functional requirements are typically elicited concurrently.

  ■ *Nonfunctional requirement.* Describes the environmental conditions or qualities required for the product to be effective. Nonfunctional requirements are sometimes known as product quality requirements or quality of service requirements. Examples of types of nonfunctional requirements include reliability, security, performance, safety, level of service, and supportability. Quality of service requirements are not the same as the quality requirements discussed from a project management perspective.

◆ **Transition requirement.** Describes temporary capabilities, such as data conversion and training requirements, and operational changes needed to transition from the current state to the future state. Once the transition to the future state is complete, the transition requirements are no longer needed.

Two other types of requirements are project requirements and quality requirements. These requirement types are not part of the business analysis effort and are not considered to be product requirements. Project and quality requirements focus on project execution and are part of the project management effort. Because project and quality requirements are outside the scope of business analysis, they are only discussed here to show context of their relationship to business analysis:

◆ **Project requirement.** Describes the actions, processes, or other conditions the project needs to meet. Examples of types of project requirements include milestone dates, contractual obligations, and constraints.

◆ **Quality requirement.** Describes any condition or criterion needed to validate the successful completion of a project deliverable or the fulfillment of other project requirements. Examples of types of quality requirements include tests, certifications, and validations.

Although project and quality requirements are part of the project management effort, collaboration is required to define all types of requirements. The project management effort comprises the management of all requirements-related deliverables, including ensuring that the definition of the product requirements is completed. When product requirements are defined, the constraints of the project need to be accounted for to ensure that the defined solution can be delivered within the time, resource, and cost parameters of the project. It would be difficult to accurately describe the work needed to deliver the solution and determine how to validate the successful completion of project deliverables without some information about the solution. Project and quality requirements, therefore, cannot be defined until the solution is somewhat defined.

Business analysis focuses on ensuring that the product is of sufficient quality through the development of nonfunctional requirements. Project management focuses on ensuring that the processes performed to deliver the solution are of sufficient quality through the development of quality requirements. When the solution adheres to nonfunctional requirements and the processes to deliver the solution adhere to quality requirements, it maximizes the probability that the solution will meet business needs.

For more information about project and quality requirements, refer to the *PMBOK® Guide* – Sixth Edition.

Figure 1-1 depicts the relationships that exist among various categories of product and project requirements, for example:

◆ A single business requirement may be supported by multiple stakeholder and solution requirements;

◆ A single stakeholder requirement may be supported by many solution requirements;

◆ Solution requirements may be written as functional or nonfunctional requirements;

◆ Because transition requirements describe the transition from the current to future state, they support the implementation of stakeholder and solution requirements;

◆ Project requirements support product requirements, as project requirements describe the work needed to deliver the unique solution(s); and

◆ Quality requirements support project requirements because they are used to validate the successful completion of a project deliverable or the fulfillment of other project requirements.

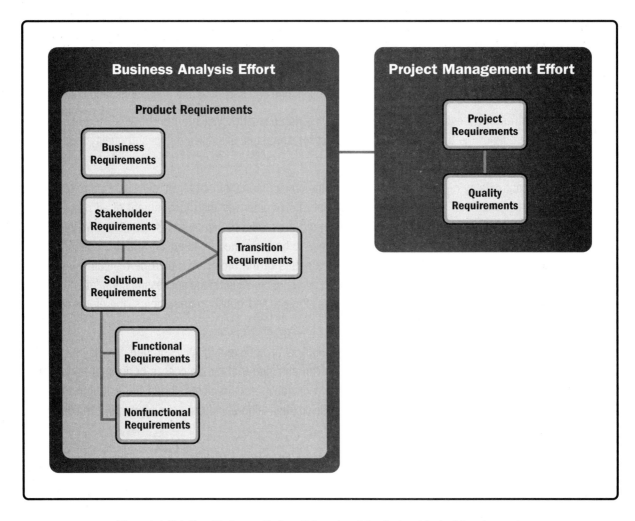

Figure 1-1. Relationship Among Various Categories of Product and Project Requirements

1.1.7.5 PRODUCT INFORMATION

Throughout the performance of the business analysis process, significant amounts of information are created, collected, analyzed, modified, consumed, and shared. Within the guide and standard, when *product information* is referred to in process descriptions as an input or as an output, the reference is being made to the most common component of product information that is relevant to the process. A choice was made not to list specific types of product information except where it could provide more context or understanding, because typically the specifics are highly dependent on life cycles and organization-specific terminology used by teams. The types of information the guide refers to as product information include:

◆ Business goals and objectives,

◆ Requirements,

◆ Analysis models,

◆ Backlogs,

- ◆ User stories,

- ◆ Acceptance criteria and definition of associated metrics,

- ◆ Product scope,

- ◆ Product risks,

- ◆ Assumptions,

- ◆ Constraints,

- ◆ Dependencies, and

- ◆ Issues.

Product information can include different types or levels of detail. For example, requirements could refer to business requirements or stakeholder requirements, and issues might be stakeholder issues or defects. Product information can take on different states as various processes consume and produce the information. For example, at different points in business analysis work, requirements can be in a verified, validated, prioritized, or approved state. The product information may be stored in a variety of forms, such as tools, documents, notes, emails, and possibly in people's minds.

Product information is by no means the only information relevant to business analysis processes. Additional kinds of information are used to create and analyze the product information throughout the course of performing business analysis. The type and form of the additional information could include the original source material from which elicitation results came, elicitation notes, emails with additional context about analysis, and verbal or written comments from stakeholders about the information.

1.1.7.6 SOLUTION

A solution is something that is produced to deliver measurable business value to meet the business need and expectations of stakeholders. It defines what a specific portfolio component, program, or project will deliver. A solution could be one or more new products, components of products, or enhancements or corrections to a product.

1.1.7.7 STAKEHOLDER

In project management, a stakeholder is an individual, group, or organization that may affect, be affected by, or perceive itself to be affected by a decision, activity, or outcome of a project. In business analysis, stakeholders also include those affected or perceived to be affected by activities and decisions related to the solution. Identifying stakeholders, analyzing them, and effectively managing their expectations are critical activities for both project management and business analysis. Each discipline performs these activities for different purposes and with a different focus; project managers identify and analyze stakeholders to best manage the project and business analysts identify and analyze stakeholders to best manage the business analysis activities. See Section 1.2.1 for more information on the product/project relationship.

In business analysis, stakeholder identification begins when business analysis activities are performed to define the business need and situation statement and continues through the development of a business case and during charter development. It is imperative that the stakeholder list be revised regularly to retain its accuracy. Throughout an initiative, several factors may occur that require further identification or analysis to be performed, such as a change in product scope or a refinement of requirements that uncovers new stakeholders. Business analysts work very closely with stakeholders, often on a day-to-day basis, and therefore, they continue to make refinements to the stakeholder register as new information becomes available. Maintaining accuracy of the stakeholder register is critical because when stakeholders are overlooked, there is a high chance that requirements will be missed.

In business analysis, understanding the stakeholders identified in the register is equally important. When stakeholder characteristics are not known or understood, the business analyst may choose techniques that are ineffective. Misunderstanding stakeholders may result in ineffectively communicating or collaborating with stakeholders throughout the entire product life cycle. For more information on stakeholder characteristics, see Section 5.2.

Stakeholders have different roles and relationships across the business analysis effort. Their involvement can change over the course of the product life cycle. Stakeholder involvement may range from being occasional contributors in surveys and focus groups to full project sponsorship that includes the provision of financial, political, or other types of support. Stakeholders may be actively involved in requirements-related activities, serving as subject matter experts (SMEs) or decision makers with regard to product scope, requirements priorities, or proposed changes to product features. Stakeholders may have interests that may be positively or negatively affected by the end solution. Different stakeholders may have competing requirements and expectations that could create conflicts for decisions about approving solution options, requirements, or allocating requirements across releases. Stakeholders may also exert influence over various aspects of the business analysis process, its deliverables, and other stakeholders to achieve a set of outcomes that satisfies their own needs and expectations. It is essential that these relationships and dependencies be identified and managed to ensure a successful business analysis process. Section 3.3.3.1 describes some of the typical relationships created and managed by business analysts, including those relationships managed with stakeholders.

1.2 FOUNDATIONAL ELEMENTS

1.2.1 RELATIONSHIP BETWEEN PRODUCTS AND PROJECTS

For organizations to remain competitive, products often evolve through the work of projects. Projects deliver solutions through new products, product enhancements, revised processes, integrated systems, restructured organizations, market research, and trained personnel. Remaining competitive, however, is not the only reason products are advanced—evolution could occur to address regulatory or compliance needs, fix inefficiencies, increase revenue, cut costs, or other reasons. Business analysis is used to identify business needs and subsequently to identify and define appropriate solutions to address those needs.

Projects are temporary endeavors undertaken to create unique products, services, or results. Business analysis focuses on products, whereas project management focuses on delivering projects to create or evolve products. Both views are essential because the concepts of products and projects are highly intertwined—a fact that cannot be ignored. Figure 1-2 represents one scenario for the relationship between projects and products in which one product evolves over the course of multiple projects.

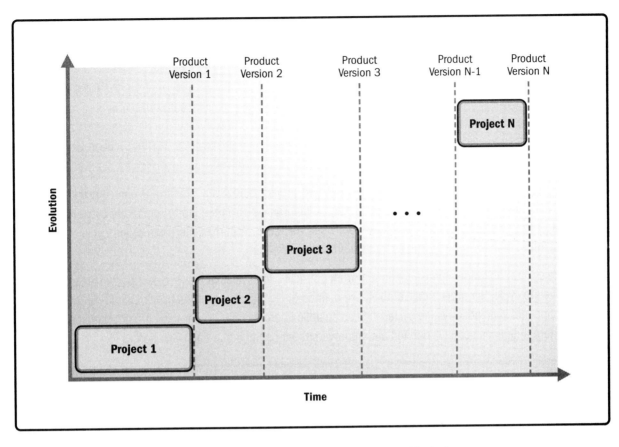

Figure 1-2. The Relationship Between Products and Projects

1.2.2 PRODUCT AND PROJECT LIFE CYCLES

A product life cycle is a series of phases that represent the evolution of a product from concept through delivery, growth, maturity, maintenance, and retirement. The number of intermediary phases that a product goes through is dependent on the longevity of the product life cycle. Projects may be implemented to evolve products, but projects are not required for this evolution. It may take multiple projects to evolve a product through the product life cycle and, in some cases, a product may evolve in the same phase.

A product life cycle may consist of multiple project life cycles. A needs assessment conducted within the product life cycle provides strategic alignment and justification for the investment of a new project. After the project is complete, an evaluation of the product is performed within the product life cycle to determine if a new project is needed to evolve the product. Business analysis focuses on the entire product life cycle, including the many projects that advance the product.

A project life cycle is the series of phases through which a project passes from its initiation to its closure. The phases can be sequential or they may overlap. The names, number, and duration of the project phases are influenced by a number of factors, including the management and control needs of the organization(s) involved in the project, the nature of the project itself, its area of application, and the complexity or volatility of the product information. The phase or phases associated with the development of features and capabilities can be unitary or composed of multiple iterations. Iterations are generally time-bounded, with a start and end or control point. At the control point, the project charter, business case, and other project baselines are reexamined based on the current environment. The project's risk exposure and evaluation of project execution compared to its performance measurement baseline are used to determine if the project should be changed, terminated, or continued as planned.

The project life cycle is influenced by many internal and external factors, including but not limited to, the unique aspects of the organization, industry, or technology employed. While every project has a clear start and end, the specific deliverables and work that take place vary widely depending on the project. The life cycle provides the basic framework for managing the project, regardless of the specific work involved.

Figure 1-3 shows the relationship between product and project life cycles, illustrating that a product life cycle is comprised of one or more project life cycles. While the diagram is not intended to model life cycle phases, keep in mind that each project life cycle may contain activities related to a part of the product life cycle (e.g., product development, product maintenance, and eventually product retirement).

Project life cycles can range along a continuum from predictive life cycles at one end to adaptive ones at the other. In a predictive life cycle, the project deliverables are defined at the beginning of the project, and any changes to the scope are managed. In an adaptive life cycle, such as an agile approach, the deliverables are developed over multiple iterations where a detailed scope is defined and approved at the beginning of each iteration.

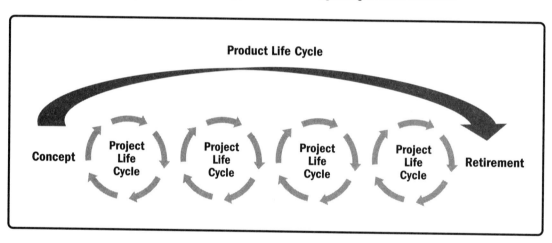

Figure 1-3. The Relationship Between Product and Project Life Cycles

1.2.3 HOW BUSINESS ANALYSIS SUPPORTS PORTFOLIO, PROGRAM, AND PROJECT MANAGEMENT

Portfolio management is the centralized management of one or more groupings of projects, programs, subsidiary portfolios, and operations to achieve strategic objectives. Programs focus on achieving a specific set of expected benefits as determined by organizational strategy and objectives, whereas projects are largely concerned with creating specific deliverables that support specific organizational objectives. Projects may or may not be part of a program. Business analysis supports portfolio, program, and project management. Business analysis competencies increase alignment between the higher-level strategies and outcomes of programs and enable portfolio, program, and project management practices and processes.

Business analysis begins with defining a situation and a complete understanding of the problem or opportunity that the organization wishes to address; this work is considered pre-project. The results of pre-project activities provide information to understand the value a given project provides the portfolio and program. When organizations lack portfolio and program management practices, the definition of the problem or opportunity should be performed at the onset of the project. Business analysis activities support portfolio management by helping to align programs and projects to organizational strategy. In portfolio, program, and project management, business analysis also involves the elicitation and analysis necessary to define the product scope, requirements, models, and other product information necessary to build a common understanding of the solution and clearly communicate product features to those responsible for developing the end product.

The business analysis processes performed as part of the Defining and Aligning Process Group produce analysis results and other outputs leveraged by portfolio management. All other business analysis activities performed outside of the Defining and Aligning Process Group help define the solution and support the work of program and project management. The Business Analysis Process Groups are defined in Section 1.3.2.

Table 1-1 provides a comparison of business analysis with project, program, and portfolio management.

Table 1-1. Comparative Overview of Business Analysis with Project, Program, and Portfolio Management

	Business Analysis	Project Management	Program Management	Portfolio Management
Definition	The set of activities performed to support the delivery of solutions that align to business objectives and provide continuous value to the organization.	The application of knowledge, skills, tools, and techniques to project activities to meet the project requirements.	The application of knowledge, skills, and principles to a program to achieve the program objectives and obtain benefits and control not available by managing program components individually.	The centralized management of one or more portfolios to achieve strategic objectives.
Focus	**Solution:** Something that is produced to deliver measurable business value to meet the business need and expectations of stakeholders (e.g., new products and enhancements to products).	**Project:** A temporary endeavor undertaken to create a unique product, service, or result.	**Program:** A group of related projects, subsidiary programs, and program activities that are managed in a coordinated way to obtain benefits not available from managing them individually.	**Portfolio:** A collection of projects, programs, subsidiary portfolios, and operations managed as a group to achieve strategic objectives.
Scope Definition	**Product scope:** The features and functions that characterize a solution.	**Project scope:** The work performed to deliver a product, service, or result with the specified features and functions.	**Program scope:** The scope that encompasses program components and the interactions and synergy between them.	**Portfolio scope:** The organizational scope that changes with the strategic objectives of the organization.
Roles	Those who identify business needs, and recommend and describe solutions through the definition of product requirements.	Those who manage the project team to meet the project objectives.	Those who ensure that program benefits are delivered as expected by coordinating the activities of a program's components.	Those who coordinate portfolio management staff, or program and project staff that may have reporting responsibilities into the aggregate portfolio.
Success	Measured by a solution's ability to deliver its intended benefits to an organization, degree of customer satisfaction, and achievement of business objectives.	Measured by product and project quality, timelines, budget compliance, and degree of customer satisfaction.	Measured by program's ability to deliver its intended benefits to an organization, and by the program's efficiency and effectiveness in delivering those benefits.	Measured in terms of the aggregate investment performance and benefit realization of the portfolio.

1.2.4 BUSINESS VALUE

Organizations employ portfolio, program, and project management to improve their abilities to deliver benefits. Business value may be defined as the net quantifiable benefit derived from a business endeavor. The benefit may be tangible, intangible, or both. In business analysis, business value is considered the return, in the form of time, money, goods, or intangibles for something exchanged. For example, tangible benefits may include monetary assets, facilities, fixtures, equity, and utility, and intangible benefits may include goodwill, brand recognition, public benefit, trademarks, compliance, and capabilities. Business value may also be created through the effective management of ongoing, well-established operations. However, the effective use of portfolio, program, and project management enables organizations to employ reliable, established processes to generate new business value by effectively pursuing new business strategies that are consistent with their mission and vision for the future.

Portfolio management ensures that an organization's programs, projects, and/or operations are aligned with its strategy. It allows organizations to define how they will pursue their strategic goals through programs and projects, and how those programs and projects will be supported by human, financial, or material resources. In doing this, portfolio management optimizes the pursuit of business value.

Program management enables organizations to effectively pursue their strategic goals through the coordinated pursuit of projects, programs, and other program-related work. Program management seeks to optimize the management of related component projects and programs to improve the generation of business value.

Project management enables organizations to efficiently and effectively generate outputs and outcomes required for the pursuit of their strategic goals by applying knowledge, processes, skills, tools, and techniques that enhance the delivery of outputs and outcomes by projects. Project management seeks to optimize the delivery of business value by improving the efficiency of organizations as they deliver new products, services, or results.

Business analysis is used to perform research and elicit sufficient information to support business decision making, to determine if and when there is value in pursuing organizational changes to address business needs, and when it makes sense, to initiate a project or program to facilitate such change. As a result, business analysis optimizes the delivery of business value by providing the information needed to make wiser investment decisions on portfolios, programs, and projects. These processes are further discussed in Sections 7.4 and 9.3, where business value is defined and the results of measurements are considered.

Business analysis also supports the elicitation necessary to specify the set of product information used by development teams to design, build, and deliver solutions once the decision to pursue an organizational change has been made.

To ensure the best chance of success, business analysis performance can be assessed periodically by using the results from evaluation to identify and act on opportunities for improving business analysis practices. As with any valuation, agreed-upon measures need to be defined up front. See Section 5.7 for details about evaluating business analysis performance during and after projects.

1.2.4.1 DETERMINING BUSINESS VALUE

A project benefit is defined as an outcome of actions, behaviors, or solutions that provide value to the sponsoring organization as well as to the project's intended beneficiaries. However, it may sometimes be difficult to measure whether projects have delivered business value because business value can mean different things to different stakeholder groups. For example, if a project introducing a new product missed its sales targets, but those who purchased the product were very satisfied with it and indicated that they would repurchase the product, then depending on whom you ask, you may obtain a different response to the question of whether this project provided business value.

Some organizations might choose to define and prioritize based on customer value instead of, or in addition to, business value. Ideally, customer and business value are aligned such that items that are of value to the customer are also of value to the business. However, this is not always the case. Even when a proposed change that is of value to the business might not be of value to the customer, the business might choose to move forward with the implementation. Similarly, something that is of value to the customer might not provide value to the business. For this reason, focusing solely on customer value is risky because the business might not receive the benefits to justify pursuing the proposed change. Business analysis is used to understand and prioritize competing definitions of value by different stakeholders. The rest of this section refers to business value, but the same concepts about defining and measuring business value also apply to customer value.

A challenge in defining business value often lies with first articulating the intended business value before the project has started, so the project team knows what to strive for, which answers the question "Why are we doing this project?" Project benefits are defined in the form of business objectives that serve as the foundation for business requirements and all other categories of product requirements. Business analysis is used to define reasonable business objectives that can be measured. For example, a business objective to which a project might contribute could be to increase revenue by US$1 million in the next calendar year.

Another challenge is articulating the business value in a measurable form or articulating or finding indirect evidence for business value. In the previous example, where the business objective was to measure revenue growth, some organizations might find it difficult to set a target revenue, baseline the revenue, or even measure revenue growth. Organizations are also sometimes hesitant to commit to achieving a target benefit. A measurement, such as customer satisfaction, can be used as a proxy or indirect evidence for revenue growth, with the assumption that there is a correlation between customer satisfaction and revenue growth. Increasing customer satisfaction is also something that is not easily measured; however, customer satisfaction surveys can be a means to quantify customer satisfaction. If the business objective is to increase customer satisfaction by three points, then customer satisfaction surveys can answer whether the business value has been achieved.

1.2.4.2 MEASURING BUSINESS VALUE

A complication is that the realization of benefits often does not happen until well after project completion. For example, when measuring revenue growth, measurement of the target revenue cannot be performed until a year after the solution has been deployed. Measurement of customer satisfaction, which is a good leading indicator that revenue growth is also on track, may be accomplished sooner. By establishing a business objective before the project starts and determining how it will be measured, the project team is able to build requirements based on the business objectives and to incorporate the process of measuring the business value into the project, which ensures that metrics are available when the project has been implemented and that measurement data can be collected. If it is known that business value will be measured by customer satisfaction survey scores, a baseline survey should be taken to determine whether satisfaction increased. Resources can also be set aside to measure whether the business value was achieved after the project was implemented to learn from this experience, which could also introduce new projects and support the development of the product roadmap.

1.2.4.3 MEASURING PROJECT SUCCESS

Project success should be tied to whether a project delivered its intended business value. *PMI's Pulse of the Profession In-Depth Report: The High Cost of Low Performance* [2] reported that organizations have consistently struggled to deliver projects that meet original goals and business intent. In 2016, only 62% of the organizations surveyed said they achieved what they set out to do, and in 2017 this measure rose to 69% [2].

The types of information that can be analyzed and documented when deciding how portfolio, program, and project success will be measured include the following:

- ◆ **Business objectives.** Measurable objectives, including the timing of when they should be measured.

- ◆ **Strategic alignment.** How well the business objectives align to the overall strategies of the organization.

- ◆ **Benefits owner.** Accountable person to monitor, record, and report realized benefits throughout the plan.

- ◆ **Measurement plan.** Plan describing what to measure, how to measure it, and when to measure whether the business objectives have been achieved.

- ◆ **Risks.** Uncertain events or conditions that could affect the achievement of business objectives.

- ◆ **Assumptions.** Assumptions that are made when defining the business objectives and how they will be achieved.

1.3 COMPONENTS OF THIS GUIDE

1.3.1 BUSINESS ANALYSIS PROCESSES

Business analysis processes describe the activities performed to conduct business analysis. Every business analysis process produces one or more outputs from one or more inputs by using appropriate business analysis tools and techniques. A process is defined as a systematic series of activities directed toward causing an end result such that one or more inputs will be acted upon to create one or more outputs.

An *input* is defined as any item that is required by a process before that process proceeds. Depending on the point in time within the product life cycle, the list of inputs may change; therefore, the processes listed in this guide represent the inputs that would apply regardless of timing. In practice, if there are better inputs available, then the process can be tailored to use them. It is important to note that organizational process assets, enterprise environmental factors, expert judgment, and the business analysis plan are commonly used as inputs into all business analysis processes and will therefore not be repeated as inputs for each process discussed within the guide.

An *output* is defined as a product, result, or service generated by a process. The output of one process generally results in:

- ◆ An input to another process;

- ◆ A business analysis deliverable; and/or

- ◆ An outcome, end result, or consequence of a process.

Business analysis is accomplished through the appropriate application and integration of logically grouped business analysis processes that are linked by the outputs they produce. Business analysis processes apply globally across industry groups. Processes may be used in parallel, contain overlapping activities, and occur multiple times throughout the product life cycle. While business analysis processes are not required, each process is recommended to varying levels of detail under different conditions. For more information about tailoring business analysis processes, see Section 1.3.4.

1.3.2 BUSINESS ANALYSIS PROCESS GROUPS

A Business Analysis Process Group is a logical grouping of business analysis processes. *The Standard for Business Analysis* defines six Business Analysis Process Groups. Each Process Group is independent of the application area or industry in which it is performed. Process Groups are not project life cycle phases; sequence and timing are not prescribed. Process Groups are revisited as one or more processes within the Process Group can be repeated on an ongoing basis throughout the project life cycle. The Executing Process Group is one such example. The processes for elicitation are ongoing and are performed for each iteration in an adaptive life cycle.

The six Business Analysis Process Groups are defined as follows:

◆ **Defining and Aligning Process Group**. The processes performed to investigate and evaluate the viability for initiating a new product or changes to or retirement of an existing product as well as defining scope and aligning products, portfolios, programs, and projects to the overall organizational strategy.

◆ **Initiating Process Group.** The process performed to define the portfolio, program, or project objectives and apply resources to a portfolio component, program, project, or project phase.

◆ **Planning Process Group.** The processes performed to determine an optimal approach for performing business analysis activities, including how they are adapted for the chosen project life cycle, and to analyze the internal and external stakeholders who will interact and influence the overall definition of the solution.

◆ **Executing Process Group.** The processes performed to elicit, analyze, model, define, verify, validate, prioritize, and approve all types of product information, ranging from backlogs to user stories and requirements to constraints.

◆ **Monitoring and Controlling Process Group.** The processes performed on an ongoing basis to assess the impact of proposed product changes within a portfolio, program, or project to assess business analysis performance and to promote ongoing communication and engagement with stakeholders.

◆ **Releasing Process Group.** The process performed to determine whether all or part of a solution should be released and to obtain acceptance that all or part of a solution is ready to be transitioned to an operational team that will take ongoing responsibility for it.

Figure 1-4 depicts the six Business Analysis Process Groups within the product and project life cycles. This diagram demonstrates that processes within the Business Analysis Process Groups can be performed within the context of a project and beyond by supporting the activities in program or portfolio management. The left side of Figure 1-4 shows the Business Analysis Process Groups that are used before a project initiates, but still within the product life cycle. The center section shows the Business Analysis Process Groups that are used during one or more iterations of a project. The right side of the figure shows the Business Analysis Process Groups that are used after a project but still within a product life cycle.

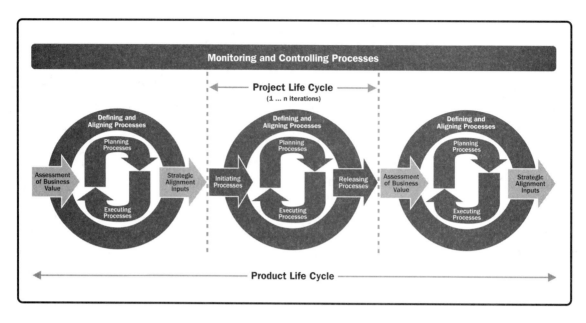

Figure 1-4. Business Analysis Process Groups Within the Product and Project Life Cycles

1.3.3 BUSINESS ANALYSIS KNOWLEDGE AREAS

Knowledge Areas are fields or areas of specialization that are commonly employed when performing business analysis. A Knowledge Area is a set of processes associated with a particular function. In this guide, the Knowledge Areas presented contain the set of processes that comprise the work of business analysis. The processes, though related, do not prescribe a sequence or order. The guide covers the following Business Analysis Knowledge Areas:

◆ **Needs Assessment.** Analyzing current business problems or opportunities to understand what is necessary to attain the desired future state.

◆ **Stakeholder Engagement.** Identifying and analyzing those who have an interest in the outcome of the solution to determine how to collaborate and communicate with them.

◆ **Elicitation.** Planning and preparing for elicitation, conducting elicitation, and confirming elicitation results to obtain information from sources.

◆ **Analysis.** Examining, breaking down, synthesizing, and clarifying information to further understand it, complete it, and improve it.

◆ **Traceability and Monitoring.** Tracing, approving, and assessing changes to product information to manage it throughout the business analysis effort.

◆ **Solution Evaluation.** Validating a full solution or a segment of a solution that is about to be or has already been implemented to determine how well a solution meets the business needs and delivers value to the organization.

Figure 1-5 illustrates the relationships that exist among the six Business Analysis Knowledge Areas. For example:

◆ The processes in the Stakeholder Engagement Knowledge Area are used throughout all business analysis efforts and interact with all the other Business Analysis Knowledge Areas;

◆ The results obtained by using the processes in the Needs Assessment Knowledge Area are the basis for work conducted using the processes in the Elicitation, Analysis, and Traceability and Monitoring Knowledge Areas;

◆ The processes in the Elicitation, Analysis, and Traceability and Monitoring Knowledge Areas tend to be used concurrently; and

◆ The processes in the Elicitation, Analysis, and Traceability and Monitoring Knowledge Areas produce results that are analyzed with the processes in the Solution Evaluation Knowledge Area, which, in turn, may trigger additional usage of the processes in the Needs Assessment Knowledge Area.

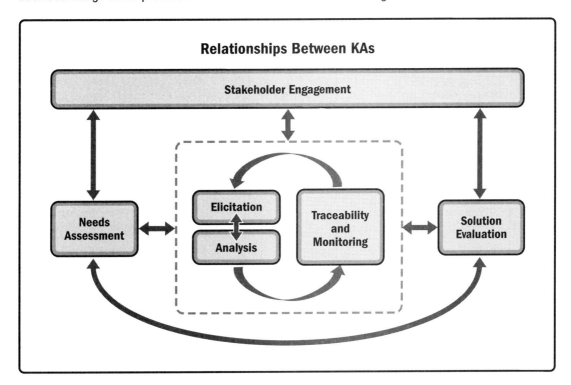

Figure 1-5. Relationships Among Knowledge Areas

The Standard for Business Analysis presents the work of business analysis as a set of processes, relating those processes to the six Business Analysis Process Groups and six Knowledge Areas. In *The Standard for Business Analysis*, the Process Groups assist with understanding how business analysis processes are performed. Within this guide, Knowledge Areas are used to group related processes to demonstrate how work is associated or logically related to collectively achieve the objectives of the Knowledge Area.

Table 1-2 maps the 35 business analysis processes within the six Business Analysis Process Groups and the six Business Analysis Knowledge Areas. The business analysis processes depicted in this table are relevant to all projects regardless of the life cycle the project is following. Within this guide, processes are numbered and presented according to the sequence they appear within each Knowledge Area. Within the standard, the sequencing and location of the processes are different, as each is presented according to the order in which it appears within each Process Group.

Table 1-2 provides the reference numbers for locating each process within the guide and standard. The reference number appearing before the process name identifies the section where the process is located in the guide and the reference number in parentheses represents the section where the process is located within the standard.

Table 1-2. Business Analysis Process Group/Knowledge Area Mapping

Knowledge Areas	Business Analysis Process Groups[A]					
	Defining and Aligning Process Group (2)	Initiating Process Group (3)	Planning Process Group (4)	Executing Process Group (5)	Monitoring and Controlling Process Group (6)	Releasing Process Group (7)
4. Needs Assessment	4.1 Identify Problem or Opportunity (2.1) 4.2 Assess Current State (2.2) 4.3 Determine Future State (2.3) 4.4 Determine Viable Options and Provide Recommendation (2.4) 4.5 Facilitate Product Roadmap Development (2.5) 4.6 Assemble Business Case (2.6)	4.7 Support Charter Development (3.1)				
5. Stakeholder Engagement	5.1 Identify Stakeholders (2.7)		5.2 Conduct Stakeholder Analysis (4.1) 5.3 Determine Stakeholder Engagement and Communication Approach (4.2) 5.4 Conduct Business Analysis Planning (4.3)	5.5 Prepare for Transition to Future State (5.1)	5.6 Manage Stakeholder Engagement and Communication (6.1) 5.7 Assess Business Analysis Performance (6.2)	
6. Elicitation			6.1 Determine Elicitation Approach (4.4)	6.2 Prepare for Elicitation (5.2) 6.3 Conduct Elicitation (5.3) 6.4 Confirm Elicitation Results (5.4)		
7. Analysis			7.1 Determine Analysis Approach (4.5)	7.2 Create and Analyze Models (5.5) 7.3 Define and Elaborate Requirements (5.6) 7.4 Define Acceptance Criteria (5.7) 7.5 Verify Requirements (5.8) 7.6 Validate Requirements (5.9) 7.7 Prioritize Requirements and Other Product Information (5.10) 7.8 Identify and Analyze Product Risks (5.11) 7.9 Assess Product Design Options (5.12)		
8. Traceability and Monitoring			8.1 Determine Traceability and Monitoring Approach (4.6)	8.2 Establish Relationships and Dependencies (5.13) 8.3 Select and Approve Requirements (5.14)	8.4 Manage Changes to Requirements and Other Product Information (6.3)	
9. Solution Evaluation	9.1 Evaluate Solution Performance (2.8)		9.2 Determine Solution Evaluation Approach (4.7)	9.3 Evaluate Acceptance Results and Address Defects (5.15)		9.4 Obtain Solution Acceptance for Release (7.1)

[A] The section number preceding each process name identifies the location of the process in the guide. The section number in parentheses following the process name identifies the location of the process in the standard.

The PMI Guide to Business Analysis

Business analysis processes are shown in the Process Group in which most of the activity takes place. When a process is performed in the Planning Process Group and its output is updated as part of the work in Executing, the process does not reappear in the Executing Process Group, but instead the process is just performed again. The iterative nature of business analysis means that processes from any group may be used throughout the product life cycle in any order. For example, when managing stakeholder engagement in Monitoring and Controlling, it may be necessary to adjust how best to engage stakeholders after gaining some experience working with them, thereby resulting in a need to revisit the Determine Stakeholder Engagement and Communication Approach process.

1.3.4. BUSINESS ANALYSIS TAILORING

Business analysis involves selecting the appropriate business analysis processes, tools, techniques, inputs, and outputs for use on a specific portfolio, program, or project. The business analyst performs this selection activity in collaboration with the project manager, sponsor, functional managers, other business analysts, or some combination thereof. This selection activity is known as tailoring business analysis.

Tailoring is necessary because each organization, portfolio, program, and project is unique; therefore, not every process, tool, or technique in this guide is necessarily required for every business analysis effort. The format of inputs and outputs listed within each process may also be tailored. For example, the output of Define and Elaborate Requirements (Section 7.3) is requirements and other product information. Requirements and other product information may be presented in the form of a requirements document, a collection of user stories, or another format deemed suitable for the situation. The inputs themselves can also be tailored, in that the inputs listed for each process are required at minimum to perform that process; however, if there are other helpful inputs available, they should be used. For example, a product roadmap may be beneficial when prioritizing product information, but is not listed as an input because a product roadmap may not always be available when prioritizing product information.

This guide provides a recommended reference for tailoring because it identifies the body of knowledge that defines business analysis that is generally recognized as good practice. Good practice does not mean that the knowledge described should always be applied uniformly to all portfolios, programs, or projects. There are different aspects of business analysis that can be tailored, including the:

◆ Business analysis methodology and techniques selected for use,

◆ Level of detail in the product information, and

◆ Business analysis deliverables.

Tailoring business analysis methodologies and practices is covered in Section 1.3.4.1. Tailoring the level of detail of product information is covered in Section 1.3.4.3. Tailoring the business analysis deliverables is covered in Section 1.3.4.4. More details about tailoring each process are covered within the process descriptions throughout the guide.

There are several factors that impact how to tailor business analysis. When deciding how to tailor business analysis, the team should consider the factors shown in Table 1-3. Table 1-3 presents the factors individually, but the cumulative effect of these factors could have a different impact on tailoring. For example, experienced stakeholders working in a highly regulated environment may require more detailed product information than they would otherwise if the environment were unregulated.

Table 1-3. Factors That Impact Tailoring Business Analysis

Tailoring Consideration Factors	How Factor Impacts Tailoring
Chosen project life cycle	Adaptive and predictive project life cycles almost always require different business analysis methodologies, different product information, and different deliverables. Tailoring business analysis based on the project life cycle is covered in more detail in Section 1.3.4.5.
Stakeholder knowledge and experience	Experienced and knowledgeable stakeholders or teams that have been working together for a while may require less detailed product information.
Location of the project participants	Distributed project participants may require detailed product information and additional deliverables to ensure communication when not face-to-face.
Business analysis experience on the team	Experienced business analysts may require less detailed business analysis practices than an inexperienced team. Teams that are not familiar with business analysis practices may need to conduct formal business analysis practices to help mature the teams.
Maturity level of the organization	Start-up organizations may not need or have formal business analysis practices or deliverables, whereas established organizations may have existing and repeatable business analysis practices.
Corporate culture	Some changes to business analysis practices are difficult or not possible without changes in corporate culture. Though improvements in business analysis processes may be justified, they may not be successful without a shift in mindset. Business analysis needs to be balanced between what is required, what is possible, and what will be accepted.
Importance or value of the project or components of the project	Highest-value projects or components of projects may warrant more rigorous business analysis practices, detailed product information, and additional formal deliverables.
Risk appetite of stakeholders and risk to the project, product, or its components	Higher risk levels may require rigorous business analysis methodology and detailed product information and additional deliverables for the riskiest components. Some stakeholders with lower risk appetite levels may want all details documented and approved.
Team stability	Irrespective of the project life cycle, when staffing volatility is a concern, there may be a need for more detailed product information and additional deliverables to reduce risk.
Size and complexity of the project	Larger or complex projects may require rigorous business analysis methodology, detailed product information, and additional interim deliverables to ensure thorough communication.
Governing standards and regulatory constraints	Regulatory constraints may require formal methodology, detailed product information, and additional deliverables to meet compliance requirements.
Outsourcing or vendor involvement	Contractual aspects of dealing with outsourced product development may require more formal business analysis practices and hand offs, more detailed project information, and additional hand-off deliverables.

1.3.4.1 BUSINESS ANALYSIS METHODOLOGY AND PRACTICES TAILORING

In some organizations, business analysts apply a business analysis methodology or business analysis practices to their work, which is either part of, or needs to align to, the overall project management or product development methodology. A methodology is a system of practices, techniques, tools, procedures, and rules used by those who work in a discipline. A practice is less formal than a methodology, is not required, and pertains to a manner in which we perform our work, typically based on preferences or recommended conventions or approaches. This guide itself is not a methodology because, although it offers practices, tools, and techniques, it does not prescribe the order, procedures, and rules for applying those elements. Individual business analysis methodologies may be derived from *The Standard for Business Analysis*. Specific methodology recommendations are outside the scope of this guide.

Some practices, techniques, and tools could be used in one methodology but not another. The order of application may also vary by methodology. Business analysis methodologies and practices may be:

◆ Developed by experts within an organization,

◆ Developed by experts outside an organization,

◆ Defined by vendors,

◆ Prescribed by a tool,

◆ Obtained from professional associations,

◆ Acquired from government agencies, or

◆ Any combination of these items.

To summarize, business analysts need to adapt elements of this guide to fit within their organization's overall methodology and any existing project or business analysis practices where value can be enhanced.

1.3.4.2 BUSINESS ANALYSIS TECHNIQUES TAILORING

Techniques describe different ways for performing a particular business analysis process or task. There are hundreds of techniques in use. Some techniques are specifically used when performing business analysis, while others are common and used by many disciplines. As the standard and this guide describe business analysis activities for all project life cycles, the techniques, too, are universal, regardless of the chosen delivery approach. While some techniques may be more helpful in one life cycle than another, most business analysis techniques are beneficial regardless of the life cycle chosen or industry in which they are performed.

The techniques discussed in this guide were chosen based on universal and common use and are not intended to be an exhaustive collection of all the options available. Within each business analysis process, a small sample of techniques is listed as guidance to highlight possible techniques a business analyst may apply when performing the process. This list is based on universal and common use and is not intended to be exhaustive. Those performing business analysis are always encouraged to learn new techniques or adapt current techniques to new situations; therefore, the techniques available to a practitioner are always changing and growing.

1.3.4.3 PRODUCT INFORMATION TAILORING

Product information, as described in Section 1.1.7.5, includes any of the information created, collected, analyzed, modified, consumed, and shared in business analysis. The product information used in business analysis is adapted most commonly based on the needs of the stakeholders, the context of a project, and the product and project life cycles in use. For more about effects of the project life cycle on the product information, see Section 1.3.4.5.

In general, most stakeholders want to contribute to or know about all the product information in scope. However, the level of detail in which the product information is explored and documented may vary according to stakeholder characteristics. Stakeholders who are experts in the domain of the project, located near one another, or in frequent communication with one another might require less detail when defining the product information. For stakeholders who are less familiar with the project domain, are physically distributed, or speak different languages, more detail may need to be included when defining product information.

The context of a project may vary with regard to the depth to which product information is defined. For example, for projects that are high risk or of high value, additional effort could be made to define highly detailed product information. Products that are regulated or are required to adhere to specific government regulations require detailed product information. Similarly, components of a project that are high risk may warrant more levels of depth in the product information than lower-risk components. When requirements are going to be reused by other projects, used to create training materials, or used to facilitate test case generation, it could be valuable to create more detailed requirements. For small and simple projects or small teams, fewer details in the product information may be sufficient. Expected high turnover in personnel or team distribution may warrant creating detailed product information.

1.3.4.4 BUSINESS ANALYSIS DELIVERABLES TAILORING

Business analysis processes produce deliverables that can be tailored. The deliverables, what they contain, and the degree of formality with which they are described vary based on the selected project life cycle and other project characteristics. Business analysis planning includes identifying the types of deliverables expected to be produced and considers maintenance, storage, and access needs.

When tailoring the deliverables, the business analyst needs to think through which stakeholders will consume them, what product information those stakeholders need to see, the level of understanding a stakeholder may have on the topic, and what will be the easiest format for the stakeholders to use. The objective is to produce deliverables that reflect what will be best for the stakeholders.

The deliverables may take the form of documents or they may exist in tools, such as requirements management tools, modeling tools, or agile tools. Typical business analysis deliverables and their most common forms are described in Table 1-4.

1.3.4.5 ADAPTING BUSINESS ANALYSIS TO THE PROJECT LIFE CYCLE

While many factors influence how or why business analysis is tailored, the primary reason to tailor business analysis is to enable the business analysis practices to work within a specific project life cycle. The project life cycle refers to the phases through which a project passes from its initiation to its closure. Project life cycles can range along a continuum from adaptive life cycles—for example, agile approaches—to predictive life cycles, such as waterfall approaches. The business analysis approach or methodology is adapted to whichever project life cycle is being followed. This section refers to adapting business analysis practices, tools, techniques, procedures, and rules to fit within the confines of the adaptive or predictive approach used.

Within the scope of the standard and guide, all the processes are applicable for use in any project life cycle; however, the timing and degree of depth with which they are performed may vary based on the project life cycle. For example, in a waterfall approach, the Conduct Elicitation process is performed mostly in the early phases of the project. This does not mean that elicitation will not occur in later phases, just less of it. In an agile approach, elicitation is performed repeatedly in each iteration throughout the entire project.

The project life cycle drives which product information is applicable or, at the very least, how the product information is named. For example, predictive life cycles tend to refer to requirements, whereas adaptive life cycles refer to this same product information by the names of user stories and acceptance criteria. However, all project life cycles will likely elicit business objectives and create models. For this reason, this guide provides specific names such as business objectives or models when the type of business analysis information being discussed is common across life cycles or specific to a process; otherwise, the guide uses the term *product information*.

Table 1-4. Deliverables, Common Formats, and Ranges of Formality

	Description	Common Formats	Low Formality	High Formality
Business Analysis Plan	Details about the business analysis approach, including tasks that are performed, deliverables to be produced, and roles to carry out the tasks	Project schedule file, project planning tool, word processing document, or spreadsheet	Informal ideas for business analysis approaches and resource needs	Formal definition of tasks, roles, and estimates as part of a work breakdown structure
Requirements Specification	Written description of the requirements and other product information	Word processing document, spreadsheets, notecards, entries in a requirements management tool, or exports or reports from a tool	Note cards stuck to a wall	Documents or tools
Business Case	Documented economic feasibility study as the basis for defining the value of project work	Physical document or presentation	A qualitative definition of value and cost	Thorough analysis, described with detailed estimates of value and cost
Elicitation Notes	Documented outputs from conducting elicitation	Documented notes, emails, or recordings	Informal rough notes straight from elicitation activities	Cleaned up and organized notes
Models	Visual representations of information	Individual model diagrams, informal sketches, or diagrams in a requirements management or modeling tool	Sketches on paper, a whiteboard, or in an artistic program	Formal diagrams in a modeling tool
Traceability Matrix	Table that links product requirements to other product information or deliverables	Spreadsheet or a requirements management tool	Spreadsheet with manual links	Links within a requirements management tool
Transition Materials	Information that is helpful to transition from current as-is state to the future state	Word processing documents, presentations, or spreadsheets	Discussion notes and written plans	Formal plans detailing tasks, data, resources, standard operating procedures, and work instructions

The project life cycle also influences when product information is created, consumed, or modified. For example, in predictive approaches, the Conduct Elicitation process could first focus on business objectives and then on stakeholder and solution requirements—all in the early phases of the project. In later phases of the project, elicitation activities may be used primarily to correct errors or uncover missing product information. In adaptive approaches, while business objectives may have been elicited in earlier iterations, product information such as user stories and acceptance criteria are elicited in every iteration until nearly the end of the project.

The tools and techniques used on a given project also vary based on the project life cycle. Some tools and techniques are applicable in any project life cycle, while others are more specific to certain life cycles, which will be discussed in the tools and techniques descriptions where applicable. It is always acceptable to use any tool or technique in any project life cycle if it helps further the business analysis.

Section 3 provides more detail about the different knowledge, skills, and personal qualities of a business analyst. However, generally speaking, business analysis competencies are applicable across all project life cycles. For example, although the choice of necessary analytical skills will vary based on the project, any of the competencies can be used in any project life cycle. While it is likely that the methods and frequency of communication could vary by project life cycle or stakeholder group, the communication skills are applicable within any life cycle. Finally, although different tools may be used in different project life cycles, the general skills related to tool knowledge are always applicable.

Table 1-5 describes the aspects of business analysis that could be tailored as well as a description of how that aspect would vary. A version of this table is included within each process description throughout the guide and explains how that process is commonly tailored for an adaptive and predictive life cycle. Like the rest of this guide, these tables are intended as a guideline or reference, because any specific project in a particular life cycle could vary from the information provided in this table. For example, when an adaptive approach is being used, it does not mean all of the recommended tailoring listed within that process for adaptive life cycles needs to be followed. It may be appropriate to use some predictive recommendations on an adaptive project because of other considerations the project team is dealing with. Similarly, some predictive tailoring descriptions imply a heavy and formal process, but predictive life cycle projects can use a lightweight approach that follows adaptive life cycle elements.

Table 1-5. Examples of Tailoring in Business Analysis

Aspects to Be Tailored	How the Aspect Is Tailored for Adaptive or Predictive Life Cycles
Process Name	The process may be called by different names in different project life cycles.
Approach	The approach could be tailored according to the level of formality to be used and the timing for performance of the activity. For example, the project life cycle may suggest when product information is created, reviewed, or refined, the frequency for those activities and whether official sign-offs are required. The approach is described using the names of the product information that are specific to the life cycle.
Deliverables	For each of the differing life cycles, the work products and specific deliverables produced by the process may vary in name and level of formality.

2

THE ENVIRONMENT IN WHICH BUSINESS ANALYSIS IS CONDUCTED

2.1 OVERVIEW

This section examines the influences within the environment and organization where business analysis is performed and discusses how these influences impact the manner in which business analysis is conducted.

The two major categories of influences discussed in this section are enterprise environmental factors and organizational process assets:

◆ **Enterprise environmental factors (EEFs).** Conditions not under the immediate control of the team that influence, constrain, or direct the portfolio, program, or project. In business analysis, these conditions influence, constrain, or direct how business analysis is conducted and are not under the control of business analysts. Any given EEF can be external or internal to an organization.

◆ **Organizational process assets (OPAs).** The plans, processes, policies, procedures, and knowledge bases specific to and used by a performing organization.

EEFs and OPAs are implicit inputs to all business analysis processes. As noted in Section 1, an important distinction between business analysis and project management is that the primary focus of project management is the project, while the primary focus of business analysis is the product. A consequence of business analysis being product focused is that some aspects are fairly independent of these influences and others are highly dependent on the influences. The following are examples of each:

◆ **Independent of influences.** Simply put, analysis is analysis. The same thought patterns used to think about a solution are used before or during a project or when considering the solution as part of a portfolio or program. In this guide, these thought processes are categorized as processes within Process Groups and Knowledge Areas and they occur whether:

■ The solution is highly complex or simple;

■ The solution is ultimately operationalized in a highly regulated environment or in a small start-up;

■ The project teams are colocated or regionally dispersed (large or small);

■ The projects in which the solution is conceptualized, designed, and developed are executed with a predictive, adaptive, or hybrid life cycle; or

■ The eventual solution implementation necessitates building something physical, building software, devising or revising business processes, or any combination thereof.

◆ **Dependent on influences.** Influences often dictate which project life cycle or life cycles are used to develop or enhance products, how business analysis processes are named, the methodology used to conduct them, the depth and style, and optionally, product information documentation, the level of formality of deliverables, and the collaboration style of a team as it works together to conduct analysis. How to bundle, slice, or split the delivery of a solution depends on environmental influences as well. For example, different deliverables or levels of collaboration could be appropriate in business analysis within a highly regulated environment as compared to a small start-up. The teams' physical working locations could change how much detail is documented about the product information and how frequently a team communicates.

Influences on how business analysis is conducted may be categorized in a similar but not identical way as influences on projects. Figure 2-1 shows the breakdown of influences into EEFs and OPAs.

EEFs influence how business analysis is conducted, and can originate from either within or outside of the enterprise. Refer to Section 2.2 for additional information on EEFs.

OPAs are internal to the enterprise. These may arise from the enterprise itself, a portfolio, a program, another project, or a combination of these. Refer to Section 2.3 for additional information on OPAs.

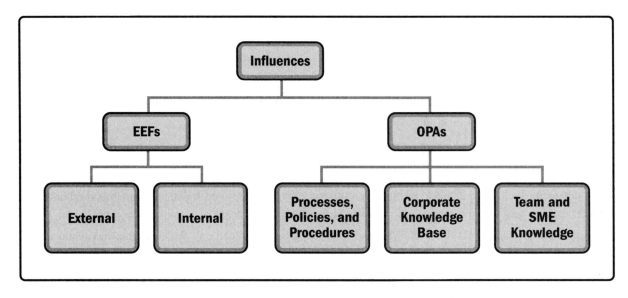

Figure 2-1. Influences on How Business Analysis Is Conducted

In addition to EEFs and OPAs, organizational systems can also impact how business analysis is conducted. System factors that impact the power, influence, interests, competencies, and political capabilities of the people to act within the organizational system are discussed further in Sections 2.4.3 and 2.4.4.

A challenge for those who are responsible for business analysis is to choose appropriate business analysis processes to perform in support of product development while working within the framework of an organization's environmental and organizational influences.

2.2 ENTERPRISE ENVIRONMENTAL FACTORS

This section examines individual EEFs. Representative examples of each factor are listed along with the areas of business analysis that are impacted. Although an individual factor may influence one or more specific aspects of business analysis, the cumulative influence of all the environmental factors on the choice of the project or product life cycle drives how they impact business analysis.

2.2.1 EXTERNAL TO THE ORGANIZATION

The following categories of EEFs are external to the organization and can impact how business analysis is performed:

◆ **Marketplace conditions.** Examples include competitors, market share, brand recognition, trademarks, and customer expectations. Marketplace conditions may impact the timing, duration, and segmentation of business analysis processes in support of product development.

◆ **Social and cultural influences and issues.** Examples include organizational politics, codes of conduct, ethics, and perceptions. Social and cultural considerations may impact the formality of business analysis efforts and how and when those responsible for business analysis collaborate with their stakeholders.

◆ **Stakeholder expectations and risk appetite.** Examples include organizational culture, organizational politics, governance structure of the organization, service levels, and customer representation. Like social and cultural considerations, stakeholder expectations and risk appetite may impact the rigor and formality of business analysis efforts and the style of collaboration with stakeholders.

◆ **Legal and contractual restrictions.** Examples of legal restrictions include country, local, or industry-specific laws and regulations related to security, data protection, business conduct, employment, and procurement. Examples of contractual restrictions include relationships with companies that provide products and/or resources to build or enhance products and the indirect relationship between an organization and the union that represents some or all of its workers (in some cases, this includes business analysts). Legal and contractual restrictions may substantially impact the formality and style of and storage, access, and audit requirements for business analysis documentation as well as how business analysis processes are conducted.

◆ **External professional standards for business analysis.** Examples include professional development organizations, such as PMI, which are setting the expectations and standards for how to conduct business analysis. These professional standards are resources for confirming or adjusting organizational business analysis practices.

The following categories of external EEFs primarily provide sources of additional information to be analyzed to support product development and enhancement. When included as part of a project, these information sources may simplify or shorten business analysis efforts in some situations, and in other situations, may increase complexity or scope:

◆ **Commercial databases.** Examples include benchmarking results, standardized cost estimating data, industry risk study information, and risk databases. Reuse of this type of information could shorten business analysis efforts.

◆ **Academic research.** Examples include studies, publications, and benchmarking results. As with commercially available information, reuse of academic research results could shorten business analysis efforts.

◆ **Government or industry standards.** Examples include regulatory agency regulations and standards related to products, production, environment, quality, and workmanship. Consideration of government or industry standards could substantially increase or decrease the complexity of the business analysis effort. Government or industry standards about the process may also influence how business analysis is conducted.

◆ **Financial considerations.** Examples include currency exchange rates, interest rates, tariffs, and geographic location. Any of these considerations may impact the scope of a business analysis effort if they need to be considered to develop or enhance the product.

◆ **Physical environmental elements.** Examples include working conditions, weather, and construction constraints caused by previous construction or geology. Consideration of the physical environment may impact the scope or complexity of a business analysis effort.

2.2.2 INTERNAL TO THE ORGANIZATION

The following EEFs are internal to the organization. They are listed along with representative examples for each factor. Most organizations are impacted by more than one of these influences. While each could have an impact on its own if it were the only influence involved, the impact made is usually the result of the cumulative effect of multiple EEFs:

◆ **Organizational culture, structure, and governance.** Examples include vision, mission, values, beliefs, cultural norms, leadership style, hierarchy and authority relationships, organizational style, ethics, and code of conduct. Additionally, the history or experience of the organization with the product under evolution or with the methods used in prior business analysis efforts can color the acceptance of the current business analysis approach. Ultimately, these factors—especially organizational values and beliefs—are the basis for the presence or absence of many of the other internal environmental factors of an organization. As such, organizational culture, structure, and governance are among the most significant internal factors that impact how business analysis is conducted. Organizational structure and governance frameworks are explored further in Sections 2.4.2 and 2.4.3.

◆ **Stakeholder expectations and risk appetite.** These considerations are internal as well as external EEFs. Examples include organizational culture, organizational politics, governance structure of the organization, service levels, and customer representation. Like social and cultural considerations, stakeholder expectations and risk appetite may impact the rigor and formality of business analysis efforts and the style of collaboration with stakeholders.

◆ **Geographic distribution of facilities and resources.** Examples include factory locations, virtual teams, shared systems, and cloud computing. Geographic distribution impacts how and when business analysts collaborate.

◆ **Market research and experimentation.** Examples include considering real customer feedback, product experiments, and prototyping feedback. Like external EEFs, information from these initiatives may simplify or shorten business analysis efforts, especially when they have been performed as part of a separate effort.

◆ **Architecture and infrastructure.** Enterprise architecture is a collection of the business and technology components needed to operate an enterprise. Business architecture is a collection of the business functions, organizational structures, locations, and processes of an organization, including documents and depictions of those elements. The business architecture is usually a subset of the enterprise architecture and is extended with the applications, information, and supporting technology to form a complete blueprint of an organization.

This blueprint includes the enterprise's existing inventory of purchased or built software used in its business operations. Infrastructure components are either part of a physical architecture or a software architecture. Infrastructure components include existing facilities, equipment, organizational telecommunications channels, information technology hardware, availability, and capacity. Architecture and infrastructure factors are taken into account during business analysis.

◆ **Information technology software.** Examples that impact how business analysis is conducted include the availability of tools to support business analysis, such as conferencing tools, modeling tools, and product requirements or backlog management tools. For more information about tools used in business analysis, see Section X3.6.

◆ **Interest and level of commitment to reuse the results of business analysis.** How business analysis is conducted and the tools used to support it are impacted by whether or not the organization intends to leverage the analysis results of past products as a starting point to enhance those products or to consider or create future products. Some organizations have little interest or commitment to reuse the results of business analysis. For organizations that practice reuse of business analysis results, this may occur at a team level, a business unit level, or an enterprise level. An organization's approach to reuse results impacts how business analysis deliverables are structured, stored, and shared when the project is completed.

◆ **Human resources management policies and procedures.** Examples include staffing and retention guidelines, employee performance reviews and training records, reward and overtime policy, cost per skill type, and time tracking. Human resource management policies and procedures may determine which individuals can conduct business analysis or may impose restrictions on who can perform the work. These policies and procedures may also impact the number of projects assigned concurrently to any one person who is responsible for business analysis. Reward and incentive policies can indirectly impact the way business analysis is conducted by influencing how stakeholders, subject matter experts, and other project team members prioritize their availability to participate in a business analysis process. For example, when busy subject matter experts are needed for business analysis for a new product, but are incentivized based on their responsibilities for other product development or operational areas, they may be less available for business analysis of that new product.

◆ **Resource policies, procedures, and availability.** Examples include contracting and purchasing constraints, certified providers and subcontractors, and collaboration agreements.

◆ **Employee capability.** Examples include existing human resources expertise, skills, competencies, and specialized knowledge. Overall skills impact the level of business analysis maturity of the organization as a whole, which has a direct impact on the quality of business analysis at the project level. The experience level of those conducting business analysis can impact the tools and techniques chosen as well as the number of individuals assigned to work together on business analysis tasks and whether those individuals need coaching support. For more information about business analyst competencies, see Appendix X3.

◆ **Security policies, procedures, and protocols.** Examples include access protocols for facilities and data, protection of personal and customer information, proprietary information policies, procedures for personal security, and levels of confidentiality.

2.3 ORGANIZATIONAL PROCESS ASSETS

Organizational process assets (OPAs) are the plans, processes, policies, procedures, and knowledge bases specific to and used by a performing organization. These assets influence how business analysis is conducted.

In general, OPAs include any work product, practice, or knowledge from any or all of the organizations involved in the project that can be used to perform or govern a project. Examples of an organization's OPAs include templates, tools, methodologies, or internally and externally developed standards in response to regulatory constraints that the organization wishes to use across projects. Process assets also include the organization's knowledge bases, such as lessons learned and results from retrospectives and other historical information. For business analysis, OPAs may additionally include the actual results of prior business analysis efforts, such as enterprise-wide, locally shared, product-specific, or project-specific requirements and models.

OPAs are implicit inputs to all business analysis processes. For example, during business analysis planning, decisions may be made about which types of OPAs should be used while conducting business analysis. During the business analysis execution processes, specific OPAs may be selected for use. Because OPAs are internal to the organization, the project team members may be able to update and add to the organizational process assets as necessary throughout the project.

Organizational process assets may be grouped into three categories:

◆ Business analysis processes, policies, and procedures;

◆ Corporate knowledge bases; and

◆ Team and subject matter expert knowledge.

Generally, business analysis processes, policies, procedures, and templates are not updated as part of the project work in support of creating or modifying a product. Updates are usually established by a global organizational function, such as a business analysis center of excellence, business analysis community of practice, business analysis shared service organization, or possibly a project management office (PMO). Some organizations encourage teams to tailor copies of templates and other assets to meet the needs of a project; other organizations require such assets to be used without modification unless they undergo an approved organization-wide change. In any event, updates to organizational business analysis processes, policies, and procedures can be applied by following the appropriate organizational change management processes.

Corporate knowledge base assets are updated throughout a project with information about business analysis performance and product information. For example, business analysis performance information from lessons learned and retrospectives and product requirements documentation and models are continually updated throughout a project. Many organizations use business analysis performance information as an input for evolving business analysis processes, policies, and procedures. In organizations with an interest and commitment to reuse the results of business analysis, product requirements and models can be used to seed projects to enhance existing products or develop new ones.

Team and SME knowledge evolves and grows over time. As team members and SMEs integrate new learnings and insights into their own personal knowledge base, the hope is that they will find ways to share that knowledge rather than using it to become "indispensable."

2.3.1 PROCESSES, POLICIES, AND PROCEDURES

As noted earlier, these OPAs are used as needed in support of the product life cycle. An organization's business analysis process, policy, and procedures include but are not limited to the following:

◆ **Guidelines and criteria.** These include the organization's set of standard processes and procedures and deliverables that satisfy the specific needs of a product and project.

◆ **Specific organizational standards.** These include policies, such as human resources policies, health and safety policies, security and confidentiality policies, quality policies, environmental policies, and audit policies.

◆ **Project life cycles.** As noted in Section 1.3.4.5, project life cycles can significantly impact the names of business analysis processes and deliverables, the formality with which they are documented, as well as when business analysis is conducted and which analysis techniques are used. They can also impact who is responsible for conducting business analysis and how much analysis to conduct. Keep in mind that organizations may use more than one life cycle approach to develop or enhance a given product, which may add an additional level of complexity to conducting business analysis.

◆ **Templates.** Examples include but are not limited to templates for business cases, business analysis plans, product requirements, use cases, user stories, backlog lists, models, risk registers, and traceability matrices.

◆ **Change control procedures for product requirements and other product information.** These procedures include the steps by which business analysis standards, policies, plans, and procedures or any business analysis product or project documents are to be modified, and how any changes are to be approved and validated.

◆ **Requirements management tool procedures.** Examples include procedures for the use of requirements management repositories, backlog management tools for product requirements, or traceability tools, as well as the configuration of such tools—whether out-of-the-box, customized, or internally developed—to support the procedures.

◆ **Financial controls procedures.** Examples include standard contract provisions that may impact how business analysis is conducted.

◆ **Issue and defect management procedures as applied to product requirements and other product information.** Examples include defining issue and defect controls, issue and defect identification and resolution, and action item tracking, along with the procedures for using any tracking tools.

◆ **Organizational communication requirements as applied to business analysis processes.** Examples include specific communication technology available, authorized communication media, record retention policies, videoconferencing, remote collaboration tools, and security requirements.

◆ **Procedures.** Examples include procedures for prioritizing, verifying, and approving product requirements.

◆ **Risk management templates.** Templates are used for identifying product risks.

◆ **Standardized guidelines.** Guidelines may include work instructions, proposal evaluation criteria, and business analysis performance measurement criteria.

◆ **Project closure guidelines or requirements.** Examples include cumulative information from lessons learned and retrospective sessions, final project audits, project evaluations, product validations, acceptance criteria, and knowledge transfer.

2.3.2 CORPORATE KNOWLEDGE BASE

In its discussion about managing project knowledge, Section 4.4 of *A Guide to the Project Management Body of Knowledge* (*PMBOK® Guide*) – Sixth Edition [5] makes a distinction between explicit knowledge and tacit knowledge. Explicit knowledge can be readily codified using words, pictures, and numbers. Tacit knowledge is personal and difficult to express, such as beliefs, insights, experience, and know-how. The *PMBOK® Guide* further states that tacit knowledge has context built in, but is very difficult to codify. It resides in the minds of individual experts or in social groups and situations, and is normally shared through conversations and interactions between people.

Much of the explicit knowledge elicited and analyzed by business analysts is stored in corporate knowledge bases, also known as repositories. In some organizations, all or part of the explicit knowledge elicited and analyzed by business analysts may be shared in conversations and interactions between people, along with tacit knowledge. For business analysis in such organizations, team members and subject matter experts act as living repositories. For additional information about team and SME knowledge, see Section 2.3.3.

Corporate knowledge repositories are used while conducting business analysis to store and retrieve product requirements and other product information and business analysis practices. These repositories can be used to research and understand as-is products and as-is business practices, procedures, and problems. They include but are not limited to the following:

- **Business knowledge repositories.** Contain versioned project and product documents, such as locally shared, enterprise-wide, product-specific, or project-specific product requirements and models. For more information about the types of requirements and models that may be included in a business knowledge repository, see Sections 7.2 and 7.3. As-built documentation is analysis and design documentation that has been updated to correspond to the released solution, and can also be considered part of the business knowledge repository. For some organizations, business knowledge is stored in requirements management tools or modeling tools; others may store this information in project folders and files.

- **Configuration management knowledge repositories.** Contain the versions of software and hardware components and baselines of all performing organizational standards, policies, and procedures.

- **Historical information and lessons learned knowledge repositories.** Examples include project records and documents relating to business analysis performance, project closure information related to business analysis, information regarding both the results of previous project and product selection decisions, previous business analysis performance information, and information from risk management processes.

- **Issue and defect management data repositories.** Contain issue and defect status, control information, issue and defect resolution, and action item results. In some organizations, issues and defects may be tracked and managed separately.

- **Data repositories for metrics.** Include metrics defined for collecting and sharing measurement data on business processes and products.

2.3.3 TEAM AND SUBJECT MATTER EXPERT (SME) KNOWLEDGE

No matter what life cycle is used, some product information may not be fully and/or formally documented. As noted in Section 1, product requirements and other product information may be stored in a variety of forms such as tools, documents, notes, emails, and in the minds of subject matter experts. For business analysis, SMEs are a rich source of information, insights, and expectations for a future state. Long-time members of product development or product enhancement teams may also have knowledge that is not formally documented; in some sense, these team members become SMEs themselves. Solutions developed using any life cycle approach, but especially adaptive life cycle approaches, often use conversations to elicit, elaborate, and analyze product requirements. Though adaptive life cycles may also use lightweight documentation, such as user stories and models, to serve as reminders to have those conversations and may use sketches of lightweight models as reminders of the results of those conversations, some of the product information may still reside in people's minds. Product teams have the responsibility for transferring the product knowledge to the newest team members, so that the team itself becomes a living and self-sustaining repository of product knowledge.

2.4 THE IMPACT OF ORGANIZATIONAL SYSTEMS ON HOW BUSINESS ANALYSIS IS CONDUCTED

2.4.1 OVERVIEW

Section 2.4.1 of *A Guide to the Project Management Body of Knowledge* (*PMBOK® Guide*) – Sixth Edition [5] defines a system as a collection of various components that together can produce results not obtainable by the individual components alone. It notes that an organizational system is composed of organizational components, which are identifiable elements within an organization that provide a particular function or group of related functions. The interaction of the various system functional components creates the organization's capabilities and influences its culture.

Organizational systems impact how business analysis is conducted by influencing:

◆ Choice of project life cycles that the organization uses, which is explored in Section 2.4.2;

◆ Type of support provided for business analysis practices and where it is located organizationally, which is explored in Section 2.4.3; and

◆ Collaboration with individuals in other functional areas, which is noted in Section 2.4.4 and explored further in Section 3.3.

A challenge for those who are responsible for business analysis is to leverage business analysis processes in support of product development while working within the framework of an organizational system. Regardless of these impacts, business analysis processes should be performed to effectively elicit, elaborate, and analyze product requirements and product information in support of sound decision making about solutions and to ensure that enough is known about a product so that it can be developed or enhanced properly.

2.4.2 ORGANIZATIONAL SYSTEMS, PROJECT LIFE CYCLES, AND BUSINESS ANALYSIS

Internal EEFs, especially those that are examples of organizational culture, such as values and beliefs, structure, and governance, determine many of the characteristics of an organizational system. They come into play when determining an organization's processes, policies, and procedures, including its choice of project life cycles and approaches to solution delivery. As noted in Section 1.3.4, the project life cycles and approaches to solution delivery that are chosen create likely scenarios for the formality with which business analysis is conducted and what tools and techniques are used. As mentioned in Section 1.3.4.5, the level of formality is a factor in deciding how business analysis deliverables are tailored. Typical considerations for conducting business analysis processes within adaptive and predictive life cycles can be found in the Knowledge Area process description sections of this guide.

2.4.3 HOW ORGANIZATIONS SUPPORT BUSINESS ANALYSIS PRACTICES

A recent PMI survey [3] of individuals who have a role related to business analysis found the following:

◆ Only 18% of respondents stated that the level of maturity in their practices is considered highly mature, optimized for continuous improvement, and established.

◆ An astounding 46% of all respondents believed the business analysis practices and the associated maturity level of practices are considered not mature or operating from an ad-hoc or "getting started" perspective.

Organizations that establish groups to support business analysis tend to evolve to a high level of business analysis capability. They tend to create high-quality standards/governance for business analysis practices and deliverables; facilitate resource sharing, methodologies, tools, and techniques; and provide learning opportunities for those who are responsible for performing this work. Examples include:

◆ Business analysis forums or communities of practice are often informal support organizations that focus on sharing and learning. These structures enable business analysts to share practices, tips and techniques, and project experiences with one another where adoption of anything learned is optional. Many forums and communities of practice sponsor "lunch and learns" or other sharing events, and may create their own corporate knowledge base. Other communities of practice operate on a remote basis and maintain continuity through online discussions within their corporate knowledge base.

◆ Business analysis centers of excellence or business analysis competency centers are more formal support organizations. Coaches and mentors for business analysis may report to these organizations. In some organizational systems, they may also have a controlling role and require compliance for:

  ■ Conducting specific business analysis processes with a specific level of formality based on how a solution or project is categorized;

  ■ Use of specific templates, forms, and tools based on solution or project categorization; and

  ■ Conformance to governance frameworks.

According to PMI's 2016 research, a significant number of organizations considered to have mature business analysis practices operate project management offices (PMOs) and enterprise project management offices (EPMOs). This research also confirmed that organizations with mature business analysis practices obtained more value from implemented solutions [2].

Business analysis shared services organizations take on all the support and controlling responsibilities listed above and also have a controlling role for resource management for business analysis. In some organizations, support organizations for business analysis are part of the PMO; in other organizations, they reside in a different functional area.

2.4.4 BUSINESS ANALYSIS COLLABORATION ACROSS ORGANIZATIONAL FUNCTIONAL AREAS

The functional areas and reporting relationships within an organizational structure have a significant impact on how business analysis is conducted as well as who participates in it and their level of participation. Section 3.3 explores the sphere of influence of business analysis and the many functional areas with which business analysts collaborate to support product development and enhancement. It provides further insights into the importance of the relationships between business analysts and other roles in other functional areas. This collaboration often requires being mindful of the impact imposed by organizational systems.

Business analysis requires a strong focus on the product. Individuals who are responsible for business analysis are often not the decision makers for products and projects even though they are often considered trusted advisors who use the product knowledge they have elicited and analyzed to advise and influence product decisions. These individuals recognize that they need to collaborate with others who hold other product and project roles, and who may belong to different functional areas. Ideally, collaboration between the business analyst and other roles occurs early and often, but sometimes those with critical roles have limited availability to collaborate. Insufficient collaboration for business analysis processes occurs when the priorities of individuals from different functional areas who are assigned to support the development or enhancement of a product are significantly different from the priorities of the business analysts. Insufficient collaboration may result in incomplete or inaccurate elicitation or review of product requirements, which cascades into incomplete or inaccurate analysis, and can have a profoundly negative impact on the product being developed or enhanced.

Obtaining sufficient collaboration may require extensive knowledge of the organization's systems, structures, culture, and governance framework. At the same time, successfully navigating organizational systems is often difficult, especially in large or complex organizational structures. To obtain sufficient collaboration and to work through the challenges that arise from the structure, governance, and culture of organizational systems, business analysts should closely collaborate with portfolio, program, and project managers and use their combined perspectives to build and share a strong understanding of organizational systems and how to successfully network within them in support of product, portfolio, program, and project initiatives. When the business analyst and portfolio, program, and project managers collaborate as closely as possible, navigating the organizational systems becomes a less daunting task, as each role leverages the knowledge and experience of the other for the betterment of the overall project.

3

THE ROLE OF THE BUSINESS ANALYST

3.1 OVERVIEW

Business analysis has been performed for decades, and despite its long-term existence, the role of the business analyst is still considered fairly new. While the number of business analysts employed is on the increase as the role continues to mature and evolve, the role of the business analyst is often misunderstood and underutilized within organizations. There are several contributing factors to this misunderstanding, including:

◆ Inconsistent expectations regarding the skills required to perform the role,

◆ Inconsistent definition of the role and how the skills are applied,

◆ Lack of understanding about the value the role provides, and

◆ Failure to recognize that business analysis practices are equally important for program and project success as program and project management practices.

This section explores the business analyst role by examining the position of the business analyst within the organizational structure, discussing the business analyst's sphere of influence in this structure, and discussing important skills that the business analyst may want to develop to be successful. This section intentionally focuses on the role rather than the profession of business analysis to make comparisons between the project manager role, the business analyst role, and other positions within the organization. Although this section uses a specific role title, the information presented here is important to anyone performing business analysis, whether they are performing business analysis with a project manager/business analyst (PM/BA) hybrid title, a business or technical title, or as part of an agile team.

This section is not intended to cover the entire spectrum of information that is currently available to explain the role; rather, it is intended to present an overview and provide a common understanding of the generally accepted key skills required of anyone performing business analysis.

3.2 DEFINITION OF A BUSINESS ANALYST

Those who perform business analysis are commonly called business analysts, but there are business analysis professionals with other job titles who also perform business analysis activities. Some business analysis professionals are specialized and therefore have a title that reflects that area of their competency: strategic business analyst, data analyst, process analyst, or systems analyst are a few examples of these roles. How an organization uses business analysis resources; where these resources functionally report; and the type of industry, type of project, and type of project life cycle being used are some of the factors that influence how organizations title those who have the responsibility for business analysis.

There are also many roles where business analysis is performed as a part of the role but is not necessarily the only responsibility. Enterprise and business architects; portfolio, program, project managers; and operational analysts are a few examples. The business analysis processes, tools, and techniques presented in this guide and standard are relevant to these individuals, too. Because there are many titles and variations of business analysis roles in use, this guide and standard use the phrase *business analysis professional* over *business analyst*. When the term *business analyst* is used, it is done for the sake of brevity and should always be considered a reference to anyone performing business analysis regardless of the title a person holds or the percentage of job function spent on the work. The objective of this guide and standard is to establish an understanding about business analysis and not job titles.

3.2.1 EVOLUTION OF THE ROLE

The evolution of the business analyst role is one of the reasons for the variety of job titles that exists today. Before business analysis was recognized as its own discipline, requirements-related activities were performed by various other roles, such as project managers, software developers, and product quality control analysts (which some organizations refer to as quality assurance analysts).

Developers did not always have the interest or communication and business skills required to work effectively with business stakeholders, and project managers often felt conflicted when they had to forego important needs of the business for the sake of the schedule and cost parameters of the project. Roles such as programmer analyst and systems analyst evolved out of the need and desire to have a dedicated resource focus on the requirements-related work and convert the business requirements into solution requirements for the technical team while ensuring that the procedures and rules that supported those requirements were well understood. While this was an improvement for project teams, these resources tended to come from IT, brought heavy technical experience, and sometimes fell short in meeting the expectations of the business.

Analyst positions on the business side began to appear for the purpose of improving the shortcomings of the technical analyst role. These positions worked well because analysts from the business side understood the day-to-day issues the business faced, understood the context where problems or opportunities existed, and were great advocates for championing the need for change. Frequently, technical expertise was lacking to understand what was possible and feasible and analytical skills were not sufficient when it came to asking probing questions or assessing results from a critical thinking perspective. Today, it is common to find business analysis resources in various areas of the business in addition to IT.

3.2.1.1 CONTINUED EVOLUTION OF THE ROLE

The role of the business analyst has continued to evolve. Trends, such as the rise of the global marketplace, geographically dispersed project teams, advances in technology, and other factors, have continued to influence the evolution of the role. Five developments in business analysis are worth highlighting, as each has been a contributing factor to broadening the role and creating variations in role title:

◆ Organizations recognizing the value of performing sufficient analysis prior to project initiation to ensure a clear and correct definition of the problem;

◆ Expansion of business analysis into specialized roles such as the enterprise business analyst who supports strategic planning efforts and portfolio managers building up portfolios with candidate project work;

◆ Acknowledgment that projects are created to deliver more than software solutions;

◆ Recognition that for business analysis services to be valuable, they need to be tailored based on project characteristics, including the selected project life cycle; and

◆ Revelation that many organizations are using a hybrid role for performing project management and business analysis activities.

These subsequent trends resulted in organizations shifting their thoughts on where to place these analytical resources within the organization and how to name and define the role. For example:

◆ Some organizations moved away from programmer or system analyst titles to recognize the value in also applying analysis practices to non-IT solutions. Examples of roles these organizations use include business process analyst, business rules analyst, business architect, and requirements analyst, among others;

◆ On the business side, some organizations use roles such as business relationship managers, business development managers, or product owners to represent the needs of the business while using technical analysts to represent IT. These organizations may utilize a business resource to perform pre-project activities such as needs analysis and business case creation and utilize the technical analysts for the requirements-related activities of the project;

◆ For organizations that have moved to an agile product delivery model, the role of the business analyst is not always discretely recognized. Those organizations will often utilize cross-functional teams, where every team member can usually play more than one role. The team takes on responsibility for business analysis, whether or not there is a team member who holds the role of a business analyst;

◆ Some organizations, recognizing the value that analytical resources provide, have specialized their analyst positions into roles, such as data analysts, usability analysts, or process improvement analysts, to capitalize on the value provided by those who target and perfect such specialization; and

◆ For those organizations recognizing that there is some overlap in the skill set utilized by project managers and business analysts, a project manager/business analyst hybrid role may be used.

Although the business analyst role has deep roots within IT, business analysis activities continue to be performed by many roles in non-IT environments. As mentioned in Section 1.1.3, business analysis can be performed when creating or enhancing a product, solving a problem, or seeking to understand customer needs. Many industries and types of projects benefit from business analysis, including construction, health care, and manufacturing. Those who perform business analysis across industries may be called by various other titles that are not included in this guide.

3.2.1.2 WHERE BUSINESS ANALYSTS COME FROM

Because the role of the business analyst has evolved as a result of these trends, it is quite common to find that the person performing business analysis did not start off with a vision to become a business analyst. Many business analysts evolved from other roles, for example, developers, product quality control analysts (referred to quality assurance analysts in some organizations), or subject matter experts from the business. The business analyst is able to bring a wide variety of skills and expertise to the position. Project teams can benefit from this wide variety of skill sets, but variation in skill sets often results in variations in how the role is performed (see Section 3.2.1.3).

Today, no matter whether the role is filled from the business or technical side, the important point is that those who perform business analysis should possess the requisite skills to facilitate collaboration from both the business and IT areas and understand stakeholder needs from all sides.

3.2.1.3 VARIATIONS CAN IMPACT QUALITY

When business analysts lack sufficient skills or the business analysis skills, experience, or competencies they hold vary widely within an organization, business analysis work is not performed consistently across programs and projects. This results in disparate applications of the role, which can lead to teams underperforming or overperforming business analysis. As with any process, reducing variance allows for more consistency in the way activities are performed and allows for repeatability, thereby providing greater effectiveness in execution.

The variation described here should not be confused with tailoring. Tailoring is the need to adjust which business analysis activities are best performed for projects of varying characteristics. For example, tailoring is performed to ensure that business analysis is correctly sized for projects of differing levels of complexity or those having different project life cycles—for example, predictive, adaptive, etc. For more information on tailoring, refer to Section 1.3.4.

The variations referred to in this section are concerned with the inconsistent application of business analysis across projects with similar characteristics. These variations can exist simply because the role is complex and the required skills needed are advanced. Business analysis skills take time to develop. Business analysts who possess different skill sets may gravitate to the business analysis activities in which they are skilled, disregarding activities where they feel ill-equipped. Variations may exist simply because business analysts are unaware of what the organization or project team expects of them or are unaware of the possible value their role can provide. For example, a business analyst who originated from the business side may feel comfortable defining the business need and writing business cases; however, when asked to interact with vendors to assess possible solution approaches, the business analyst may feel inadequate to facilitate the vendor review sessions and incapable of asking probing questions to examine the vendor offerings. In this scenario, business analysis activities are underperformed and a host of undesirable outcomes may result.

3.2.1.4 HOW TO ADDRESS BUSINESS ANALYST VARIANCE

When inconsistent execution of business analysis is a root cause for poor project performance or occurs in an area that places a priority on the consistency of business analysis practices, organizations should explore the inconsistencies to identify why variances in business analysis are present. Possibly, the business analyst position has evolved, creating a moving target to which current business analysts may aspire. Perhaps the discipline lacks a standard process within the organization, or business analysts are being recruited from many areas of the organization but lack formal training. Whatever the reasons are, efforts should be taken to understand the causes.

Organizations may also want to understand the competency level of business analysts both as a whole and at an individual level. In this case, the organization should define the business analyst skills it requires and compare that list to the skills of the existing business analysis resources employed within the organization. A skills analysis such as this is used to identify deficiencies so that measures and plans can address any skill gaps. These gaps can be addressed by augmenting staff with highly trained and certified practitioners such as PMI Professional in Business Analysis (PMI-PBA)® certification holders, by implementing training programs, by establishing a mentorship program, or many other options.

Organizations may also consider self-reflection on past project work to assess where business analysis has worked well and where it hasn't, and then leverage this information to make process and people decisions on future projects. By understanding the types of business analysis skills that a project team is looking for and keeping an accurate inventory of the skills present across business analyst resources, the organization is better able to assign the right mix of business analyst skill sets to future projects.

To minimize variances in the execution of the business analyst role, organizations should consider what structures are lacking. Examples of how organizations add structure into the role of the business analyst include:

◆ Establishment of a consistent and repeatable business analysis approach that is administered centrally for use across all programs and projects;

◆ Adoption of industry/best practice standards when the organization does not have a defined process in place;

◆ Creation of clear job descriptions for business analysts;

◆ Development of a career path, career framework, and competency ladder to provide guidance on the skills required to advance to the next level within the business analyst job family;

◆ Establishment of interview checklists and objective methods for evaluating future business analyst new hires; and

◆ Support of professional development opportunities for business analysts by encouraging involvement in professional associations like PMI, involvement in local PMI chapter events and conferences, or by providing funding for on-demand or classroom training.

3.3 THE BUSINESS ANALYST'S SPHERE OF INFLUENCE

3.3.1 OVERVIEW

Business analysts may lead, but they do not oversee project resources; this is the work of the project manager. A lead business analyst may oversee the work of less experienced business analysts on the team, or a manager of business analysis may be responsible for managing a pool of business analyst resources from an assignment or allocation perspective. At the project level, it is the project manager who is responsible for resource allocation, scheduling, and work progress, including that of business analysts.

Business analysts *do* manage stakeholder engagement, which is often considered an area of overlap with project managers. Looking more closely, business analysts have different objectives from project managers; therefore, each role manages engagement with stakeholders for different purposes. The business analyst's objective is to ensure that stakeholders remain engaged throughout the entire business analysis process so that the information required to build the solution is attained through ongoing discovery and collaboration and the solution design ultimately meets the needs of the business. The business analyst needs to be aware of stakeholder expectations, availability, and individual interests and the impact each has on the ability to successfully elicit the product requirements. When the dynamics are a cause for one stakeholder group to overpower or shut down another, or when a particular stakeholder becomes disinterested in the solution and begins to withdraw in requirements workshops, it is the business analyst's responsibility to take charge and resolve these situations. Because stakeholder relationships are managed across the project by the project manager, the best tactic is for the business analyst and project manager to work together when stakeholder situations arise regarding the solution. More information about the business analyst's role in managing stakeholder relationships can be found in Section 5.

A business analyst works with stakeholders to elicit and analyze business analysis information and evolve and develop the product requirements and other information necessary to achieve a common understanding of the product features across the product team. This makes relationship building and management a very important aspect of the business analyst role. Business analysts maintain a range of relationships that influence the business analysis work. Figure 3-1 highlights some of the stakeholder relationships that business analysts need to manage within their sphere of influence.

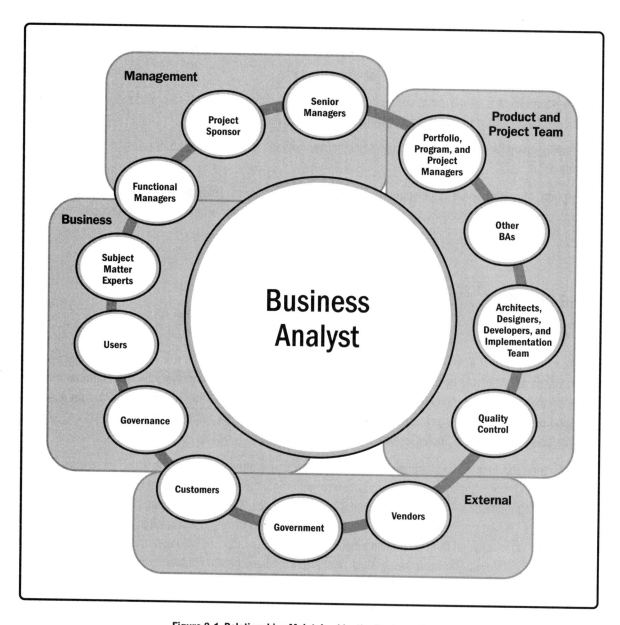

Figure 3-1. Relationships Maintained by the Business Analyst

3.3.2 THE PRODUCT

The business analyst has accountability for leading stakeholders through a comprehensive process to ensure the successful delivery of the optimal solution. The process begins with a needs assessment and concludes with solution evaluation; all activities are product focused. A product can be tangible or intangible—for example, an organizational structure, a process, or a service.

Almost all of the confusion that occurs on programs and projects between the roles and responsibilities of the project manager and business analyst can be cleared up by understanding that the objectives for each role are different. Project managers are responsible for the successful delivery of the project, while business analysts are responsible for the successful delivery of the product. A product focus requires an understanding of strategy to align proposed solutions and enable the achievement of organizational and business objectives. The product focus is, therefore, much broader than the project focus. The focus on product versus project is a fundamental difference between the roles of the project manager and business analyst. To learn more about the project versus product perspective, refer to Section 1.2.1.

The skills presented in this section and the processes described within Sections 4 through 9 help business analysts successfully deliver solutions to the organizations that hire and employ them.

3.3.3 THE ORGANIZATION

The position of the business analyst within the organization can be very different depending on how the organization leverages the skills of the business analyst. When positioned properly, the business analyst can be a trusted advisor to the business and a liaison to any technical resources. A business analyst can be considered a critical resource on assigned programs and projects and can be considered a leader within the organization. Business analysts require direct access to key stakeholders, so leaders such as the sponsor or project manager can help ensure access by removing any roadblocks that preclude the business analyst from obtaining clear communications with the stakeholders.

As depicted in Figure 3-1, business analysts form a lot of relationships; therefore, relationship building is a critical skill. Business analysts are in an interesting position within the organization, as they have responsibility for leading and influencing stakeholders without possessing the supervisory authority, title, or rank to do so. This can be one of the hardest aspects of the business analyst role, especially when the business analyst lacks the underlying soft skills to make this happen. Business analysts can strengthen their leadership abilities by building trust and demonstrating honesty, integrity, and transparency with those they interact with.

3.3.3.1 BUSINESS ANALYST RELATIONSHIPS

While the major relationships a business analyst develops and manages are vast, the number of relationships that need to be managed increases as the size and complexity of the project or program increases. The following are some of the typical relationships created and managed by business analysts, along with a description of the value that each relationship provides to the organization and the business analyst:

◆ **Business stakeholders and customers.** In some organizations and on some programs and projects, the solution developed is delivered internally to business stakeholders. These stakeholders may also be referred to as "the customer" when the solution is addressing a problem or opportunity directly for their business area.

Other solutions are developed to service stakeholders who are external to the organization, and typically these stakeholders may be referred to as the customer. Business analysts develop strong relationships with those who will be affected by the development of the solution, whether business stakeholder or customer, as it is their needs that the business analyst is ensuring are addressed in the end product. The category of business stakeholders is a broad one, covering all those with an interest in the business; therefore, it can be made up of other role types, such as subject matter experts or users.

◆ **Design team.** Business analysts support the design team by serving as the business advocate and sharing information about the business need and current state environment. The business analyst can review design proposals and provide feedback that the design team values and considers.

◆ **Governance.** Depending on the industry, organization, complexity, and risk level of the solution, business analysts often find a need to collaborate with one or more roles within the governance category. Roles considered part of governance include legal, risk, release management, change control boards, DevOps (which some organizations use to coordinate activities and improve collaboration between development and operational areas), a PMO or business analysis center of excellence head, or compliance auditors or officers. Such stakeholders can provide important insights regarding regulations, auditing obligations, business rules, and required organizational processes the product team is obligated to support and adhere to. Business analysts form collaborative relationships with governance roles to ensure that the product development process, including the management of requirements and product information, is performed as required.

◆ **Government.** Relationships may need to be established with government agencies at the state, federal, or international level. Typically, product teams are constrained in process or design aspects based on rules and regulations that need to be followed. Business analysts may develop points of contact in these agencies who can provide guidelines, requirements, or answers to questions.

◆ **Functional managers.** Building relationships with functional managers can help a business analyst remove roadblocks, obtain subject matter expert resources to participate in elicitation sessions, and gain key insights into business problems or opportunities of significance to the business. Building rapport with managers provides the business analyst with a strong advocate on the business side who can lend support when issues arise over scope or priorities.

◆ **Portfolio and program managers.** Business analysts lend analytical expertise to portfolio and program managers to analyze business problems, recommend viable options, and support decision making about which projects to pursue and how best to prioritize projects and project activities. Business analysts perform business case development and feasibility analysis to support portfolio and program management activities.

◆ **Project manager.** The business analyst and project manager can greatly influence the success of the project when a strong relationship and partnership is established between the two roles. The project manager/business analyst working relationship should be built upon mutual trust and respect, and all efforts should be made to accentuate each other's strengths. Collaboration is essential to provide a united front to the sponsor, stakeholders, and other project team members. Communication should be aligned, and each role should be able to support the other in most activities.

◆ **Project sponsor.** The sponsor champions the product and project, and the business analyst advocates on behalf of the sponsor. The business analyst works closely with the sponsor to define the problem or opportunity and identify solutions to address the business need. The business analyst champions the change throughout the project life cycle, serving as the business advocate—a communication bridge to the project team. The business analyst ensures that the business vision is addressed in the solution.

◆ **Product team.** The product team consists of the resources who act together in conducting the work to develop a product. Members of the project team are members of the product team, but not all product team members may be included on the project team. A product team member is anyone a business analyst interacts with when performing the work of business analysis. Some roles, such as enterprise and business architects, lend support across the organization, including supporting business analysis, but may not be directly allocated as a resource on a project team.

◆ **Project team.** The project team is a group of individuals who act together in performing the work of the project to achieve its objectives. Regardless of the project life cycle selected, the business analyst should strive for a strong relationship with the project team and should be considered a key member. When an organization or project life cycle does not recognize the role of the business analyst, this does not mean the work of business analysis is overlooked by the project team. A scrum team will have a scrum master, a product owner, and the development team. On projects using an agile approach, business analysts learn that their role responsibilities depend on the needs of the project team and that business analysis responsibilities may be spread across roles. Therefore, the relationship to the project team is always critical, but the business analyst's responsibilities may shift based on the selected project life cycle.

◆ **Product quality control (QC).** Developing a good working relationship with the product quality control team, which some organizations refer to as a quality assurance (QA) testing team, provides several benefits. Product quality control analysts are detail oriented and, over time, become experts in the products/solutions they test. This experience is valuable to the business analyst seeking insights into existing solutions. QC analysts are great candidates to review the business analysis deliverables to look for inconsistencies, areas where communications are not clear, or requirements that are not testable. QC analysts should attend requirements review sessions to help business analysts find errors or inconsistencies in requirements and use the experience as an opportunity to ensure a sufficient level of understanding about requirements to conduct the testing activities. QC analysts may even support the business analyst with transition activities. Business analysts can perform a similar review to support QC, looking for errors and issues with test cases and helping QC figure out what to test and by stressing areas of higher risk where testing requires heavier focus.

◆ **Relationship with other business analysts.** Business analysts also manage relationships with other business analysts throughout the organization. Business analysis work may be split across multiple roles, where one business analyst takes responsibility for development of the business case and business requirements and others work with stakeholders to define the requirements for a particular stakeholder group. Still other business analysts may be assigned responsibility over developing the solution and transition requirements. Regardless of how work is divided, business analysts build and promote relationships with other business analysts.

When business analysts report into a single functional area, establishing relationships with peer business analysts may be easier than in organizations where business analysts are distributed. Some organizations may establish a business analysis community of practice or a center of excellence to enable collaboration among business analysts. Whether formal structures are in place to enable these relationships or not, business analysts can seek to build a network of business analysts across their organization to learn and share best practices. Senior business analysts and business analyst managers support the profession by increasing the business analysis competency levels and capabilities of business analysis within the organization.

◆ **Subject matter experts (SMEs).** Business analysts work with a vast number of SMEs across all business analysis activities, but do so most heavily during elicitation and analysis. The business analyst leverages a variety of soft skills to maintain good working relationships with SMEs. When SMEs lack respect for the business analyst or perceive that there is a lack of credibility, honesty, or transparency with the business analyst, the level of SME engagement declines and the overall quality of the elicitation sessions suffers.

3.3.4 BUSINESS ANALYSIS AND INDUSTRY KNOWLEDGE

Business analysts have an interest in monitoring and staying well informed of changes occurring within the industries where they perform business analysis. Business analysts leverage industry information to understand how trends may impact solutions currently implemented in the organization, processes currently in place, or existing projects, including their associated requirements and proposed solutions.

These trends include but are not limited to:

◆ Product development,

◆ New and changing market niches,

◆ Customer preferences and buying habits,

◆ Government and international regulations,

◆ Changes impacting existing or proposed solutions, and

◆ Business analysis and portfolio and program standards and practices.

3.3.5 PROFESSIONAL DEVELOPMENT

In addition to maintaining relationships with peer business analysts on the job, many business analysts seek to build a network of business analyst relationships outside of work. These external relationships provide the opportunity to obtain and transfer knowledge, find solutions to some of the challenges the business analyst may be facing, obtain insights on emerging trends in the profession, and collaborate with other like-minded professionals.

Because the profession of business analysis is vast, it is difficult for business analysts to get to a point where they feel they have mastered the discipline. Professional development is ongoing in the business analysis profession, and continuing to acquire knowledge is very important. Business analysts also learn by sharing, teaching, coaching, and mentoring other business analysts who are in need of learning. Through technology, there are numerous online communities where business analysts can share templates, white papers, webinars, and other training materials to support one another's professional development needs. Obtaining professional certification can also contribute to one's professional development.

3.3.6 EDUCATING ACROSS DISCIPLINES

In addition to mentoring peer business analysts, there is often a need to educate personnel across the organization on elicitation and modeling techniques or on specific tools the business analyst may be using to collaborate with stakeholders.

Business analysts may need to demonstrate the value of business analysis, increase the acceptance of business analysis within the organization, or advance the efficacy of the business analysis center of excellence. They may serve as internal ambassadors to educate others about the value that business analysis provides to organizational and project success.

3.4 BUSINESS ANALYST COMPETENCIES

3.4.1 OVERVIEW

Proficient business analysts possess a variety of skills that enable them to operate successfully at a senior level. Sections 3.4.2 through 3.4.7 present a summary of the knowledge, skills, and personal qualities a business analyst may consider developing to perform effectively in the role. These competencies are further elaborated in Appendix X3. The skill list provided is not intended to be exhaustive, but instead highlights those skills that are most heavily used. The list of skills can serve as a checklist for business analysts to gauge and measure their personal competencies and to highlight areas where future professional development efforts may be targeted.

3.4.2 ANALYTICAL SKILLS

Analytical skills are utilized by the business analyst to process information of various types and at various levels of detail, break the information down, look at it from different viewpoints, draw conclusions, distinguish the relevant from the irrelevant, and apply information to formulate decisions or solve problems. The analytical skills category is composed of creative thinking, conceptual and detailed thinking, decision making, design thinking, numeracy, problem solving, research skills, resourcefulness, and systems thinking.

3.4.3 EXPERT JUDGMENT

Expert judgment relates to the skills and knowledge obtained from acquiring expertise in an application area, Knowledge Area, discipline, industry, etc., as appropriate for the activity being performed. It includes the skills and knowledge acquired through the collective acquisition of business and project experience. Expert judgment is an important component of a business analyst's decision-making process because previous experiences often have parallels to challenges that a business analyst might be facing. Expert judgment includes the skills to apply acquired knowledge and enterprise environmental factors and organizational process assets to perform work effectively. Expert judgment includes enterprise/organizational knowledge, business acumen, industry knowledge, life cycle knowledge, political and cultural awareness, product knowledge, and standards.

3.4.4 COMMUNICATION SKILLS

Communication skills are utilized to provide, receive, or elicit information from various sources. Due to the number of relationships and interactions that business analysts are required to manage and the amount of information that needs to be exchanged, these skills are some of the most critical ones for the business analyst to master. The communication skills category includes active listening, communication tailoring, facilitation, nonverbal and verbal communication, visual communication skills, professional writing, and relationship building.

3.4.5 PERSONAL SKILLS

Personal skills are skills and quality attributes that identify the personal attributes of an individual. Stakeholders, project team members, and peers use the skills and quality attributes in this category to critique how effective a business analyst is on a personal level. When a business analyst is viewed as being strong in any or all of these skills and attributes, he or she is able to build credibility. The personal skills category is composed of adaptability, ethics, learning, multitasking, objectivity, self-awareness, time management, and work ethic.

3.4.6 LEADERSHIP SKILLS

Leadership involves focusing the efforts of a group of people toward a common goal and enabling them to work as a team. Business analysts leverage these skills to lead disparate groups of stakeholders through various forms of elicitation, to sort through stakeholder differences, to help the business reach decisions on requirements and priorities, and ultimately to gain buy-in to transition a solution into the business environment. The leadership category is comprised of change agent skills, negotiation skills, personal development skills, and skills to enable the business analyst to become a trusted advisor.

3.4.7 TOOL KNOWLEDGE

Tool knowledge is composed of various categories of tools that, if mastered, enable the practitioner to work more effectively. Business analysts use various software and hardware products to help them interact with stakeholders and get work done. The tool knowledge category is comprised of communication and collaboration tools, desktop tools, reporting and analysis tools, requirements management tools, and modeling tools.

For more information regarding the individual knowledge, skills, and personal qualities comprising each skill category in Sections 3.4.2 through 3.4.7, refer to Appendix X3.

4

NEEDS ASSESSMENT

Needs Assessment includes the processes used to analyze a current business problem or opportunity, analyze current and future states to determine an optimal solution that will provide value and address the business need, and assemble the results of the analysis to provide decision makers with relevant information for determining whether an investment in the proposed solution is viable.

The Needs Assessment processes are:

4.1 Identify Problem or Opportunity—The process of identifying the problem to be solved or the opportunity to be pursued.

4.2 Assess Current State—The process of examining the current environment under analysis to understand important factors that are internal or external to the organization, which may be the cause or reason for a problem or opportunity.

4.3 Determine Future State—The process of determining gaps in existing capabilities and a set of proposed changes necessary to attain a desired future state that addresses the problem or opportunity under analysis.

4.4 Determine Viable Options and Provide Recommendation—The process of applying various analysis techniques to examine possible solutions for meeting the business goals and objectives and to determine which of the options is considered the best possible one for the organization to pursue.

4.5 Facilitate Product Roadmap Development—The process of supporting the development of a product roadmap that outlines, at a high level, which aspects of a product that are planned for delivery over the course of a portfolio, program, or one or more project iterations or releases, and the potential sequence for the delivery of these aspects.

4.6 Assemble Business Case—The process of synthesizing well-researched and analyzed information to support the selection of the best portfolio components, programs, or projects to address the business goals and objectives.

4.7 Support Charter Development—The process of collaborating on charter development with the sponsoring entity and stakeholder resources using the business analysis knowledge, experience, and product information acquired during needs assessment and business case development efforts.

Figure 4-1 provides an overview of the Needs Assessment processes. The business analysis processes are presented as discrete processes with defined interfaces, although, in practice, they overlap and interact in ways that cannot be completely detailed in this guide.

Needs Assessment Overview

4.1 Identify Problem or Opportunity

.1 Inputs
   .1 Assessment of business value
   .2 Elicitation results (unconfirmed/confirmed)
   .3 Enterprise environmental factors
.2 Tools & Techniques
   .1 Benchmarking
   .2 Competitive analysis
   .3 Document analysis
   .4 Interviews
   .5 Market analysis
   .6 Prototyping
.3 Outputs
   .1 Business need
   .2 Situation statement

4.5 Facilitate Product Roadmap Development

.1 Inputs
   .1 Business goals and objectives
   .2 Required capabilities and features
.2 Tools & Techniques
   .1 Facilitated workshops
   .2 Feature model
   .3 Product visioning
   .4 Story mapping
.3 Outputs
   .1 Product roadmap

4.2 Assess Current State

.1 Inputs
   .1 Enterprise and business architectures
   .2 Organizational goals and objectives
   .3 Situation statement
.2 Tools & Techniques
   .1 Business architecture techniques
   .2 Business capability analysis
   .3 Capability framework
   .4 Capability table
   .5 Elicitation techniques
   .6 Glossary
   .7 Pareto diagrams
   .8 Process flows
   .9 Root cause and opportunity analysis
   .10 SWOT analysis
.3 Outputs
   .1 Current state assessment

4.6 Assemble Business Case

.1 Inputs
   .1 Business goals and objectives
   .2 Feasibility study results
   .3 Product roadmap
   .4 Recommended solution option
   .5 Required capabilities and features
   .6 Situation statement
.2 Tools & Techniques
   .1 Document analysis
   .2 Facilitated workshops
   .3 Glossary
   .4 Product visioning
   .5 Story mapping
.3 Outputs
   .1 Business case
   .2 Product scope

4.3 Determine Future State

.1 Inputs
   .1 Business need
   .2 Current state assessment
   .3 Enterprise and business architectures
   .4 Situation statement
.2 Tools & Techniques
   .1 Affinity diagram
   .2 Benchmarking
   .3 Capability table
   .4 Elicitation techniques
   .5 Feature model
   .6 Gap analysis
   .7 Kano analysis
   .8 Process flows
   .9 Purpose alignment model
   .10 Solution capability matrix
.3 Outputs
   .1 Business goals and objectives
   .2 Required capabilities and features

4.7 Support Charter Development

.1 Inputs
   .1 Business case
   .2 Product scope
.2 Tools & Techniques
   .1 Document analysis
   .2 Facilitated workshops
   .3 Glossary
   .4 Interviews
.3 Outputs
   .1 Charter
   .2 Shared product information

4.4 Determine Viable Options and Provide Recommendation

.1 Inputs
   .1 Business goals and objectives
   .2 Enterprise and business architectures
   .3 Required capabilities and features
   .4 Situation statement
.2 Tools & Techniques
   .1 Benchmarking
   .2 Cost-benefit analysis
   .3 Elicitation techniques
   .4 Feature injection
   .5 Group decision-making techniques
   .6 Real options
   .7 Valuation techniques
   .8 Weighted ranking
.3 Outputs
   .1 Feasibility study results
   .2 Recommended solution option

Figure 4-1. Needs Assessment Overview

KEY CONCEPTS FOR NEEDS ASSESSMENT

Needs Assessment processes guide the investment decisions made by organizations. During portfolio and program management, business analysis results are used to ensure that the performance of the portfolio or program continues to provide the expected business value; that new initiatives align with organizational strategy and portfolio and program objectives; that proposed portfolio components, programs, and projects are well vetted and scrutinized with accurate information; and that all aspects of a proposed solution are analyzed for value and risk. During project work, similar alignment activities occur to ensure that the initiative stays aligned to organizational strategies.

Needs Assessment activities are performed to assess the internal and external environments and current capabilities of the organization to determine a set of viable solution options, any one of which, if pursued, would help the organization address the business need. These activities provide information that decision makers can use when determining which strategic initiatives to pursue, which activities to perform, and which components of portfolios to implement or terminate. The results provide the contextual information used when initiating portfolio components, programs, or projects and establishing portfolio, program, or project and product scope.

Understanding the business problems and opportunities with stakeholders is important for all programs and projects; the degree to which a Needs Assessment is formally documented depends upon organizational, cultural, environmental, market, and possibly regulatory constraints.

4.1 IDENTIFY PROBLEM OR OPPORTUNITY

Identify Problem or Opportunity is the process of identifying the problem to be solved or the opportunity to be pursued. The key benefit of this process is the formation of a clear understanding of the situation that the organization is considering to address. If the problem or opportunity is not thoroughly understood, the organization may pursue a solution that does not address the business need. The inputs, tools and techniques, and outputs of the process are depicted in Figure 4-2. Figure 4-3 depicts the data flow diagram for the process.

Figure 4-2. Identify Problem or Opportunity: Inputs, Tools and Techniques, and Outputs

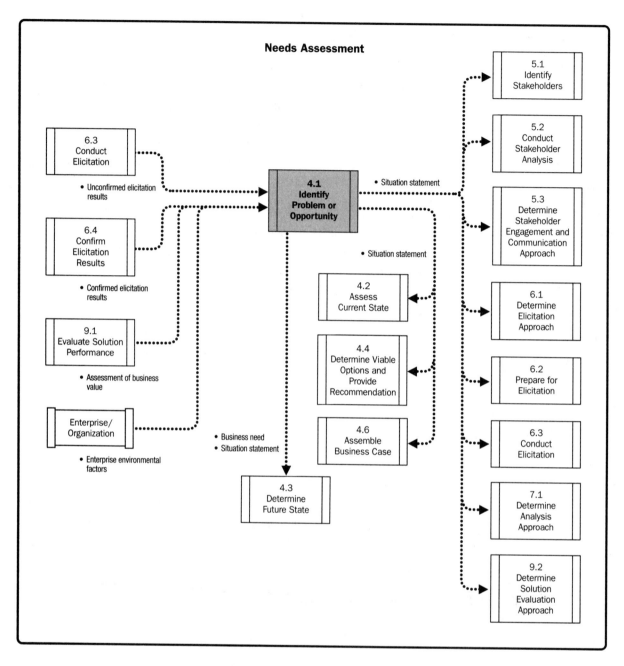

Figure 4-3. Identify Problem or Opportunity: Data Flow Diagram

Part of the work performed within Needs Assessment is to identify the problem being solved or the opportunity that needs to be addressed. To avoid focusing on the solution too soon, emphasis is placed on understanding the current environment and analyzing the information uncovered. Asking questions such as "What problem are we solving?" or "What opportunity might transform how we service our customers?" allows for exploring the situation with stakeholders without jumping directly into a solution.

Various types of elicitation are performed to draw out sufficient information to fully identify the problem or opportunity. Once there is a broad understanding of the situation, it is necessary to elicit relevant information to understand the magnitude of the problem or opportunity. Lack of data can result in proposing solutions that are either too small or too large compared to the problem at hand. This process occurs in conjunction with Section 6.3 on Conduct Elicitation, as much of the information needed to identify the problem or opportunity is obtained through effective elicitation.

Once the problem is understood, a situation statement is drafted by documenting the current problem that needs to be solved or the opportunity to be explored. Drafting a situation statement ensures a solid understanding of the problem or opportunity that the organization plans to address. The situation statement is reviewed and approved with key stakeholders to ensure that the solution team has correctly assessed the situation. If the situation statement is not properly understood, or if the stakeholders have a different idea of the situation, there is a risk that the wrong solution will be identified. The business problem or opportunity is defined in support of portfolio and program management activities and occurs pre-project, as it provides the basis from which a business case will be developed.

4.1.1 IDENTIFY PROBLEM OR OPPORTUNITY: INPUTS

4.1.1.1 ASSESSMENT OF BUSINESS VALUE

Described in Section 9.1.3.1. In business analysis, business value refers to the time, money, goods, or intangibles in return for something exchanged. Business analysis involves reviewing implemented or partially implemented solutions to assess whether the business value that the organization expected to provide is being delivered. When there is a significant variance between expected and actual value, Needs Assessment activities are performed to analyze the situation and uncover any resulting problems or opportunities. The assessment of business value, when negative, is used to determine whether a problem exists and to what severity. When the business value exceeds the value that was expected, the situation that is analyzed is considered an opportunity because the organization can pursue it to further enhance the positive results being received. Solution assessment activities need to be performed on an ongoing basis, because, over time, an organization may change its value expectations for a solution.

4.1.1.2 ELICITATION RESULTS (UNCONFIRMED/CONFIRMED)

Described in Sections 6.3.3.1 and 6.4.3.1. Elicitation results consist of the business analysis information obtained from elicitation activities. Results of prior discussions can take many forms, such as sketches, diagrams, models, and notes on flipcharts, sticky notes, or index cards. Past results of prior discussions and elicitation activities may be used as a starting point to learn enough about the situation to adequately understand the context of the problem or the opportunity being investigated. Through analysis and continued collaboration, the elicitation results used to identify the problem or opportunity may transition from unconfirmed to confirmed, demonstrating the iterative nature of elicitation and analysis within business analysis.

4.1.1.3 ENTERPRISE ENVIRONMENTAL FACTORS (EEFs)

Described in Sections 2.2.1 and 2.2.2. EEFs are conditions, not under the immediate control of the team, that influence, constrain, or direct the portfolio, program, or project. While performing Needs Assessment activities, including researching an existing problem or opportunity, a variety of EEFs may be reviewed to better understand the situation being investigated. Some examples include:

◆ Contractual restrictions that can impose relationships with vendors or third-party suppliers that might be factors contributing to an existing problem;

◆ Legal and governing restrictions, such as federal, state, local, and international laws and industry standards, that can impose constraints or additional requirements;

◆ Marketplace conditions that may pose issues that impede the chance of success with a current product, such as shifting competitor attitudes or the image of the organization in the marketplace;

◆ Social and cultural influences that can impact customer buying habits, imposing positive or negative impacts on the products being offered; and

◆ Stakeholder expectations and risk appetite that may influence the solution options that the business is willing or able to accept.

4.1.2 IDENTIFY PROBLEM OR OPPORTUNITY: TOOLS AND TECHNIQUES

4.1.2.1 BENCHMARKING

Benchmarking is a comparison of an organization's practices, processes, and measurements of results against established standards or against what is achieved by a "best in class" organization within its industry or across industries. The objective is to obtain insights into how successful organizations perform. Benchmarking results can be used to identify areas where organizational performance requires improvement. Benchmarking is not a technique unique to the business analysis profession, but it is one in which business analysis skills are used to analyze the results.

Once a broad understanding of the situation is obtained, it is necessary to gather relevant data to understand the magnitude of a problem or opportunity. The business analyst should attempt to measure the size of a problem or opportunity to help determine an appropriately sized solution. When data cannot be feasibly collected or insufficient information exists within an organization to understand a current state, benchmarking results may be used to provide information. Benchmarking is further discussed in Section 2.4.5.3 of *Business Analysis for Practitioners: A Practice Guide.*

4.1.2.2 COMPETITIVE ANALYSIS

Competitive analysis is a technique for obtaining and analyzing information about an organization's external environment. Results of competitive analysis may identify competitor strengths that impose threats or may uncover an area of weakness an organization has in comparison to its competition. These gaps are important to recognize if an organization is to remain competitive. Discoveries may identify gaps where customer needs are not being met or are being completely overlooked, providing an opportunity to develop products to address the void or identify new markets for existing products. Competitive analysis is a component of market analysis. Competitive analysis is further discussed in Section 2.4.5.3 of *Business Analysis for Practitioners: A Practice Guide*. For information on market analysis, see Section 4.1.2.5.

4.1.2.3 DOCUMENT ANALYSIS

Document analysis is an elicitation technique used to analyze existing documentation to identify information relevant to the requirements. While identifying problems or opportunities, this technique involves reviewing information relevant to the business need. For example, strategic goals and objectives, performance goals and results, customer survey results, documentation about current processes, and business rules might be analyzed. The objective is to identify and review the most relevant information to support analysis efforts when determining the problem or opportunity. For more information on document analysis, see Section 6.3.2.3.

4.1.2.4 INTERVIEWS

Interviews are a formal or informal approach to elicit information from individuals or groups of stakeholders by asking questions and documenting the responses provided by the interviewees. Interviews with key stakeholders can produce a wealth of information to support the identification of a problem or opportunity. Follow-up interviews can be performed to discover the finer details of the situation being examined. Interviews are one of several elicitation techniques that can be used to discover information needed to develop the situation statement. For more information on interviews, see Section 6.3.2.6.

4.1.2.5 MARKET ANALYSIS

Market analysis is a technique used to obtain and analyze market characteristics and conditions for the organization's market area and then overlay this information with the organization's plans and projections for growth. Information pertaining to any number of characteristics can be researched—for example, market size, trends, growth rates, customers, products, distribution channels, opportunities, threats, and many others. The information obtained is used by the organization in decision making, specifically to influence decisions regarding investments in future products. Market analysis results can be used to support strategic planning initiatives and provide context for future elicitation.

Analysis results may uncover threats such as shifting consumer preferences, new competitors entering the marketplace, new regulations, or downward trends in buying habits. A thorough market analysis includes information about the industry and market in which an organization operates, competitors, areas of risk and constraints, and projections such as expected sales growth or market share. This information is valuable when analyzing the business for problems or opportunities.

4.1.2.6 PROTOTYPING

Prototyping is a method of obtaining early feedback on requirements by providing a model of the expected solution before building it. When identifying problems or opportunities, this technique is useful to learn and discover what is valuable from the perspective of the customer. Low-fidelity prototyping, using models that provide a visual representation of what may eventually evolve into a product's design, may be particularly valuable for identifying problems and opportunities in projects using an adaptive approach to development. Low-fidelity prototyping may also be useful for any situation in which visual communication is more effective than verbal communication. For more information on prototyping, see Section 6.3.2.8.

4.1.3 IDENTIFY PROBLEM OR OPPORTUNITY: OUTPUTS

4.1.3.1 BUSINESS NEED

A business need is the impetus for a change in an organization, based on an existing problem or opportunity. It provides the rationale for why organizational changes are being proposed and why a new portfolio component, program, or project is being considered. Once clearly defined, it is used to provide context when discussing the future state, solution options, and business requirements.

4.1.3.2 SITUATION STATEMENT

In business analysis, a situation statement is an objective statement of a problem or opportunity that includes the statement itself, the situation's effect on the organization, and the resulting impact. The situation statement provides a concise format for presenting the problem or opportunity statement. Organizations may have other preferred formats. The important point is not so much the format but rather to ensure that the team discusses and agrees on the situation prior to discussing solutions. Refer to Section 2.3.4 in *Business Analysis for Practitioners: A Practice Guide* for an example of how to document a situation statement.

4.1.4 IDENTIFY PROBLEM OR OPPORTUNITY: TAILORING CONSIDERATIONS

Adaptive and predictive tailoring considerations for Identify Problem or Opportunity are described in Table 4-1.

Table 4-1. Adaptive and Predictive Tailoring for Identify Problem or Opportunity

Aspects to Be Tailored	Typical Adaptive Considerations	Typical Predictive Considerations
Name	Identify Problem or Opportunity	
Approach	Performed prior to portfolio, program, or project initiation during an early planning iteration; the degree to which Needs Assessment is formally performed depends upon organizational, cultural, environmental, market, and/or regulatory constraints.	Performed prior to portfolio, program, or project initiation, Needs Assessment is performed as a more formal process where the situation statement is drafted, reviewed, and approved.
Deliverables	Adaptive projects often create a brief statement of project intent. In whatever format it takes, the statement of intent typically states the business objectives, value propositions, benefits, goals, milestones, customers and partners, etc., that were identified as part of a strategic planning effort and are part of the project. It may also include very high-level user epics that are later broken down into user stories when the story is selected as a feature of a release. Situations involving higher risk or in regulated industries may require a documented situation statement.	Documented situation statement. Any models needed to assess the situation.

4.1.5 IDENTIFY PROBLEM OR OPPORTUNITY: COLLABORATION POINT

All levels of management can serve as sources of information to provide the context and history behind a problem or opportunity. These managers can also remove barriers that stand in the way of gaining access to other key stakeholders who hold needed information. Sometimes the information these managers possess is difficult to obtain because of management availability and scheduling difficulties. When this occurs, business analysts may need to work with proxies who serve as alternates.

4.2 ASSESS CURRENT STATE

Assess Current State is the process of examining the current environment under analysis to understand important factors that are internal or external to the organization, which may be the cause or reason for a problem or opportunity. The key benefit of this process is that it provides a sufficient understanding of the existing state of the organization, providing context for determining which elements of the current state will remain unchanged and which changes are necessary to achieve the future state. The inputs, tools and techniques, and outputs of the process are depicted in Figure 4-4. Figure 4-5 depicts the data flow diagram for the process.

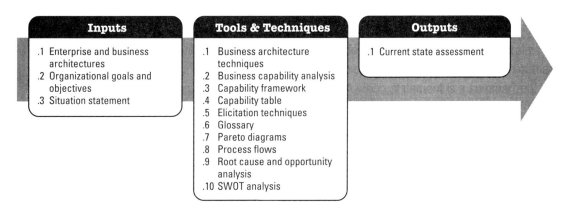

Figure 4-4. Assess Current State: Inputs, Tools and Techniques, and Outputs

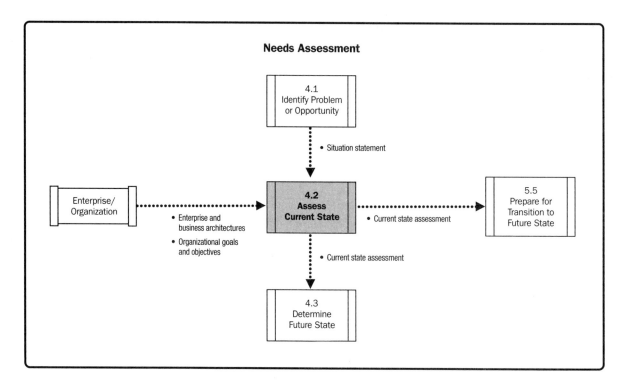

Figure 4-5. Assess Current State: Data Flow Diagram

Assessing the current state involves researching and analyzing various aspects of the existing organizational environment to understand a situation of concern or interest to the business. The area of analysis may involve a portfolio, program, or project; a department or business unit within the organization; an aspect of the competitive environment; a particular product; or any number of other areas. Various factors can be analyzed, such as the organizational structure, current capabilities, culture, processes, policies, enterprise and business architectures, capacities such as human resources and capital, and external factors. It is common for the information obtained as part of this process to be more detailed than the information analyzed as part of defining the problem or opportunity, since ongoing elicitation activities have continued to cultivate the information. Assess Current State occurs in conjunction with Section 6.3 on Conduct Elicitation.

Evaluating the current capabilities of the organization is a significant focus during a current state assessment. A capability is a function, process, service, or other proficiency of an organization. Capabilities enable an organization to achieve its strategy. The analysis of a problem and its associated root causes allow an organization to identify the capabilities that will be needed or need to be matured to address the business need. Any limiting factors, along with the associated root causes for such factors, are captured and the capabilities or features required to address these duly noted.

Current state assessments are performed to learn enough about the problem or opportunity to adequately understand the situation without the need for conducting a full analysis of requirements. Information about the current state may be obtained through various elicitation methods such as document analysis, interviews, observation, and surveys.

Business analysis activities should be focused on analyzing the areas relevant for defining the situation statement and should be careful not to lead to analysis of areas that are out of scope or not helpful for the eventual definition of the future state. In situations where the current state has recently been assessed in sufficient detail, it is sometimes possible to use that knowledge as the basis for defining the future state without conducting yet another current state assessment. In some organizations, the analytical resources who conduct current state assessments may be a different team of analysts from the analytical resources who perform business analysis on the project if one is approved and initiated.

4.2.1 ASSESS CURRENT STATE: INPUTS

4.2.1.1 ENTERPRISE AND BUSINESS ARCHITECTURES

Described in Section 2.2.2. Enterprise architecture is a collection of business and technology components needed to operate an enterprise. Enterprise architecture is assembled in the form of a schematic or model. Models can be analyzed to understand the strategic and operational impacts that a change will have on various aspects of the enterprise. Business architecture is a subset of the enterprise architecture and contains components such as the business functions, organizational structures, locations, and processes of an organization, including documents and depictions of those elements.

Enterprise and business architectures are a fundamental input into the current state assessment because they visually and holistically depict different aspects of the enterprise and organizational structures that need to be understood for future business analysis work. These architectures provide the most value when they are current, but even outdated models can be leveraged and used as a starting point for conversation with business stakeholders. When architecture models do not exist, business analysis can be performed to begin to develop the aspects of the models most relevant to the situation being analyzed. Aside from architecture models, the actual systems or data supported by the systems can be reviewed from a high level to understand key data components, current relationships, and business rules. This work can be performed using the support of an enterprise or business architect.

4.2.1.2 ORGANIZATIONAL GOALS AND OBJECTIVES

Organizational goals define the measurable targets that a business establishes in order to deliver on its strategy. Organizational objectives are the statements aimed at directing the actions of the organization to reach its goals. Goals are typically broad based and span one or more years. Objectives enable goals, are more specific, and tend to be of shorter term, often with durations of 1 year or less. Goals and objectives provide criteria that are used when making decisions regarding which programs or projects are best pursued.

Existing organizational goals and objectives may be reviewed as part of the current state analysis. Organizational goals and objectives are often revealed in internal corporate strategy documents and business plans. These documents and plans may be reviewed to acquire an understanding of the industry and its markets, the competition, products currently available, potential new products, and other factors used in developing organizational strategies. If corporate strategy documents and plans are not available for review, it may be necessary to interview stakeholders to determine this information. Organizational goals and objectives are further discussed in Section 2.4.1 of *Business Analysis for Practitioners: A Practice Guide*.

4.2.1.3 SITUATION STATEMENT

Described in Section 4.1.3.2. The situation statement provides an objective statement about the problem or opportunity the business is looking to address, along with the effect and impact the situation has on the organization. The assessment of the current state is compared against the situation statement to determine the impact of a problem or opportunity on the existing organizational environment.

4.2.2 ASSESS CURRENT STATE: TOOLS AND TECHNIQUES

4.2.2.1 BUSINESS ARCHITECTURE TECHNIQUES

Business architecture techniques are organizational frameworks available to model business architecture, each providing different approaches for analyzing various aspects of the business. These models can serve as checklists, frameworks, or job aids for assessing the current state and can be used to guide strategy decisions within the organization, specifically at the portfolio and program levels.

4.2.2.2 BUSINESS CAPABILITY ANALYSIS

Business capability analysis is a technique used to analyze performance in terms of processes, people skills, and other resources used by an organization to perform its work. Historical data obtained from analyzing current capabilities are used to understand trends and determine what measures will be helpful guidelines for determining whether a capability is performing as it should be in the current state. The historical data are used to establish performance standards by which current and future performance is evaluated. In the current state, the objective is to determine a specification by which business capabilities can be assessed and performance measured and monitored on an ongoing basis. In the future state, this specification can be used to establish a benchmark for future performance.

4.2.2.3 CAPABILITY FRAMEWORK

A capability framework provides a set of descriptions about the key skills, knowledge, behaviors, abilities, systems, and overall competencies of value to an organization. The capabilities analyzed can be for people or products. Capability frameworks may include information about physical, financial, informational, or intellectual capabilities. Some capabilities are available because of the availability of assets that support them. A physical capability could be the usage of machinery for construction, which requires both the machinery itself and individuals with the capability to operate it, and an intellectual capability could be copyrights and intellectual property. Capabilities for people are typically listed by role or position. This information supports improved decision making with regard to training, hiring, or allocating people resources to processes or projects. Capability frameworks may contain information about the competencies that enable the organization to operate today and may be used as a starting point when performing a gap analysis to identify the capabilities needed to achieve the future state. There are many different formats for presenting capability information; Tables 4-2 and 4-3 show two ideas for people- and product-focused discussions. The rows and columns could be changed or switched in either table. Some organizations refer to these types of frameworks as maturity models.

Table 4-2. Capability Framework Sample Format for Analyzing People Capabilities

Capability Framework—Business Analysis Job Family					
Business Analyst	**Entry Level**	**Intermediate**	**Senior I**	**Senior II**	**Senior III**
Capability 1	Describes how an individual demonstrates the capability at each level				
Capability 2					
Capability 3					

Table 4-3. Capability Framework Sample Format for Analyzing Product Capabilities

Categories to Be Measured	Maturity Levels				
	Level 0	**Level 1**	**Level 2**	**Level 3**	**...**
People	<criteria about people resources>				
Process	<criteria about process and methodology>				
Technology	<criteria about technology or tools>				

4.2.2.4 CAPABILITY TABLE

Capability tables are used for analyzing capabilities in a current or future state. Within future-state analysis, the model can be used to display the capabilities needed to solve a problem or seize an opportunity. The technique can be applied to depict the relationship between a situation, its root causes, and the capabilities needed to address the situation. The model can provide an easy way to visualize current problems, the associated root causes, and the proposed new capabilities or features that if pursued, could address the problem. Today, different forms of capability tables exist. Table 4-4 shows a sample format of one possible way to structure a capability table. Capability tables are further discussed and an example is provided in Section 2.4.5.1 of *Business Analysis for Practitioners: A Practice Guide*.

Table 4-4. Capability Table Sample Format

Problem/Current Limitations	Root Cause(s)	New Capability/Feature
Problem #1	1st root cause for problem #1	• New capability • New capability
	2nd root cause for problem #1	• New capability
	3rd root cause for problem #1	• New capability
Problem #2	1st root cause for problem #2	• New capability • New capability
	2nd root cause for problem #2	• New capability

4.2.2.5 ELICITATION TECHNIQUES

Elicitation techniques are used to draw information from various sources. Information about the current state may be obtained through various elicitation methods as described in Section 6.3 on Conduct Elicitation. A few common techniques that are effective during current state analysis are document analysis, interviews, observation, and questionnaires and surveys:

◆ **Document analysis.** An elicitation technique used to analyze existing documentation and identify relevant product information. Many documents found within an organization can provide relevant information about the current state, such as training materials, product literature, standard operating procedures, or deliverables from past projects. For more information on document analysis, see Section 6.3.2.3.

◆ **Interviews.** A formal or informal approach to elicit information from stakeholders. Interviews can be scheduled with various stakeholders who possess key information about the current state, such as the users of an existing solution or participants in existing processes where problems have been identified. For more information on interviews, see Section 6.3.2.6.

◆ **Observation.** An elicitation technique that provides a direct way of eliciting information about how a process is performed or a product is used, by viewing individuals in their own environment performing their jobs or tasks and performing processes. Through observation, the observer can experience the current state firsthand. For more information on observation, see Section 6.3.2.7.

◆ **Questionnaires and surveys.** Written sets of questions designed to quickly accumulate information from a large number of respondents. Surveys can be developed to elicit information about the current state—for example, areas where customers or business stakeholders may wish to see improvements or have concerns or existing problems. When confidentiality is made part of the process, participants may be more willing to provide information that they would not otherwise provide in a face-to-face forum like an interview. For more information on questionnaires and surveys, see Section 6.3.2.9.

For more information about elicitation techniques, see Section 6.3.2.

4.2.2.6 GLOSSARY

In business analysis, a glossary provides a list of definitions for terms and acronyms about a product. A glossary should be started as early as possible in portfolio, program, or project analysis to support common language; therefore, it is a technique that is commonly started with needs assessment activities. It may be possible to reuse a common glossary maintained as part of the organization's business architecture or from past project archives. For more information on glossaries, see Section 7.3.2.3.

4.2.2.7 PARETO DIAGRAMS

A Pareto diagram is a histogram that can be used to communicate the results of root cause analysis. Pareto diagrams are a special form of vertical bar chart used to emphasize the most significant factor among a set of data. The vertical axis can depict any category of information that is important to the product team, such as cost or frequency, or consequences such as time or money. The horizontal axis can display the categories of data being measured—for example, types of problems or cause categories. When analyzing problems, the vertical axis might depict the frequency at which different types of problems are occurring, how many times a cause category was identified, or the total cost associated with resolving different product issues. The data results are displayed in descending order, which easily draws attention to the problems, causes, or costs that have the greatest significance and thereby require the most attention. The format of a Pareto diagram helps demonstrate the 80/20 principle whereby 80% of problems can be related back to 20% of the causes. Pareto diagrams are also known as Pareto charts. The process of creating these visuals is called Pareto analysis. Figure 4-6 shows a sample format of a Pareto diagram.

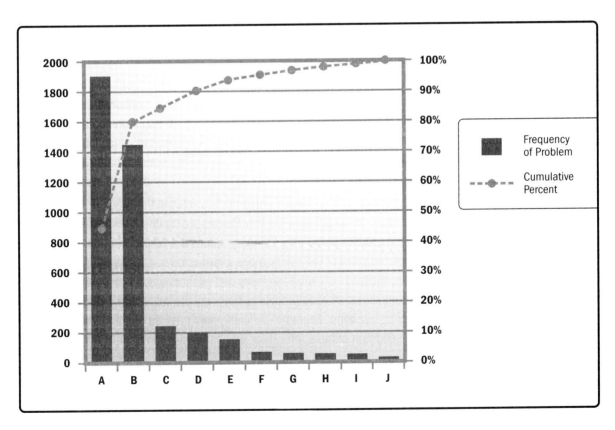

Figure 4-6. Pareto Diagram Sample Format

4.2.2.8 PROCESS FLOWS

Process flows describe business processes and the ways stakeholders interact with those processes. Process flows can be used to document current as-is processes of the business. The diagrams provide visual context for discussions with stakeholders and the product team about how the existing environment performs its work. The models can also be used to analyze the ways in which a process contributes to a given problem. Value stream maps—a variation of process flows—can be used to identify process steps that add value (value stream) and those that do not add value (waste). The information can be used to identify areas where a process might be streamlined to eliminate inefficiencies. For more information on process flows, see Section 7.2.2.12.

4.2.2.9 ROOT CAUSE AND OPPORTUNITY ANALYSIS

Once a situation is discovered, documented, and agreed upon, it needs to be analyzed before being acted upon. After the problem to be solved or the opportunity to pursue has been agreed upon, the problem or opportunity can be broken down into either the root causes or opportunity contributors so that a viable and appropriate solution can be recommended. Two techniques commonly used to perform this analysis are the following:

◆ **Root cause analysis.** Techniques used to determine the basic underlying reason for a variance, defect, or risk. When applied to business problems, root cause analysis can be used to discover the underlying causes of a problem so that solutions can be devised to reduce or eliminate them.

◆ **Opportunity analysis.** Techniques used to study the major facets of a potential opportunity to determine the possible changes in products offered to enable its achievement. Opportunity analysis may require additional work to study the potential markets an organization may consider entering.

Several techniques can be used to analyze root causes and opportunities, including the following:

◆ **Cause-and-effect diagrams:**

■ *Fishbone diagram.* A version of a cause-and-effect diagram used to depict a problem and its root causes in a visual manner. These diagrams are snapshots of the current situation and high-level causes of why a problem is occurring. They help trace the undesirable effects of issues back to their root causes. Use of this technique helps the product team avoid jumping to a solution without understanding the true causes of why an issue is occurring.

The fishbone diagram uses a fish image, where the problem (effect) is listed at the head and the causes and subcauses of the problem are placed on the bones of the fish. Causes are grouped into categories and each grouping branches off from the backbone of the fish. Category names are placed in rectangular boxes to easily identify the groupings. The structure of the fish provides a layout to visually assess the relationships between the causes and effects, and helps organize the ideas and connections. The model is often a good starting point when first analyzing root causes to problems; however, the technique will not be sufficient for understanding all root causes. Fishbone diagrams are commonly referred to as cause-and-effect or Ishikawa diagrams. Figure 4-7 shows a sample format for a fishbone diagram. The fishbone diagram is further discussed and an example is provided in Section 2.4.4.2 of *Business Analysis for Practitioners: A Practice Guide.*

- *Interrelationship diagram.* A special type of cause-and-effect diagram that depicts related causes and effects for a given situation. Interrelationship diagrams help uncover the most significant causes and effects involved in a situation. They are helpful for visualizing complex problems that have seemingly unwieldy relationships among multiple variables. In some cases, the cause of one problem may be the effect of another. An interrelationship diagram can help stakeholders understand the relationships between causes and effects and can identify which causes are the primary ones producing a problem. Interrelationship diagrams are most useful for identifying relationships among root causes, but like fishbone diagrams, they are not sufficient for understanding all root causes.

Constructing an interrelationship diagram helps participants isolate each dimension of a problem individually without using a strict linear process. Focusing on the individual dimension allows participants to concentrate on and analyze manageable pieces of a situation. When the analysis is complete, the diagram sheds considerable light on the problem, but only after the entire diagram has been assembled. Figure 4-8 shows an interrelationship diagram format. Interrelationship diagrams are further discussed and an example is provided in Section 2.4.4.2 of *Business Analysis for Practitioners: A Practice Guide.*

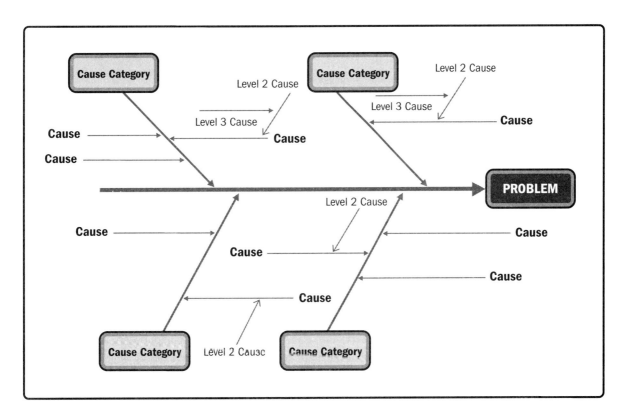

Figure 4-7. Fishbone Diagram Sample Format

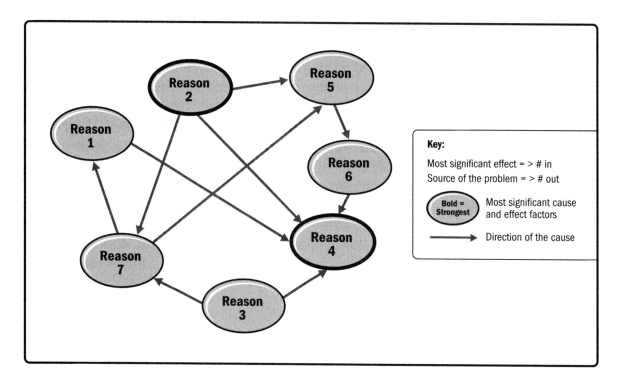

Key:

Most significant effect = > # in
Source of the problem = > # out

Bold = Strongest — Most significant cause and effect factors

→ Direction of the cause

Figure 4-8. Interrelationship Diagram Sample Format

◆ **Five-Whys.** A technique that suggests anyone trying to understand a problem needs to ask why it is occurring up to five times in order to thoroughly understand the problem's causes. The technique does not advocate having a person literally ask the participant the question "Why?" five times; rather, it promotes ongoing questioning to engage the participant in deeper levels of discussion provoked by more targeted questioning. The facilitator or interviewer discusses a problem and continues to explore why the situation is occurring until the root cause becomes clearer, typically uncovering the root cause after five rounds of questioning. The Five-Whys technique is further discussed in Section 2.4.4.1 of *Business Analysis for Practitioners: A Practice Guide.*

4.2.2.10 SWOT ANALYSIS

SWOT analysis is a technique for analyzing the strengths (S) and weaknesses (W) of an organization, project, or option, and the opportunities (O) and threats (T) that exist externally. This technique can be used to assess organizational strategy, goals, and objectives and to facilitate discussions with stakeholders when discussing high-level and important aspects of an organization, especially as they pertain to a specific situation. SWOT is a widely used tool to help understand high-level views surrounding a business need. SWOT can be used to create a structured framework for breaking down a situation into its root causes or contributors.

SWOT investigates the situation internally and externally as follows:

◆ **Internally:**

  ■ Shows where the organization has current strengths to help solve a problem or take advantage of an opportunity.

  ■ Reveals or acknowledges weaknesses that need to be alleviated to address a situation.

◆ **Externally:**

- Identifies potential opportunities in the external environment to mitigate a problem or seize an opportunity.

- Shows threats in the market or external environment that could impede success in addressing the business need.

Figure 4-9 shows a SWOT diagram format. SWOT diagrams are further discussed and an example is provided in Section 2.4.2 of *Business Analysis for Practitioners: A Practice Guide.*

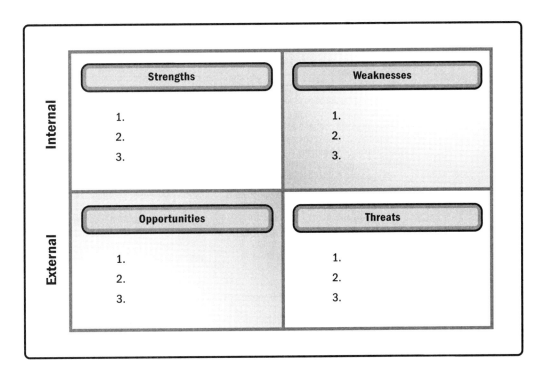

Figure 4-9. SWOT Diagram Sample Format

4.2.3 ASSESS CURRENT STATE: OUTPUTS

4.2.3.1 CURRENT STATE ASSESSMENT

The current state assessment is an understanding of the current mode of operations, or the as-is state of the organization. It is a culmination of the analysis results obtained from examination of the existing organizational environment. Typical information captured during the analysis of the current state might be a high-level overview of the existing business context. Examples include models and textual descriptions about existing business processes, key stakeholders, enterprise and business architectures, existing products, and how these items are impacted by the problem or opportunity presented in the situation statement.

A current state assessment may be nothing more than an understanding of the current state and may not necessarily include formalized documentation. Based on the size of the problem, the type and complexity of the project and industry, and various other factors, it may not be necessary to document the results of the current state assessment. If the organization maintains thorough enterprise and business architectures, it may also be sufficient to leverage these organizational process assets in lieu of creating additional as-is documentation for the project.

4.2.4 ASSESS CURRENT STATE: TAILORING CONSIDERATIONS

Adaptive and predictive tailoring considerations for Assess Current State are described in Table 4-5.

Table 4-5. Adaptive and Predictive Tailoring for Assess Current State

Aspects to Be Tailored	Typical Adaptive Considerations	Typical Predictive Considerations
Name	Not necessarily a formally named process; performed as part of initial planning or iteration 0.	Assess Current State (or as-is analysis)
Approach	As-is analysis can be performed throughout the project, as each iteration may focus the as-is discussion on a slice of the overall context. The as-is environment will continue to change, and therefore, will need to be continually assessed to understand how changes in the current state might impact proposed work within the backlog.	As-is analysis is performed up front as a starting point to provide context for future business analysis work. If a recent current state assessment is available, it may be possible to leverage historical information and avoid conducting another current state assessment.
Deliverables	Just enough modeling in order to move forward on discussions regarding the future state. The scope of analysis and, hence, the deliverables are focused on the context necessary for the early iterations of development work or to provide context when developing a lightweight business case.	As-is models may be completed to a detailed level. Models constructed may cover the entire problem space up front before requirements elicitation begins. May include models produced in a process modeling tool. The information assembled from the current state assessment may be packaged into a current state assessment document leveraging a standardized template.

4.2.5 ASSESS CURRENT STATE: COLLABORATION POINT

Business stakeholders contribute deep business knowledge and provide a holistic view of the current state, including historical information that the business analyst needs to start the current state assessment. Relationships with these stakeholders are some of the first ones a business analyst will establish. If a project is initiated, the business stakeholders and business analyst should maintain their collaboration across the entire product development life cycle.

4.3 DETERMINE FUTURE STATE

Determine Future State is the process of determining gaps in existing capabilities and a set of proposed changes necessary to attain a desired future state that addresses the problem or opportunity under analysis. The key benefit of this process is the resulting identification of a set of capabilities required for the organization to be able to transform from the current state to the desired future state and satisfy the business need. The inputs, tools and techniques, and outputs of the process are depicted in Figure 4-10. Figure 4-11 depicts the data flow diagram for the process.

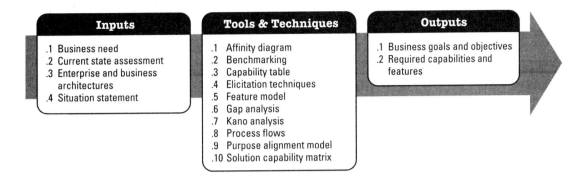

Figure 4-10. Determine Future State: Inputs, Tools and Techniques, and Outputs

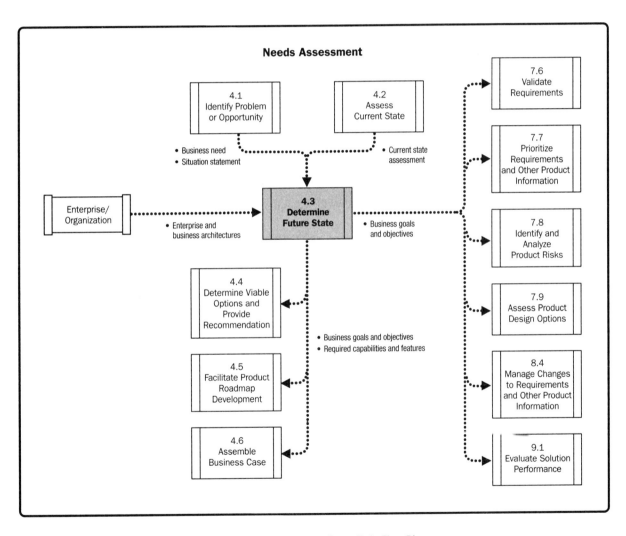

Figure 4-11. Determine Future State: Data Flow Diagram

Determining the future state involves conducting further elicitation and analysis to define the changes necessary to address the business need to determine which existing capabilities should remain or which new capabilities should be added. In some situations, it may only be necessary to recommend process changes without adding new capabilities or other resources. For more complex situations, like those that span various departments or divisions or involve a highly sophisticated product, the future state may involve adding a combination of new capabilities, including process changes, new machinery, highly skilled staff, physical plants or properties, new training initiatives, new or enhanced IT systems, or a completely redesigned product and determining how to integrate these new elements with existing capabilities.

The future state may involve:

◆ New work that the organization will take on;

◆ Outsourcing to acquire capabilities that the organization cannot obtain on its own;

◆ Applying existing resources in a different manner; or

◆ Combinations of enhanced, new, or acquired capabilities.

Business analysis is performed to determine which combination of capabilities will best address the stated problem or opportunity. The product team works through discussions using information obtained during the current state analysis about the situation and organizational capabilities. The team develops a clear definition of what the future state will look like, including identification of the capabilities and features required to enable the organization to transform from its current as-is state into this proposed to-be future. The required capabilities and features described here identify what is needed, but do not prescribe a recommended solution. Further analysis is required to evaluate how the capabilities and features will be delivered. Part of this analysis involves obtaining a thorough understanding about how users or customers define value.

Once an understanding about the future state is obtained, business goals and objectives are created to succinctly communicate what the business wants a portfolio, program, or project to deliver. The business goals and objectives here should not be confused with the organizational goals and objectives that were reviewed as part of analyzing the current state. Business goals and objectives align to the organizational goals and objectives, but they are at a lower level because they specify stated targets that the business is seeking to achieve. The term *business* is used here to represent the area of the organization experiencing the problem or desiring to achieve an opportunity, and represents the area of the organization that has an interest in and willingness to sponsor the need for the change.

4.3.1 DETERMINE FUTURE STATE: INPUTS

4.3.1.1 BUSINESS NEED

Described in Section 4.1.3.1. Business need is the impetus for the change an organization will undertake to address an existing problem or opportunity. The business need guides the business goals and objectives of the future state. It provides the rationale for why the organization desires the change. The business need provides relevant data needed to formulate the desired future state.

4.3.1.2 CURRENT STATE ASSESSMENT

Described in Section 4.2.3.1. Provides the foundational information about the current environment that becomes the starting point from which the future state is based. The current state assessment may include information regarding different aspects about the current environment that can be referenced when determining which changes will be necessary to address the problem or opportunity. Before recommending new capabilities, a review of the existing capabilities occurs to understand the starting point or baseline from which the product team is working.

4.3.1.3 ENTERPRISE AND BUSINESS ARCHITECTURES

Described in Section 4.2.1.1. Enterprise and business architectures comprise a collection of the business and technology components needed to operate an enterprise. Architecture frameworks provide information about the current state that can be used as a starting point for discussions about the future state. Enterprise and business architectures support the product team in understanding which capabilities are present today and help the team draw conclusions about which new or enhanced capabilities will be needed in the future state.

4.3.1.4 SITUATION STATEMENT

Described in Section 4.1.3.2. Provides a context for understanding the problem or opportunity that exists today. It is the starting point from which the future state can be built. The future state is designed to solve or address the problem/opportunity the organization is addressing.

4.3.2 DETERMINE FUTURE STATE: TOOLS AND TECHNIQUES

4.3.2.1 AFFINITY DIAGRAM

As future state discussions begin, various capabilities might be proposed for addressing the problem or opportunity under analysis. Future state considerations begin at a broad level. Through ongoing exploration and communication, the product team sifts through different ideas and alternatives. These might be discovered through brainstorming, a companion technique to the affinity diagram. Brainstorming is described in Section 5.1.2.1.

Affinity diagrams display categories and subcategories of ideas that cluster or have an affinity to one another. When defining future state considerations, affinity diagrams are used to process a large set of information or ideas into a manageable set of data organized by categories. For problem solving, affinity diagrams help organize related causes of a problem or opportunity. The ability to group data by a common theme allows insights to be identified that might not be possible to uncover when considering the information separately. Figure 4-12 shows a sample format of an affinity diagram. Affinity diagrams are further discussed and an example is provided in Section 2.4.5.2 of *Business Analysis for Practitioners: A Practice Guide*.

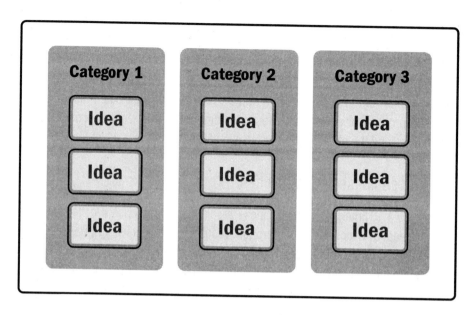

Figure 4-12. Affinity Diagram Sample Format

4.3.2.2 BENCHMARKING

Benchmarking is a comparison technique used to compare one set of practices, processes, and measurements of results against another. During future state analysis, this technique provides another way to determine new capabilities by conducting a comparison against benchmarking studies of external organizations that have solved similar problems or seized opportunities that the organization is considering pursuing. Benchmarking studies often guide final recommendations to address the situation as well as highlight which recommendations not to pursue. For more information on benchmarking, see Section 4.1.2.1.

4.3.2.3 CAPABILITY TABLE

Capability tables relate the identified problems within the current state to their associated root causes and the capabilities required to address the problem in the future state. This technique is a good choice for a model to relate the information obtained during the current state analysis with the information resulting from the future state discussions. The model depicts aspects of the current state alongside the features or capabilities required to address the problem and achieve the future state. For more information on capability tables, see Section 4.2.2.4.

4.3.2.4 ELICITATION TECHNIQUES

Elicitation techniques are used to draw information from different sources. Information about the future state may be obtained through various elicitation methods, as described in Section 6.3 on Conduct Elicitation. A few common techniques that are effective during future state analysis include brainstorming and facilitated workshops:

◆ **Brainstorming.** Used to identify a list of ideas within a short period of time. During future state analysis, the product team conducts conversations about potential capabilities that the organization might consider for addressing the situation. Brainstorming is a viable technique to help product teams create an initial list of capabilities. A companion technique is the affinity diagram described in Section 4.3.2.1. For more information on brainstorming, see Section 5.1.2.1.

◆ **Facilitated workshops.** Structured meetings led by a skilled, neutral facilitator and a carefully selected group of stakeholders to collaborate and work toward a stated objective. Because facilitated workshops support interactivity, collaboration, and improved communications among participants, the technique is a viable elicitation technique for a team to use when defining the future state. For more information on facilitated workshops, see Section 6.3.2.4.

For more information about elicitation techniques, see Section 6.3.2.

4.3.2.5 FEATURE MODEL

Feature models provide a visual representation of all the features of a solution arranged in a tree or hierarchical structure. The strength of the model is its ability to help visually and logically group feature sets. The model can be utilized to parse out groups of features or capabilities to help facilitate discussions about different future state options that the organization may wish to consider. Different versions of a feature model can be created, with each representing a possible future state alternative. For more information on feature models, see Section 7.2.2.8.

4.3.2.6 GAP ANALYSIS

Gap analysis is a technique for comparing two entities, usually the as-is and to-be state of a business. During Needs Assessment, gap analysis is performed by examining the differences between the current and future states. The current state assessment includes a thorough exploration of elements in the existing environment—for example, processes, systems, staff, and a variety of environmental factors necessary to understand how the organization operates today. The future state assessment includes an exploration of the capabilities required to address the problem or opportunity. Gap analysis is performed by comparing the required capabilities against the existing capabilities and identifying the difference, or "gap." This gap refers to the missing capabilities that the organization needs to acquire to address the business need in the future state. Gap analysis is further discussed in Section 2.4.7 of *Business Analysis for Practitioners: A Practice Guide*.

4.3.2.7 KANO ANALYSIS

Kano analysis is a technique used to model and analyze product features by considering the features from the viewpoint of the customer. Kano analysis can be used to help a product team understand the level of importance of features being considered for the future state. During Kano analysis, product features are grouped into one of five categories and plotted on a grid. The vertical axis is used to measure the degree of customer satisfaction that the feature will provide, and the horizontal axis shows how well the product is expected to satisfy or deliver the feature. When placing product features into the Kano categories, the grouping is determined by considering the customer's viewpoint or perception of the feature. This categorization helps the product team understand how each feature is expected to contribute to the customer's satisfaction level. A Kano survey is used to collect the data necessary to plot on the grid. The discoveries made during Kano analysis provide good information that the team can consider when prioritizing customer needs. A Kano model can also be used to analyze products.

There are five product feature categories commonly used in a Kano model. Some organizations elect to use only the first three. A description of each is as follows:

◆ **Basic.** Features that provide little satisfaction to stakeholders, but, when missing from the end solution, cause extreme dissatisfaction. Stakeholders do not give a lot of thought to the features in this category because it is assumed that the final solution will include them.

◆ **Performance.** Features that stakeholders think about, desire, and use to consciously evaluate the final solution. These features can either satisfy or dissatisfy the stakeholder, depending on how well the solution addresses them.

◆ **Delighters.** Features that differentiate the product from competitors' products and are sometimes referred to as the "wow" factor. Delighters play off of emotion. When these features are present, they provide extreme satisfaction to the stakeholder. When they are not present, typically stakeholders are not even aware that the feature is possible and the stakeholder is not consciously dissatisfied.

◆ **Indifferent.** Features that neither satisfy nor dissatisfy a customer. The customer does not care whether these features are included or not. These features plot along the horizontal axis of the Kano model.

◆ **Reverse.** Features that decrease a stakeholder's satisfaction level when present and increase it when excluded from the final product.

Customer perceptions can change over time. A competitor may add a similar "wow" factor to their products or improve upon a "wow" factor, which in turn will decrease the uniqueness of the original product; features that once were delighters turn into performance features, or even basic features, as customer expectations evolve.

Figure 4-13 shows a sample format of a Kano model.

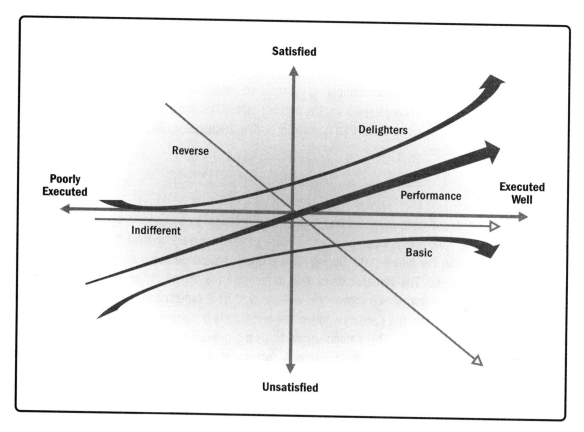

Figure 4-13. Kano Model Sample Format

4.3.2.8 PROCESS FLOWS

Process flows are used to depict the business processes in the current state and used as a starting point for discussions concerning the changes desired and required for the future state. Process flow modeling is a good technique for performing what-if analysis to walk through various future state scenarios with key stakeholders. The diagrams and flows produced during process flow modeling can be modified to reflect and analyze various future states to support decision making. Various simulation packages exist where process flows are automated and proposed changes simulated to analyze various elements of the future state before solution options are developed and projects are initiated to implement the changes. For more information on process flows, see Section 7.2.2.12.

4.3.2.9 PURPOSE ALIGNMENT MODEL

The purpose alignment model is a technique that provides a framework to support strategic or product decision making. The framework is used to categorize options by aligning them with the business purpose they support. The model can become a basis for forming decisions about which options to pursue and how to pursue them.

The model helps a product team link business strategy to product strategy. For example, it can be used to work through features in a product backlog to determine the value a feature holds for the organization or a release. For future state analysis, understanding the alignment of product options with business purposes helps the product team consider different solution options and which features to address and when. For more information on product backlogs, see Section 7.3.2.4.

While this technique is typically used as a basis for making strategic or high-level product decisions, some organizations also use it to analyze and facilitate discussions about product requirements and features, including the value each provides. These discussions, in turn, can become an input into prioritization activities. The remainder of this section focuses on using a purpose alignment model to categorize product features.

At the project level, product features are placed on a quadrant matrix considering two factors: criticality and market differentiation. A product feature that is determined to be highly critical may be needed for the organization to stay in business or meet regulations. A product feature rated as a market differentiator may contribute to the organization's ability to gain market share, increase sales, or surpass competitor offerings. The discussions a product team works through when determining how best to position the feature on the grid promotes a shared understanding about value. The analysis provides information to help determine which features the organization should invest in. The four categories of purposes in the model and the actions that might be taken from a feature perspective are as follows:

◆ **Differentiating.** Features in this category are mission critical and provide high market differentiation. They can help the organization gain market share, improve its competitive advantage, and outrival its competitors. Organizations need to continually invest in this area to excel, provide uniqueness, and stay ahead of the competition. When they do, customers will consider the organization to be an innovator.

◆ **Parity.** Features here help the organization maintain its parity in the marketplace. Investments in parity features may be mission critical, but they do not provide the organization with a competitive advantage. Features in this category simply ensure that the business stays on par with competitor offerings.

◆ **Partner.** Features assigned here are not considered mission critical, but if provided, they would enable the organization to differentiate itself in the market. As a result, an organization will look externally for a partner company to provide these features but will not invest in these features itself. A viable partner would be an organization that today is differentiated by offering these features.

◆ **Who cares.** Features in this category are neither differentiating nor mission critical to the organization. Features that end up in this category are generally not built.

Figure 4-14 shows a sample format of a purpose alignment model.

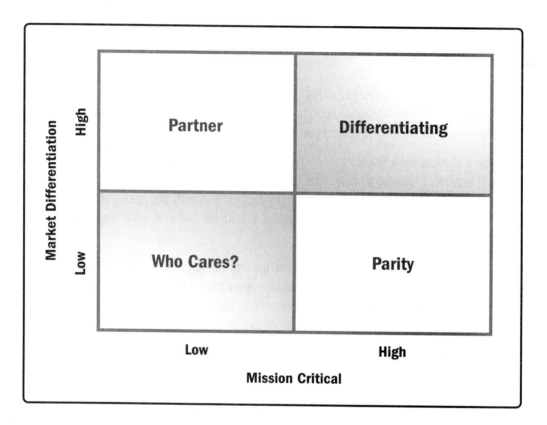

Figure 4-14. Purpose Alignment Model Sample Format

4.3.2.10 SOLUTION CAPABILITY MATRIX

A solution capability matrix is a model that provides a simple visual way to examine capabilities and solution components in one view, identifying where capabilities will be addressed in the new solution. When timing information is added, the product team can use the model during planning discussions to understand when different solution components are expected to be delivered.

The matrix can be presented with capabilities listed down the left column and the components of the solution across the top. An X placed at the point of intersection between column and row indicates when the capability is covered by a component of the solution. Product teams can utilize a solution capability matrix to understand which capabilities are covered in the solution or a solution component. The Xs may be replaced with a version number or an iteration number if the team wishes to communicate when a capability will be addressed in the solution. Today, different forms of solution capability matrices exist. Table 4-6 shows a sample format for one possible way of structuring a solution capability matrix.

Table 4-6. Solution Capability Matrix Sample Format

	Solution Component A	Solution Component B	Solution Component C	Solution Component D	Solution Component ... *n*
Capability 1			X		
Capability 2	X				
Capability 3		X		X	
Capability 4					
Capability 5			X		
Capability ... *n*					

4.3.3 DETERMINE FUTURE STATE: OUTPUTS

4.3.3.1 BUSINESS GOALS AND OBJECTIVES

Business goals and objectives identify what the business expects the portfolio, program, or project to deliver. Business goals and objectives align to the organizational goals and objectives, but are at a lower level because they specify stated targets that the business is seeking to achieve.

4.3.3.2 REQUIRED CAPABILITIES AND FEATURES

The required capabilities and features identify the list of net changes the organization needs to obtain in order to achieve the desired future state. The capabilities and features listed do not prescribe a solution. Additional analysis is still needed to determine how these capabilities and features will be delivered.

4.3.4 DETERMINE FUTURE STATE: TAILORING CONSIDERATIONS

Adaptive and predictive tailoring considerations for Determine Future State are described in Table 4-7.

Table 4-7. Adaptive and Predictive Tailoring for Determine Future State

Aspects to Be Tailored	Typical Adaptive Considerations	Typical Predictive Considerations
Name	Not a formally named process and performed as part of backlog refinement, business modeling, initial planning, or iteration 0.	Determine Future State
Approach	Teams explore the future state in slices and discuss it in terms of themes, goals, and objectives. Some organizations may take a broader or organizational viewpoint to this work. Typically, some high-level information on the future state is formed at either project initiation or as part of iteration 0, but that information is constantly evolving as new information emerges. Future state information is reviewed prior to each iteration to ensure that the capabilities required for the future state are known and understood.	To-be analysis is performed up front prior to initiating a project to understand the business goals and objectives. Results from gap analysis are understood to define required capabilities. The to-be state is fully defined and understood before moving forward on proposing viable solution approaches. The future state definition is formally documented, reviewed, and approved with the business.
Deliverables	The future state definition may be represented in lightweight documentation. Models utilized to facilitate discussions involve a low level of formality and are often developed on whiteboards or flipcharts. The future state definition is captured and made available to the team on an ongoing basis. Other deliverables may include roadmaps, story maps, and product backlog.	A future state definition can be documented within a tool or within a formal document such as a business case. Models built to assist in defining the future state are often formalized, created with a modeling tool, and archived for future reference.

4.3.5 DETERMINE FUTURE STATE: COLLABORATION POINT

In some organizations, the analytical resources involved in needs assessment activities may be a different team of analysts from the analytical resources who perform business analysis on the project if one is approved and initiated. Business analysts will often find themselves collaborating with peers who report into different organizational structures or who are supporting other programs and projects.

4.4 DETERMINE VIABLE OPTIONS AND PROVIDE RECOMMENDATION

Determine Viable Options and Provide Recommendation is the process of applying various analysis techniques to examine possible solutions for meeting the business goals and objectives and to determine which of the options is considered the best possible one for the organization to pursue. The key benefits of this process are that it validates the feasibility of proposed solutions and promotes the best course of action for executives and decision makers to meet the business goals and objectives. The inputs, tools and techniques, and outputs of the process are depicted in Figure 4-15. Figure 4-16 depicts the data flow diagram for the process.

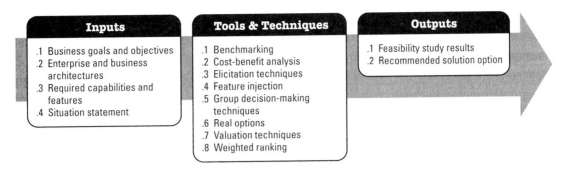

Figure 4-15. Determine Viable Options and Provide Recommendation: Inputs, Tools and Techniques, and Outputs

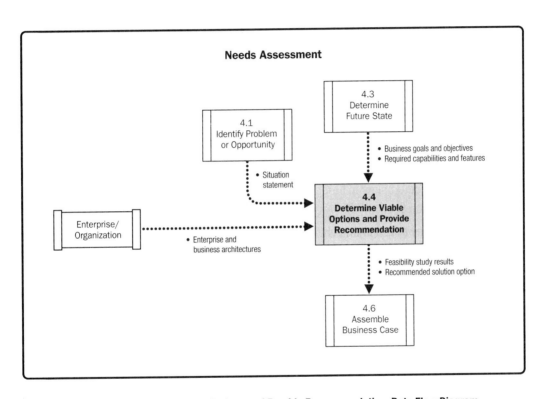

Figure 4-16. Determine Viable Options and Provide Recommendation: Data Flow Diagram

Determining viable options entails conducting discussions with stakeholders and product team members and performing further analysis to define a list of possible solution recommendations to address the business need. The product team considers the information from the current and future state analysis when formulating these options. The product team also determines the solution approach for each option. The solution approach is a high-level definition about the considerations and steps necessary to deliver the solution and thereby transition the business from the current to the future state.

Stakeholders often propose solutions without fully understanding the context around the situation. Presenting the results of needs analysis to key decision makers, including the rationalization why the viable options are being chosen, can reduce the likelihood that an unfit solution will be chosen.

Determining viable options and providing a recommendation entails the following activities:

◆ **Identifying viable options.** Using the results of the current and future state analysis to determine which solution options are best for the business to consider.

◆ **Conducting feasibility analysis.** Evaluating different factors to determine the feasibility of the options under consideration. Organizations may dictate that the results of the feasibility analysis be captured in a formal document using an approved template, but the level of formality followed depends on organizational standards. Common elements analyzed for each of the options under consideration include the following:

■ *Constraints.* Any limitations that restrict the option under consideration. For more information on constraints, see Section 7.8.

■ *Assumptions.* Any factors that are unknown and are assumed to be true, real, or certain for each option without actual proof or demonstration. For more information on assumptions, see Section 7.8.

■ *Product risks.* Uncertain events or conditions that may have a positive or negative effect on the successful delivery of the solution. For more information on product risks, see Section 7.8.

■ *Dependencies.* Any relationships upon which a solution depends for successful implementation. Dependencies introduce a level of risk; therefore, a solution option with several dependencies may be deemed riskier and determined to be less viable than an option with no dependencies. For more information on dependencies, see Section 7.8.

■ *Culture.* An enterprise environmental factor that can impact both the success of the business analysis effort and the portfolio, program, or project. A lack of acceptance across the organization could potentially limit both the success and expected value of the final solution.

■ *Operational feasibility.* The receptivity of the organization to the change and whether the change can be sustained after it is implemented.

■ *Technology feasibility.* Refers to whether the necessary technology and technical skills exist or can be affordably obtained to adopt and support the solution option. It also includes whether the proposed change is compatible with other parts of the technical infrastructure.

■ *Supportability.* A category of nonfunctional requirements used to evaluate the cost, level of effort, and ease with which each option can be maintained and managed by the organization over time.

■ *Cost-effectiveness feasibility.* An initial, high-level estimate of costs and value of the benefits that the option is expected to deliver. During feasibility analysis, this estimate is not intended to be a complete cost-benefit analysis.

■ *Time feasibility.* The assessment of whether the solution option can be delivered within the time constraints specified. Time constraints may be imposed by the organization, business, or external factors.

■ *Value.* The business value that the solution option will provide to the organization. It includes a discussion of how value may change over time.

■ *Validation.* Provides the assurance that the solution will meet the needs of the customer and other identified stakeholders. Each option will require a different approach and level of effort to validate its alignment to the business objectives. Some options may prove more difficult or costly to validate, which may be of significant interest to the organization when assessing the overall viability of an option.

Constraints, assumptions, product risks, and dependencies are analyzed as part of Section 7.8.

The feasibility analysis should provide sufficient information to compare the list of possible or viable options, and may result in the elimination of some options that are then considered infeasible. Typically, there is not just one factor, such as cost or time, that will determine whether an option is feasible, so the determination of feasibility is best analyzed when several of the factors mentioned above are considered.

◆ **Defining preliminary product scope.** Determining the high-level scope defined in terms of the capabilities that each option will provide. At this stage, what is known about the product scope remains at a high level.

◆ **Defining high-level transition requirements.** Identifying high-level transition considerations, such as data conversion or training requirements required to transition the organization to the specified solution. Attention should be given to draw out the significant differences in transition needs between each option.

◆ **Recommending the most viable option.** A recommendation put forth to identify the option considered the most viable, assuming that more than one option remains viable after the feasibility analysis is completed. The option that is selected is identified, along with the rationale explaining why that selection was made over the other options.

If only one option is judged to be feasible after the analysis is completed, that option, in most cases, will be recommended. When there are no viable options to address the business need, one option is to recommend that nothing be done. When faced with two or more feasible options, the remaining choices can be arranged in rank order, based on how well each one meets the business need. A technique such as weighted ranking is a good choice to perform this analysis.

4.4.1 DETERMINE VIABLE OPTIONS AND PROVIDE RECOMMENDATION: INPUTS

4.4.1.1 BUSINESS GOALS AND OBJECTIVES

Described in Section 4.3.3.1. Business goals and objectives identify what the business is expecting the portfolio, program, or project to deliver. Each of the viable options under consideration will be assessed to determine how well it satisfies the stated business goals and objectives. Each option will satisfy the goals and objectives differently, and some options will satisfy them far better than others under consideration.

4.4.1.2 ENTERPRISE AND BUSINESS ARCHITECTURES

Described in Section 4.2.1.1. Enterprise and business architectures provide insights into the current state of the organization. When presenting viable options, each option can be analyzed and explained within the context of existing architectures. Doing this helps frame up the size and complexity of each option in terms that decision makers can more easily relate to and understand.

4.4.1.3 REQUIRED CAPABILITIES AND FEATURES

Described in Section 4.3.3.2. The required capabilities and features identify the list of net changes the organization is looking to obtain in order to achieve the desired future state. Each proposed option will address the capabilities and features differently. Which capabilities and features are covered determines the product scope for each option. Initially, discussions begin at a high level, but as options are formulated, discussed, and further refined, some capabilities may be determined to be more valuable than others and adjustments made to the solution approaches under consideration.

4.4.1.4 SITUATION STATEMENT

Described in Section 4.1.3.2. The situation statement is an objective statement of a problem or opportunity that includes the statement itself, the situation's effect on the organization, and the resulting impact. The situation statement provides context for discussions when identifying a list of viable options.

4.4.2 DETERMINE VIABLE OPTIONS AND PROVIDE RECOMMENDATION: TOOLS AND TECHNIQUES

4.4.2.1 BENCHMARKING

Benchmarking is a comparison of an organization's practices, processes, and measurements of results against established standards or against what is achieved by a "best in class" organization within its industry or across industries. Benchmarking results can help stimulate ideas for formulating a list of viable options. For more information on benchmarking, see Section 4.1.2.1.

4.4.2.2 COST-BENEFIT ANALYSIS

Cost-benefit analysis is a financial analysis tool used to compare the benefits provided by a portfolio component, program, or project against its costs. It is commonly used to identify the most viable option from a set of options. Cost-benefit analysis is often conducted prior to project initiation, as part of portfolio or program management activities. Completing a cost-benefit analysis requires an understanding of financial analysis, so business analysis resources may often seek out the support of a financial analyst within their organization to assist with this work. The results of the cost-benefit analysis are included in the business case to demonstrate why the solution option selected and proposed is considered the most viable choice. Organizations often have standards that dictate when and how to perform a cost-benefit analysis, including which financial valuation methods to employ. To perform a cost-benefit analysis, at least one valuation technique is applied to make the financial assessment. Valuation techniques are defined in Section 4.4.2.7.

4.4.2.3 ELICITATION TECHNIQUES

Elicitation techniques are used to draw information from different sources. The information required to formulate a list of viable options is obtained by applying various elicitation techniques, as described in Section 6.3. For example, prototyping can be used to determine whether an option is viable by developing a prototype model to assess stakeholder expectations against the model. Prototypes help eliminate uncertainties about options, thereby reducing product-related risks. For more information on prototyping, see Section 6.3.2.8. For more information about elicitation techniques, see Section 6.3.2.

4.4.2.4 FEATURE INJECTION

Feature injection is a framework and set of principles used to deliver successful outcomes by improving and expediting how a product team develops and analyzes product requirements. The framework is popular with teams that use adaptive development methods. The idea is to focus discussions and analysis on the features where there can be an immediate return of value. In predictive life cycle methods, stakeholders provide a vast amount of information up front, teams analyze the collective set of information, and a set of product requirements is developed from the entire collection of information. Feature injection challenges this traditional approach by guiding the team to analyze only those features that are deemed to be of the highest value. The objective is to reduce the amount of time that teams spend analyzing low-value requirements. Using feature injection, product teams work backwards, focusing on value first and then on features to attain the value. Feature injection follows a three-step approach:

◆ **Step 1: Determine the business value.** The team discusses the expected or required value that the business seeks to achieve (the outcome). A technique like the purpose alignment model may help guide these discussions, but other value models can be used as well. When the team reaches a common understanding about expected value, it moves on to Step 2.

◆ **Step 2: Inject features.** Step 2 involves "injecting" or determining the features that will enable the business to achieve the value stated in Step 1. The product team determines the minimal set of features required to deliver the expected value. Each feature is presented in the form of a scenario. Modeling is used to promote these discussions.

◆ **Step 3: Spot examples.** Step 3 is about elaborating details. The business is asked to talk through examples that deviate from the scenario modeled in Step 2. Step 3 is used to uncover variations in processing or exceptions. The examples discussed here help the team develop a shared understanding of all the scenarios that the solution has to support; therefore, these scenarios expand product scope.

Feature injection focuses team discussions on higher-value features. Discoveries are applied when formulating different solution options.

4.4.2.5 GROUP DECISION-MAKING TECHNIQUES

Group decision-making techniques are techniques that can be used in a group setting to bring participants to a final decision on an issue or topic under discussion. Group decision-making techniques can be used in conjunction with other techniques to decide on the recommended solution option. The team establishes how decisions will be made during business analysis planning to avoid misunderstandings or conflict at the point when decisions are needed. For more information on group decision-making techniques, see Section 8.3.2.7.

4.4.2.6 REAL OPTIONS

Real options is a decision-making thought process that can be used on projects that follow an adaptive delivery model. The objective of the technique is to approach decision making with the same level of thinking used to approach a stock option where a decision is made about whether to pursue an option (e.g., a decision and at what point in time). Two fundamental principles are applied to decision making with real options. The first is to reduce the number of decisions that need to be made in the short term, and the second is to delay all decision making until as late as possible. Delayed decision making provides a product team with more time to discover and improve its knowledge base; it reduces uncertainties and avoids making decisions based on assumptions. Delayed decision making allows a product team to keep its options open and does not commit the team to choices at a point in time when information is scarce. As with options trading, options in the real options framework have expiration dates; waiting too long will result in the option expiring (i.e., the option will no longer have value for the business). Applying this decision framework to adaptive projects, teams can apply real options principles when making decisions about which stories to include in an iteration or when to begin business analysis activities to elaborate a story. Real options is a technique to help teams determine when to make decisions, not how or why.

4.4.2.7 VALUATION TECHNIQUES

Valuation techniques quantify the return or value that an option will provide. Valuation techniques are utilized when conducting a cost-benefit analysis to establish criteria for objectively assessing a solution. A variety of techniques is available. Which techniques are used may depend on organizational standards. Some of the more common valuation techniques include the following:

- **Internal rate of return (IRR).** The projected annual yield of an investment, incorporating both initial and ongoing costs. The value signifies the interest rate at which the net present value of all the cash flows will equal zero. IRR is a measure of return to cost; therefore, the higher the IRR, the higher the return a solution option is expected to deliver.

- **Net present value (NPV).** The future value of expected benefits expressed in the value that those benefits have at the time of investment. NPV takes into account current and future benefits, inflation, and factors in the yield that could be obtained through investing in financial instruments as opposed to a portfolio component, program, or project. NPV provides insight into whether an investment will provide value; the higher the NPV, the greater the amount of value an option is expected to provide.

- **Payback period (PBP).** The time needed to recover an investment, usually in months or years. The longer the PBP, the greater the risk.

- **Return on investment (ROI).** The percentage return on an initial investment. ROI is calculated by taking the total projected net benefits and dividing them by the cost of the investment. The costs may be direct costs, but a more accurate value to use is the total cost of ownership, which factors in direct and indirect costs. ROI provides an estimate of profitability; therefore, the higher the value, the better an investment is estimated to be.

In some organizations, a specific factor may be required by policy, such as an NPV or return of a specific level. Value may not always be expressed in terms of financial value; other valuation techniques may prove to be more useful in those situations. Valuation techniques are further discussed in Section 2.5.6 of *Business Analysis for Practitioners: A Practice Guide*.

4.4.2.8 WEIGHTED RANKING

Weighted ranking is a technique used to support objective decision making. It is typically performed with the use of a weighted ranking matrix. A weighted ranking matrix or table is used to weight, rate, and score each criterion against a set of options. A weight is established for each criterion, commonly based on how important it is to the overall objective. In this approach, each option is rated as to how well it meets each individual criterion independent of other options, using a common scale. The weight and rating are multiplied together to obtain a criteria score, and all criteria scores are added together and compared to determine the preferred choice. Care is taken when determining the weighted criteria to ensure that they align with the business goals and objectives identified in Section 4.3. Table 4-8 shows a sample format of a weighted ranking matrix. The weighted ranking matrix is further discussed and an example is provided in Section 2.5.5.1 of *Business Analysis for Practitioners: A Practice Guide*.

Table 4-8. Weighted Ranking Matrix Sample Format

Items to Be Ranked	Criteria (Weight)				Total Votes	Final Rank[A]
	Criteria 1 (Weight 0.2)	Criteria 2 (Weight 0.4)	Criteria 3 (Weight 0.3)	Criteria 4 (Weight 0.1)		
Option #1	3 x 0.2 = 0.6	2 x 0.4 = 0.8	0	3 x 0.1 = 0.3	1.7	2
Option #2	0	0	2 x 0.3 = 0.6	2 x 0.1 = 0.2	0.8	3
Option #3	1 x 0.2 = 0.2	3 x 0.4 = 1.2	1 x 0.3 = 0.3	2 x 0.1 = 0.2	1.9	1

[A] 0 = Does not satisfy; 1 = Lightly satisfies; 2 = Partially satisfies; 3 = Fully satisfies

4.4.3 DETERMINE VIABLE OPTIONS AND PROVIDE RECOMMENDATION: OUTPUTS

4.4.3.1 FEASIBILITY STUDY RESULTS

Feasibility study results are the summarized outcomes obtained from the completion of the feasibility analysis. The results are assembled into a package that is conducive to supporting executive review and decision making. Many organizations may require the use of a standardized template to package and communicate the results of the study. Although a recommended option will accompany the communication package, sufficient information pertaining to each of the viable options considered should be provided in case decision makers do not favor the preferred choice.

4.4.3.2 RECOMMENDED SOLUTION OPTION

The recommended solution option is the solution choice determined to be the best course of action for addressing the business need. This recommendation is the best option, considering the results and factors of the completed analysis, including the financial analysis results. The recommended solution option should include a summary of why the option was chosen, along with a high-level description of the process utilized to reach the decision. If any subjective criteria were applied in the decision-making process, these, too, should be included. At the portfolio or program level, analysis results are reviewed and a decision and recommendation is reached, which consists of the best course of action for the portfolio or program. At the project level, the recommended solution is a high-level description of the product(s) to be developed.

4.4.4 DETERMINE VIABLE OPTIONS AND PROVIDE RECOMMENDATION: TAILORING CONSIDERATIONS

Adaptive and predictive tailoring considerations for Determine Viable Options and Provide Recommendation are described in Table 4-9.

Table 4-9. Adaptive and Predictive Tailoring for Determine Viable Options

Aspects to Be Tailored	Typical Adaptive Considerations	Typical Predictive Considerations
Name	Not a formally named process; performed as part of iteration 0 or later iterations.	Determine Viable Options and Provide Recommendation, business case analysis, or feasibility study
Approach	High-level vision of the solution and an early version of product scope might be created. Initial solution options are evaluated during iteration 0. Tasks can be created as "spikes" to investigate the feasibility of a solution during an iteration.	Viable options are identified, feasibility studies completed, and a recommended solution is selected prior to portfolio, program, or project initiation. Project and product scope are determined and agreed to up front, and adherence to both are managed throughout the course of the program or project.
Deliverables	Solution options are rarely documented and instead just implemented in the final product. Functional or technical spikes might be performed to research or investigate viable options for implementing user stories.	Feasibility study results and recommended solution option.

4.4.5 DETERMINE VIABLE OPTIONS AND PROVIDE RECOMMENDATION: COLLABORATION POINT

Architects and designers are valuable contributors when determining the viability of a solution because they lend their expertise to assess constraints, dependencies, technical feasibilities, and the alignment of proposed options against existing architectures. Project managers may fulfill the role of SME, lending expertise to share insights related to costs, risks, scheduling, and resourcing for the options being discussed. Financial analysts provide assistance in performing the financial analysis using one or more of the valuation techniques to evaluate the options.

4.5 FACILITATE PRODUCT ROADMAP DEVELOPMENT

Facilitate Product Roadmap Development is the process of supporting the development of a product roadmap that outlines, at a high level, which aspects of a product are planned for delivery over the course of a portfolio, program, or one or more project iterations or releases, and the potential sequence for the delivery of these aspects. The key benefit of this process is that it creates shared expectations among stakeholders for the deliverables and the potential order in which they will be delivered. The inputs, tools and techniques, and outputs of the process are depicted in Figure 4-17. Figure 4-18 depicts the data flow diagram for the process.

Figure 4-17. Facilitate Product Roadmap Development: Inputs, Tools and Techniques, and Outputs

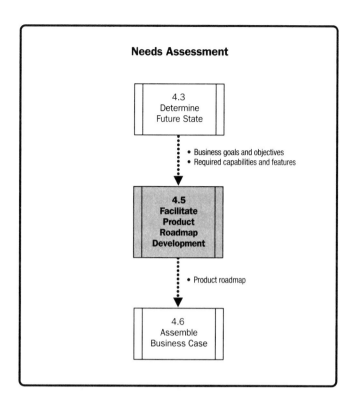

Figure 4-18. Facilitate Product Roadmap Development: Data Flow Diagram

In business analysis, product roadmaps provide important information about a product, providing insight about the product vision and how the product will support organizational strategy, business goals, and objectives over time. Organizational strategy is achieved through portfolio components, programs, and projects, and the product roadmap helps tie organizational strategy and the product vision to an executable plan to achieve the strategic goals and objectives through delivery of the product. At the portfolio level, product portfolio roadmaps can be created to set vision, strategy, and timing for a group of products.

The process of developing a product roadmap is a collaborative effort and brings together resources from the business and development team to form a shared understanding of what is being requested and why. The process can also entail the development of different "what if" scenarios used by the team in reviewing various planning and delivery options and in making and solidifying their final decisions. Discussions begin at a high level, focusing on the product vision, and continue through the lower levels of details, ultimately defining product releases and which features will be provided in each release. Milestones can be included on a roadmap to show when objectives that are important for delivering a strategic objective are to be met.

Several key elements are typically elicited and documented in the product roadmap, including the following:

◆ **Strategy information.** Information about how the product supports the overall organizational strategy (e.g., it provides better market positioning or improved customer satisfaction).

◆ **Portfolio.** Relationship of the product to the portfolio and how the product relates to other products in the portfolio.

◆ **Program.** Relationship of the product to the program and how the product relates to other products in the program.

- ◆ **Initiatives.** Overview information about different projects being considered or currently in development related to the product.

- ◆ **Product vision.** Explanation of the product, intended customers, and how needs are to be met. The product vision ties together what is being developed with why it is being developed.

- ◆ **Success criteria.** Metrics that can be used to determine solution success.

- ◆ **Market forces.** Any external market forces that influence or shape the development of the product.

- ◆ **Product releases.** Identification of the expected product releases, and the themes or high-level features that each includes. When specifying product releases, some high-level assumptions regarding the project life cycle may need to be made.

- ◆ **Features.** Capabilities that the product will provide, paired to the product releases. Features are typically prioritized and explained from the viewpoint of how each supports the organizational strategy and business goals and objectives.

- ◆ **Timelines.** Expected window in which the feature sets will be delivered (generally a three- to six-month horizon for projects following a predictive life cycle and shorter for adaptive approaches).

Product roadmaps may be assembled in the form of a text-based document or they may take the form of a visual model. Organizations may use product roadmap software to build and communicate product roadmap information. Regardless of whether the roadmap is formally or informally developed, it is crucial for product information to be assembled and shared with stakeholders and product team members to bring awareness to the expected growth and development of the product and how it will assist the organization in achieving its goals and objectives.

Product roadmaps are used internally, but they also provide valuable information to customers, vendors, and others who are external to the organization. It may be necessary to adjust the type and level of information provided to different recipients. For example, external customers may not need to know or be interested in how products align to the organizational strategy. Items considered confidential in nature may also need to be removed from external viewing. Release dates shared with customers may need to be broad, covering a time range rather than a specific date so communicated dates are more reliable and customers are not discouraged if the dates fluctuate. Internal recipients will also have differing communication requirements; product managers will desire the most detailed information about the product.

4.5.1 FACILITATE PRODUCT ROADMAP DEVELOPMENT: INPUTS

4.5.1.1 BUSINESS GOALS AND OBJECTIVES

Described in Section 4.3.3.1. Business goals and objectives identify the deliverables for the portfolio, program, or project. Products are developed to solve the business need; therefore, they need to align to the stated business goals and objectives.

4.5.1.2 REQUIRED CAPABILITIES AND FEATURES

Described in Section 4.3.3.2. The required capabilities and features identify the list of net changes that the organization will need to obtain to achieve the desired future state. Required capabilities and features can be reflected in the product roadmap to communicate the expected timing of delivery.

4.5.2 FACILITATE PRODUCT ROADMAP DEVELOPMENT: TOOLS AND TECHNIQUES

4.5.2.1 FACILITATED WORKSHOPS

Facilitated workshops use a structured meeting led by a skilled, neutral facilitator and a carefully selected group of stakeholders to collaborate and work toward a stated objective. Facilitated workshops can be used to elicit the information required to develop the product roadmap. Because facilitated workshops support interactivity, collaboration, and improved communications among participants, the technique is a viable elicitation technique for performing this work. For more information on facilitated workshops, see Section 6.3.2.4.

4.5.2.2 FEATURE MODEL

A feature model is a scope model that visually represents all the features of a solution arranged in a tree or hierarchical structure. An existing feature model can be referenced or a new one created to identify a list of features for the product roadmap. A facilitated workshop can be conducted to identify the features and prioritize the feature list into a product roadmap. For more information on feature models, see Section 7.2.2.8.

4.5.2.3 PRODUCT VISIONING

Product visioning is a technique used to set the high-level direction for a product or a product release. It entails conducting conversations with team members to visualize and obtain agreement about what the team envisions for the product. Product visioning is performed by using one more elicitation techniques, such as collaborative games. It typically results in the development of a written or visual deliverable to ensure a shared understanding of the product and its direction—for example, a vision statement or a product box. A vision statement is a summarized, high-level description about the expectations for a product, such as the target market, users, major benefits, and what differentiates the product from others in the market. Vision statements provide enough guidance to the development team to ensure that its members collectively share a common understanding about the product without including a thoroughly vetted feature list. For more information on collaborative games and developing a product box, see Section 6.3.2.2.

4.5.2.4 STORY MAPPING

Story mapping is a technique used to sequence user stories, based upon their business value and the order in which their users typically perform them, so that teams can arrive at a shared understanding of what will be built. Story maps help communicate the features and product components that the product team will be responsible for delivering. Stories written during the development of the product roadmap typically are written at a high level and may exist as epics. Epics are later decomposed into other epics or individual stories. The output from this technique provides insightful information used in the development of the product roadmap. For more information on story maps, see Section 7.2.2.16.

4.5.3 FACILITATE PRODUCT ROADMAP DEVELOPMENT: OUTPUTS

4.5.3.1 PRODUCT ROADMAP

A product roadmap provides a high-level view of product features, along with the sequence in which the features will be built and delivered. It is used to communicate how a product will develop and mature over time. Product roadmaps include information about the product vision and the evolution of the product throughout its life cycle. Product roadmaps are used as a planning tool to understand a product and how it will continue to support organizational strategy as it is further refined and enhanced. Product roadmaps should be aligned with the goals and milestones identified as part of the strategic planning effort.

4.5.4 FACILITATE PRODUCT ROADMAP: TAILORING CONSIDERATIONS

Adaptive and predictive tailoring considerations for Facilitate Product Roadmap are described in Table 4-10.

Table 4-10. Adaptive and Predictive Tailoring for Facilitate Product Roadmap

Aspects to Be Tailored	Typical Adaptive Considerations	Typical Predictive Considerations
Name	Facilitate Product Roadmap	
Approach	Visual representation of a roadmap is broken out by themes and features and may cover a short-term or long-term view. It is revised as new features are identified and priorities are adjusted. The value of the product changes regularly as adjustments are made to the feature set. Roadmaps can be created for single products or for an entire portfolio.	Roadmaps might show high-level milestones, features, or product components. The product roadmap covers a longer time frame (e.g., 12 months) and change is infrequent. When changes are proposed, they need to be assessed for impact to previously stated and expected value. Roadmaps can be created for single products or for an entire portfolio.
Deliverables	Product roadmap	

4.5.5 FACILITATE PRODUCT ROADMAP: COLLABORATION POINT

Portfolio and program managers can serve as valuable sources of information needed for the development of the roadmap. They are key contributors in defining how a new product aligns to organizational strategy and relates to other products in the portfolio or program, and they can work closely with the business analyst to transfer this knowledge.

4.6 ASSEMBLE BUSINESS CASE

Assemble Business Case is the process of synthesizing well-researched and analyzed information to support the selection of the best portfolio components, programs, or projects to address business goals and objectives. The key benefit of this process is that it helps organizations scrutinize programs and projects in a consistent manner, enabling the decision makers to determine whether a program and/or project is worth the required investment. The inputs, tools and techniques, and outputs of the process are depicted in Figure 4-19. Figure 4-20 depicts the data flow diagram for the process.

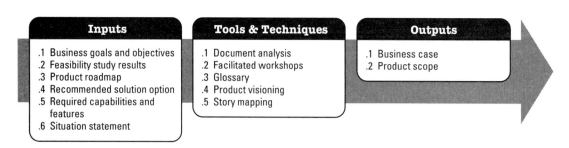

Inputs	Tools & Techniques	Outputs
.1 Business goals and objectives .2 Feasibility study results .3 Product roadmap .4 Recommended solution option .5 Required capabilities and features .6 Situation statement	.1 Document analysis .2 Facilitated workshops .3 Glossary .4 Product visioning .5 Story mapping	.1 Business case .2 Product scope

Figure 4-19. Assemble Business Case: Inputs, Tools and Techniques, and Outputs

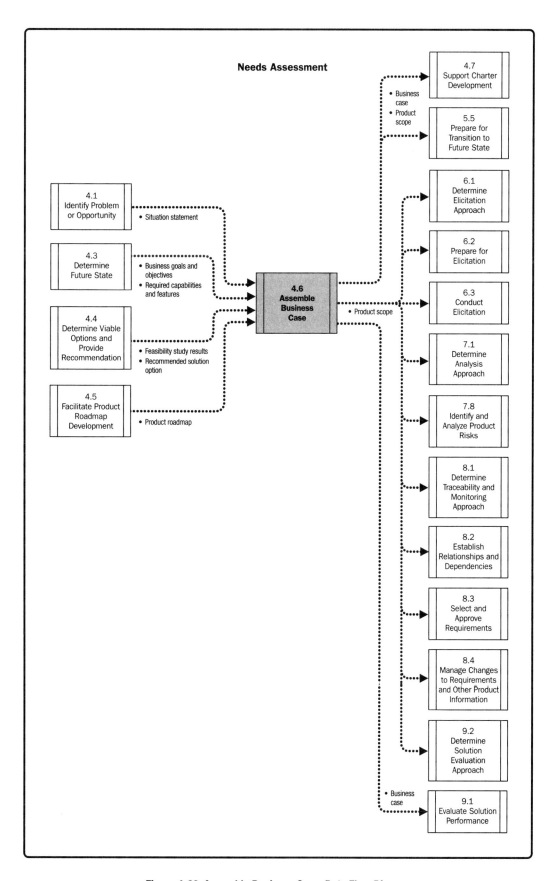

Figure 4-20. Assemble Business Case: Data Flow Diagram

Assemble Business Case consists of the work performed to assemble and package the information required by key decision makers to evaluate portfolio components, programs, or projects and determine whether a portfolio component, program, or project is worth pursuing. A business case provides a documented economic feasibility study, establishing the validity of the benefits to be delivered by a portfolio, program, or project. A business case presents information to establish whether the organization should address a problem or opportunity. The business case explores the nature of the problem or opportunity, presents its root causes or contributors to success, and looks at many facets that contribute to a complete recommendation. Much of the analysis completed during Needs Assessment is used in the development of the business case. The business case provides the key information required to establish the objectives and serves as a major input to the charter. Identifying the value that is expected from pursuing the proposed change and making sure the value proposition is being clearly communicated is a critical component of the business case.

Not all business problems or opportunities require a formal business case. Executives in an organization may approve portfolio components, programs, or projects based on competitive pressure, government mandate, or executive inclination. In those cases, a charter may be used to initiate the portfolio component, program, or project. A formally documented business case and charter are commonly requirements in large or highly regulated companies. Though the formality of a business case may not always be useful in smaller organizations or in some organizations that have adopted an adaptive approach, the thought process of defining the problem/opportunity, analyzing the situation, making recommendations, and defining evaluation criteria is applicable to all organizations.

In most instances, the analysis performed in the business case helps organizations select the best portfolio components, programs, or projects to invest in and meet the needs of the business. Business cases help organizations scrutinize portfolio components, programs, and projects in a consistent manner. When this process is embraced, organizations should consistently make better decisions.

When a business case is produced, the organization may require the use of a standardized, preapproved business case template. Often, an organization has its own requirements for what to include in a business case and employs a set of templates or business case software to simplify and standardize the process. A common set of components in any business case should minimally include the following:

◆ **Problem/opportunity.** Specify what is prompting the need for action. Use a situation statement or equivalent to document the business problem or opportunity to be addressed through a portfolio component, program, or project. Include relevant data to assess the situation and identify which stakeholders or stakeholder groups are affected.

◆ **Analysis of the situation.** Describe how a potential solution will support and contribute to the business goals and objectives. Include root cause(s) of the problem or the main contributors to an opportunity. Support the analysis through relevant data to confirm the rationale. Include needed capabilities versus existing capabilities. The gaps between these will form the portfolio, program, or project objectives.

◆ **Recommendation.** Present the results of the feasibility analysis for each potential option. Specify any constraints, assumptions, risks, and dependencies for each option. Rank in order the alternatives and list the recommended one; include why it is recommended and why the others are not. Summarize the cost-benefit analysis for the recommended option. Include the implementation approach, including milestones, dependencies, roles, and responsibilities. The work products produced in Section 4.4 provide the necessary research and background information to develop the business case and support decision makers with sufficient evidence that the action being requested is necessary and viable.

◆ **Evaluation.** Include a plan for measuring benefits realization. This plan typically includes metrics for evaluating how the solution contributes to goals and objectives. It may necessitate additional work to capture and report those metrics. This plan is formed by concurrently performing the Determine Solution Evaluation Approach, described in Section 9.2.

When a business case is created, it becomes a valued input to the initiation of a portfolio component, program, or project, providing the team with a concise and comprehensive view of the business need and the approved solution for that need. More than a simple input, a business case is a living document that is constantly referenced throughout a portfolio, program, or project. It may be necessary to review and update a business case based on what is discovered as a portfolio, program, or project progresses over time.

The development of a business case may be driven by many factors, including:

◆ Market demand,

◆ Organizational need,

◆ Customer request,

◆ Strategic opportunities,

◆ Technological advancement,

◆ Legal or regulatory requirement,

◆ Ecological impacts, and

◆ Social needs.

In multiphase initiatives, the business case may be periodically reviewed to ensure that the portfolio component, program, or project is on track to deliver the business benefits. In the early stages of the initiative, periodic review of the business case by the sponsoring organization helps confirm that the initiative is still aligned with the business case. The sponsor should agree to the scope and limitations of the business case and acts as a key stakeholder with responsibility to approve the business case prior to the start of the initiative.

Although both adaptive and predictive project life cycles recognize the business case as a key input for initiating project-related work, adaptive methods will assemble "just enough" of the content to get started. With adaptive approaches, features will continue to be added as the solution is further refined; therefore, the business case will not contain the full list of benefits, as it would in a predictive approach. Adaptive methods will estimate cost and schedule from a very high level and then progressively expand upon this information through the iterative development cycle, while predictive methods will complete all this analysis up front.

4.6.1 ASSEMBLE BUSINESS CASE: INPUTS

4.6.1.1 BUSINESS GOALS AND OBJECTIVES

Described in Section 4.3.3.1. Business goals and objectives specify stated targets that the business is seeking to achieve. A common link between business goals and objectives and portfolio components, programs, or projects is the business case. Business goals and objectives are included in the business case to provide context regarding what the business expects to achieve by pursuing the proposed change.

4.6.1.2 FEASIBILITY STUDY RESULTS

Described in Section 4.4.3.1. Feasibility study results are the summarized results obtained from the completion of the feasibility analysis. The results are included in the business case to provide supporting information to decision makers who will determine whether the portfolio component, program, or project should be initiated. Decision makers can review the results to obtain an understanding about the proposed solutions that were analyzed and why each was considered a viable option. The feasibility results also support why the recommended solution option is being recommended.

4.6.1.3 PRODUCT ROADMAP

Described in Section 4.5.3.1. A product roadmap provides a high-level view of product features, along with the sequence in which the features will be built and delivered. The key information from the product roadmap is included within the business case to provide decision makers with insights into how the product is envisioned to evolve over time.

4.6.1.4 RECOMMENDED SOLUTION OPTION

Described in Section 4.4.3.2. The recommended solution option is the solution choice determined to be the best course of action for addressing the business need. The recommended solution option is showcased within the business case, along with the supporting information that provides the rationalization for its selection.

4.6.1.5 REQUIRED CAPABILITIES AND FEATURES

Described in Section 4.3.3.2. The required capabilities and features identify the list of net changes the organization will need to obtain in order to achieve the desired future state. The capabilities and features required for the recommended solution are listed in the business case to provide decision makers with insight into which capabilities and features are required when the recommended solution option being recommended is pursued.

4.6.1.6 SITUATION STATEMENT

Described in Section 4.1.3.2. The situation statement is an objective statement of a problem or opportunity that includes the statement itself, the situation's effect on the organization, and the resulting impact. The situation statement is included in the business case to clearly communicate the problem or opportunity that the proposed solution is addressing. The situation statement is intended to help those reviewing the business case to understand the problem or opportunity that the organization is facing and minimize quick judgments about potential solutions.

4.6.2 ASSEMBLE BUSINESS CASE: TOOLS AND TECHNIQUES

4.6.2.1 DOCUMENT ANALYSIS

Document analysis is an elicitation technique used to analyze existing documentation and identify relevant product information. When assembling a business case, documentation from several different sources is reviewed to obtain the relevant information needed to build the business case. The most relevant documents used are the outputs produced from earlier Needs Assessment processes. For more information on document analysis, see Section 6.3.2.3.

4.6.2.2 FACILITATED WORKSHOPS

Facilitated workshops use a structured meeting led by a skilled, neutral facilitator and a carefully selected group of stakeholders to collaborate and work toward a stated objective. Because facilitated workshops support interactivity, collaboration, and improved communication among participants, the technique is a good choice when a team needs to elicit information and amass support to assemble the business case. For more information on facilitated workshops, see Section 6.3.2.4.

4.6.2.3 GLOSSARY

In business analysis, a glossary provides a list of definitions for terms and acronyms about a product. When assembling a business case, a glossary provides a common vocabulary about terms that the stakeholders and product team may be unfamiliar with and focuses specifically on the terms requiring clarity to understand the information in the business case. When the product team shares a glossary across the portfolio, program, or project, a link to the shared glossary should be provided either within the business case or team workspace. For more information on glossaries, see Section 7.3.2.3.

4.6.2.4 PRODUCT VISIONING

Product visioning is a technique that a product team can use to obtain a shared understanding about the product and set a high-level direction for its development. Product visioning involves discussions to help the team evolve its ideas about the product. A vision statement or similar output that clearly defines the goal and rationale for building the solution is included in the business case to provide decision makers with the same understanding of the product that the team shares. For more information on product visioning, see Section 4.5.2.3.

4.6.2.5 STORY MAPPING

Story mapping is a technique used to sequence user stories, based upon their business value and the order in which their users typically perform them, so that teams can arrive at a shared understanding of what will be built. Story maps help communicate the features and product components that the product team will be responsible for delivering. Product components can be assigned to product releases to communicate when features will be delivered. When included in the business case, story maps provide insightful information to those responsible for determining whether to approve the portfolio component, program, or project. Stories written for inclusion into a business case are typically written at a high level and may exist as epics. Epics are later split into other epics or individual stories. For more information on story maps, see Section 7.2.2.16.

4.6.3 ASSEMBLE BUSINESS CASE: OUTPUTS

4.6.3.1 BUSINESS CASE

A business case provides a documented economic feasibility study, establishing the validity of the benefits, in terms of value, to be delivered by a portfolio component, program, or project. The business case is the common link between the business goals and objectives and the portfolio components, programs, or projects established to execute the business strategy. Business goals and objectives may have any number of business cases to support them. An approved business case is used as input when creating a charter to initiate a portfolio component, program, or project. Business cases are assembled as one of the final process steps in Needs Assessment.

4.6.3.2 PRODUCT SCOPE

Product scope is defined as the features and functions that characterize a solution. The product scope varies based on which viable option from Determine Viable Options and Provide Recommendation, described in Section 4.4, is selected. Decision makers may accept the recommended option put forth in the business case, choose an alternative approach, or defer or reject the business case. If the business case is approved, whichever solution approach is approved defines the initial product scope. At this point, product scope is understood at a high level by the capabilities and features associated with the selected option. Product scope continues to be refined as the product team furthers analysis. Throughout an initiative, product scope may be revised in response to changing business needs, risks, or one or more constraints imposed by budget or schedule.

4.6.4 ASSEMBLE BUSINESS CASE: TAILORING CONSIDERATIONS

Adaptive and predictive tailoring considerations for Assemble Business Case are described in Table 4-11.

Table 4-11. Adaptive and Predictive Tailoring for Assemble Business Case

Aspects to Be Tailored	Typical Adaptive Considerations	Typical Predictive Considerations
Name	Not a formally named process; performed as part of project chartering.	Assemble Business Case
Approach	An initial set of features is developed, with more added over time. Estimates are just detailed enough to continue. Includes enough information in the business case to move forward with a decision. The feasibility of the solution is validated early by delivering higher-risk features in early iterations. Return on investment is attained more quickly than with predictive methods, as features are delivered iteratively. The budget might be focused on how much the sponsor has to spend instead of on an assessment of costs. Scope is determined by addressing highest-prioritized features first. As features are added over time, the assessment of benefits/value changes.	Create a thorough list of product features, rigorous estimate, fully defined list of benefits, list of risks, assumptions, constraints, and dependencies. Requires a formal sign-off against a fully elaborated business case. Considered a higher-risk approach over adaptive methods because feasibility is not validated until late in the initiative. Return on investment is attained at completion of the entire initiative. The business case includes cost estimates. The benefits are estimated and not realized until implementation. Funding is typically sought to cover the entire product development cycle.
Deliverables	Lightweight business case that is revisited and revised.	Formalized detailed business case.

4.6.5 ASSEMBLE BUSINESS CASE: COLLABORATION POINT

At the point of business case development, a portfolio component, program, or project is not yet initiated, but the resource who will serve as sponsor should the business case get approved is typically known. The proposed sponsor is the business champion for this change. The sponsor writes the business case with the support of the business analyst or provides information to support its development. The sponsor provides a wealth of information about the business need and current state environment. The sponsor may be the point of contact to pitch and promote the change and seek approval of the business case among the key decision makers. A business analyst partners with the sponsor to see how to support the sponsor through the approval process.

4.7 SUPPORT CHARTER DEVELOPMENT

Support Charter Development is the process of collaborating on charter development with the sponsoring entity and stakeholder resources using the business analysis knowledge, experience, and product information acquired during needs assessment and business case development efforts. The key benefit of this process is that it enables a smooth transition from the business case to charter development and provides stakeholders with a foundational understanding of the portfolio, program, or project objectives, including product scope and requirements. The inputs, tools and techniques, and outputs of the process are depicted in Figure 4-21. Figure 4-22 depicts the data flow diagram for the process.

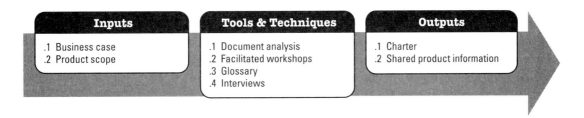

Inputs	Tools & Techniques	Outputs
.1 Business case .2 Product scope	.1 Document analysis .2 Facilitated workshops .3 Glossary .4 Interviews	.1 Charter .2 Shared product information

Figure 4-21. Support Charter Development: Inputs, Tools and Techniques, and Outputs

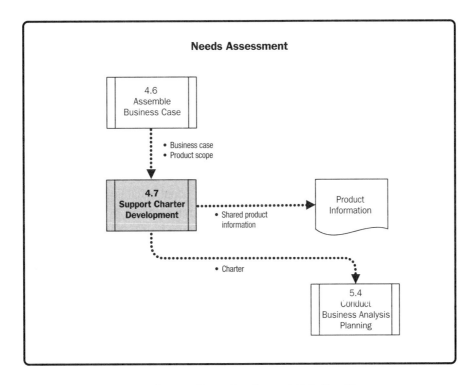

Figure 4-22. Support Charter Development: Data Flow Diagram

A *portfolio charter* is a document issued by a sponsor that authorizes and specifies the portfolio structure and links the portfolio to the organization's strategic objectives. A *program charter* authorizes the program management team to use organizational resources to execute the program and links the program to the organization's strategic objectives. A *project charter* is issued by the project initiator or sponsor to formally authorize the existence of a project and provides the project manager with the authority to apply organizational resources to project activities. A *charter* establishes the scope boundaries and creates a documented record of the initiation of the portfolio component, program, or project.

The charter is used to establish a partnership between the business and the product development team by creating internal agreements within the organization to ensure the proper delivery of the solution. The charter provides the context needed to plan the scope management processes and serves as a communication mechanism by which senior managers can formally accept and commit to the initiative. Developing a charter provides an opportunity to hold discussions about key roles and responsibilities. Decisions are included in the charter to delegate authority and set expectations across the team. The effort to develop a charter helps set the objective of the portfolio, program, or project, as it clearly communicates what needs to be accomplished. Business analysis activities support portfolio, program, and project charter development.

Development of the charter should be a collaborative effort involving various resources from across the team, including product development, the sponsor, customers, and other stakeholders. The development of the charter should be supported by the analytical resources who participated in the Needs Assessment activities, specifically those who were responsible for development of the business case. The initiator or sponsor should be at the appropriate level to procure funding and commit resources to the initiative. The process of creating a charter establishes a shared understanding of the solution, the risks, resource requirements, high-level schedule, and success criteria resulting in attainment of the business goals and objectives. The charter helps align stakeholders' expectations with the portfolio, program, or project's purpose, and demonstrates how stakeholder participation in the initiative and the associated phases can ensure that overall expectations are achieved.

Information in the charter is presented at a high level, but is more detailed than the information assembled when recommending the proposed solution in Section 4.4. Information in the charter focuses on a tactical discussion about how the portfolio component, program, or project will be performed, including information about the elements required to deliver the chosen solution to the business. Information about initial financial resources and the internal and external stakeholders who will interact and influence the overall outcome of the initiative are identified. The higher-level information provided in a charter serves as the starting point for communicating the tactical needs of the portfolio, program, or project and is used to develop detailed elements in later processes. For example, the information in the charter is later elaborated upon when the scope statement is developed and a detailed description of the scope elements is defined and progressively elaborated throughout the initiative. The summary budget information in the charter is the basis from which detailed costs will later be developed.

Information that is commonly part of a charter includes:

◆ Description and purpose;

◆ Business goals/objectives;

◆ High-level product and portfolio, program, or project scope;

◆ Risks;

◆ Summary milestone schedule;

- ◆ Summary budget information;

- ◆ High-level risks and dependencies;

- ◆ Success criteria; and

- ◆ Information about internal and external parties related to the portfolio, program, or project, which are affected by the result or execution of the portfolio component, program, or project—for example, the sponsor(s), customers, team members, groups and departments participating in the initiative, and other people or organizations affected by the initiative.

The size of the charter varies depending on the complexity of the portfolio, program, or project and the information known at the time of its creation. At a minimum, the charter should provide a high-level description and characteristics of the solution so that detailed requirements can later be developed. A formal documented charter is commonly required in large or highly regulated companies. Although this formality may not always apply in smaller organizations or in some organizations that have adopted an adaptive approach, the thought processes conducted in Needs Assessment to define the problem or opportunity, analyze the situation, make recommendations, and define evaluation criteria establish the fundamental groundwork for creating a charter and are applicable to all organizations.

Chartering validates alignment of the portfolio, program, or project to the strategy and ongoing work of the organization regardless of how formal an output is required. A charter requires enough information to secure funding for a portfolio, program, or project and to authorize a team to begin work. In some organizations—typically those that follow predictive life cycles—the charter is a large, formal document that requires approval and sign-off. In other organizations—typically those employing adaptive life cycles—the deliverable may be a lightweight charter and verbal authorization to proceed. If a formal charter is not produced, comparable information needs to be acquired or developed and used as a basis for the detailed project scope statement. Organizations that do not produce a formal charter usually perform an informal analysis to identify the content necessary for further scope planning. In some organizations, the charter may be developed before a decision is made on whether to use a predictive or adaptive project life cycle.

4.7.1 SUPPORT CHARTER DEVELOPMENT: INPUTS

4.7.1.1 BUSINESS CASE

Described in Section 4.6.3.1. The business case describes pertinent information to determine whether the initiative is worth the required investment. The needs assessment and business case build the foundation for determining the objectives of the portfolio component, program, or project, and serve as inputs to a charter. Typically, the business need and the cost-benefit analysis are contained in the business case to justify and establish boundaries for the portfolio component, program, or project, which is necessary information when creating a charter.

4.7.1.2 PRODUCT SCOPE

Described in Section 4.6.3.2. Product scope is defined as the features and functions that characterize a solution. During charter development, initial product scope is established by the inclusion of high-level product requirements. The charter may also include information about out-of-scope features to clearly identify any features that have been deferred or cut from the scope.

4.7.2 SUPPORT CHARTER DEVELOPMENT: TOOLS AND TECHNIQUES

4.7.2.1 DOCUMENT ANALYSIS

Document analysis is an elicitation technique used to analyze existing documentation to identify relevant product information. It can be used to identify information used in the development of the charter. Reviewing organizational charts to identify a potential list of stakeholders or existing business architecture models to understand areas of the business impacted by the proposed change are two examples of how existing documentation can be reviewed to elicit information to develop a charter. For more information on document analysis, see Section 6.3.2.3.

4.7.2.2 FACILITATED WORKSHOPS

Facilitated workshops use a structured meeting led by a skilled, neutral facilitator and a carefully selected group of stakeholders to collaborate and work toward a stated objective, such as the development of product requirements. Facilitated workshops are used to elicit information needed in the development of the charter. Because facilitated workshops support interactivity, collaboration, and improved communication among participants, the technique is a practical elicitation technique to use when developing a charter and obtaining stakeholder consensus on the information included in it. For more information on facilitated workshops, see Section 6.3.2.4.

4.7.2.3 GLOSSARY

In business analysis, a glossary provides a list of definitions for terms and acronyms about a product. When developing a charter, a glossary can provide a common vocabulary about terms with which the stakeholders and product team are unfamiliar or that are commonly misunderstood, focusing specifically on the terms requiring clarity to understand the information in the charter. If the product team is sharing a glossary across the portfolio, program, or project, a link to the shared glossary can be provided from the charter or team workspace. For more information on glossaries, see Section 7.3.2.3.

4.7.2.4 INTERVIEWS

An interview is a formal or informal approach to elicit information from stakeholders. It is a viable technique for eliciting information necessary in the development of the charter. Interviews are scheduled with various stakeholders who possess key information. The information obtained from interviews can be used to initiate the charter or fill in information gaps when other elicitation techniques were used previously. For more information on interviews, see Section 6.3.2.6.

4.7.3 SUPPORT CHARTER DEVELOPMENT: OUTPUTS

4.7.3.1 CHARTER

A charter establishes the scope boundaries and creates a documented record of the initiation of the portfolio component, program, or project. It is used to establish a partnership between the business and the product development team by establishing internal agreements within the organization to ensure proper delivery of the portfolio, program, or project. Business analysis is used in the development of the charter. In predictive life cycles, typically the individual assigned to perform business analysis supports the sponsor with this work. In adaptive life cycles, a sponsor may create the charter, but a product owner might contribute to the business analysis work to support charter development.

4.7.3.2 SHARED PRODUCT INFORMATION

Shared product information consists of the compilation of all the information discussed and shared across the product team during collaboration. When the charter is collaboratively developed, the product team obtains a common understanding about the solution that the portfolio component, program, or project is commissioned to deliver. Building a shared understanding reduces the risk that the product team may develop an end solution that is out of alignment with stakeholder expectations and enables the team to work more effectively during development efforts.

4.7.4 SUPPORT CHARTER DEVELOPMENT: TAILORING CONSIDERATIONS

Adaptive and predictive tailoring considerations for Support Charter Development are described in Table 4-12.

Table 4-12. Adaptive and Predictive Tailoring for Support Charter Development

Aspects to Be Tailored	Typical Adaptive Considerations	Typical Predictive Considerations
Name	Charter Development	Support Charter Development
Approach	Created as an entire team, before the initiative starts with lightweight information about the initiative, why it is pursued, high-level scope, capabilities, and success criteria. Decisions made during charter development discussions will be revisited across iterations to ensure that ongoing work remains in alignment with the vision set forth at the start of the initiative.	Created before the initiative starts with detailed information about the portfolio components, program, or project; why it is pursued; high-level scope; capabilities; and success criteria. Once approved, the guidelines set forth in the charter are followed. The charter information will not change unless the changes being proposed are approved by those with the authority to do so.
Deliverables	Charter developed to sufficient level to obtain a shared understanding about initiative and solution. May include models that define scope—for example, context diagram.	Formal charter, multipage document. May include models that define scope—for example, context diagram. Assembled in a document created from a standardized organizational template.

4.7.5 SUPPORT CHARTER DEVELOPMENT: COLLABORATION POINT

Portfolio, program, and/or project managers work alongside the business analyst to translate the business case into a portfolio, program, or project charter.

5

STAKEHOLDER ENGAGEMENT

Stakeholder Engagement includes the processes to identify and analyze those with an interest in the solution, determining how best to engage, communicate, and collaborate with them; establish a shared understanding of the business analysis activities required to define the solution; and conduct periodic assessment of the business analysis process to ensure its effectiveness. This section presents Stakeholder Engagement from a business analysis perspective.

Within business analysis, the Stakeholder Engagement processes are as follows:

5.1 Identify Stakeholders—The process of identifying the individuals, groups, or organizations that may impact, are impacted, or are perceived to be impacted by the area under assessment.

5.2 Conduct Stakeholder Analysis—The process of researching and analyzing quantitative and qualitative information about the individuals, groups, or organizations that may impact, are impacted, or are perceived to be impacted by the area under assessment.

5.3 Determine Stakeholder Engagement and Communication Approach—The process of developing appropriate methods to effectively engage and communicate with stakeholders throughout the product life cycle, based on an analysis of their needs, interests, and roles within the business analysis process.

5.4 Conduct Business Analysis Planning—The process performed to obtain shared agreement regarding the business analysis activities the team will be performing and the assignment of roles, responsibilities, and skill sets for the tasks required to successfully complete the business analysis work.

5.5 Prepare for Transition to Future State—The process of determining whether the organization is ready for a transition and how the organization will move from the current to the future state to integrate the solution or partial solution into the organization's operations.

5.6 Manage Stakeholder Engagement and Communication—The process of fostering appropriate involvement in business analysis processes, keeping stakeholders appropriately informed about ongoing business analysis efforts, and sharing product information with stakeholders as it evolves.

5.7 Assess Business Analysis Performance—The process of considering the effectiveness of the business analysis practices in use across the organization, typically in the context of considering the ongoing deliverables and results of a portfolio component, program, or project.

Figure 5-1 provides an overview of the Stakeholder Engagement processes. The business analysis processes are presented as discrete processes with defined interfaces, although, in practice, they overlap and interact in ways that cannot be completely detailed in this guide.

Stakeholder Engagement Overview

5.1 Identify Stakeholders

.1 Inputs
  .1 Elicitation results (unconfirmed/ confirmed)
  .2 Enterprise and business architectures
  .3 Situation statement
.2 Tools & Techniques
  .1 Brainstorming
  .2 Interviews
  .3 Organizational charts
  .4 Process flows
  .5 Questionnaires and surveys
.3 Outputs
  .1 Stakeholder register

5.2 Conduct Stakeholder Analysis

.1 Inputs
  .1 Elicitation results (unconfirmed/confirmed)
  .2 Enterprise and business architectures
  .3 Situation statement
  .4 Stakeholder register
.2 Tools & Techniques
  .1 Job analysis
  .2 Persona analysis
  .3 RACI model
  .4 Stakeholder maps
.3 Outputs
  .1 Updated stakeholder register

5.3 Determine Stakeholder Engagement and Communication Approach

.1 Inputs
  .1 Situation statement
  .2 Updated stakeholder register
.2 Tools & Techniques
  .1 Elicitation techniques
  .2 Persona analysis
  .3 RACI model
  .4 Retrospectives and lessons learned
  .5 Stakeholder maps
.3 Outputs
  .1 Stakeholder engagement and communication approach

5.4 Conduct Business Analysis Planning

.1 Inputs
  .1 Business analysis performance assessment
  .2 Charter
  .3 Enterprise environmental factors
  .4 Planning approaches from all other Knowledge Areas
  .5 Product risk analysis
.2 Tools & Techniques
  .1 Burndown charts
  .2 Decomposition model
  .3 Estimation techniques
  .4 Planning techniques
.3 Outputs
  .1 Business analysis plan

5.5 Prepare for Transition to Future State

.1 Inputs
  .1 Business case
  .2 Current state assessment
  .3 Product risk analysis
  .4 Product scope
  .5 Requirements and other product information
  .6 Solution design
  .7 Stakeholder engagement and communication approach
.2 Tools & Techniques
  .1 Elicitation techniques
  .2 Group decision-making techniques
  .3 Job analysis
  .4 Prioritization schemes
  .5 Process flows
  .6 SWOT analysis
  .7 User story
.3 Outputs
  .1 Readiness assessment
  .2 Transition plan

5.6 Manage Stakeholder Engagement and Communication

.1 Inputs
  .1 Stakeholder engagement and communication approach
  .2 Updated stakeholder register
.2 Tools & Techniques
  .1 Elicitation techniques
.3 Outputs
  .1 Improved stakeholder engagement and communication

5.7 Assess Business Analysis Performance

.1 Inputs
  .1 Business analysis plan
  .2 Business analysis organizational standards
  .3 Business analysis performance metrics and measurements
  .4 Business analysis work products
.2 Tools & Techniques
  .1 Burndown charts
  .2 Elicitation techniques
  .3 Process flows
  .4 Retrospectives and lessons learned
  .5 Root cause and opportunity analysis
  .6 Variance analysis
.3 Outputs
  .1 Business analysis performance assessment

Figure 5-1. Stakeholder Engagement Overview

KEY CONCEPTS FOR STAKEHOLDER ENGAGEMENT

Stakeholder Engagement involves the activities performed to analyze the needs and characteristics of stakeholders to understand how best to identify, involve, communicate, and work with them in a collaborative manner. Stakeholder Engagement is not unique to business analysis, but when performed within the discipline, the objective is to ensure the best engagement with stakeholders across the business analysis processes.

Much of the work in business analysis involves communication. Stakeholder Engagement processes raise awareness about those who have a connection, either directly or indirectly, to the situation under analysis or the solution. When there is clarity on who needs to be included and involved in the business analysis process and an effort is made to partner and apply practices that are supportive and collaborative, then there are tremendous benefits gained for business analysis and across portfolio, program, and project management. Stakeholder Engagement is about ensuring optimal representation and ongoing interest and involvement from the stakeholder community.

5.1 IDENTIFY STAKEHOLDERS

Identify Stakeholders is the process of identifying the individuals, groups, or organizations that may impact, are impacted, or are perceived to be impacted by the area under assessment. The key benefit of this process is that it helps determine whose interests should be taken into account throughout the business analysis–related activities. The inputs, tools and techniques, and outputs of the process are depicted in Figure 5-2. Figure 5-3 depicts the data flow diagram for the process.

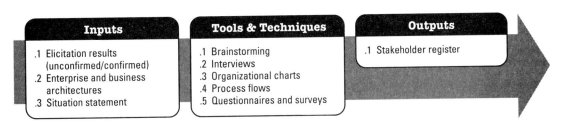

Figure 5-2. Identify Stakeholders: Inputs, Tools and Techniques, and Outputs

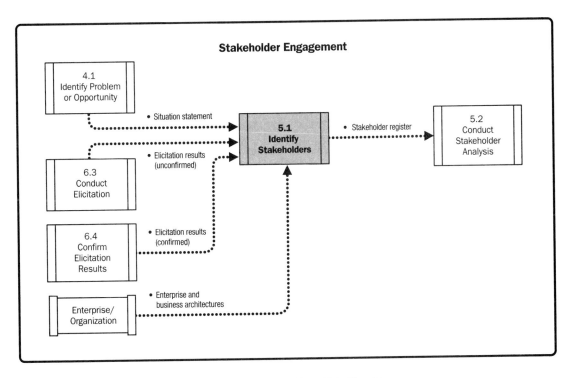

Figure 5-3. Identify Stakeholders: Data Flow Diagram

According to the *PMBOK® Guide*, a stakeholder is an individual, group, or organization that may affect, be affected by, or perceive itself to be affected by a decision, activity, or outcome of a portfolio, program, or project. In business analysis, a stakeholder is an individual, group, or organization that may affect, be affected by, or perceive itself to be affected by the solution; therefore, these individuals and organizations can be termed *product stakeholders.*

Product stakeholders participate in the discovery of requirements and contribute in requirements elicitation by sharing business analysis information from which product requirements are eventually formed. Anyone who initially identifies or perceives him- or herself as a product stakeholder may later have that disposition changed as more information is discovered about the situation and product requirements. Product teams will use the definition of product scope and analysis results produced as the solution evolves to make adjustments to the stakeholder list. Within this standard and guide, the term *stakeholder* refers to those affected by the solution; hence, *product* stakeholder is assumed.

Because stakeholder identification is performed as part of business analysis and portfolio, program, and project management, there is the potential for much overlap in effort. Collaboration can ensure that business analysis and portfolio, program, and project management efforts avoid redundancy and gaps and the partnership between roles provides for a better end result.

5.1.1 IDENTIFY STAKEHOLDERS: INPUTS

5.1.1.1 ELICITATION RESULTS (UNCONFIRMED/CONFIRMED)

Described in Sections 6.3.3.1 and 6.4.3.1. Elicitation results consist of the business analysis information obtained from completed elicitation activities. Elicitation occurs across the entire business analysis process. At any point in time, unconfirmed and confirmed elicitation results are available as a source of data for identifying stakeholders. Even results that are unconfirmed can prove valuable when identifying additional areas where potential stakeholders may exist. Sometimes unconfirmed elicitation results will prompt a follow-up discussion with stakeholders, which then leads to further discovery of stakeholders and other product-related information. Through analysis and continued collaboration, the elicitation results used to identify stakeholders can transition from unconfirmed to confirmed, demonstrating the iterative nature of elicitation and analysis within business analysis.

5.1.1.2 ENTERPRISE AND BUSINESS ARCHITECTURES

Described in Section 4.2.1.1. Enterprise and business architectures are a collection of the business and technology components needed to operate an enterprise, including business functions, organizational structures, locations, and processes of an organization. Enterprise and business architectures often contain models and textual descriptions about roles throughout the organization. This information can be utilized as a source for identifying stakeholders. Architecture models can be shared with stakeholders, which may help participants recall missing stakeholders that need to be added to the stakeholder register.

5.1.1.3 SITUATION STATEMENT

Described in Section 4.1.3.2. The situation statement provides an objective statement about the problem or opportunity the business is looking to address, along with the effect and impact the situation is having on the organization. This context is required for determining the scope boundary to guide which stakeholders to include in the stakeholder register.

5.1.2 IDENTIFY STAKEHOLDERS: TOOLS AND TECHNIQUES

5.1.2.1 BRAINSTORMING

Brainstorming is an elicitation technique that can be used to identify a list of ideas in a short period of time (e.g., a list of risks, stakeholders, or potential solution options). Brainstorming is conducted in a group environment and is led by a facilitator. A topic or issue is presented and the group is asked to generate as many ideas as possible about the topic. Ideas are provided freely and rapidly, and all ideas are accepted. Because the discussion occurs in a group setting, participants feed off of one another's inputs to generate additional ideas. The responses are documented in front of the group, so progress is continually fed back to the participants. The facilitator takes on an important role to ensure that all participants are involved in the discussion, and that no individual monopolizes the session or critiques or criticizes the ideas offered by others. Brainstorming is comprised of two parts: idea generation and analysis. The analysis is conducted to turn the initial list of ideas into a usable form of information. Brainstorming can be used during stakeholder identification to build an initial list of stakeholder names. Brainstorming is further discussed in Section 3.3.1.1 of *Business Analysis for Practitioners: A Practice Guide*.

5.1.2.2 INTERVIEWS

An interview is a formal or informal approach to elicit information from stakeholders. Interviews can be conducted with stakeholders, such as a sponsor or operational managers, to identify the list of stakeholders who will be involved in one or more aspects of the business analysis effort. For more information on interviews, see Section 6.3.2.6.

5.1.2.3 ORGANIZATIONAL CHARTS

Organizational charts are models that depict the reporting structure within an organization or within a part of an organization. These models can be reviewed to facilitate the discovery of stakeholder groups or individuals who may be impacted by or have a potential impact on the solution under analysis.

Existing organizational charts can be used as a starting point or, when these charts are not accessible or nonexistent, new ones can be built from scratch. Organizational charts are best finalized by collaborating with the representatives or individuals being modeled. Based on the size of the organization and how the organizational charts are being used across the business analysis effort, the business analyst determines whether it makes sense to take a role organizational chart down to the individual stakeholder level. If the goal is only to identify the number of groups impacted by the proposed solution, the role organizational chart may be the sufficient level of detail required.

Roles may be conducted differently across the organization and may vary regionally or by the type of customer supported. Stakeholders from the same group may use a product differently. When uncovered during stakeholder analysis, such variations can be reflected in the stakeholder register and can be reflected in a persona that the team creates to further analyze the role. The ultimate goal when reviewing organizational charts is to uncover all the stakeholders who will have needs that will have to be met by the solution and that may have requirements to provide. An oversight of just one role type can result in implementing a solution that fails to meet the needs of hundreds or even thousands of customers. Organizational charts are further discussed in Section 3.3.1.2 of *Business Analysis for Practitioners: A Practice Guide*.

5.1.2.4 PROCESS FLOWS

Process flows visually document the steps or tasks that people perform in their jobs or when they interact with a product. These models are typically well understood by business stakeholders, so they make for a great tool to facilitate discussions around missing stakeholders or to validate a stakeholder register that has already been started. When identifying stakeholders, the discussion can be focused on understanding the roles responsible for performing existing processes or roles that interact with the outputs produced from these processes. Process flows can be constructed to envision the future state, and any new stakeholders can then be identified by reviewing how work will be performed in the future. For more information on process flows, see Section 7.2.2.12.

5.1.2.5 QUESTIONNAIRES AND SURVEYS

Questionnaires and surveys are written sets of questions designed to quickly accumulate information from a large number of respondents. Surveys can be used to collect information to establish or maintain a stakeholder list. For more information on questionnaires and surveys, see Section 6.3.2.9.

5.1.3 IDENTIFY STAKEHOLDERS: OUTPUTS

5.1.3.1 STAKEHOLDER REGISTER

In project management, a stakeholder register is a project document that includes the identification, assessment, and classification of project stakeholders. In business analysis, any individual, group, or organization that may affect, be affected by, or be perceived to be affected by the proposed or intended solution is added to the stakeholder register.

5.1.4 IDENTIFY STAKEHOLDERS: TAILORING CONSIDERATIONS

Adaptive and predictive tailoring considerations for Identify Stakeholders are described in Table 5-1.

Table 5-1. Adaptive and Predictive Tailoring for Identify Stakeholders

Aspects to Be Tailored	Typical Adaptive Considerations	Typical Predictive Considerations
Name	Identify Stakeholders	
Approach	Stakeholders are identified during initial planning, often using brainstorming, and can be revisited at any point throughout the adaptive life cycle as stakeholders are discovered.	List of stakeholders is identified during business analysis planning and can be revisited/revised if the product scope changes or elicitation and analysis activities identify new stakeholders.
Deliverables	Might be a list of stakeholders noted in lightweight documentation or models may just involve brainstorm results.	Stakeholder register; may require the use of an approved stakeholder register template.

5.1.5 IDENTIFY STAKEHOLDERS: COLLABORATION POINT

Enterprise and business architects model aspects of the organization, including information pertaining to internal human resources and supporting external people resources that have relationships to the enterprise. Architects may be able to share models depicting current organizational units, roles, and skills to augment stakeholder identification activities.

5.2 CONDUCT STAKEHOLDER ANALYSIS

Conduct Stakeholder Analysis is the process of researching and analyzing quantitative and qualitative information about the individuals, groups, or organizations that may impact, are impacted, or are perceived to be impacted by the area under assessment. The key benefit of this process is that it provides important insights about stakeholders that can be used when choosing elicitation and analysis techniques, selecting which stakeholders are appropriate to involve at different times in the business analysis efforts, and determining the best communication and collaboration methods to use. The inputs, tools and techniques, and outputs of the process are depicted in Figure 5-4. Figure 5-5 depicts the data flow diagram for the process.

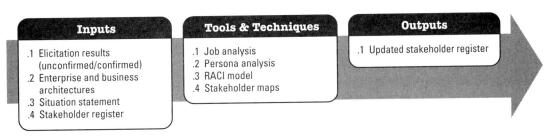

Figure 5-4. Conduct Stakeholder Analysis: Inputs, Tools and Techniques, and Outputs

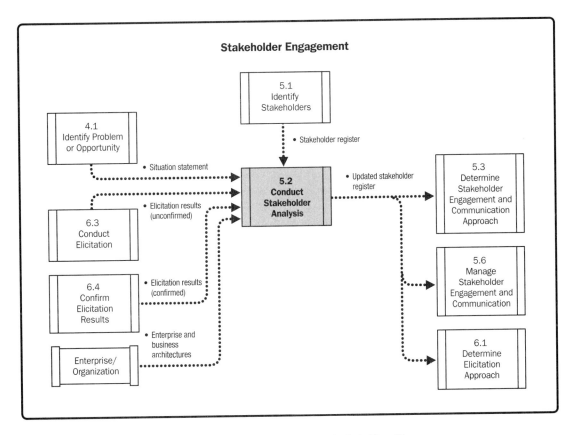

Figure 5-5. Conduct Stakeholder Analysis: Data Flow Diagram

Stakeholder analysis is performed to systematically review and consider quantitative and qualitative information to understand stakeholder characteristics and to determine the interests and positions that the stakeholders have in the solution. Such analysis is often conducted during planning so the product team can understand the stakeholder impacts and influences on the business analysis process as early as possible. The results of stakeholder analysis are used to develop effective approaches to interact and communicate with stakeholders throughout the project and specifically the requirements-related activities.

Stakeholder analysis is performed iteratively and is revisited throughout the project as new stakeholders are discovered or existing stakeholder relationships or characteristics change. Refinements to the product scope may result in the addition or removal of stakeholders. Early planning will produce the initial stakeholder list, but further stakeholder identification will maintain it. When a large number of stakeholders is identified, stakeholder analysis may involve grouping the stakeholder list by common characteristics, which helps streamline analysis.

Any number of characteristics may be analyzed during stakeholder analysis to develop clearer insights about the stakeholders identified in Section 5.1. The information gleaned from this analysis helps with decision making, when establishing roles and responsibilities, and in determining how best to engage and collaborate with stakeholders. The analysis can also be used to determine which stakeholders should be engaged based on the situation. Some characteristics might include the following:

◆ **Attitude.** Identifies who is and who is not supportive, interested, or motivated to support the work and accept the recommended solution option.

◆ **Experience.** Provides understanding about the industry, organization, and solution experience the stakeholder may provide the team during the business analysis effort.

◆ **Interests.** Identifies stakeholders who obtain positive or negative gains from the solution. This, in turn, may impose positive and negative impacts to the requirements-related activities.

◆ **Level of influence.** Detects those who have influence within the organization or product team that may hinder or support the proposed solution.

Any number of characteristics can be chosen for analyzing stakeholders. The product team works together to determine which characteristics to consider. Stakeholder analysis and characteristics are further discussed in Section 3.3 of *Business Analysis for Practitioners: A Practice Guide.*

5.2.1 CONDUCT STAKEHOLDER ANALYSIS: INPUTS

5.2.1.1 ELICITATION RESULTS (UNCONFIRMED/CONFIRMED)

Described in Sections 6.3.3.1 and 6.4.3.1. Elicitation results consist of the business analysis information obtained from completed elicitation activities. Past results of prior discussions and elicitation activities may be used when analyzing characteristics about stakeholders. Even when elicitation results are unconfirmed, the information can serve as a starting point for performing this work. Through analysis and continued collaboration, the elicitation results used to perform stakeholder analysis may transition from unconfirmed to confirmed, demonstrating the iterative nature of elicitation and analysis within business analysis.

5.2.1.2 ENTERPRISE AND BUSINESS ARCHITECTURES

Described in Section 4.2.1.1. Enterprise and business architectures are a collection of the business and technology components needed to operate an enterprise, including business functions, organizational structures, locations, and the processes of an organization. Enterprise and business architectures contain models and textual descriptions about the various roles within the organization. Such information can be utilized as a starting point when beginning to analyze stakeholders.

5.2.1.3 SITUATION STATEMENT

Described in Section 4.1.3.2. The situation statement provides objective information to understand the problem or opportunity that the business is looking to address, along with the organizational impact. This context is required during stakeholder analysis to make the determinations and categorizations about stakeholders and how each is impacted by the recommended solution option.

5.2.1.4 STAKEHOLDER REGISTER

Described in Section 5.1.3.1. A stakeholder register is a product document that includes the identification, assessment, and classification of project stakeholders. In business analysis, any individual, group, or organization that may affect, be affected by, or be perceived to be affected by the proposed or intended solution is added to the stakeholder register. The stakeholder register provides the most current list of stakeholders for performing a stakeholder analysis. The register is maintained during business analysis and portfolio, program, and project management activities.

5.2.2 CONDUCT STAKEHOLDER ANALYSIS: TOOLS AND TECHNIQUES

5.2.2.1 JOB ANALYSIS

Job analysis is a technique that can be used to identify the job requirements and competencies required to perform effectively in a specific job or role. It can be used to determine training needs, as a precursor to writing a job posting, or to support a performance appraisal process. The technique is often used when a new job is created or when an existing job is modified to draft the job description and assist in identifying a recommended list of qualifications for the position.

The output of job analysis may include details such as a high-level description of the work, a depiction of the work environment, a detailed list of the activities a person is expected to perform, a listing of the preferred interpersonal skills, or a list of required training, degrees, and certifications.

The results of job analysis can be used during business analysis to gain insights into stakeholder roles, which is especially helpful when the project entails replacing or revising workflow and business processes. When the solution will involve the creation of one or more new roles, this technique may be used to specify the tasks required for the new positions and the qualities and characteristics needed to be successful in the job. Job analysis is further discussed in Section 3.3.3.1 of *Business Analysis for Practitioners: A Practice Guide*.

5.2.2.2 PERSONA ANALYSIS

A persona is a fictional character created to represent an individual or group of stakeholders, termed a *user class*. For an individual class, a persona can include any number of descriptive features the team decides are worth capturing—for example, a name, narrative, goals, behaviors, motivations, hobbies, environment, demographics, and/or skills. The persona narrative, if included, tells a story about the user class. The objective is to analyze usage information or draw out stakeholder requirements to determine how a user class interacts with a solution. A persona can range in size from a summary paragraph to a one- to two-page description, depending on the characteristics the team agrees to capture. Unlike a stakeholder, a persona may or may not have an interest in the outcome of the project and can be a user with no influence over the solution.

Persona analysis is a technique that can be used to analyze a class of users or process workers, to understand their needs or product design and behavior requirements. During stakeholder analysis, the results of persona analysis can provide insights that can be used to structure a more effective business analysis approach. Personas can be used in product development or IT systems development to design or map out user experiences. Although it may not be possible to obtain requirements for every stakeholder on the stakeholder register, stakeholders can be grouped into user classes and a persona built to understand the needs of each by the class that represents them.

The main difference between a persona and a stakeholder is that the persona is a fictional representation and a stakeholder is an actual person. The main difference in describing personas and stakeholders is that personas include more detail about how the person or group operates within the problem or solution space. For example, personas might describe device literacy, preferred methods for performing tasks, and frequency of performing specific actions. Generally, this kind of in-depth information is not needed for all stakeholders, and is therefore applied to only the most critical or most impacted stakeholders. Persona analysis is further discussed in Section 3.3.3.2 of *Business Analysis for Practitioners: A Practice Guide.*

5.2.2.3 RACI MODEL

A RACI model is a common type of responsibility assignment matrix that uses Responsible, Accountable, Consult, and Inform designations to define the involvement of stakeholders in activities. Portfolio, program, or project managers may develop a RACI model to identify roles and responsibilities for a body of work. In business analysis, a RACI can be developed to communicate the roles and responsibilities of those involved in the business analysis effort. Product teams should avoid assuming that everyone involved in the business analysis process will understand their roles and work assignments. Stakeholders can be confused when they participate on more than one project team and fulfill differing roles. Stakeholders may also have confusion about the roles they are assigned versus the roles they desire. Determining roles and responsibilities with a RACI model helps minimize confusion and conflicts, especially in areas where responsibilities appear to overlap.

Stakeholder analysis involves describing how stakeholders may be categorized by classifications, such as their power, influence, impact, or interest. Such classifications can help determine the level of involvement stakeholders may have, as well as the roles they hold within the business analysis process. Engagement-level classifications, such as unaware, resistant, neutral, supportive, and leading, can be used to consider the current and desired level of engagement of any stakeholder or stakeholder group with the product or project, which will be taken into consideration as part of formulating the stakeholder engagement approach during planning.

These classifications, in turn, may be used to determine what signifies an appropriate level of involvement and how to classify stakeholders within the RACI model. The RACI model demonstrates that stakeholders can have different levels of involvement at different points within a product or project life cycle or within different business analysis processes. The RACI model will highlight single points of accountability and those situations where there is joint accountability. The RACI classifications are as follows:

◆ R—Role or person "responsible" for performing the task.

◆ A—Role or person "accountable" for the completion/quality of the task; final approver.

◆ C—Role or person who may be "consulted" to obtain information to complete the task.

◆ I—Role or person who is in some manner impacted by the task, and hence, needs to be "informed" or kept up to date on the progress and work being performed to complete the task.

Table 5-2 shows a sample format of a RACI model. RACI models are further discussed and an example is provided in Section 2.3.1 of *Business Analysis for Practitioners: A Practice Guide.*

Table 5-2. RACI Model Sample Format

	Role 1	Role 2	Role 3	Role 4	Role 5	Role ... *n*
Task 1	A	C	R		C	
Task 2	A	I	R	C	C	
Task 3	I	A	R	C	C	
Task 4		A	R	C	I	
Task 5	R	A	I	I	C	
Task ... *n*						

5.2.2.4 STAKEHOLDER MAPS

Stakeholder maps are a collection of techniques used for analyzing how stakeholders relate to one another and to the solution under analysis. Several stakeholder mapping techniques exist. The stakeholder matrix and onion diagram are just two of these and are explained below:

◆ **Stakeholder matrix.** A stakeholder matrix is a technique that uses a quadrant or matrix to analyze a set of stakeholders. The *x* and *y* axes are labeled with the names of the variables the product team chooses to analyze by, for example:

   ■ *Influence.* How much the stakeholder may influence product requirements, and

   ■ *Impact.* How significantly the solution will impact the stakeholder once it is implemented.

Each stakeholder name or group name is placed in one of the four quadrants, as depicted in Figure 5-6. A matrix analyzing impact to influence would result in the following relationships:

   ■ *High influence/low impact.* Stakeholders categorized in this group may serve as product champions or advocates for the solution team and business analysis effort. This category includes decision makers who are not directly impacted by the solution but may manage one or more stakeholder groups that are. Although this group of stakeholders may defer the functional requirements work to subject matter experts (SMEs) reporting to them, it is still prudent to maintain open communications with stakeholders in this category to leverage their support and advocacy.

- *High influence/high impact.* This quadrant signifies a critical group of stakeholders to engage with during the business analysis process and requirements-related activities. These stakeholders are critical sources for requirements; therefore, planning should allocate a significant amount of the total business analysis effort to these stakeholders. Stakeholders here require frequent communication and are important resources with whom to build a strong partnership and trusting relationship because they have the influence to make or break an initiative.

- *Low influence/low impact.* These stakeholders should not be ignored, and should be included in initial discussion to validate that their relationship is assessed correctly. These stakeholders may find that their requirements are some of the last to be factored into the final product or may have the value of such requirements ranked so low that the requirements are never implemented by the solution team. Stakeholders here may have no impact and may have no interest or awareness of the effort. The stakeholders in this category should be monitored to ensure that their relationship to the solution does not change as the solution definition evolves.

- *Low influence/high impact.* Stakeholders categorized in this group are also critical sources for requirements. Although the stakeholders themselves may not hold significant power within the organization, they could be represented by an individual who does. Stakeholders here may represent a significant portion of the product requirements; therefore, this is an area where adequate time should be spent understanding the situation and later eliciting requirements. Attention should be given to ensure that communication is reaching this stakeholder group and that any concerns they have are known and addressed. Stakeholders in this group may represent those expected to adapt to the implemented solution once it is built.

Figure 5-6 shows a sample format of a stakeholder matrix.

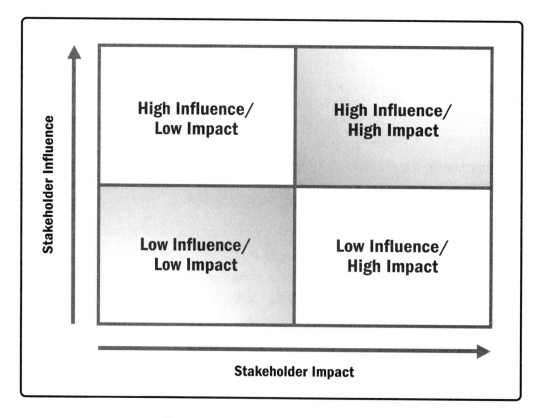

Figure 5-6. Stakeholder Matrix Sample Format

The PMI Guide to Business Analysis

◆ **Onion diagram.** An onion diagram is a technique that can be used to model relationships between different aspects of a subject. In business analysis, an onion diagram can be created to depict the relationships that exist between stakeholders and the solution. The solution may represent one or more products. The stakeholders can be internal or external to the organization. Once built, this model can help the team analyze stakeholders by representing the strength or significance of the relationships of the people to the solution. Stakeholders modeled closest to the center of the onion represent those who have the closest or strongest relationship to the solution—for example, end users or product development stakeholders. Stakeholders modeled on the outer portion of the onion represent those with a less significant relationship. The team can decide the meaning of the layers or relationships being modeled. One example is as follows:

  ■ *Layer 1.* Those directly involved with the development of the solution.
  ■ *Layer 2.* Stakeholders whose activities are directly enhanced or modified by the implemented solution.
  ■ *Layer 3.* Stakeholders who work or interact with those who are directly impacted by the implemented solution.
  ■ *Layer 4.* External stakeholders.

Figure 5-7 shows a sample format of an onion diagram.

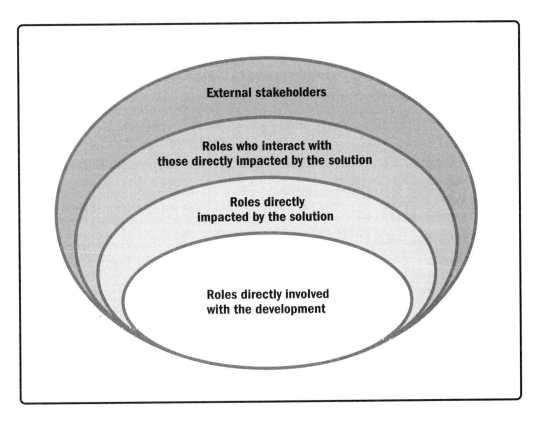

Figure 5-7. Onion Diagram Sample Format

The onion diagram is a good choice when the team is looking for a concise way to communicate information about stakeholder relationships. Other methods, such as brainstorming or analyzing organizational charts, work well as companion techniques to help teams identify the stakeholder roles that need to be depicted in the onion diagram. For more information on organizational charts, see Section 5.1.2.3. For more information on brainstorming, see Section 5.1.2.1.

5.2.3 CONDUCT STAKEHOLDER ANALYSIS: OUTPUTS

5.2.3.1 UPDATED STAKEHOLDER REGISTER

The results of stakeholder analysis may include the addition or modification of stakeholder names or the addition or modification of any of the supporting information pertaining to stakeholder characteristics. Maintaining an accurate stakeholder register is critical to successful business analysis because the oversight of any one stakeholder could result in the loss of critical product requirements. Table 5-3 shows a sample format of a stakeholder register.

Table 5-3. Stakeholder Register Sample Format

Stakeholder	Roles	Attitude	Interests	Level of Impact	Level of Influence	Communication Preferences	Location	Success Criteria	Work Hours

5.2.4 CONDUCT STAKEHOLDER ANALYSIS: TAILORING CONSIDERATIONS

Adaptive and predictive tailoring considerations for Conduct Stakeholder Analysis are described in Table 5-4.

Table 5-4. Adaptive and Predictive Tailoring for Conduct Stakeholder Analysis

Aspects to Be Tailored	Typical Adaptive Considerations	Typical Predictive Considerations
Name	Stakeholder or Persona Analysis	Stakeholder Analysis
Approach	Stakeholder interests and influences as related to expected solution value; performed during initial planning or early iterations and can be revisited prior to the start of an iteration when specific details regarding stakeholders are required for the next iteration.	Any number of stakeholder characteristics analyzed; performed during business analysis planning and can be revisited/revised if the product scope changes, as elicitation and analysis activities identify new stakeholders needing to be analyzed, or across the project life cycle as stakeholder attitude and influence levels may change.
Deliverables	May include stakeholder maps, personas, models, or lightweight documentation.	Stakeholder register that includes a listing of stakeholder names and characteristics.

5.2.5 CONDUCT STAKEHOLDER ANALYSIS: COLLABORATION POINT

Project managers and business analysts encounter an overlap with regard to stakeholder analysis activities because both roles have a vested interest in understanding stakeholder characteristics and managing stakeholders. On adaptive life cycle projects, the overlap or interest and responsibility may exist between any roles performing this analysis. To ensure that redundancy of effort is avoided, business analysts and portfolio, program, and project managers should complete this work collaboratively. Each role provides a unique perspective, with portfolio, program, and project managers analyzing stakeholders for impacts to the portfolio, program, and project, respectively, and business analysts analyzing stakeholders for impacts to the solution and to ensure an effective business analysis process. For the sake of the stakeholders, the product team needs to operate as a cohesive unit and avoid making uncoordinated and redundant requests of stakeholders.

5.3 DETERMINE STAKEHOLDER ENGAGEMENT AND COMMUNICATION APPROACH

Determine Stakeholder Engagement and Communication Approach is the process of developing appropriate methods to effectively engage and communicate with stakeholders throughout the product life cycle, based on an analysis of their needs, interests, and roles within the business analysis process. The key benefit of this process is that it provides a clear, actionable approach to engage stakeholders throughout business analysis and requirements-related activities, so that stakeholders receive the right information, through the best communication methods and frequency to satisfy the needs of the initiative and meet stakeholder expectations.

The inputs, tools and techniques, and outputs of the process are depicted in Figure 5-8. Figure 5-9 depicts the data flow diagram for the process.

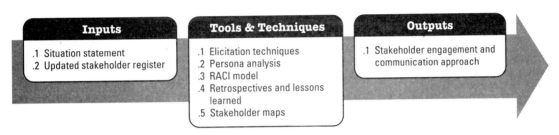

Figure 5-8. Determine Stakeholder Engagement and Communication Approach: Inputs, Tools and Techniques, and Outputs

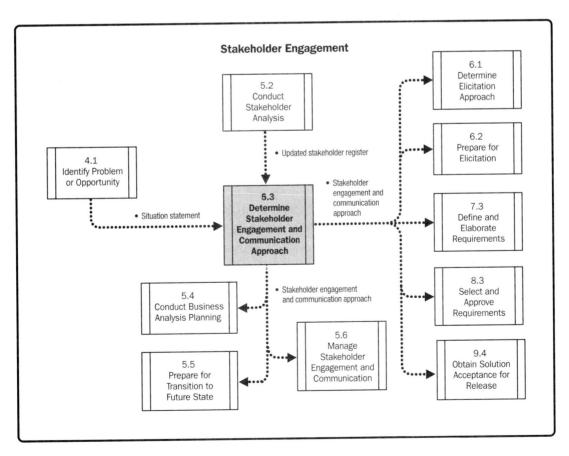

Figure 5-9. Determine Stakeholder Engagement and Communication Approach: Data Flow Diagram

Determining stakeholder engagement and communication means devising different ways to secure an optimal level of commitment from stakeholders at appropriate points in the product life cycle. The stakeholder engagement and communication approach is developed by taking into consideration the results of stakeholder analysis, relevant organizational norms and standards, and lessons learned from past engagements with stakeholders.

A stakeholder engagement and communication approach often has five components:

◆ The level of involvement of each stakeholder or stakeholder group, often based on the RACI and other characterizations of stakeholders as summarized in the stakeholder register;

◆ The approaches for making decisions, such as decision by consensus, decision by sponsor, or decision by weighted analysis. These decision-making approaches are typically defined collaboratively with stakeholder input, taking organizational norms and standards into account;

◆ The approach for obtaining approvals, including who can approve requirements and other product information and who can reject requirements. The approach for approvals also includes the necessary level of approval formality, such as whether sign-off is required, and if it is, whether an electronic signature or email approval is acceptable;

◆ How product and project information will be structured, stored, and maintained in support of keeping stakeholders and others informed. Organizational standards for standard knowledge repositories, requirements management tools, modeling tools, agile team tools, and record retention policies often drive the options that are available. Within these options, wherever possible, stakeholder preferences are considered; and

◆ How stakeholders will be kept up to date about product and project efforts, taking into account which stakeholders need which information, as well as stakeholder preferences for the level of detail of communication, frequency of communication, and the time zones where the stakeholders are located. Additionally, organizational options for communication media and tools will be considered, such as specific communication technology available, authorized communication media, videoconferencing, remote collaboration tools, and security requirements. Within these options, wherever possible, stakeholder preferences are considered.

When dealing with stakeholders who are external to the organization, the same factors have to be considered, such as the best method and timing for delivering communications. Communication to external stakeholders may be initiated from and channeled through single points of contact at both the initiating and receiving ends to ensure consistency in messaging.

For business analysis, there is rarely a one-size-fits-all way to communicate requirements and other product information to all stakeholders. Yet, when tailoring considerations make communication very complex, communication to stakeholders may become very time-consuming. The following questions help to determine what and how to communicate and who might do the communicating:

◆ Who actually uses this kind of information?

◆ Does this information need to be in a formal document?

◆ Does this information need to be written at all, or can it be conveyed in some other way?

Communication approaches are further discussed in Sections 3.4.11 of *Business Analysis for Practitioners: A Practice Guide.*

There is significant overlap between the business analysis perspective of stakeholder engagement and communication and how portfolio, program, and project managers view it. Although overlaps exist, the focus is somewhat different between roles. For example, business analysts are responsible for stakeholder engagement during product development, while portfolio, program, and project managers are responsible for stakeholder engagement within their purview. It is imperative for business analysts to work with portfolio, program, and project managers to determine which stakeholders need to be involved in the product life cycle and their appropriate level of involvement, and to avoid redundancies and inconsistencies in communications. Additionally, business analysts often rely on portfolio, program, and project managers, or work with them, to negotiate and secure the desired commitment from the stakeholders.

Taking time to consider how best to engage and communicate with stakeholders is accomplished in many ways, ranging from the highly formal to the very informal. In organizations with a need or desire for formality, the stakeholder engagement and communication approach becomes a component of a formal business analysis plan, which is discussed in more detail in Section 5.4. Efforts using an adaptive life cycle also require communication/collaboration to be successful; "planning communication" is inherent in the life cycle itself and is not an activity that is formally performed.

No matter how formally or informally one plans out engagement and communication, the thought process is critical for successful product development. In its absence, stakeholders may end up being involved on an ad-hoc basis or whenever they have time to spare. In such situations, a product team risks not obtaining sufficient stakeholder involvement for elicitation, analysis, and decision making; not having a good balance of stakeholder interests represented; and not considering stakeholder preferences for communication, all of which can adversely impact solution decisions and development.

5.3.1 DETERMINE STAKEHOLDER ENGAGEMENT AND COMMUNICATION APPROACH: INPUTS

5.3.1.1 SITUATION STATEMENT

Described in Section 4.1.3.2. The situation statement is an objective statement of a problem or opportunity. The statement, along with a list of stakeholders identified in the stakeholder register, provides context to understand the analysis area and guide decisions about the engagement and communication approach.

5.3.1.2 UPDATED STAKEHOLDER REGISTER

Described in Section 5.2.3.1. The updated stakeholder register contains the results of stakeholder analysis, including the addition or modification of stakeholder names and any supporting information pertaining to stakeholder characteristics. The characterization of the stakeholders obtained through stakeholder analysis is a key factor for determining how a stakeholder will best participate in product development activities.

5.3.2 DETERMINE STAKEHOLDER ENGAGEMENT AND COMMUNICATION APPROACH: TOOLS AND TECHNIQUES

5.3.2.1 ELICITATION TECHNIQUES

Elicitation techniques are used to draw information from sources. As part of determining the stakeholder engagement and communication approach, it's important to work directly with the stakeholders to understand their mindset, what they need, and what will work best for them to engage. Doing so also helps develop or enhance good relationships with them. A few common elicitation techniques that can support determining the stakeholder engagement and communication approach are brainstorming, facilitated workshops, and interviews:

◆ **Brainstorming.** A technique used to identify a list of ideas in a short period of time. It can be used to generate ideas for communication approaches and how to keep all stakeholders engaged. For more information on brainstorming, see Section 5.1.2.1.

- ◆ **Facilitated workshops.** Structured meetings led by a skilled, neutral facilitator and a carefully selected group of stakeholders to collaborate and work toward a stated objective. The structure of a facilitated workshop promotes an efficient and focused meeting for the stakeholders to discuss engagement and communication. For more information on facilitated workshops, see Section 6.3.2.4.

- ◆ **Interviews.** A technique used to elicit information for the stakeholder engagement and communication approach. They can be scheduled with various stakeholders who possess key information at times that are convenient for them. When necessary, individual interviews can provide each stakeholder with an opportunity to speak candidly about concerns regarding stakeholder engagement. For more information on interviews, see Section 6.3.2.6.

For more information on elicitation techniques, see Section 6.3.2.

5.3.2.2 PERSONA ANALYSIS

A persona is a fictional character created to represent an individual or group of stakeholders. When stakeholder types have been characterized by personas, continuing analysis to look for patterns may suggest effective ways to engage and communicate with them. For more information on persona analysis, see Section 5.2.2.2.

5.3.2.3 RACI MODEL

The RACI model is a common type of responsibility assignment matrix that uses responsible, accountable, consult, and inform designations to define the involvement of stakeholders in activities. A RACI model can be used to present the desired level of involvement of each stakeholder or stakeholder group for different business analysis activities. The results of RACI modeling can be used to understand assigned responsibilities and how best to engage and communicate with the stakeholders and groups identified. For more information on RACI models, see Section 5.2.2.3.

5.3.2.4 RETROSPECTIVES AND LESSONS LEARNED

Retrospectives and lessons learned use past experience to plan for future work. An optimal stakeholder engagement and communication approach may consider recommendations provided from past projects or prior iterations, or may apply past lessons about approaches that worked well for similar product development efforts. For more information on retrospectives and lessons learned, see Section 5.7.2.4.

5.3.2.5 STAKEHOLDER MAPS

Stakeholder maps help with the analysis of stakeholder characteristics such as the power, influence, impact, and interest of stakeholder groups. Ongoing stakeholder mapping and consideration of the current and desired level of engagement by stakeholders is part of determining the stakeholder engagement and communication approach. For more information on stakeholder maps, see Section 5.2.2.4.

5.3.3 DETERMINE STAKEHOLDER ENGAGEMENT AND COMMUNICATION APPROACH: OUTPUTS

5.3.3.1 STAKEHOLDER ENGAGEMENT AND COMMUNICATION APPROACH

The stakeholder engagement and communication approach summarizes agreements for the level of involvement of each stakeholder or stakeholder group; the approaches for making decisions and obtaining approvals; how product and project information are structured, stored, and maintained in support of keeping stakeholders and others informed; and how stakeholders are kept up to date about product and project information and efforts.

5.3.4 DETERMINE STAKEHOLDER ENGAGEMENT AND COMMUNICATION APPROACH: TAILORING CONSIDERATIONS

Adaptive and predictive tailoring considerations for Determine Stakeholder Engagement and Communication Approach are described in Table 5-5.

Table 5-5. Adaptive and Predictive Tailoring for Determine Stakeholder Engagement and Communication Approach

Aspects to Be Tailored	Typical Adaptive Considerations	Typical Predictive Considerations
Name	Not a formally named process	Determine Stakeholder Engagement and Communication Approach
Approach	The product owner, representing stakeholder needs and preferences for communication, and the rest of the team verbally agree on the format and level of detail of product information to be communicated. Stakeholder engagement and communication is taken into account as part of overall preliminary and ongoing collaborative team planning. When team members are colocated, most communication can occur in person.	Planning ideas about whom to engage, what information to communicate, and how to engage and communicate with stakeholders are incorporated into the business analysis plan. Planning activities occur prior to the start of elicitation. May specify the format and level of detail of product information to be communicated and how that will vary by stakeholder or stakeholder group.
Deliverables	Not a separate deliverable.	Stakeholder engagement and communication approach becomes a component of the business analysis plan.

5.3.5 DETERMINE STAKEHOLDER ENGAGEMENT AND COMMUNICATION APPROACH: COLLABORATION POINT

Senior managers have the broadest understanding of whether stakeholder priorities are complementary or conflicting. Product teams can work together to vet the stakeholder engagement and communication approach with senior managers, especially when organizational priorities or politics have an impact on stakeholder participation. Collaboration with portfolio, program, and project managers is essential to ensure that stakeholder engagement and communication approaches are aligned.

5.4 CONDUCT BUSINESS ANALYSIS PLANNING

Conduct Business Analysis Planning is the process performed to obtain shared agreement regarding the business analysis activities the team will be performing and the assignment of roles, responsibilities, and skill sets for the tasks required to successfully complete the business analysis work. The results of this process are assembled into a business analysis plan that may be formally documented and approved or may be less formal depending on how the team operates. Whether the plan is formally documented or not, the results from all of the planning processes should be considered in the overall approach. Failing to make planning decisions can result in a less than optimal approach when performing the business analysis work. The key benefit of this process is that it sets expectations by encouraging discussion and agreement on how the business analysis work will be undertaken and avoids confusion regarding roles and responsibilities during execution.

The inputs, tools and techniques, and outputs of the process are depicted in Figure 5-10. Figure 5-11 depicts the data flow diagram for the process.

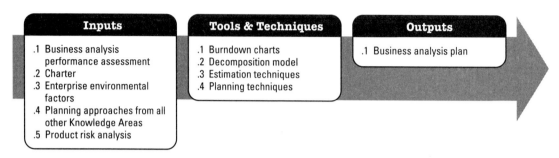

Inputs	Tools & Techniques	Outputs
.1 Business analysis performance assessment .2 Charter .3 Enterprise environmental factors .4 Planning approaches from all other Knowledge Areas .5 Product risk analysis	.1 Burndown charts .2 Decomposition model .3 Estimation techniques .4 Planning techniques	.1 Business analysis plan

Figure 5-10. Conduct Business Analysis Planning: Inputs, Tools and Techniques, and Outputs

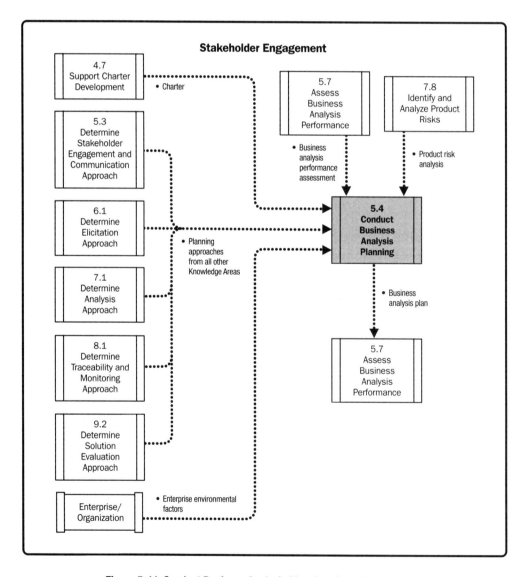

Figure 5-11. Conduct Business Analysis Planning: Data Flow Diagram

The PMI Guide to Business Analysis

The process of conducting business analysis planning has three main objectives:

◆ Aggregates all of the Knowledge Area approaches into a cohesive set of agreements and decisions about how business analysis will be conducted,

◆ Produces an estimation of the level of effort for business analysis activities, and

◆ Assembles a business analysis plan from the component approaches and the estimates.

The activities associated with each of these components are accomplished in markedly different ways for efforts that use a plan-driven, predictive life cycle as opposed to those using a change-driven, adaptive life cycle. These differences are explained in this section and in Section 5.4.4.

When developing the business analysis plan, it is a good practice to provide explanations for the planning choices made. For example, for projects using an adaptive life cycle, the depth and cadence of analysis activities will be planned differently from projects that use a predictive life cycle. Explaining why planning choices were selected provides context for those who review the plan and provides a rationale for the decisions made.

Solutions developed using a predictive life cycle typically use a plan-driven approach for estimation and planning. Estimates are usually created for each role involved in an effort, either from the beginning to the end of the effort or broken out by phases. The level of detail of the estimates may vary, depending on the planning techniques chosen. From a business analysis perspective, this means that separate time estimates are created for the expected effort needed to complete each discrete business analysis task. Once the tasks are estimated, they are structured into an appropriate work plan.

Teams that develop solutions using a change-driven, adaptive life cycle still need to think about business analysis tasks, the level of effort and duration of tasks, dependencies and constraints, and the sequence of activities. However, with the possible exception of tasks to refine large or complex product backlog items that the team may soon develop, business analysis effort and business analysis tasks are not typically broken out as separate line items for estimating and planning purposes.

For an adaptive life cycle approach, as part of a planning session that deliberately occurs at the release level, prioritization is typically used as a primary planning factor. For planning that deliberately occurs at the beginning of each iteration, prioritization and just-in-time estimating are used to select the product backlog items that the team will commit to deliver, following which those items are broken down into tasks. Some teams using an adaptive approach will also break out and estimate time for refining or *making ready* large or complex items that are part of the current iteration or are next in line in a product backlog but have not yet been made *ready*—that is to say, sufficiently understood to begin development.

Despite these differences, there is still a need to allow time for business analysis planning as part of product development. No matter what type of life cycle is used, the thought process of planning for business analysis still needs to occur.

5.4.1 CONDUCT BUSINESS ANALYSIS PLANNING: INPUTS

5.4.1.1 BUSINESS ANALYSIS PERFORMANCE ASSESSMENT

Described in Section 5.7.3.1. A business analysis performance assessment summarizes what has been learned about the effectiveness of the business analysis processes and the business analysis techniques used in past efforts. As part of planning how to conduct business analysis for an upcoming effort, business analysis performance assessments may suggest ways to adapt business analysis processes and techniques to optimize their value in working with a group of stakeholders.

5.4.1.2 CHARTER

Described in Section 4.7.3.1. A charter formally authorizes the existence of a portfolio component, program, or project; establishes its boundaries; and creates a record of its initiation. A charter provides an initial understanding of scope and provides the context and rationale for a product development initiative. Together with the business analysis planning approaches (see Section 5.4.1.4), it becomes the basis for identifying which aspects of business analysis should be conducted and for estimating the level of effort involved.

5.4.1.3 ENTERPRISE ENVIRONMENTAL FACTORS (EEFS)

Described in Sections 2.2.1 and 2.2.2. EEFs are conditions, not under the immediate control of the team, that influence, constrain, or direct the portfolio, program, or project. The influences of EEFs are often considered when examining all the Knowledge Area approaches that are part of the business analysis plan to ensure its reasonability. See Section 5.4.1.4 for a listing of these approaches. Among the EEFs to consider are the following:

◆ Factors that may influence the formality of business analysis efforts and how and when those responsible for business analysis collaborate with their stakeholders include social and cultural influences and issues, stakeholder expectations and risk appetite, legal and contractual restrictions, and government or industry standards. Additionally, organizational culture, structure, governance, and geographic distribution of facilities and resources often have the greatest influence over how business analysis is conducted. Human resource management policies and procedures may impact the availability of individuals to be involved, along with the capability and skill level of the individuals selected.

◆ Factors that may influence the choice of techniques and tools in support of business analysis include the availability of tools to support business analysis, such as conferencing tools, modeling tools, and product requirements or backlog management tools, and any security policies, procedures, and protocols that may be associated with them.

◆ Factors that may influence or constrain the results of business analysis include enterprise architecture, organizational commitment to reuse existing products, and even the results of previous business analysis efforts. A commitment to reuse may lead some organizations to have templates for business analysis plans for different types of products or projects. Such templates contain frequently used approaches from all of the Knowledge Areas that a team may reuse as-is or reuse with modification.

5.4.1.4 PLANNING APPROACHES FROM ALL OTHER KNOWLEDGE AREAS

The planning approaches from the other Knowledge Areas can be consolidated into an overall business analysis plan. Along with the charter, they are the basis for considering the complexity and duration of business analysis activities and figure into any estimates developed that have business analysis effort associated with them. These components are:

◆ Stakeholder engagement and communication approach, described in Section 5.3.3.1;

◆ Elicitation approach, described in Section 6.1.3.1;

◆ Analysis approach, described in Section 7.1.3.1;

◆ Traceability and monitoring approach, described in Section 8.1.3.1; and

◆ Solution evaluation approach, described in Section 9.2.3.1.

5.4.1.5 PRODUCT RISK ANALYSIS

Described in Section 7.8.3.1. The product risk analysis includes the consolidated results from identifying and analyzing product risks. Higher-risk or more complex products and projects may require additional work effort to address the risks or the complexity.

5.4.2 CONDUCT BUSINESS ANALYSIS PLANNING: TOOLS AND TECHNIQUES

5.4.2.1 BURNDOWN CHARTS

A burndown chart is a graphical representation used to count the remaining quantity of some trackable aspect of a project over time. Burndown charts help visualize progress, stalled efforts, or backsliding where the remaining quantity of what is being tracked increases over time. Typically, teams working within an adaptive life cycle use burndown charts to track the remaining product backlog items in a backlog from iteration to iteration. Some adaptive practitioners track hours of work remaining or tasks remaining, although other adaptive practitioners would be wary that detailed tracking of hours or tasks could lead to micromanagement of the team's work.

For efforts using an adaptive life cycle, it is common for the work during early iterations to reveal a number of adjustments for requirements and the product backlog items with which they are associated. New requirements and product backlog items also tend to emerge in early iterations as more is learned about the solution. This additional work that is uncovered adds to the number of product backlog items remaining, which may cause a bump in the burndown chart. Such volatility is expected initially as part of using an adaptive life cycle; however, when the number of product backlog items remaining keeps increasing from iteration to iteration as development and delivery proceeds, or when progress flattens and stalls, there may be causes for concern. Thus, from a business analysis perspective, examining the trends seen in burndown charts could suggest modifications either to how business analysis is conducted or the amount of time devoted to it.

Figure 5-12 is an example of tracking remaining product backlog items in a backlog that might represent the normal course of events in a project using an adaptive life cycle, where there is initially an increase in the number of product backlog items remaining in early iterations, followed by a steady decrease.

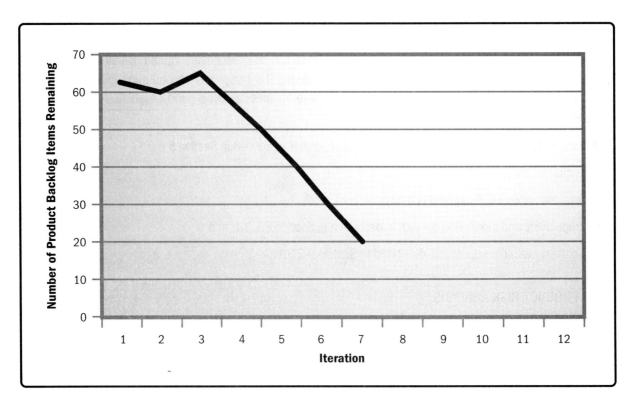

Figure 5-12. Conduct Business Analysis Planning: Typical Burndown Chart for Product Backlog Items

5.4.2.2 DECOMPOSITION MODEL

A decomposition model is an analysis model used to break down information described at a high level into a hierarchy of smaller, more discrete parts. For estimation purposes, typical objects often analyzed with decomposition may include scope, work products, deliverables, processes, functions, or any other object types that can be subdivided into smaller elements. For product development efforts where discrete business analysis tasks and deliverables are estimated separately, decomposition models can be used to identify what needs to be estimated and ultimately sequenced into a business analysis work plan. Decomposition models are further discussed in Section 3.5.2.2 of *Business Analysis for Practitioners: A Practice Guide.*

5.4.2.3 ESTIMATION TECHNIQUES

Estimation techniques are used to provide a quantitative assessment of likely amounts or outcomes. Typical estimation techniques for an effort can include one or more of the following:

◆ **Affinity estimating.** A form of relative estimation, in which team members organize product backlog items into groups where each product backlog item is about the same size, or where team members use the notion of T-shirt size—e.g., small, medium, large, and extra-large—as an estimation scale.

◆ **Bottom-up estimating.** A method of estimating duration or cost by aggregating the estimates of the lower-level tasks. A decomposition model often identifies these lower-level tasks.

◆ **Delphi.** Used to support gaining consensus through anonymous estimating as well as to support decision making. For more information on Delphi, see Section 8.3.2.4.

◆ **Estimation poker.** A collaborative relative estimation technique in which there is an agreed-upon scale used for the relative estimates. Examples of scales include:

- The mathematical Fibonacci series: 0, 1, 1, 2, 3, 5, 8, 13, 21, 34 . . . ; and

- A modified Fibonacci series to which other numbers have been added. One such scale commonly in use is 0, 1, 2, 3, 5, 8, 13, 20, 40, and 100.

Each person participating in estimation poker is given a series of cards with the agreed-upon scale. Team members typically will converge upon a reference estimate for one of their project's product backlog items, often using a Delphi or wide-band Delphi approach (see Section 8.3.2.4). The reference estimate is then used as a basis for subsequent relative estimates for each additional product backlog item that is to be estimated. Team members hold up cards that represent their estimates of the level of effort required in the context of their agreed-upon reference estimate, expressed within the chosen scale. Those who created the highest and lowest estimates explain their rationale, following which everyone estimates again. The process repeats until convergence is achieved.

◆ **Relative estimation.** A technique for creating estimates that are derived from performing a comparison against a similar body of work rather than estimating based on absolute units of cost or time. Relative estimation is similar, but not identical, to analogous estimation, which is usually based on historical data. For relative estimation, a team agrees on some way to represent an estimate for one product backlog item and then estimates other product backlog items in comparison to that agreed-upon estimate.

◆ **Wide-Band Delphi.** A variation of the Delphi technique where there is more communication and interpersonal collaboration to bring convergence to widely differing estimates that have been developed separately for the same task or product backlog item by a number of different individuals. Some organizations take a formal approach to wide-band Delphi, where all estimates are created anonymously by a team of experts and the members of that team collaborate to discuss the estimates and then re-estimate anonymously. Other organizations apply wide-band Delphi in an informal way, where those who created the highest and lowest estimates explain their rationale, following which everyone re-estimates. Irrespective of the approach taken, the process repeats until convergence is achieved.

5.4.2.4 PLANNING TECHNIQUES

Typical planning techniques may include one or more of the following:

◆ **Product backlog.** The product backlog is the list of all product backlog items, typically user stories, requirements, or features, that need to be delivered for a solution. Individual items in the backlog are estimated as part of selecting, in prioritized order, those items that the team is about to commit to deliver in an upcoming iteration. The business analysis effort for any product backlog item focuses on making sure that product backlog items meet the definition of *ready*, as described in Section 7.3.2.2. Making a product backlog item ready helps the team refine its business understanding of that item to the point where it has enough information to begin development. Although teams using an adaptive approach frequently allocate effort to make product backlog items ready, including time to look ahead at items that are likely to be selected for delivery within the next iteration or two, that time is typically not split out separately, but rather is considered part of the time needed to deliver the item. That said, some teams do account separately for additional time to refine the backlog. For more information on product backlogs, see Section 7.3.2.4.

In an adaptive life cycle, the timing of work done by a team to plan and commit to what is going to be delivered depends upon which adaptive approach the team uses. When using an adaptive approach, backlog management and kanban boards may be used as part of planning. For more information on backlog management, see Section 7.7.2.1. For more information on kanban boards, see Section 7.7.2.4.

◆ **Rolling wave planning.** This is an iterative planning technique in which the work to be accomplished in the near term is planned in detail, while the work in the future is planned at a higher level. From the perspective of business analysis, business analysts working as part of a predictive life cycle could be responsible for or could work with the project manager to create rolling wave estimates for business analysis tasks at intervals specified within the overall project schedule. For planning within an adaptive life cycle, rolling wave planning can be used at the release level to determine those features and functions for the current or next release. Similarly, within the context of rolling wave planning, progressive elaboration or further analysis identifies the specific features and epics to be included in the current release, and also incorporates new information into plans as the project progresses.

◆ **Story mapping.** A technique used in planning for projects that use an adaptive life cycle. Story mapping is used to sequence user stories, based upon their business value and the order in which their users typically perform them, so that teams can arrive at a shared understanding of what will be built. From the perspective of planning for business analysis, story mapping can help suggest when more effort may need to be spent on analysis. For more information on story mapping, see Section 7.2.2.16.

◆ **Work breakdown structure (WBS).** A planning technique for projects using a predictive life cycle. WBS is a hierarchical decomposition of the total scope of work to be carried out by the project team to accomplish the project objectives and create the required deliverables. Often, a WBS is subdivided by project phase and by component or deliverable within that phase. The WBS becomes the basis for creating a schedule that sequences the work that needs to be accomplished, based on estimates, priorities, dependencies, and constraints. For projects using a predictive life cycle, a WBS is typically created initially during planning and then revised at regularly scheduled intervals, such as phase gates. From the perspective of business analysis, business analysts would be responsible for the portion of the WBS that focuses on business analysis tasks.

5.4.3 CONDUCT BUSINESS ANALYSIS PLANNING: OUTPUTS

5.4.3.1 BUSINESS ANALYSIS PLAN

A business analysis plan, if formally documented, may be a subplan of the portfolio, program, or project management plan or may be a separate plan. It defines the business analysis approach through the assembly of the sub-approaches across all Knowledge Areas. A business analysis plan can include an estimation of level of effort for business analysis activities. It covers the entire business analysis approach, from stakeholder engagement to decisions about how to manage requirements. It is broader than a requirements management plan, which focuses on how requirements will be elicited, analyzed, documented, and managed. Whether formally documented or not, the business analysis plan provides a summary of the agreements reached for all of its components.

Whenever a written business analysis plan is a required document, it should be written in a manner that will be easily understood, because it will be reviewed and may need to be approved by key stakeholders.

For more information on business analysis plans, see Section 3 of *Business Analysis for Practitioners: A Practice Guide*.

5.4.4 CONDUCT BUSINESS ANALYSIS PLANNING: TAILORING CONSIDERATIONS

Adaptive and predictive tailoring considerations for Conduct Business Analysis Planning are described in Table 5-6.

Table 5-6. Adaptive and Predictive Tailoring for Conduct Business Analysis Planning

Aspects to Be Tailored	Typical Adaptive Considerations	Typical Predictive Considerations
Name	Not a formally named process; performed as part of initial planning or iteration 0	Conduct Business Analysis Planning
Approach	Some teams formulate their approach to business analysis planning by deciding how they will conduct discovery and backlog refinement. The level of effort needed for business analysis is rarely estimated separately from the time needed to design and develop or enhance the product. Instead, it is part of the overall planning for future iterations.	Plan includes business analysis tasks, level of effort, roles, and responsibilities. Prior to beginning any elicitation activities, the business analysis plan is assembled using the component plans from other Knowledge Areas. The level of effort required for elicitation, analysis, traceability and monitoring, and evaluation activities is estimated. Approval or sign-off is obtained for the entire plan.
Deliverables	Rarely a separate deliverable. Some teams capture specific analysis tasks when creating the list of tasks for each iteration to a burndown chart or add something to the project charter about business analysis as part of authorizing the resources for the project. Some results of business analysis planning are reflected in the definition of ready.	Business analysis plan, including work breakdown structure.

5.4.5 CONDUCT BUSINESS ANALYSIS PLANNING: COLLABORATION POINT

The business analyst should build the business analysis plan collaboratively with key stakeholders to ensure engagement, achieve alignment, and attain buy-in. A plan that is constructed with the project team provides a sense of ownership to those involved and sets expectations by bringing awareness to how the work will be performed. The project sponsor is interested in aspects of the plan when additional costs to the project may be incurred, such as travel for workshop attendees and specialized business analysis tools required for the effort. For adaptive approaches, any light planning that is done will be performed as a project team.

Planning is an area where project managers and business analysts will find their roles overlapping, especially with respect to stakeholder identification and engagement, communication, risk identification, estimating, and development of work plans. The business analyst should work closely with the project manager to avoid redundancy of effort and to reduce the risk of inconsistent results.

5.5 PREPARE FOR TRANSITION TO FUTURE STATE

Prepare for Transition to Future State is the process of determining whether the organization is ready for a transition and how the organization will move from the current to the future state to integrate the solution or partial solution into the organization's operations. The key benefits of this process are that the organization can successfully adopt the changes resulting from the implementation of the new solution or solution component, and that any product or program component or overall program benefit anticipated for the solution can be sustained after it is put into operation. The inputs and outputs of this process are depicted in Figure 5-13. Figure 5-14 is a data flow diagram for this process.

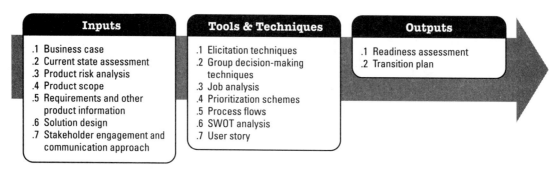

Inputs	Tools & Techniques	Outputs
.1 Business case .2 Current state assessment .3 Product risk analysis .4 Product scope .5 Requirements and other product information .6 Solution design .7 Stakeholder engagement and communication approach	.1 Elicitation techniques .2 Group decision-making techniques .3 Job analysis .4 Prioritization schemes .5 Process flows .6 SWOT analysis .7 User story	.1 Readiness assessment .2 Transition plan

Figure 5-13. Prepare for Transition to Future State: Inputs, Tools and Techniques, and Outputs

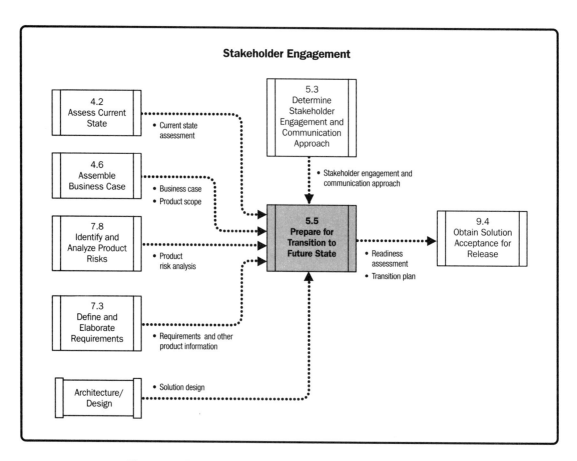

Figure 5-14. Prepare for Transition to Future State: Data Flow Diagram

Preparing for transition involves assessing the readiness of the organization to successfully transition from product development to operations and creating a plan to identify the requirements for making the transition successful. A transition readiness assessment addresses the ability and the interest of an organization to work within the future state or to use its capabilities. The readiness assessment is used to identify any gaps in readiness that are considered risks to achieving the end state, along with risk responses for addressing them. A transition readiness assessment may also incorporate the results from an organizational readiness assessment, which may look at an organization's overall readiness to incorporate any change and could include looking at the influences of the organization's EEFs and its organizational process assets. Organizational readiness can be measured against a maturity model, if one is available, so that an organization's maturity in terms of practices, procedures, and culture can be compared to that of other organizations. Comparing an organization's readiness to the readiness of similar organizations may reveal competitive opportunities or challenges that may be associated with the transition.

Preparing for transition to the future state identifies and utilizes transition requirements. Transition requirements describe temporary capabilities, such as data conversion and training requirements, and operational changes needed to transition from the current state to the future state. Transition requirements may also be discovered while modeling, defining and elaborating product requirements, or as part of a feasibility analysis—for example, when determining viable options.

Preparing for transition to the future state necessitates taking all the known transition requirements and readiness factors into account to support the creation of a plan for how the transition will occur. Frequently used strategies for planning a transition include:

◆ Massive one-time cutover to the future state;

◆ Staged release of the future state by a target segment, such as by region or by type of customer or type of employee;

◆ Time-boxed coexistence of the current and future state, with a final cutover on a specific future date; and

◆ Permanent coexistence of the current and future state.

No matter what strategy is selected, business analysis supports the creation of a transition plan, developed collaboratively with all the roles responsible for transition. The plan addresses all transition requirements, including the development of all the communication, rollout, training, procedure updates, business recovery updates, and collateral needed to successfully cut over and adapt to the future state. The transition plan is coordinated with other anticipated releases that enable the future state. It ensures that implementation occurs at a time when the business can accept the changes including any interruptions caused by the transition itself, and that the rollout is not in conflict with other in-process programs and project work. The transition plan may need to adjust as additional transition requirements emerge, including addressing deficiencies in organizational readiness.

The transition plan may contain or reference transition requirements expressed in whatever style is appropriate for the organization. The plan often includes a checklist of transition activities with no-later-than completion dates. In its most formal format, it has a prescribed schedule developed in collaboration with and managed by those responsible for project management and operations.

Successful product releases depend on delivering the solution with its expected capabilities and preparing the people who are going to use it. For some products, a successful release also depends upon having the operational environment set up or converted. For large or complex products, customer bases, or dispersed user bases, success may not be possible without a thoughtfully considered and executed transition plan.

Large organizations that use predictive life cycles typically have a very formal approach to transition to a future state. Yet, irrespective of organizational size, the execution of transition activities is an area where predictive and adaptive life cycles both rely on rigor and discipline and sometimes automation to transition a solution to its operational area, so that the transition will be as smooth and as seamless as possible. With that rigor and discipline in mind, transition plans are often initially considered early in a product's life cycle to gain a sense of what it will take to accomplish the transition.

5.5.1 PREPARE FOR TRANSITION TO FUTURE STATE: INPUTS

5.5.1.1 BUSINESS CASE

Described in Section 4.6.3.1. The business case describes pertinent information to determine whether the initiative is worth the required investment. The business case provides the context for the transition and a basis for prioritizing transition activities.

5.5.1.2 CURRENT STATE ASSESSMENT

Described in Section 4.2.3.1. The current state assessment is the culmination of the analysis results produced during the assessment of the current state. This assessment can be examined in conjunction with the solution design to identify differences between them, so as to consider how to handle those differences. Typical differences are areas where the solution design:

◆ Provides less functionality than the current state,

◆ Replaces current state functionality with new or improved capabilities, and

◆ Provides capabilities that previously did not exist in the current state.

5.5.1.3 PRODUCT RISK ANALYSIS

Described in Section 7.8.3.1. The product risk analysis includes the consolidated results from identifying and analyzing product risks. Higher-risk or more complex products and projects may require additional work effort to address the risks or the complexity as part of the transition.

5.5.1.4 PRODUCT SCOPE

Described in Section 4.6.3.2. Product scope is defined as the features and functions that characterize a solution. Understanding the product scope may be the basis for deciding how the transition should proceed and what special resources and coordination will be needed.

5.5.1.5 REQUIREMENTS AND OTHER PRODUCT INFORMATION

Described in Section 7.3.3.1. Requirements and other product information include all information about a solution and are the culmination of results from elicitation and analysis activities. Transition requirements are part of the requirements and other product information. Transition requirements describe temporary capabilities, such as data conversion and training requirements, and operational changes needed to transition from the current state to the future state. Any of the modeling or textual techniques used to define and elaborate business, stakeholder, and solution requirements—especially, but not exclusively, nonfunctional requirements—may reveal transition requirements. Very often, transition requirements emerge during a discussion of other requirements and product information.

5.5.1.6 SOLUTION DESIGN

The solution design is a crucial input for preparing for the transition to the future state, as it determines the future state. The solution design normally includes specifications and diagrams. These specifications and diagrams are typically based on the product information that has been identified and elaborated by business analysis, but go beyond what can be specified by business analysis alone. When possible and appropriate, the solution design should exploit the features of the business and enterprise architecture. The solution design may also include business procedure specifications with process flows. The solution design may be compared to the proposed solution design option. Such an assessment may provide insights on design challenges that will need to be addressed as part of the transition to the future state. For more information on assessing solution design options, see Section 7.9.

5.5.1.7 STAKEHOLDER ENGAGEMENT AND COMMUNICATION APPROACH

Described in Section 5.3.3.1. The stakeholder engagement and communication approach summarizes all the agreements for governing how stakeholders will be engaged and communicated with across the portfolio, program, or project. The approach identifies which stakeholders should be involved in preparing for the transition and how best to collaborate with them. Without the participation of key stakeholders in transition activities, transition work may be poorly executed.

5.5.2 PREPARE FOR TRANSITION TO FUTURE STATE: TOOLS AND TECHNIQUES

5.5.2.1 ELICITATION TECHNIQUES

Elicitation techniques are used to draw out information from sources. A few common techniques that are effective when preparing for transition to a future state are brainstorming, facilitated workshops, and interviews:

◆ **Brainstorming.** Used to identify a list of ideas in a short period of time. Brainstorming helps move a product team from thinking about product development to thinking through a transition. For more information on brainstorming, see Section 5.1.2.1.

◆ **Facilitated workshop.** A structured meeting led by a skilled, neutral facilitator and a carefully selected group of stakeholders to collaborate and work toward a stated objective. Facilitated workshops create an opportunity to gain synergy by sharing ideas for the transition. They can also increase a sense of ownership in the solution by the stakeholders who participate in these sessions, which may in turn help with the actual transition itself. For more information on facilitated workshops, see Section 6.3.2.4.

◆ **Interviews.** Can be used to elicit information to prepare for the transition to the future state. Interviews with key stakeholders, including those whose daily work is likely to be impacted by the transition, may be used to assess readiness for the transition, as well as to elicit transition requirements. Individual interviews are often used to assess readiness so that each stakeholder can speak candidly about concerns for the transition. For more information on interviews, see Section 6.3.2.6.

For more information on elicitation techniques, see Section 6.3.2.

5.5.2.2 GROUP DECISION-MAKING TECHNIQUES

Group decision-making techniques can be used to bring participants to a final decision on an issue or topic under discussion. Decision-making techniques can help reach decisions about the best approaches for moving a solution from a development environment into an operational environment. For more information on group decision-making techniques, see Section 8.3.2.7.

5.5.2.3 JOB ANALYSIS

Job analysis is a technique that is used to identify job requirements and competencies required to perform effectively in a specific job or role. It can be used to determine training needs, as a precursor to writing a job posting, or to support a performance appraisal process. As part of preparing for the transition to the future state, job analysis is used to think through what is needed to hire and train people for new roles that may be needed to support the future state. For more information on job analysis, see Section 5.2.2.1.

5.5.2.4 PRIORITIZATION SCHEMES

Prioritization schemes are different methods used to prioritize requirements, features, or any other product information. Prioritization may be used as part of preparing for a transition in any situation where it becomes necessary to conduct a transition in segments. Typical reasons for segmenting a transition include:

◆ Need to handle a large number of transition requirements or readiness issues,

◆ Presence of complex transition requirements or issues, and

◆ Need to make the transition at multiple sites.

For more information on prioritization schemes, see Section 7.7.2.5.

5.5.2.5 PROCESS FLOWS

A process flow visually documents the steps or tasks that people perform in their jobs or when they interact with a product. Some of the process flows comprising the requirements and other product information provide the basis for training materials on the new procedures that will be in place once the transition takes place. Additional process flows may be created, when necessary, to describe the transition processes themselves to make it easier for those responsible for the transition to know what needs to be done. For more information on process flows, see Section 7.2.2.12.

5.5.2.6 SWOT ANALYSIS

SWOT analysis is a technique for analyzing the strengths (S) and weaknesses (W) of an organization, project, or option, and the opportunities (O) and threats (T) that exist externally. A SWOT analysis focused on transition can help prepare the product team for making the transition. The analysis can provide a way for the participants to express their expectations and concerns for the transition at a high level, by stating these concerns as strengths, weaknesses, opportunities, and threats. Readiness issues may surface from the weaknesses and threats that are identified. For more information on SWOT analysis, see Section 4.2.2.10.

5.5.2.7 USER STORY

User stories are a method to document stakeholder requirements from users' point of view with a focus on the value or benefit achieved by users with the completion of that story. For solutions developed using an adaptive life cycle, some transition requirements may be expressed as user stories. Transition user stories may focus on topics such as expectations for training materials and communications, about the rollout of the future state, or on new procedures. For more information on user stories, see Section 7.3.2.9.

5.5.3 PREPARE FOR TRANSITION TO FUTURE STATE: OUTPUTS

5.5.3.1 READINESS ASSESSMENT

A transition readiness assessment determines the ability and the interest of an organization to transition to the future state or to use its capabilities. The assessment is used to identify any gaps in readiness that are considered risks to achieving the end state, along with risk responses for addressing them. A readiness assessment may take the form of a report that provides the results of a readiness evaluation or it may take the form of a readiness checklist, where readiness characteristics can be checked off to reveal where there are transition elements still requiring attention.

There are often some unique aspects to each transition that stem from the specific products or organization being evaluated for readiness. There are also some generic aspects to transition readiness assessments that apply to all organizations or all organizations within an industry. Such generic aspects may be found in readiness assessments based on that industry's maturity model.

5.5.3.2 TRANSITION PLAN

A transition plan is based on the readiness assessment as well as the transition strategy. From a business analysis perspective, a transition plan encompasses actionable and testable transition requirements. While there are some generic aspects to transition plans that can be repeated from solution to solution, other aspects may be highly focused on the products and industries included in the transition, as well as the specific organization in which the transition is occurring. Transition strategy considerations are further discussed in Section 6.11 of *Business Analysis for Practitioners: A Practice Guide*.

5.5.4 PREPARE FOR TRANSITION TO FUTURE STATE: TAILORING CONSIDERATIONS

Adaptive and predictive tailoring considerations for Prepare for Transition to Future State are described in Table 5-7.

Table 5-7. Adaptive and Predictive Tailoring for Prepare for Transition to Future State

Aspects to Be Tailored	Typical Adaptive Considerations	Typical Predictive Considerations
Name	**Prepare for Transition to Future State**	
Approach	For small, incremental releases to production, there will be transition tasks in a story or separate transition stories to push the release to production. For implementations in large-scale environments, many or all of the predictive considerations for transition may be used, even in situations where product segments were delivered for feedback as soon as they were production ready.	A readiness assessment and transition requirements are used to determine a transition strategy and as the basis of transition planning. It includes information to support operational procedures, training collateral, service-level agreements, rollout collateral, coordination with other releases, and contingency plans.
Deliverables	Format can vary from being part of the "definition of done" or transition user stories all the way to formal plans for large-scale product releases. For some organizations, rather than a plan per se, thinking about transition may manifest itself in setting up a reserved block of time or specific iteration to accomplish the transition, coordinated with the operational area that will own the solution, including time to clean up technical debt.	A readiness assessment and transition plan, potentially including a readiness checklist and a schedule.

5.5.5 PREPARE FOR TRANSITION TO FUTURE STATE: COLLABORATION POINT

Preparing for and implementing a transition requires close collaboration among those conducting business analysis and project management, and the individuals on readiness teams and release management teams.

The knowledge gained from business analysis about the existing solution, the replacement solution, and transition requirements are used when defining the transition activities. Governance roles provide feedback about opportunities and threats arising from the transition requirements and defined transition activities. For implementation in large-scale environments, the collaboration may take the form of a DevOps approach, where development, quality control, and operations (IT and business operations) collaborate to support rapidly releasing a solution by operationalizing it in small segments, each of which provides additional functionality to its users. DevOps would provide coordination for the transition among all the teams involved.

5.6 MANAGE STAKEHOLDER ENGAGEMENT AND COMMUNICATION

Manage Stakeholder Engagement and Communication is the process of fostering appropriate involvement in business analysis processes, keeping stakeholders appropriately informed about ongoing business analysis efforts, and sharing product information with stakeholders as it evolves. The key benefits of this process are that it promotes continuous stakeholder participation in the business analysis process and in defining the solution, and maintains ongoing communication with stakeholders. The inputs, tools and techniques, and outputs of the process are depicted in Figure 5-15. Figure 5-16 depicts the data flow diagram for the process.

Manage Stakeholder Engagement and Communication focuses on monitoring the participation of stakeholders in business analysis activities, ensuring that stakeholders remain engaged throughout and assessing whether their participation is sufficient for them to have a clear understanding of the requirements and other product information.

Project team members who conduct business analysis often work very closely with those responsible for removing roadblocks when managing stakeholder engagement and communication, because there is more to stakeholder engagement than their participation in business analysis activities.

In organizations where the stakeholder engagement and communication approach is formally documented, the resolution of some engagement and communication concerns sometimes necessitates updates to the stakeholder engagement and communication approach.

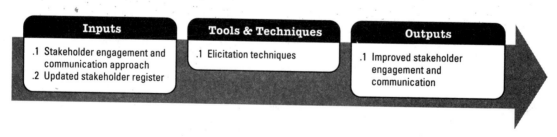

Inputs	Tools & Techniques	Outputs
.1 Stakeholder engagement and communication approach .2 Updated stakeholder register	.1 Elicitation techniques	.1 Improved stakeholder engagement and communication

Figure 5-15. Manage Stakeholder Engagement and Communication: Inputs, Tools and Techniques, and Outputs

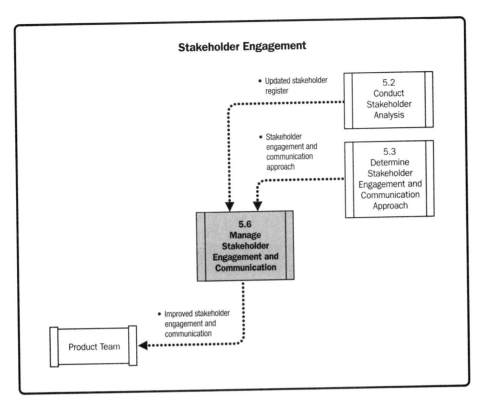

Stakeholder Engagement

Figure 5-16. Manage Stakeholder Engagement and Communication: Data Flow Diagram

5.6.1 MANAGE STAKEHOLDER ENGAGEMENT AND COMMUNICATION: INPUTS

5.6.1.1 STAKEHOLDER ENGAGEMENT AND COMMUNICATION APPROACH

Described in Section 5.3.3.1. The stakeholder engagement and communication approach summarizes all the agreements for governing how stakeholders will be engaged and communicated with across the portfolio, program, or project. The agreements within the stakeholder engagement and communication approach provide the norms for ensuring that stakeholders remain involved and continue to actively participate and that communication is open and ongoing throughout the entire product development life cycle.

5.6.1.2 UPDATED STAKEHOLDER REGISTER

Described in Section 5.2.3.1. The updated stakeholder register includes the identification, assessment, and characterization of project or product stakeholders. The characterization of the stakeholders is a key factor for assessing whether or not the engagement of and communication with a particular stakeholder is optimal at any point in time.

5.6.2 MANAGE STAKEHOLDER ENGAGEMENT AND COMMUNICATION: TOOLS AND TECHNIQUES

5.6.2.1 ELICITATION TECHNIQUES

Elicitation techniques are used to draw out information from sources. Managing engagement and communication requires exploring necessary changes to the ways that stakeholders are engaged or communication is conducted across business analysis activities. This kind of exploration can be framed by the recommendations established in the stakeholder engagement and communication approach. Elicitation reveals the perspective of the stakeholders and enables product teams to brainstorm solutions to any communication or engagement challenges that may arise. When eliciting information about engagement or communication challenges, care should be taken to involve those who are responsible for removing roadblocks. In some organizations, politics or perception may make it prudent to avoid separating stakeholder engagement and communication for business analysis from overall stakeholder engagement and communication concerns. For more information on elicitation techniques, see Section 6.3.2.

5.6.3 MANAGE STAKEHOLDER ENGAGEMENT AND COMMUNICATION: OUTPUTS

5.6.3.1 IMPROVED STAKEHOLDER ENGAGEMENT AND COMMUNICATION

Improved stakeholder engagement and communication are the result of directing efforts and team collaboration toward addressing business analysis engagement and communication concerns as they arise. For challenges that arise, those responsible for business analysis often address the concerns by closely working with and relying upon those who have management responsibilities, authority, and/or the responsibility to remove roadblocks.

5.6.4 MANAGE STAKEHOLDER ENGAGEMENT AND COMMUNICATION: TAILORING CONSIDERATIONS

Adaptive and predictive tailoring considerations for Manage Stakeholder Engagement and Communication are described in Table 5-8.

Table 5-8. Adaptive and Predictive Tailoring for Manage Stakeholder Engagement and Communication

Aspects to Be Tailored	Typical Adaptive Considerations	Typical Predictive Considerations
Name	Not a formally named process	Manage Stakeholder Engagement and Communication
Approach	Typically use regularly scheduled (often daily), very short (no more than 15 minutes) team meetings to uncover existing or potential roadblocks where stakeholder engagement and communication is not optimal; appropriate team members then work to immediately remove these roadblocks as they are uncovered.	Business analysts raise stakeholder engagement concerns with stakeholders directly or at regularly scheduled status meetings, risk meetings, and in conversations with project management.
Deliverables	Possible changes to "ground rules" or other written rules of engagement.	Improved engagement and communication as reflected in changes to approaches, plans, issue logs, and other documents.

5.6.5 MANAGE STAKEHOLDER ENGAGEMENT AND COMMUNICATION: COLLABORATION POINT

Business analysts collaborate with team members responsible for removing roadblocks to address stakeholder engagement concerns and support project managers who have responsibility for stakeholder engagement on the project. Sponsors provide authority to ensure that roadblocks are removed and that necessary stakeholders are supportive and continue to fulfill their role and obligations to the work. Subject matter experts (SMEs) may assist with removing roadblocks and encouraging stakeholders to remain involved in supporting the product, and can help find resolutions to engagement and communication issues. In some organizations, an area responsible for organizational development/change management (OD/CM) may collaborate to resolve engagement and communication concerns.

5.7 ASSESS BUSINESS ANALYSIS PERFORMANCE

Assess Business Analysis Performance is the process of considering the effectiveness of the business analysis practices in use across the organization, typically in the context of considering the ongoing deliverables and results of a portfolio component, program, or project. Practices that are working well at the project level can be elevated to best practices and standards for use by the organization across future projects. The key benefit of this process is that it provides the opportunity to adjust business analysis practices to meet the needs of a project, its team, and ultimately, the organization. The inputs, tools and techniques, and outputs of the process are depicted in Figure 5-17. Figure 5-18 depicts the data flow diagram for the process.

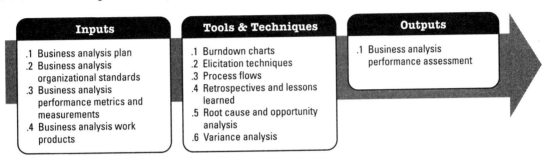

Inputs	Tools & Techniques	Outputs
.1 Business analysis plan .2 Business analysis organizational standards .3 Business analysis performance metrics and measurements .4 Business analysis work products	.1 Burndown charts .2 Elicitation techniques .3 Process flows .4 Retrospectives and lessons learned .5 Root cause and opportunity analysis .6 Variance analysis	.1 Business analysis performance assessment

Figure 5-17. Assess Business Analysis Performance: Inputs, Tools and Techniques, and Outputs

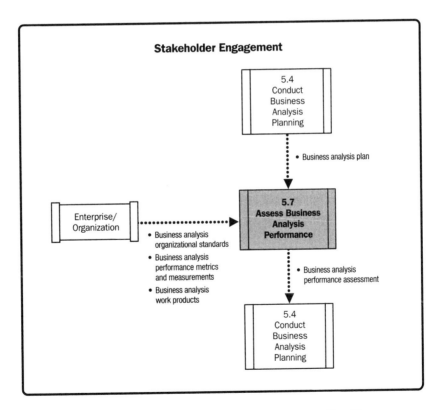

Figure 5-18. Assess Business Analysis Performance: Data Flow Diagram

The assessment of business analysis performance is an activity typically undertaken by organizations that continually strive to improve their practices and processes in support of the delivery of value to their stakeholders.

A primary purpose of assessing business analysis performance is to gain insights from product development experiences to consider which business analysis tools and techniques are working well and which present challenges. Examples of what might be assessed include the following:

◆ How well did the techniques used meet the needs of the participants and other stakeholders?

◆ Were elicitation and analysis conducted efficiently?

◆ Was there sufficient time to conduct business analysis?

◆ Were stakeholders sufficiently engaged?

◆ Were any stakeholders missed?

◆ Were any requirements missed or not sufficiently understood?

◆ Are there product defects that directly relate to the quality or completeness of business analysis efforts?

For those tools and techniques that present challenges, the goal of assessing business analysis performance is to identify improvements and act on them, or replace the challenging tools and techniques with other tools and techniques that might be more effective. For those techniques that work well, the goal of assessing business analysis performance is to consider whether there are opportunities to promote or increase the usage of such techniques on other projects.

When there are large variations in expected levels of effort or in adherence to schedule or commitments to deliver, it is worthwhile to investigate whether improvements in business analysis practices could help address the underlying causes of these variations. As part of assessing business analysis performance, concerns related to the skills of the individuals conducting business analysis may be identified and addressed with training, coaching, or, when necessary, assignment of another individual to focus on business analysis.

5.7.1 ASSESS BUSINESS ANALYSIS PERFORMANCE: INPUTS

5.7.1.1 BUSINESS ANALYSIS PLAN

Described in Section 5.4.3.1. The business analysis plan includes decisions about how business analysis processes will be conducted and how decisions will be made. A business analysis plan can be compared to what was actually performed to obtain insights for planning better in the future. A business analysis work plan, a subcomponent of a business analysis plan, may include level of effort estimates, and those estimates can be compared to the actual work effort to help the team improve future estimates.

5.7.1.2 BUSINESS ANALYSIS ORGANIZATIONAL STANDARDS

Described in Section 2.3. These standards may include expectations for how business analysis will be conducted and what tools might be used to support business analysis efforts. These standards may also include key performance indicators (KPIs) established at an organizational level for business analysis. Business analysis organizational standards are part of the benchmark from which business analysis performance can be assessed.

5.7.1.3 BUSINESS ANALYSIS PERFORMANCE METRICS AND MEASUREMENTS

Business analysis performance metrics are qualitative or quantitative measures or inferences used to evaluate the effectiveness of business analysis practices. Some of the metrics tie to the usage and the perception of the effectiveness of the business analysis practices themselves; others focus on problems with requirements as an indicator of underlying problems with business analysis practices. Still others view large variances in the actual level of effort, duration, or degree of completion for business analysis activities from what was expected as a reason to consider whether improvements to business analysis practices are warranted. The data obtained from measurements may also be inputs to the assessment of business analysis performance.

Examples of possible metrics for business analysis practices, which, when measured, could quantitatively indicate that there may be problems with their effectiveness, include:

◆ Percentage of all defects that are requirements defects;

◆ Percentage of missed requirements;

◆ Number of missed business objectives;

◆ Percentage of unstable, volatile requirements (requirements that continue to change many times well after initial elicitation and analysis has been conducted);

◆ Average time to obtain customer acceptance on requirements;

◆ Percentage of teams conducting lessons learned or retrospectives where business analysis practices are among the topics discussed and improvements then made to business analysis practices;

◆ Percentage of teams using standard business analysis templates;

◆ Percentage of completion of business analysis deliverables;

◆ Slippage in delivery dates for business analysis deliverables;

◆ Counts of requirements by their "state" (such as proposed, approved, in progress, completed, deferred, rejected, canceled, and implemented);

◆ Number of open issues or questions about the requirements;

◆ Number of comments from stakeholders indicating that they are dissatisfied, uncomfortable with, or concerned about the business analysis activities or those who are conducting business analysis; and

◆ KPIs and service-level agreements (for organizations that define acceptable levels of performance as KPIs).

The team should agree how these metrics will be measured and what calculations will be used, if any. For example, percentage of missed requirements could be calculated by performing a comparison of the number of requirements identified after some point in time as compared to the total number of requirements identified up to this point.

For solutions developed using an adaptive approach, a lack of stability can be a particularly valuable indicator. While changes are expected and embraced during an adaptive life cycle, there is an expectation that stability will increase as the project proceeds. Other metrics for adaptive projects to consider include the number of open issues/ questions about user stories or the percentage of stories ready for development, based on the agreed-upon definition of ready, in time for iteration planning.

When looking at any metrics associated with business analysis performance, it is very important to be cautious, because these metrics can rarely isolate poor business analysis practices as the sole cause of project and product development problems; problems with other aspects of product development may be equal or more important contributors to the problems that these metrics surface.

5.7.1.4 BUSINESS ANALYSIS WORK PRODUCTS

As part of verifying requirements during a product development effort, the quality of the business analysis deliverables that may specify, describe, or visually illustrate requirements and other product information can be assessed against benchmarks established within business analysis organizational standards. Problems discovered while verifying requirements and trends indicating that the same types of problems occur in many efforts may be caused by using an inappropriate business analysis technique, an inability of the practitioners to use the technique, an inability of stakeholders to participate in using the technique, or insufficient detail obtained using the technique. Any of these types of problems are worth considering as part of assessing business analysis performance.

5.7.2 ASSESS BUSINESS ANALYSIS PERFORMANCE: TOOLS AND TECHNIQUES

5.7.2.1 BURNDOWN CHARTS

A burndown chart is a graphical representation of the remaining quantity of some trackable aspect of a project over time. From a business analysis perspective, when a burndown chart reveals stalled efforts, or negative progress after several iterations have been completed, it becomes important to determine whether poor or incomplete analysis of the product requirements or insufficient time allowed for this work is contributing to the team's problems, as well as whether other project factors are involved or are the sole cause of the problem. A slowdown in team velocity may be observed in a slowdown or stall in the burndown of the product backlog items remaining. For solutions delivered using an adaptive approach, such a slowdown can mean that the user stories are not sliced or defined correctly or are not sliced in a way that defines and delivers increments of value. For more information on burndown charts, see Section 5.4.2.1.

5.7.2.2 ELICITATION TECHNIQUES

Elicitation techniques are used to draw out information from sources. A few common techniques that are effective for assessing business analysis performance are brainstorming, facilitated workshops, interviews, and questionnaires and surveys:

◆ **Brainstorming.** Used to identify a list of ideas in a short period of time. Because brainstorming has a ground rule where every idea is okay, it creates an environment where team members can identify performance problems and potential solutions that they might have otherwise kept to themselves. For more information on brainstorming, see Section 5.1.2.1.

◆ **Facilitated workshop.** A structured meeting led by a skilled, neutral facilitator that works toward a stated objective. Assessing business analysis performance within a facilitated workshop helps a discussion on performance stay focused. For more information on facilitated workshops, see Section 6.3.2.4.

◆ **Interviews.** Used for eliciting information about business analysis performance from team members. Individual interviews provide an opportunity for team members to speak candidly about concerns they may have. For more information on interviews, see Section 6.3.2.6.

◆ **Questionnaires and surveys.** Written sets of questions designed to quickly accumulate information from a large number of respondents. They can also be used to quickly obtain anonymous feedback from a small group. Surveys can be developed to elicit information about areas where team members wish to see improvements in performance or have concerns. If confidentiality is made part of the process, participants may be more willing to provide information that they would not otherwise provide in a face-to-face forum like an interview. For more information on questionnaires and surveys, see Section 6.3.2.9.

For more information on elicitation techniques, see Section 6.3.2.

5.7.2.3 PROCESS FLOWS

Process flows visually document the steps or tasks that people perform in their jobs. They can be used to model any kind of activity, including business analysis activities. Drawing and analyzing the flow of business analysis activities can support the identification of possible process-related causes of problems. For more information on process flows, see Section 7.2.2.12.

5.7.2.4 RETROSPECTIVES AND LESSONS LEARNED

Retrospectives and lessons learned use past experience to plan for future work:

◆ **Retrospectives.** Meetings scheduled on a regular basis or conducted when a body of work is completed, such as at the conclusion of an iteration. Retrospectives are most commonly used in adaptive life cycles. The agenda for these meetings provides an opportunity for each team member to state the following:

■ What is working well?

■ What is not working or is unclear?

■ What needs to change? What are opportunities for improvement? What changes can we make now?

Retrospectives may benefit from the use of collaborative games. For more information on collaborative games, see Section 6.3.2.2.

Retrospectives generally focus on the specific effort that is under way. Likewise, the recommendations made during retrospectives are generally for that specific effort, although they may also be elevated for wider use within an organization when applicable.

◆ **Lessons learned.** Meetings to discuss, analyze, and document feedback about completed project activities. They are typically conducted by teams that develop solutions using a predictive life cycle. The same questions as used above for retrospectives apply to lessons learned sessions.

The biggest differences between lessons learned and retrospectives are in the timing with which issues raised during these meetings are addressed and the formality around documenting the results. Retrospectives occur regularly and frequently. For adaptive life cycles, they usually follow the delivery and demo of a completed segment or slice of the solution. Retrospectives may also be scheduled on a once-a-week basis, irrespective of delivery. Retrospectives are conducted in a highly collaborative fashion, and the decisions made are most often implemented with little formal documentation. Lessons learned are conducted at the end of a phase, such as a project closeout or program completion, or when events occur that provide learning opportunities. For predictive approaches, they are often held at the end of stage gates or development phases. Although lessons learned can be conducted more frequently, these typically happen less frequently than retrospectives during a project and may be driven by the occurrence of an event versus a fixed schedule. Learnings discussed are formally documented and stored in a repository for reference or follow-up action. Project teams leverage the lessons learned during the current project or as input when planning future projects.

Lessons learned and retrospectives are further discussed in Sections 3.4.6.1 and 3.4.6.2 of *Business Analysis for Practitioners: A Practice Guide.*

5.7.2.5 ROOT CAUSE AND OPPORTUNITY ANALYSIS

Root cause and opportunity analysis techniques are used to analyze problems and opportunities. When applied to assessing business analysis performance, root cause and opportunity analysis can be used to discover the underlying reasons behind business analysis performance challenges or to identify the reasons why some business analysis practices are working very well. The root cause of some problems may originate in the skill level of the business analysis practitioners or in other aspects of product development, rather than in the business analysis practices themselves. For more information on root cause and opportunity analysis, see Section 4.2.2.9.

5.7.2.6 VARIANCE ANALYSIS

Variance is a quantifiable deviation, departure, or divergence from a known baseline or expected value. Variance analysis is a technique for determining the cause and degree of difference between the baseline and actual performance.

Irrespective of product life cycle, as part of verifying requirements, when there are significant differences between the expected format and content of a business analysis work product and what was actually produced, variance analysis may be applied to consider the causes of the differences.

For solutions developed using an adaptive life cycle, business analysis effort is rarely examined in isolation from an effort or schedule perspective, because the focus is on the end-to-end delivery of small, production-ready segments of product capabilities for demonstration and feedback. Product backlog items are small enough so that a designation of *done* or *not done* replaces tracking percent completion of any product backlog item or the tasks within it. That said, some teams using an adaptive approach may conduct variance analysis on the results observed in burndown charts to consider whether their business analysis practices are contributing to significant deviations from what was expected.

For solution development conducted using a predictive life cycle, where business analysis effort is tracked separately, variance analysis may suggest some underlying causes for variances in the percentage of business analysis completion or schedule variances that, in turn, may impact which business analysis techniques are used, to what degree they are used, and which parties would participate in using the techniques.

As previously mentioned, when looking at any metrics associated with business analysis performance, it is important to be cautious, because these metrics can rarely isolate poor business analysis practices as the sole cause of project and product development problems; problems with other aspects of product development may be equal or more important contributors to the problems that these metrics surface.

5.7.3 ASSESS BUSINESS ANALYSIS PERFORMANCE: OUTPUTS

5.7.3.1 BUSINESS ANALYSIS PERFORMANCE ASSESSMENT

A business analysis performance assessment summarizes what has been learned about the effectiveness of the business analysis processes in general and of the business analysis techniques that have been used in particular. In some cases, it may also reflect on the skill of the individuals who are conducting business analysis or the degree or quality of participation of stakeholders. Practices that are working well at the program or project level can be recommended for elevation to best practices and standards for use by the entire organization for future programs and projects. For those tools and techniques that present challenges, recommendations may be made for improvements or for the replacement of the challenging tools and techniques with other tools and techniques. Performance concerns related to individuals conducting business analysis or stakeholder participants are also identified and can be addressed with training, coaching, or, when necessary, assignment of other individuals to focus on business analysis. Some organizations track the proposed recommendations in logs.

5.7.4 ASSESS BUSINESS ANALYSIS PERFORMANCE: TAILORING CONSIDERATIONS

Adaptive and predictive tailoring considerations for Assess Business Analysis Performance are described in Table 5-9.

Table 5-9. Adaptive and Predictive Tailoring for Assess Business Analysis Performance

Aspects to Be Tailored	Typical Adaptive Considerations	Typical Predictive Considerations
Name	Not a formally named process; performed as part of Conducting Retrospectives	Assess Business Analysis Performance or Conduct Lessons Learned
Approach	Follows the principle of "inspect and adapt," where teams conduct regular and frequent reviews of practices throughout the development of the solution. These reviews are conducted at least at the end of each iteration and take action on findings to adjust business analysis practices for the next iteration. The changes are implemented in the very next iteration.	The business analyst contributes to lessons learned as part of project management's monitoring and control, at the conclusion of a work effort, at milestones, and as indicated by ongoing events. Business analysts may also analyze performance individually using metrics defined in planning. Follow-up on lessons learned can take place whenever these sessions occur during product development. When assessments occur after product development is well under way, or after it has been completed, the recommendations are more likely to be applied to future product development efforts rather than the one for which the assessment has been made.
Deliverables	Recommendations for changes to practices or participants may be communicated verbally or documented.	Recommendations for changes to practices can be documented as a separate business analysis assessment document. In organizations with more formal processes or governance, they could be documented with modifications to workflows, work instructions, templates, approach, or configuration in requirements management tools.

5.7.5 ASSESS BUSINESS ANALYSIS PERFORMANCE: COLLABORATION POINT

For work efforts conducted using an adaptive life cycle, project team members share responsibility for inspecting and adapting all their practices, including those used for business analysis. For work efforts conducted using a predictive life cycle, team members who hold other roles may provide insights into how well the analysis deliverables created by the business analyst support their efforts or how the business analysis processes as a whole meet their needs. One of the key roles providing these insights is a quality control analyst.

6

ELICITATION

Elicitation includes the processes of planning and preparing for elicitation, conducting elicitation, and confirming elicitation results. Elicitation draws information such as needs, requirements, and other product information from various sources.

The Elicitation processes are:

6.1 Determine Elicitation Approach—The process of thinking through how elicitation activities will be conducted, which stakeholders will be involved, which techniques may be used, and the order in which the elicitation activities are best performed.

6.2 Prepare for Elicitation—The process of organizing and scheduling resources and preparing necessary materials for an individual elicitation activity.

6.3 Conduct Elicitation—The process of applying various elicitation techniques to draw out information from stakeholders and other sources.

6.4 Confirm Elicitation Results—The process of performing follow-up activities on the elicitation results, determining an appropriate level of formality to use, reviewing with stakeholders for accuracy and completeness, and comparing to historical information.

Figure 6-1 provides an overview of the Elicitation processes. The business analysis processes are presented as discrete processes with defined interfaces, although, in practice, they overlap and interact in ways that cannot be completely detailed in this guide.

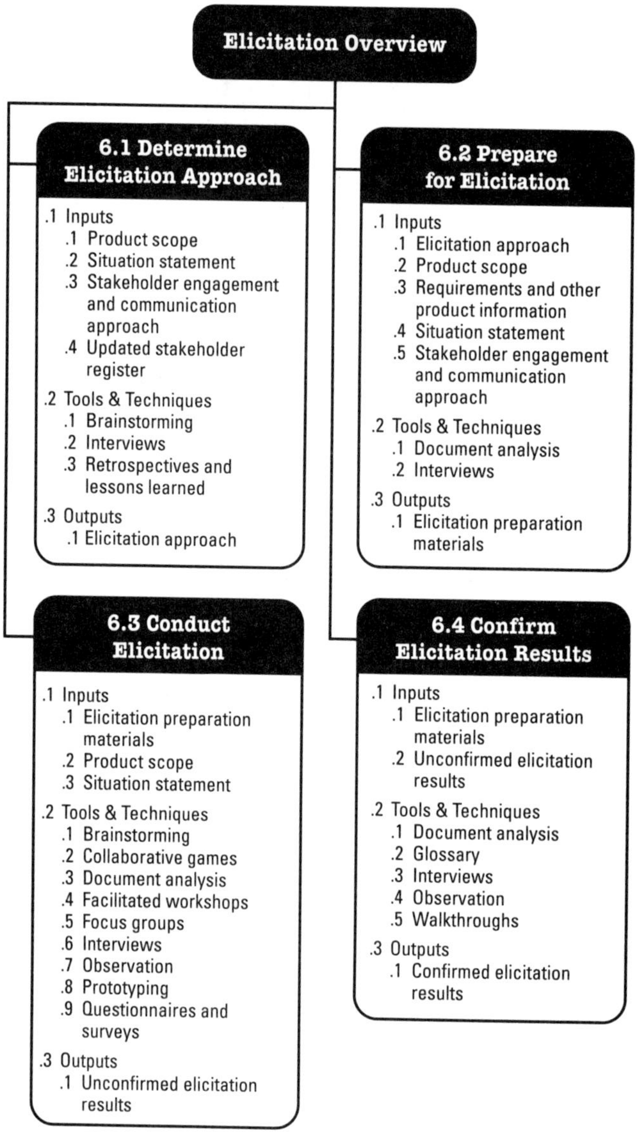

Figure 6-1. Elicitation Overview

KEY CONCEPTS FOR ELICITATION

Elicitation is the activity of drawing out information from stakeholders and other sources. It is more than collecting or gathering product information, because the terms *collecting* or *gathering* imply that stakeholders already have product information that is ready to be collected or gathered. Stakeholders often have wants, needs, and ideas, but they may not be able to express these clearly. Elicitation relies on knowledge and experience to identify the appropriate approaches and techniques to draw out information from a variety of sources. The back-and-forth interaction between the business analyst and stakeholders to obtain a shared understanding of product information is more accurately described using the term *Elicitation*.

Elicitation is highly cyclical. It is repeated multiple times for each level of abstraction in product information. For instance, all Elicitation processes would be performed to define business requirements and once again to define more detailed product requirements, such as stakeholder or solution requirements. Although the same business analyst may not be the one defining the different levels of abstraction in product information, the Elicitation processes are repeated throughout the product and project life cycles. Even when Elicitation is being performed to understand a single concept, such as the current state of an existing process, the processes are iterated through multiple times to obtain perspectives from different sources or fill in gaps in information.

Elicitation is also performed iteratively with analysis to progressively elaborate information. When business analysis information is analyzed, the quantity sometimes decreases, because extraneous information is removed. When the results are vague and open to interpretation, additional questions need to be asked and more elicitation activities conducted.

Figure 6-2 shows the iterative nature of elicitation and analysis. Elicitation and analysis activities are often performed concurrently. The process shown in Figure 6-2 is repeated for each level of abstraction of product information and for each concept until the analysis produces no further questions and the information is reduced to a depiction of the solution to the business problem or opportunity, or the risk of incomplete information is acceptable to move forward.

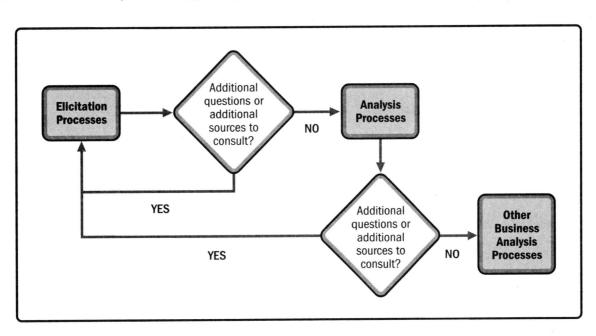

Figure 6-2. The Iterative Nature of Elicitation and Analysis

Projects using adaptive life cycles go through the elicitation and analysis processes within each project iteration. Because the features and functionality are divided among many iterations, elicitation and analysis are also divided among each iteration and happen in shorter cycles but more frequently throughout the project. Projects that use a predictive life cycle perform most of the elicitation and analysis up front within a project.

6.1 DETERMINE ELICITATION APPROACH

Determine Elicitation Approach is the process of thinking through how elicitation activities will be conducted, which stakeholders will be involved, which techniques may be used, and the order in which the elicitation activities are best performed. The key benefits of this process are efficient use of stakeholder time, effective stakeholder collaboration, and an organized approach to elicitation. The inputs, tools and techniques, and outputs of the process are depicted in Figure 6-3. Figure 6-4 depicts the data flow diagram for the process.

Figure 6-3. Determine Elicitation Approach: Inputs, Tools and Techniques, and Outputs

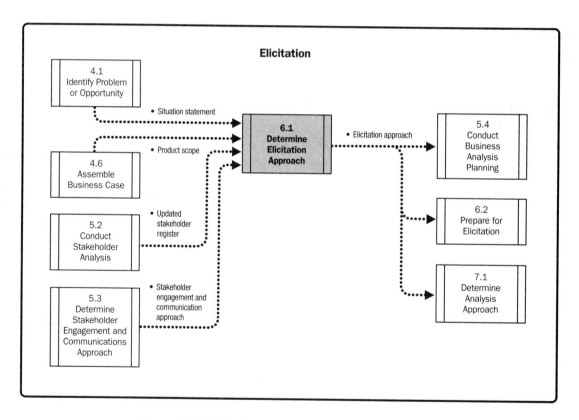

Figure 6-4. Determine Elicitation Approach: Data Flow Diagram

The elicitation approach is used to help formulate ideas about how to structure the elicitation activities. The work needed to create the elicitation approach involves thinking through how best to coordinate and conduct elicitation. Some of the elements in an elicitation approach include, but are not limited to, the following:

◆ **What information to elicit.** What is needed to define the problem, solve the problem, or answer the question?

◆ **Where to find that information.** Where is that information located: in what document, from what source, in whose mind?

◆ **How to obtain the information.** What method will be used to acquire the information from the source?

◆ **When to conduct the elicitation activities.** In what order should the elicitation activities be sequenced and when should the elicitation activities be scheduled?

A well-thought-out approach to elicitation provides the following benefits:

◆ Clear idea of the necessary information to define a problem, effect an improvement, or produce a solution;

◆ Minimization of unnecessary elicitation activities;

◆ Valuable results from each elicitation activity;

◆ Efficient and predicable use of stakeholder time to elicit the information; and

◆ Better overall focus on the entire elicitation process.

6.1.1 DETERMINE ELICITATION APPROACH: INPUTS

6.1.1.1 PRODUCT SCOPE

Described in Section 4.6.3.2, the product scope is defined as the features and functions that characterize a solution. The product scope provides context and defines the boundaries to determine what information to elicit with the goal of further detailing the scope items. Depending on what type of information is being elicited, there may already be some product information available that can be leveraged. For instance, if the team is determining or refining the elicitation approach to elicit solution requirements, stakeholder and business requirements may already be available to provide a better basis on what information to elicit.

6.1.1.2 SITUATION STATEMENT

Described in Section 4.1.3.2. The situation statement describes the problem or opportunity that the business is interested in addressing, providing context when determining what information to elicit.

6.1.1.3 STAKEHOLDER ENGAGEMENT AND COMMUNICATION APPROACH

Described in Section 5.3.3.1. The stakeholder engagement and communication approach summarizes all the agreements for governing how stakeholders will be engaged and communicated with across the portfolio, program, or project. It contains information on how to effectively interact with stakeholders. There may be certain stakeholder preferences that signal which elicitation techniques are best to use for a particular stakeholder or stakeholder group. For instance, some stakeholders may prefer one-on-one interaction, whereas others may prefer group collaboration techniques.

6.1.1.4 STAKEHOLDER REGISTER

Described in Section 5.2.3.1. The stakeholder register contains information on who may impact or be impacted by the area under analysis, along with profile information about stakeholders or stakeholder groups. Information contained within the register can be used to determine an optimal approach to perform the elicitation activities. For example, a stakeholder's role on a project or position within the organization may determine which details and/or perspectives he or she can provide. One might also conclude that senior stakeholders may have less availability and be more difficult to schedule for group elicitation activities.

6.1.2 DETERMINE ELICITATION APPROACH: TOOLS AND TECHNIQUES

6.1.2.1 BRAINSTORMING

Brainstorming is an elicitation technique used to identify a list of ideas within a short period of time. Brainstorming may be used to identify a list of sources to elicit from as well as which elicitation techniques to use. For more information on brainstorming, see Section 5.1.2.1.

6.1.2.2 INTERVIEWS

An interview is a formal or informal approach to elicit information from stakeholders. It is performed by asking prepared and/or spontaneous questions and documenting the responses. The business analyst may want to interview subject matter experts (SMEs) to discover other sources of information to elicit from, to obtain stakeholder preferences for the Elicitation process, or to learn about a stakeholder's experience and comfort level with one or more of the techniques being considered. For more information on interviews, see Section 6.3.2.6.

6.1.2.3 RETROSPECTIVES AND LESSONS LEARNED

Retrospectives and lessons learned leverage past experiences to plan for the future. To create the elicitation approach, business analysts may need to rely on their past experience or the experience from individuals or groups with specialized knowledge or training in:

◆ Tailoring the elicitation approach to meet project needs,

◆ Identifying the most authentic sources of information to be elicited,

◆ Determining the best techniques to use, and

◆ Articulating dependencies and interactions among the elicitation activities.

Retrospectives and lessons learned, combined with experience and expert judgment, can be used to tailor the elicitation approach to ensure the best fit for the project. For more information on retrospectives and lessons learned, see Section 5.7.2.4.

6.1.3 DETERMINE ELICITATION APPROACH: OUTPUTS

6.1.3.1 ELICITATION APPROACH

The elicitation approach describes how Elicitation will be performed, what information to elicit, where to find that information, how to obtain the information, and when to conduct the elicitation activities. It can be documented or it can be a thought process performed to prepare for the forthcoming elicitation effort. Whether formally documented or not, the decisions and thought process used to plan elicitation activities can be shared with the project team to ensure that everyone is aware of the forthcoming activities and their role. The elicitation approach may be referred to as an elicitation plan in more formal life cycles. For information about creating an elicitation approach, refer to Sections 3.4.7 and 4.3 in *Business Analysis for Practitioners: A Practice Guide.*

6.1.4 DETERMINE ELICITATION APPROACH: TAILORING CONSIDERATIONS

Adaptive and predictive tailoring considerations for Determine Elicitation Approach are described in Table 6-1.

Table 6-1. Adaptive and Predictive Tailoring for Determine Elicitation Approach

Aspects to Be Tailored	Typical Adaptive Considerations	Typical Predictive Considerations
Name	Not a formally named process	Determine Elicitation Approach
Approach	Though some high-level planning might occur, most of the elicitation approach is defined early in each iteration for the elicitation that will occur during that iteration. Because elicitation is often performed to refine product backlog items up to a few iterations ahead of being developed, the elicitation approach defined is often for more than the work being developed in the current iteration. Collaborative elicitation techniques may be selected to obtain information from stakeholders.	A high-level elicitation approach is defined early, during a planning phase. The elicitation approach is refined throughout the portfolio, program, or project.
Deliverables	Not a separate deliverable. The elicitation approach is not formally documented but is complete when the team obtains a shared understanding of what is expected during the elicitation activities.	Detailed elicitation approach residing in a business analysis plan.

6.1.5 DETERMINE ELICITATION APPROACH: COLLABORATION POINT

Because of constraints, Elicitation is sometimes scaled back, but doing this can introduce additional portfolio, program, project, and product risks that may result in rework or defects in the product. Obtaining early support and buy-in from portfolio, program, or project managers, and any functional managers, regarding the amount of Elicitation that is appropriate supports planning, sets expectations, and reduces risks. When deciding the order of business analysis activities, these roles may work together to determine how resource availability will impact sequencing decisions.

6.2 PREPARE FOR ELICITATION

Prepare for Elicitation is the process of organizing and scheduling resources and preparing necessary materials for an individual elicitation activity. The key benefits of this process are that the elicitation activities are organized and effectively performed and participants understand up front why they are involved and what is required of them. The inputs, tools and techniques, and outputs of the process are depicted in Figure 6-5. Figure 6-6 depicts the data flow diagram for the process.

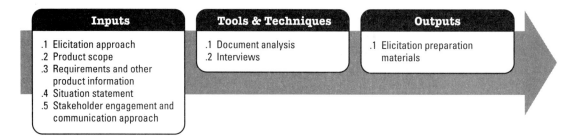

Inputs	Tools & Techniques	Outputs
.1 Elicitation approach .2 Product scope .3 Requirements and other product information .4 Situation statement .5 Stakeholder engagement and communication approach	.1 Document analysis .2 Interviews	.1 Elicitation preparation materials

Figure 6-5. Prepare for Elicitation: Inputs, Tools and Techniques, and Outputs

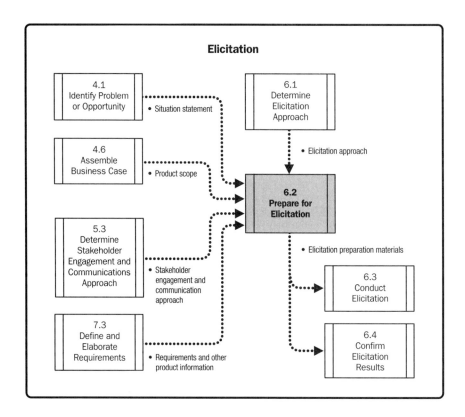

Figure 6-6. Prepare for Elicitation: Data Flow Diagram

Elicitation preparation is the planning performed prior to the start of an elicitation activity. Preparation materials are for the benefit of the facilitator to ensure that Elicitation is conducted effectively and time spent with stakeholders is efficient and provides maximum value. For large elicitation engagements, the preparation may actually be more time-consuming than the elicitation activity itself. For elicitation activities that do not involve other people, such as document analysis, the preparation might be brief.

Preparation depends on the purpose of Elicitation and the chosen elicitation technique. For large workshops, a presentation document may be created to help guide the discussion. If collaborative games are being used, preparation will include the setup for the game, as well as thinking through the instructions. Informal preparation notes may also be created to help with facilitation. Preparation notes can be used to measure the progress achieved against what was planned and can be used to adjust expectations for future elicitation activities.

The following activities may be performed to prepare for an elicitation activity:

◆ **Determine the objective.** Set an objective for each elicitation activity to ensure that each is effectively performed. The objective is the reason why the elicitation activity is being undertaken. Elicitation activities should provide some value and benefit to justify the time it takes to obtain the needed information.

◆ **Determine the participants.** Identifying the required participants for an elicitation activity is crucial. Not having the right participants may result in the need to reschedule the elicitation activity. If the activity is held, it may run less effectively or miss the set objective. Less experienced participants may not have the background they need to provide the information being sought; they may require additional time to be brought up to speed or may need to be trained if they are unfamiliar with the elicitation techniques being used.

◆ **Identify the resources.** Some elicitation activities require supporting materials, such as access to existing systems or documents. These resources can be procured during preparation.

◆ **Identify the questions for the elicitation activity.** Questions may be prepared prior to conducting Elicitation to ensure that the objectives for the elicitation activity are achieved. The business analyst may also want to think through how elicitation results will be captured and whether any assistance is required to conduct Elicitation, and coordinate with those resources in advance.

◆ **Set the agenda.** The topics to be discussed or researched and general time boundaries may be provided to participants in advance so they are aware of what is expected of them. If prework is required of any of the participants, it is recommended to consult with them beforehand, to ensure that they are prepared. Any preparation materials should be distributed, such as presentations, notes, or models to baseline and/or guide the elicitation activity. Analysis models might be created as part of preparation for elicitation activities, so that the models can be used to identify questions to be asked or topics to be reviewed during Elicitation. This process can be performed in parallel with Section 7.2.

◆ **Schedule the elicitation activity.** Schedule the appropriate amount of time for each stakeholder group. Secure any supporting materials, such as the meeting room, projectors, whiteboards, flipcharts, and writing tools, for the elicitation activity.

More information on how to prepare for Elicitation can be found in Section 4.4 of *Business Analysis for Practitioners: A Practice Guide*.

6.2.1 PREPARE FOR ELICITATION: INPUTS

6.2.1.1 ELICITATION APPROACH

Described in Section 6.1.3.1. The elicitation approach explains how Elicitation will be performed, including the elicitation activities that will be conducted. Elicitation activities will require preparation to ensure that they provide value. The participant list can also be derived from elicitation planning efforts.

6.2.1.2 PRODUCT SCOPE

Described in Section 4.6.3.2. The product scope is defined as the features and functions that characterize a solution. The product scope provides context to determine the objectives of the elicitation activity and to subsequently prepare the questions and set the agenda. There may be additional sources of information that can be consulted for context.

6.2.1.3 REQUIREMENTS AND OTHER PRODUCT INFORMATION

Described in Section 7.3.3.1. Requirements and other product information include all the information about a solution and are the culmination of results from elicitation and analysis activities. Requirements and other product information provide context to determine the objectives of the elicitation activity and to subsequently prepare the questions and set the agenda. Previously elicited requirements or models may be used to guide the elicitation activity. Visual representations are often easier for most audiences to follow along with and provide feedback on. For information on visual models, see Section 7.2.

6.2.1.4 SITUATION STATEMENT

Described in Section 4.1.3.2. The situation statement provides an objective statement of the problem or opportunity that the proposed solution is looking to address. The situation statement is used to determine the objective of the elicitation activity and to subsequently prepare the questions and set the agenda.

6.2.1.5 STAKEHOLDER ENGAGEMENT AND COMMUNICATION APPROACH

Described in Section 5.3.3.1. The stakeholder engagement and communication approach summarizes all the agreements for governing how stakeholders will be engaged and communicated with across the portfolio, program, or project. It defines the preferences and needs of stakeholders to best engage and communicate with them. These needs and preferences are taken into consideration when determining the elicitation approach and deciding on which elicitation techniques to use. It is revisited when preparing for the elicitation activity, in case the elicitation needs to be tailored to specific stakeholder preferences.

6.2.2 PREPARE FOR ELICITATION: TOOLS AND TECHNIQUES

6.2.2.1 DOCUMENT ANALYSIS

Document analysis is an elicitation technique used to analyze existing documentation to identify relevant product information. It can be used to obtain information that is readily available within existing document repositories, reducing the amount of elicitation time needed with stakeholders. The results of document analysis can be used to support elicitation preparation. Elicited information can be used to formulate agendas, identify questions for an elicitation activity, or provide context and background information prior to engaging with stakeholders directly. For more information on document analysis, see Section 6.3.2.3.

6.2.2.2 INTERVIEWS

An interview is a formal or informal approach used to elicit information from stakeholders. Preliminary interviews may support elicitation preparation by clarifying objectives with those who may take part in elicitation activities or discussing preparation steps and materials so participants know what will be expected of them prior to and during elicitation. Elicited information can be used to formulate agendas, identify questions for an elicitation activity, or provide context and background information prior to bringing a group of stakeholders together. For more information on interviews, see Section 6.3.2.6.

6.2.3 PREPARE FOR ELICITATION: OUTPUTS

6.2.3.1 ELICITATION PREPARATION MATERIALS

Elicitation preparation materials are items created to maximize the probability of meeting elicitation activity objectives, while optimizing the time spent with elicitation participants. Elicitation preparation materials may be formal or informal, depending on the preference of the facilitator. Preparation materials may include:

◆ Elicitation activity objectives,

◆ An agenda,

◆ Background information,

◆ Questions to be discussed,

◆ Ground rules and/or instructions to support an elicitation technique, and

◆ Presentation materials and/or product information, including models, to help structure the elicitation activity.

6.2.4 PREPARE FOR ELICITATION: TAILORING CONSIDERATIONS

Adaptive and predictive tailoring considerations for Prepare for Elicitation are described in Table 6-2.

Table 6-2. Adaptive and Predictive Tailoring for Prepare for Elicitation

Aspects to Be Tailored	Typical Adaptive Considerations	Typical Predictive Considerations
Name	Not a formally named process; performed as part of Backlog Refinement or Elaboration	Prepare for Elicitation
Approach	Preparation is performed whenever elicitation is to be conducted. Elicitation of high-level product information occurs within iteration 0, and elicitation of more detailed product information occurs within subsequent iterations. Elicitation within an iteration may clarify information for the current iteration or elaborate on product information one to two iterations ahead.	Preparation is performed whenever elicitation is to be conducted. Elicitation of high-level product information occurs at the portfolio and program level, and elicitation of more detailed product information occurs within an analysis phase of a project.
Deliverables	Elicitation is frequent, with the goal of elaborating just enough information; preparation materials are lightweight.	Scope of elicitation is larger; preparation materials may be more detailed.

6.2.5 PREPARE FOR ELICITATION: COLLABORATION POINT

Stakeholders may be consulted in advance so they are aware of what is expected of them and can be alerted if there are preparation activities they are required to complete in advance of the elicitation. Sufficient communication is provided beforehand so that stakeholders can secure time on their calendars.

6.3 CONDUCT ELICITATION

Conduct Elicitation is the process of applying various elicitation techniques to draw out information from stakeholders and other sources. The key benefit of this process is that it obtains information from the appropriate sources to sufficiently define and elaborate requirements and other product information. The inputs, tools and techniques, and outputs of the process are depicted in Figure 6-7. Figure 6-8 depicts the data flow diagram for the process.

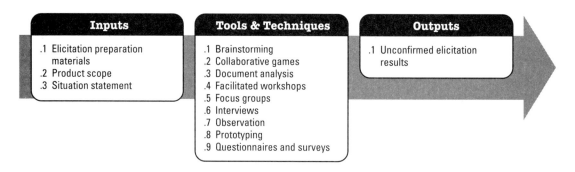

Inputs	Tools & Techniques	Outputs
.1 Elicitation preparation materials .2 Product scope .3 Situation statement	.1 Brainstorming .2 Collaborative games .3 Document analysis .4 Facilitated workshops .5 Focus groups .6 Interviews .7 Observation .8 Prototyping .9 Questionnaires and surveys	.1 Unconfirmed elicitation results

Figure 6-7. Conduct Elicitation: Inputs, Tools and Techniques, and Outputs

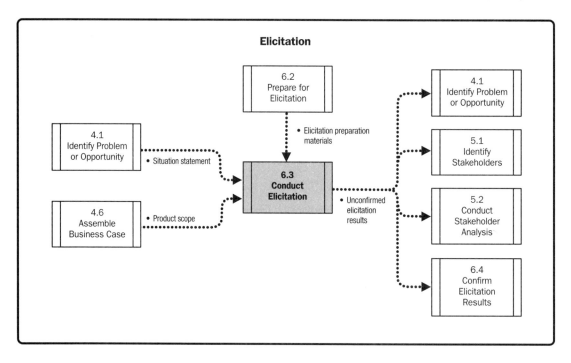

Figure 6-8. Conduct Elicitation: Data Flow Diagram

There are three stages during an elicitation activity that are applicable regardless of the elicitation technique used:

◆ **Introduction.** The introduction sets the stage, sets the pace, and establishes the overall purpose for the elicitation activity.

◆ **Body.** The body is where the questions are asked and the answers are given or uncovered.

◆ **Close.** The close provides a graceful termination to the particular activity.

Follow-up activities support elicitation and are used to confirm elicitation results. Information may be consolidated and confirmed with participants once elicitation completes or follow-up may be performed concurrently while conducting elicitation. Following up on elicitation activities is further discussed in Section 6.4. For information on how to conduct elicitation activities, see Section 4.5 of *Business Analysis for Practitioners: A Practice Guide.*

6.3.1 CONDUCT ELICITATION: INPUTS

6.3.1.1 ELICITATION PREPARATION MATERIALS

Described in Section 6.2.3.1. Elicitation preparation materials are items created to maximize the probability of meeting elicitation activity objectives, while optimizing the time spent with participants of elicitation activities. Elicitation preparation materials are used while conducting elicitation to structure and guide the elicitation activity.

6.3.1.2 PRODUCT SCOPE

Described in Section 4.6.3.2. The product scope is defined as the features and functions that characterize a solution. Product scope is used when developing the objectives for the elicitation activity and when conducting elicitation to ensure that discussions remain on topic.

6.3.1.3 SITUATION STATEMENT

Described in Section 4.1.3.2. The situation statement provides an objective statement of the problem or opportunity that the proposed solution is looking to address. The situation statement, along with any additional context obtained while preparing for the elicitation activity, can be used to ensure shared understanding among elicitation participants about the topics to be discussed and will help guide elicitation discussions.

6.3.2 CONDUCT ELICITATION: TOOLS AND TECHNIQUES

6.3.2.1 BRAINSTORMING

Brainstorming is an elicitation technique that can be used to identify a list of ideas within a short period of time—for example, a list of risks, stakeholders, or potential solution options. Brainstorming is conducted in a group environment and is led by a facilitator. Output generated from the group is often greater than the output that could be received from the same group if ideas were recorded individually. Brainstorming is a technique that is commonly used in conjunction with other elicitation techniques, such as focus groups or workshops. For more information on brainstorming, see Section 5.1.2.1.

6.3.2.2 COLLABORATIVE GAMES

Collaborative games are a collection of elicitation techniques that foster collaboration, innovation, and creativity to achieve the goal of the elicitation activity. Collaborative games use game play to encourage team participation and enhance engagement. They can help product teams with problem solving, team building, and decision making. The tools required to play collaborative games are typically simple and require minimal setup—for example, whiteboards, flipcharts, markers, and sticky notes. There are many types of collaborative games. The following are just a few:

◆ **Product box.** An elicitation technique that uses game play to focus on the features of a product that are important to the customer. The objective is to divide the participants into teams, asking each team to design a box that represents how the product would be packaged. A plain box and art supplies are provided and each team is asked to decorate the box, marketing the product in a manner that would entice a customer to purchase it. The team's use of colors, designs, and slogans identifies the product benefits and features that customers expect the product to possess. Because the size of the box limits the information that can be presented, the technique provides insights into the benefits and features that customers find most valuable.

◆ **Speedboat.** An elicitation technique that uses game play to elicit information about product features that customers/stakeholders find problematic. A picture of a boat with several anchors is drawn on a large sheet of paper. Participants are asked to think about characteristics of the current product that they do not like and to place a few words describing the problem on each anchor. Anchors can be added to the picture until all issues are raised. The team then discusses each anchor and assesses how much faster the boat might go if the anchor is removed. The technique provides a team approach to identifying product issues and quantifying the impacts of the problems raised. The game provides a nonconfrontational and indirect approach to eliciting information about product issues and downplays the stigma associated with directly informing a product team about product deficiencies. There are variations on the speedboat activity, such as sailboat, which is similar but uses sails to encourage the recognition of positive influences rather than anchors to identify negative ones.

◆ **Spider web.** An elicitation technique used to discover unknown relationships between the product being analyzed and other products. The technique helps product teams identify competitive aspects of a product and may lead to changes in product scope. Participants can be any type of stakeholder, but when the technique is used to drive innovation, customers are the optimal participants because they often provide uncommon insights about products. The technique is performed by drawing a circle in the middle of a large sheet of paper to represent the product. Participants are given a few minutes to brainstorm other products that might be related in some way to the product listed. Participants are invited to draw pictures around the circle to represent the products they identified. Relationships are then drawn between the products. Participants explain the nature of the relationships as they draw them. Spider web can be played using a variety of materials to symbolize the products and relationships. The use of different materials allows participants to show variances in importance or risk between different products, and relationships. When complete, the paper looks like a tangled spider web with many colors and symbols.

6.3.2.3 DOCUMENT ANALYSIS

Document analysis is an elicitation technique used to analyze existing documentation to identify relevant product information. Benefits of using document analysis include:

◆ Information received from individuals may be subjective or individuals may not have an accurate view of the information, whereas documented information tends to be more objective;

◆ Documents may contain information that no one individual has;

◆ Written documentation may provide more background and explanations than an individual explaining the same material;

◆ Documents may have enough information to use as a starting point, thereby saving significant stakeholder time during in-person elicitation activities; and

◆ Up-to-date documentation can be a good source of information regarding the structure and capabilities of any product.

When using document analysis, it is important to recognize the accuracy and relevancy of the information being used. Current state documentation may represent business or technical constraints that no longer apply. Outdated information may still be relevant if used appropriately as a historical baseline from which future elicitation can be based. Document analysis is a viable technique to use to gain an understanding of the business environment and situation prior to engaging directly with stakeholders. Document analysis is further discussed in Section 4.5.5.2 of *Business Analysis for Practitioners: A Practice Guide*.

6.3.2.4 FACILITATED WORKSHOPS

Facilitated workshops use a structured meeting led by a skilled, neutral facilitator and a carefully selected group of stakeholders to collaborate and work toward a stated objective. When the objective is focused on bringing cross-functional stakeholders together to define and discuss product information, the workshop is commonly termed a requirements workshop. Workshops are considered a primary technique for quickly defining product information across multiple domains and reconciling stakeholder differences. Because of their interactive group nature, well-facilitated sessions can build trust, foster relationships, and improve communication among the participants, which can lead to increased stakeholder consensus. For a well-facilitated workshop, the individual who conducts the meeting should be experienced as a facilitator. Other techniques, such as brainstorming and collaborative games, can be used in facilitated workshops to help achieve the objectives of the meeting. Facilitated workshops are further discussed in Section 4.5.5.3 of *Business Analysis for Practitioners: A Practice Guide*.

6.3.2.5 FOCUS GROUPS

Focus groups bring together prequalified stakeholders and subject matter experts (SMEs) to learn about their expectations and attitudes about a proposed solution. Focus groups provide an opportunity to obtain feedback directly from customers and/or end users. Sessions are facilitated in a manner that allows for healthy team dynamics, a free flow of ideas, and a sufficient level of feedback to meet the session objectives. Focus groups are further discussed in Section 4.5.5.4 of *Business Analysis for Practitioners: A Practice Guide*.

6.3.2.6 INTERVIEWS

An interview is a formal or informal approach used to elicit information from stakeholders. It is performed by asking prepared and/or spontaneous questions and documenting the responses. Interviews are often conducted on an individual basis between an interviewer and an interviewee, but they may also involve multiple interviewers and/or multiple interviewees. Interviewing experienced project participants, stakeholders, and subject matter experts helps identify and define the features and functions of the desired solution. Interviews may also be used to build relationships and trust with stakeholders by taking the time to understand their situation and any potential pain points. Interviews conducted for this purpose may not have documented results. Interviews are further discussed in Section 4.5.5.5 of *Business Analysis for Practitioners: A Practice Guide*.

6.3.2.7 OBSERVATION

Observation is an elicitation technique that provides a direct way of obtaining information about how a process is performed or a product is used by viewing individuals in their own environment performing their jobs or tasks. It is particularly helpful to observe detailed processes because stakeholders may have difficulty recalling specifics when discussing their work. Stakeholders may also be unaware of their actions or inactions and therefore may be unable to communicate them. Observation is usually performed with the observer viewing the process worker performing the work, but it can also be performed with the observer experiencing or performing the task firsthand. The objective of observation is to uncover information that stakeholders are not able or willing to provide and to use the information in the formulation of product requirements. The main drawback of the observation technique is that people may act differently when they are being observed. Observation is further discussed in Section 4.5.5.6 of *Business Analysis for Practitioners: A Practice Guide*.

6.3.2.8 PROTOTYPING

Prototyping is a method of obtaining early feedback on requirements by providing a model of the expected solution before building it. Prototypes are also known as proof of concepts (PoC). Because prototypes are tangible, stakeholders are able to visualize and possibly experiment with a model of the product rather than discussing abstract representations of the requirements. This provides an opportunity to validate a conceptual working solution against an existing set of requirements to look for potential gaps in requirements. Prototypes support the concept of progressive elaboration through the iterative cycles of mockup creation, user experimentation, feedback generation, and prototype revision. A prototype can be a mockup of the real result, as in an architectural model, or it can be an early version of the product itself. A few common kinds of prototypes are the following:

◆ **Storyboarding.** A prototyping technique that shows sequence or navigation through a series of images or illustrations.

◆ **Wireframes.** Diagrams that represent a static blueprint or schematic of a user interface used to identify basic functionality.

◆ **Evolutionary.** A prototype that is the actual finished solution in process.

Prototyping is further discussed in Section 4.5.5.7 of *Business Analysis for Practitioners: A Practice Guide*.

6.3.2.9 QUESTIONNAIRES AND SURVEYS

Questionnaires and surveys are written sets of questions designed to quickly accumulate information from a large number of respondents. Survey respondents can represent a diverse population and are often dispersed over a wide geographical area. As a form of elicitation, this technique has the benefit of reaching a large group of people for a relatively small cost. A typical concern with surveys is ensuring a sufficient response rate. Questionnaires and surveys are further discussed in Section 4.5.5.8 of *Business Analysis for Practitioners: A Practice Guide*.

6.3.3 CONDUCT ELICITATION: OUTPUTS

6.3.3.1 UNCONFIRMED ELICITATION RESULTS

Unconfirmed elicitation results consist of the information obtained from completed elicitation activities. The results of elicitation activities may be documented either formally or informally. Documentation can range in formality, from capturing a snapshot of a whiteboard that contains preliminary requirements to information recorded in requirements management tools. The primary documented result is a set of elicitation notes that comprise a wealth of information for performing other business analysis processes. The results may come in the form of sketches, diagrams, models, flipcharts, photos, videos, audio recordings, sticky notes, or index cards, to name a few.

6.3.4 CONDUCT ELICITATION: TAILORING CONSIDERATIONS

Adaptive and predictive tailoring considerations for Conduct Elicitation are described in Table 6-3.

Table 6-3. Adaptive and Predictive Tailoring for Conduct Elicitation

Aspects to Be Tailored	Typical Adaptive Considerations	Typical Predictive Considerations
Name	Backlog Refinement or Elaboration	Conduct Elicitation
Approach	Elicitation is frequent, with the goal of elaborating just enough information. Elicitation of high-level product information occurs to develop the backlog, and elicitation of more detailed product information happens within subsequent iterations. Elicitation within an iteration may be done to clarify information for the current iteration or to elaborate on product information one to two iterations ahead.	Elicitation of high-level product information occurs at the portfolio and program level, and elicitation of more detailed product information occurs within an analysis phase of a project. However, as changes are made in later phases, elicitation processes are repeated.
Deliverables	Shared understanding of elicitation results may not be documented, documented just enough, or represented in models.	Comprehensive and documented elicitation results.

6.3.5 CONDUCT ELICITATION: COLLABORATION POINT

When business analysis is performed by more than one business analyst, the team of analysts will work together to ensure that the roles and responsibilities for each are clear, the team is effectively working, and duplication of effort is avoided. In situations where there is only one business analyst on the team, the portfolio, program, project manager, or someone else on the product team may support the elicitation effort—for example, by taking notes—to allow the business analyst to focus on facilitation.

6.4 CONFIRM ELICITATION RESULTS

Confirm Elicitation Results is the process of performing follow-up activities on the elicitation results, determining an appropriate level of formality to use, reviewing with stakeholders for accuracy and completeness, and comparing to historical information. The key benefit of this process is that it validates that stakeholders and the elicitation results were understood during Elicitation. The inputs, tools and techniques, and outputs of the process are depicted in Figure 6-9. Figure 6-10 depicts the data flow diagram for the process.

Figure 6-9. Confirm Elicitation Results: Inputs, Tools and Techniques, and Outputs

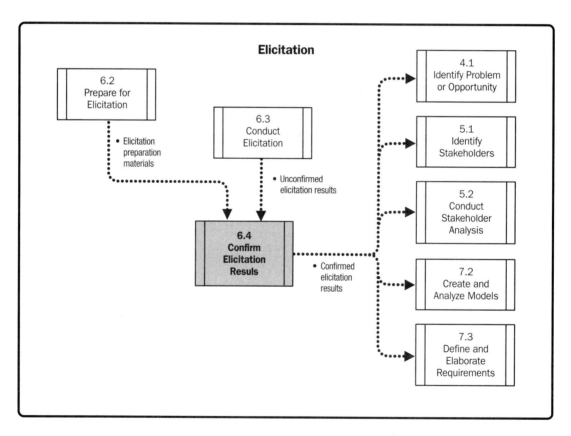

Figure 6-10. Confirm Elicitation Results: Data Flow Diagram

During Elicitation, information may be captured via multiple media, such as whiteboards, flipcharts, meeting notes, and recording devices. Elicitation results may need to be:

◆ Refined and/or corrected and extraneous information eliminated;

◆ Organized, categorized, and consolidated;

◆ Compared against previously elicited information, and discrepancies followed up on during future elicitation;

◆ Converted to an appropriate level of formality based on stakeholder needs; and

◆ Packaged for distribution.

Elicitation results can be confirmed in different ways. Elicitation results might be distributed to the participants who originally provided the information with the goal of confirming their accuracy. Other times, it may be sufficient to ask attendees to clarify and correct information during elicitation, thereby performing and confirming elicitation concurrently. Concurrent confirmation is considered a common practice in adaptive life cycles.

Both approaches can be equally effective based on the situation but also ineffective under certain conditions. For example, confirming results directly during elicitation is not preferred when key stakeholders send delegates or subordinates to participate in the elicitation activity on their behalf. A separate review and confirmation cycle may not be optimal when stakeholders are not willing to take time outside of elicitation to review and approve the results. The team should discuss and agree on how elicitation results will be reviewed and confirmed when determining the best elicitation approach for the program or project.

6.4.1 CONFIRM ELICITATION RESULTS: INPUTS

6.4.1.1 ELICITATION PREPARATION MATERIALS

Described in Section 6.2.3.1. Elicitation preparation materials are items created to maximize the probability of meeting elicitation activity objectives, while optimizing the time spent with elicitation participants or physical resources. Elicitation preparation materials that were used to structure the elicitation activity, such as previously elicited product information, may be updated based on information learned during elicitation and compared with the elicitation results to determine whether there are issues or gaps that require additional elicitation. For this reason, Section 6.4 on Confirm Elicitation Results is often performed in conjunction with Sections 7.2 on Create and Analyze Models and 7.3 on Define and Elaborate Requirements.

6.4.1.2 UNCONFIRMED ELICITATION RESULTS

Described in Section 6.3.3.1. Unconfirmed elicitation results consist of the business analysis information obtained from completed elicitation activities. The results from elicitation, documented in various formats, are consolidated and organized in a manner that can be reviewed, understood, and validated by those who provided the information or against the original source materials. Unconfirmed elicitation results evolve into confirmed elicitation results upon the completion of this process.

6.4.2 CONFIRM ELICITATION RESULTS: TOOLS AND TECHNIQUES

6.4.2.1 DOCUMENT ANALYSIS

Document analysis is an elicitation technique used to analyze existing documentation to identify relevant product information. Document analysis can be used to compare elicitation results to historical information, such as existing procedures or existing materials used during elicitation activities, to confirm accuracy. For more information on document analysis, see Section 6.3.2.3.

6.4.2.2 GLOSSARY

A glossary is a list of definitions for terms and acronyms about a product. The glossary is used to provide the product team with a common understanding about the terms being used in conversations and throughout other business analysis outputs—for example, in requirements documents, models, user stories, etc. Glossaries are a helpful tool when confirming elicitation results to enable product teams to reach agreement on the meaning of terms and to identify terms that are being used differently across the product team, organization, or industry. For more information on glossaries, see Section 7.3.2.3.

6.4.2.3 INTERVIEWS

An interview is a formal or informal approach used to elicit information from stakeholders. It is performed by asking prepared and/or spontaneous questions and documenting the responses. When necessary, follow-up interviews may be conducted to obtain confirmation of elicitation results and clarifications on any discrepancies from an elicitation activity. For more information on interviews, see Section 6.3.2.6.

6.4.2.4 OBSERVATION

Observation is an elicitation technique that provides a direct way of obtaining information about how a process is performed or a product is used by viewing individuals in their own environment performing their jobs or tasks. Observation can be used to cross-check non-observation elicitation results with actuality. For more information on observation, see Section 6.3.2.7.

6.4.2.5 WALKTHROUGHS

A walkthrough is a peer review in which the author of the materials walks the peer reviewers through the authored information. A walkthrough may be conducted to review the results of elicitation to obtain confirmation that the results are accurate at this point in time, or to clarify any discrepancies raised. For more information on walkthroughs, see Section 7.6.2.4.

6.4.3 CONFIRM ELICITATION RESULTS: OUTPUTS

6.4.3.1 CONFIRMED ELICITATION RESULTS

Elicitation results consist of the business analysis information obtained from completed elicitation activities. Confirmed elicitation results signify that the product team has reached a common understanding and agrees to the accuracy of the information elicited. Confirmed elicitation results may be obtained after a group of stakeholders reviews the materials provided upon completion of elicitation or they can be obtained concurrently as elicitation is performed.

6.4.4 CONFIRM ELICITATION RESULTS: TAILORING CONSIDERATIONS

Adaptive and predictive tailoring considerations for Confirm Elicitation Results are described in Table 6-4.

Table 6-4. Adaptive and Predictive Tailoring for Confirm Elicitation Results

Aspects to Be Tailored	Typical Adaptive Considerations	Typical Predictive Considerations
Name	Not a formally named process; performed as part of Backlog Refinement or Elaboration	Confirm Elicitation Results
Approach	Elicitation is conducted and the results confirmed concurrently.	Elicitation may be conducted and confirmed concurrently or confirmation may occur at a point in time after elicitation has been completed.
Deliverables	Shared understanding of elicitation results may be documented or represented in models.	Acknowledgment that elicitation results are accurate. Elicitation results are typically comprehensive and documented.

6.4.5 CONFIRM ELICITATION RESULTS: COLLABORATION POINT

Elicitation results are often confirmed with subject matter experts, the product owner, the sponsor, and/or portfolio, program, or project managers to ensure that the information captured is accurate. The business analyst maintains communications with these roles to keep participants engaged and informed as elicitation activities progress and the information obtained evolves.

7

ANALYSIS

Analysis includes the processes to examine and document product information in sufficient detail to ensure that it reflects the stakeholders' needs, aligns to their goals and business objectives, and enables the identification of viable solution designs.

The Analysis processes are:

7.1 Determine Analysis Approach—The process of thinking ahead about how analysis will be performed, including what will be analyzed; which models will be most beneficial to produce; and how requirements and other product information will be verified, validated, and prioritized.

7.2 Create and Analyze Models—The process of creating structured representations, such as diagrams, tables, or structured text, of any product information to facilitate further analysis by identifying gaps in information or uncovering extraneous information.

7.3 Define and Elaborate Requirements—The process of refining and documenting requirements and other types of product information at the appropriate level of detail, format, and level of formality required for various audiences.

7.4 Define Acceptance Criteria—The process of obtaining agreement as to what would constitute proof that one or more aspects of a solution have been developed successfully.

7.5 Verify Requirements—The process of checking that requirements are of sufficient quality.

7.6 Validate Requirements—The process of checking that the requirements meet business goals and objectives.

7.7 Prioritize Requirements and Other Product Information—The process of understanding how individual pieces of product information achieve stakeholder objectives, and using that information, along with other agreed-upon prioritization factors, to facilitate ranking of the work.

7.8 Identify and Analyze Product Risks—The process of uncovering and examining assumptions and uncertainties that could positively or negatively affect success in the definition, development, and the expected results of the solution.

7.9 Assess Product Design Options—The process of identifying, analyzing, and comparing solution design options based on the business goals and objectives, expected costs of implementation, feasibility, and associated risks, and using the results of this assessment to provide recommendations regarding the design options presented.

Figure 7-1 provides an overview of the Analysis processes. The business analysis processes are presented as discrete processes with defined interfaces, although, in practice, they overlap and interact in ways that cannot be completely detailed in this guide.

Analysis Overview

7.1 Determine Analysis Approach

.1 Inputs
 .1 Elicitation approach
 .2 Product scope
 .3 Situation statement
 .4 Traceability and monitoring approach

.2 Tools & Techniques
 .1 Brainstorming
 .2 Document analysis
 .3 Retrospectives and lessons learned

.3 Outputs
 .1 Analysis approach

7.5 Verify Requirements

.1 Inputs
 .1 Analysis approach
 .2 Business analysis organizational standards
 .3 Compliance or regulatory standards
 .4 Requirements and other product information

.2 Tools & Techniques
 .1 INVEST
 .2 Peer reviews

.3 Outputs
 1. Verified requirements and other product information

7.6 Validate Requirements

.1 Inputs
 .1 Acceptance criteria
 .2 Analysis approach
 .3 Business goals and objectives
 .4 Requirements and other product information

.2 Tools & Techniques
 .1 Delphi
 .2 Goal model and business objectives model
 .3 Traceability matrix
 .4 Walkthroughs

.3 Outputs
 .1 Validated requirements and other product information

7.2 Create and Analyze Models

.1 Inputs
 .1 Analysis approach
 .2 Confirmed elicitation results
 .3 Requirements and other product information

.2 Tools & Techniques
 .1 Context diagram
 .2 Data dictionary
 .3 Data flow diagram
 .4 Decision tree and decision table
 .5 Ecosystem map
 .6 Entity relationship diagram
 .7 Event list
 .8 Feature model
 .9 Goal model and business objectives model
 .10 Modeling elaboration
 .11 Organizational chart
 .12 Process flows
 .13 Prototypes, wireframes, and display-action-response models
 .14 Report table
 .15 State table and state diagram
 .16 Story mapping
 .17 System interface table
 .18 Use case diagram
 .19 User interface flow

.3 Outputs
 .1 Analysis models

7.7 Prioritize Requirements and Other Product Information

.1 Inputs
 .1 Analysis approach
 .2 Business goals and objectives
 .3 Change requests
 .4 Relationships and dependencies
 .5 Requirements and other product information

.2 Tools & Techniques
 .1 Backlog management
 .2 Goal model and business objectives model
 .3 Iteration planning
 .4 Kanban board
 .5 Prioritization schemes
 .6 Story mapping
 .7 Traceability matrix

.3 Outputs
 .1 Prioritized requirements and other product information

7.3 Define and Elaborate Requirements

.1 Inputs
 .1 Analysis approach
 .2 Analysis models
 .3 Confirmed elicitation results
 .4 Relationships and dependencies
 .5 Stakeholder engagement and communication approach

.2 Tools & Techniques
 .1 Business rules catalog
 .2 Definition of ready
 .3 Glossary
 .4 Product backlog
 .5 Requirements management tool
 .6 Story elaboration
 .7 Story slicing
 .8 Use case
 .9 User story

.3 Outputs
 .1 Requirements and other product information

7.8 Identify and Analyze Product Risks

.1 Inputs
 .1 Analysis approach
 .2 Business goals and objectives
 .3 Enterprise environmental factors
 .4 Product scope
 .5 Requirements and other product information

.2 Tools & Techniques
 .1 Context diagram
 .2 Ecosystem map
 .3 Elicitation techniques
 .4 Estimation techniques
 .5 Organizational chart
 .6 Process flows
 .7 Product backlog
 .8 Risk burndown chart
 .9 Risk register
 .10 Root cause and opportunity analysis
 .11 SWOT analysis

.3 Outputs
 .1 Product risk analysis

7.4 Define Acceptance Criteria

.1 Inputs
 .1 Analysis approach
 .2 Analysis models
 .3 Requirements and other product information
 .4 Solution evaluation approach

.2 Tools & Techniques
 .1 Behavior-driven development
 .2 Definition of done
 .3 Story elaboration

.3 Outputs
 .1 Acceptance criteria

7.9 Assess Product Design Options

.1 Inputs
 .1 Business goals and objectives
 .2 Enterprise and business architectures
 .3 Prioritized requirements and other product information

.2 Tools & Techniques
 .1 Affinity diagram
 .2 Brainstorming
 .3 Competitive analysis
 .4 Focus groups
 .5 Product backlog
 .6 Real options
 .7 Vendor assessment

.3 Output
 .1 Viable product design options

Figure 7-1. Analysis Overview

The PMI Guide to Business Analysis

KEY CONCEPTS FOR ANALYSIS

Analysis is the process of examining, breaking down, synthesizing, and clarifying information to further understand, complete, and improve it. Analysis is one of the primary activities performed on any portfolio, program, or project, and typically warrants the commitment of a significant amount of effort. Beyond analyzing, modeling, and documenting product information, analysis completes the set of product information by ensuring that it is correct, conforms to standards, can be traced to goals, has inherent risks identified, and can be turned into the product design.

Analysis can be performed on any product information; however, there is a focus on requirements-related information. The type of product information and the format it takes are highly dependent on the project life cycle. Analysis processes are often performed iteratively and in conjunction with elicitation processes.

7.1 DETERMINE ANALYSIS APPROACH

Determine Analysis Approach is the process of thinking ahead about how analysis will be performed, including what will be analyzed; which models will be most beneficial to produce; and how requirements and other product information will be verified, validated, and prioritized. The key benefit of this process is that it supports a shared understanding of the business analysis work to be performed to develop the solution. The inputs, tools and techniques, and outputs of the process are depicted in Figure 7-2. Figure 7-3 depicts the data flow diagram for the process.

Inputs
.1 Elicitation approach
.2 Product scope
.3 Situation statement
.4 Traceability and monitoring approach

Tools & Techniques
.1 Brainstorming
.2 Document analysis
.3 Retrospectives and lessons learned

Outputs
.1 Analysis approach

Figure 7-2. Determine Analysis Approach: Inputs, Tools and Techniques, and Outputs

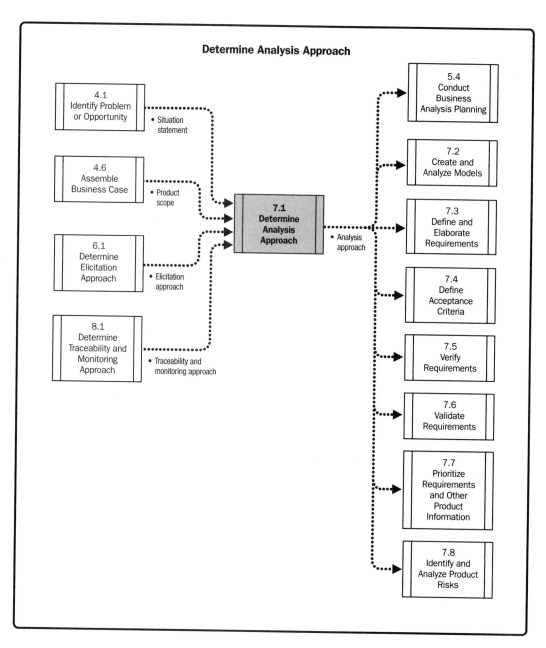

Figure 7-3. Determine Analysis Approach: Data Flow Diagram

The analysis approach identifies the relevant types of product information that will be considered during business analysis. It includes an idea of the models that would be beneficial to produce, the requirements attributes that need to be captured, and an explanation about how product information will be verified, validated, and prioritized.

When using a predictive delivery approach, the analysis approach should also define the requirements life cycle for the portfolio, program, or project. The requirements life cycle represents the various phases or states through which a requirement moves as it is defined, elaborated, verified, validated, and prioritized. When using an adaptive delivery approach, the requirement states may be more implicit. User stories may be stated as not ready, ready, or done, where done is coupled to the delivery and acceptance of that portion of the solution that satisfies the requirement.

Requirements attributes are further discussed in Section 5.2.3.1 of *Business Analysis for Practitioners: A Practice Guide*.

The analysis approach uses the requirements architecture defined in Section 8.1, which specifies how requirements, models, and other product information relate to one another. The analysis approach also identifies which analysis models are most appropriate and how they will trace to one another. The analysis approach defines which analysis activities are pertinent, which templates to start from when documenting requirements, which tools to use, and how any of those might be modified. For organizations with less formal documentation needs, the analysis approach may specify whether snapshots of sketches or informal notes from analysis sessions need to be kept or when more formal documentation is advisable.

An analysis approach involves thinking about what analysis activities and techniques are likely to be useful, when they should be used, who should be involved, and which format is appropriate for any artifacts produced, based on a variety of factors, including complexity, risk, and value. In adaptive life cycles, determining the analysis approach may not be formally named, but the activities to determine the analysis approach are still similar. Determining the analysis approach should include:

◆ When and how models will be created and analyzed, which models are most appropriate, which stakeholders will be using and reviewing the models, which modeling language to use, and how detailed the models should be;

◆ When requirements definition and elaboration will occur and the level of depth that is appropriate for the requirements;

◆ An approach for defining acceptance criteria that describes when and what level of acceptance criteria to capture;

◆ An approach for verification to understand who will be involved in verifying requirements, when verification will occur and how frequently, and how best to ensure that requirements are well written, understood, and compliant with any standards;

◆ How to validate requirements to understand what information is used for validation and who should be involved in ensuring that the requirements achieve the business goals and objectives;

◆ A prioritization approach early in the portfolio, program, or project to ensure that stakeholders have correct expectations about how priorities will be determined and who has the authority to decide priorities;

◆ An approach to identify and manage risks to ensure that important risks are not overlooked during analysis activities; and

◆ An approach for assessing product design early so that the level and timing of design work is agreed upon.

Not all techniques need to be decided upon before analysis begins, but by thinking ahead, it is more likely that business analysts will be prepared to use a variety of techniques. Part of planning for analysis includes determining which types of analysis tools and techniques would be most beneficial given what is known about the participants, portfolio, program, or project at any given point in time. Some analysis might not be planned until it is time to perform the analysis, and, in other cases, the predefined analysis approach will just be updated when needed. Planning for various analysis approaches is further discussed in Section 3 of *Business Analysis for Practitioners: A Practice Guide*.

Analysis is most effective when it is conducted concurrently with elicitation. Analysis frequently provokes relevant and important questions about the situation, requiring more elicitation. Regardless of the project life cycle used, elicitation and analysis are usually iterative and intertwined; therefore, determining the analysis approach is an activity that will be performed repeatedly throughout the duration of a portfolio, program, or project.

7.1.1 DETERMINE ANALYSIS APPROACH: INPUTS

7.1.1.1 ELICITATION APPROACH

Described in Section 6.1.3.1. The elicitation approach explains how elicitation will be performed, including the elicitation activities that will be conducted. Business analysis teams use the elicitation approach as a starting point for determining some aspects of the analysis approach. The planned elicitation techniques and their outputs might influence which analysis techniques are applicable. The timing of individual elicitation activities will affect when related analysis activities happen. The timing of stakeholder involvement in elicitation activities will impact the timing of analysis based on when elicitation outputs will be ready. However, elicitation does not need to be complete to start analysis, and in fact, small increments of both are often performed concurrently.

7.1.1.2 PRODUCT SCOPE

Described in Section 4.6.3.2. Product scope is defined as the features and functions that characterize a solution. The product scope defines the boundaries within which analysis takes place.

7.1.1.3 SITUATION STATEMENT

Described in Section 4.1.3.2. The situation statement provides an objective statement about the problem or opportunity the business is looking to address, along with the effect and impact the situation is having on the organization. The situation statement provides context about the problems or opportunities being analyzed to help determine what information will need to be analyzed and how it might need to be analyzed. Business analysts are confronted with different types of information, and the situation statement helps separate out irrelevant information that might interfere with proper analysis.

7.1.1.4 TRACEABILITY AND MONITORING APPROACH

Described in Section 8.1.3.1. The traceability and monitoring approach defines the traceability and change management processes for the portfolio, program, project, or product. One of the components of that approach is how the requirements, models, and other product information relate to one another, which is an important input for selecting analysis techniques that support creating models, using the models together, and identifying requirements from the models.

7.1.2 DETERMINE ANALYSIS APPROACH: TOOLS AND TECHNIQUES

7.1.2.1 BRAINSTORMING

Brainstorming is a technique used to identify a list of ideas within a short period of time. When determining the analysis approach, brainstorming is helpful to identify analysis tools and techniques, including ones that might be outside a business analyst's typical tool set. For more information on brainstorming, see Section 5.1.2.1.

7.1.2.2 DOCUMENT ANALYSIS

Document analysis is an elicitation technique used to analyze existing documentation to identify relevant product information. Document analysis can help determine which existing models in the organization could be used as a starting point for analysis, thereby affecting which analysis activities need to be performed and how long they will take. For more information on document analysis, see Section 6.3.2.3.

7.1.2.3 RETROSPECTIVES AND LESSONS LEARNED

Retrospectives and lessons learned use past experience to plan for future work. When determining an analysis approach, retrospectives and lessons learned can leverage past analysis experiences to plan for future analysis work. When determining the analysis approach, review what worked and what may require improvement in a past similar situation. Retrospectives and lessons learned, combined with experience and expert judgment, are the basis for tailoring the analysis approach to fit the needs of the portfolio, program, or project and organization. For more information on retrospectives and lessons learned, see Section 5.7.2.4.

7.1.3 DETERMINE ANALYSIS APPROACH: OUTPUTS

7.1.3.1 ANALYSIS APPROACH

The analysis approach describes how analysis will be performed; how to verify, validate, and prioritize requirements and other product information; how risks will be identified and analyzed; how design options will be assessed; and which techniques and templates are expected to be used to perform any analysis. The analysis approach includes which requirements attributes need to be captured and how the requirements architecture impacts analyzing models. It also describes what other information or models from the organization might be used during analysis. This output will likely be updated throughout the course of the portfolio, program, or project.

7.1.4 DETERMINE ANALYSIS APPROACH: TAILORING CONSIDERATIONS

Adaptive and predictive tailoring considerations for Determine Analysis Approach are described in Table 7-1.

Table 7-1. Adaptive and Predictive Tailoring for Determine Analysis Approach

Aspects to Be Tailored	Typical Adaptive Considerations	Typical Predictive Considerations
Name	Not a formally named process	Determine Analysis Approach
Approach	Describes the types of product information to be defined and refined during analysis. Though some high-level planning might occur, most of the analysis approach is defined just before or early in each iteration for the analysis that will occur during that iteration. Analysis performed in one iteration might not be used by the development team until a later iteration.	A high-level analysis approach is defined early, during a planning phase. The analysis approach is refined throughout the portfolio, program, or project. It describes types of product information to be defined and refined during analysis.
Deliverables	Not a separate deliverable.	Detailed analysis approach resides in a business analysis plan.

7.1.5 DETERMINE ANALYSIS APPROACH: COLLABORATION POINT

Based on their own experiences, business analysts work together as peers to help identify analysis tools, templates, and techniques that might be relevant. Collaboration with other business analysts who may be responsible for different aspects of product information is also recommended to avoid duplication of effort and to ensure continuity of analysis activities.

7.2 CREATE AND ANALYZE MODELS

Create and Analyze Models is the process of creating structured representations, such as diagrams, tables, or structured text, of any product information to facilitate further analysis by identifying gaps in information or uncovering extraneous information. The key benefit of this process is that it helps convey information in an organized manner that provides clarity and helps achieve correctness and completeness. The inputs, tools and techniques, and outputs of the process are depicted in Figure 7-4. Figure 7-5 depicts the data flow diagram for the process.

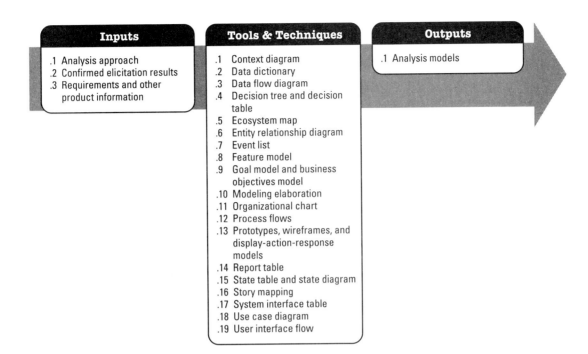

Inputs	Tools & Techniques	Outputs
.1 Analysis approach .2 Confirmed elicitation results .3 Requirements and other product information	.1 Context diagram .2 Data dictionary .3 Data flow diagram .4 Decision tree and decision table .5 Ecosystem map .6 Entity relationship diagram .7 Event list .8 Feature model .9 Goal model and business objectives model .10 Modeling elaboration .11 Organizational chart .12 Process flows .13 Prototypes, wireframes, and display-action-response models .14 Report table .15 State table and state diagram .16 Story mapping .17 System interface table .18 Use case diagram .19 User interface flow	.1 Analysis models

Figure 7-4. Create and Analyze Models: Inputs, Tools and Techniques, and Outputs

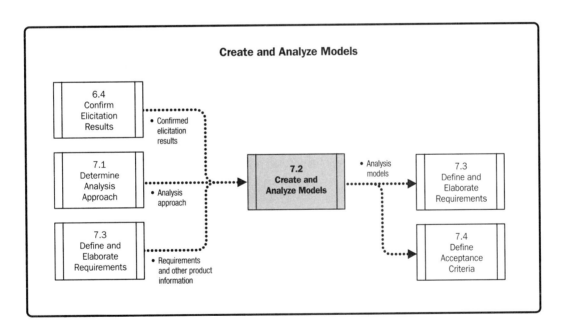

Figure 7-5. Create and Analyze Models: Data Flow Diagram

Models are visual representations of information, in the form of diagrams, tables, or structured text, that effectively arrange and convey a lot of information in a concise manner. Create and Analyze Models includes both developing the analysis models determined by the analysis approach and using those models to improve the overall product information. Analyzing models is helpful for finding gaps in information and identifying extraneous information by exploring the solution from multiple perspectives. Models provide context to discussions and analysis and provide for better understanding of complex relationships and concepts. Often, models can convey information more clearly than textual descriptions. Models provide a concise format to present information and can be used to clarify and discover information with stakeholders. Analyzing models involves looking at a few pieces of information, not necessarily the whole set of information, and finding patterns to explore the problem space further.

When performed in conjunction with elicitation, creating and analyzing models can be solitary or interactive activities. Creating and analyzing activities are highly iterative. Drafts of models are created based on the confirmed elicitation results. Those models might go back through elicitation sessions to identify new information to be refined and reanalyzed in the models. The Create and Analyze Models process is often performed concurrently with Sections 7.5 on Verify Requirements and 7.6 on Validate Requirements.

Models are important inputs to business analysis activities that occur outside of the Create and Analyze Models process, including:

◆ Defining and elaborating requirements;

◆ Building a shared understanding of the information;

◆ Mapping the relationships and dependencies within and across portfolios, programs, and projects;

◆ Finding information gaps that require additional elicitation;

◆ Identifying stakeholders who weren't previously included;

◆ Facilitating stakeholder understanding of the information during elicitation or review;

◆ Assessing capability gaps between the current and future states of a product;

◆ Analyzing changes to identify which areas of a product are impacted;

◆ Understanding what is of value for users;

◆ Prioritizing product information or projects in a portfolio;

◆ Estimating business analysis work; and

◆ Providing a business perspective on architectural designs.

The previous activities might require updates to existing models or the creation of new models.

The models are organized into five categories: (1) scope models (bounding the solution), (2) process models (how the solution will be used), (3) rule models (rules the solution needs to enforce), (4) data models (data used in a process or system and its life cycle), and (5) interface models (how the solution interacts with other systems and users). By analyzing the solution from these five different views or categories of models, a business analyst can obtain a complete picture of the product. The models are organized by category in Table 7-2.

Table 7-2. Models Organized by Category

Category	Example Models	Example Models
Scope Models	Models that structure and organize the features, functions, and boundaries of the business domain being analyzed	• Context diagram • Ecosystem map • Event list • Feature model • Goal and business objectives model • Organizational chart (Section 5.1.2.3) • Use case diagram
Process Models	Models that describe the business processes and ways in which stakeholders interact with those processes	• Process flow • Use case (Section 7.3.2.8) • User story (Section 7.3.2.9)
Rule Models	Models of concepts and behaviors that define or constrain aspects of a business in order to enforce established business policies	• Business rules catalog (Section 7.3.2.1) • Decision table • Decision tree
Data Models	Models that document the data used in a process or system and its life cycle	• Data dictionary • Data flow diagram • Entity relationship diagram • State diagram • State table
Interface Models	Models that assist in understanding specific systems and their relationships within a solution and with users	• Display-action-response model • Prototype • Report table • System interface table • User interface flow • Wireframe

There are many modeling languages, and each has its strengths and weaknesses. A few example languages are discussed in Section 4.10.6 of *Business Analysis for Practitioners: A Practice Guide*.

There is no single model that shows everything that is useful in a portfolio, program, or project. Similarly, no situation ever requires all models to be created. Some models are more useful in certain domains than others. Some models that are useful to complete business analysis might be created by more technical resources on the team. Business analysis involves choosing the models that are most useful given what is known about the situation and determining who best to collaborate with to create and review them. While models can provide clarity over textual descriptions, some analysis models may require that text be used to elaborate upon the visual to help stakeholders understand how to read and interpret the model. In these cases, text and visual elements work nicely together to relay the proper level of information.

The techniques section of this process describes many choices of models that can be used for analysis purposes. In Section 7.2.2.10, there is one technique, modeling elaboration, which is not a model; rather, it describes how to use models together to confirm completeness or find gaps. A few models are described in other locations in this guide; their sections are identified in Table 7-2. There are also models not described in this guide. Business analysts may use different models or even find it necessary to craft a new model in some cases.

7.2.1 CREATE AND ANALYZE MODELS: INPUTS

7.2.1.1 ANALYSIS APPROACH

Described in Section 7.1.3.1. The analysis approach, which defines how to conduct analysis, includes a list of candidate models to be created. As the models are analyzed, new model types might need to be created and the analysis approach may need to be updated. The analysis approach also describes the requirements architecture that describes which models are most likely to relate to one another for modeling elaboration. For information on modeling elaboration, see Section 7.2.2.10.

7.2.1.2 CONFIRMED ELICITATION RESULTS

Described in Section 6.4.3.1. Confirmed elicitation results signify that the product team has reached a common understanding about the elicitation results and agrees on the accuracy of the information elicited. Confirmed elicitation results include notes, requirements, and other outputs from completed elicitation activities. These results include the information that is needed to create first-draft models. As the models are created and analyzed for gaps, the business analyst may discover additional questions about scope, processes, rules, data, or interfaces that will require additional elicitation.

7.2.1.3 REQUIREMENTS AND OTHER PRODUCT INFORMATION

Described in Section 7.3.3.1. Requirements and other product information include all information about a solution and are the culmination of results from elicitation and analysis activities. The subset of this information that is most relevant as an input is any previously defined requirements, acceptance criteria, and other analysis models. As work progresses, the volume of requirements and other product information will grow or be refined, providing additional context to create new models or analyze existing ones.

7.2.2 CREATE AND ANALYZE MODELS: TOOLS AND TECHNIQUES

7.2.2.1 CONTEXT DIAGRAM

A context diagram is a scope model that shows all the direct system and human interfaces to systems within a solution. A context diagram clearly depicts the in-scope systems and any inputs or outputs, including the systems or actors providing or receiving them.

Like ecosystem maps, which are described in Section 7.2.2.5, context diagrams are generally created early to define scope and can be updated as new information is identified. They also help identify interface requirements and data requirements. Figure 7-6 shows a sample format of a context diagram. Context diagrams are further discussed and an example is provided in Section 4.10.7.3 of *Business Analysis for Practitioners: A Practice Guide.*

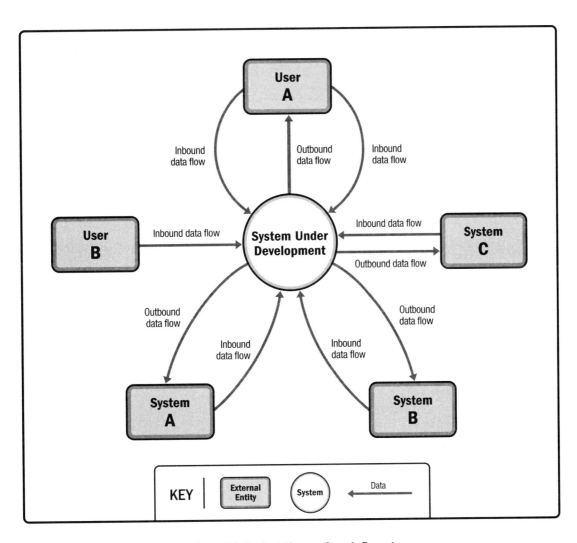

Figure 7-6. Context Diagram Sample Format

7.2.2.2 DATA DICTIONARY

A data dictionary is a data model that lists the data fields and attributes of those fields for a data object. The data fields are additional details for the data objects in an entity relationship diagram, which are described in Section 7.2.2.6. The attributes specify information about the fields, including business rules enforced by data.

Data dictionaries are often created after other data models have first been used to identify the data objects and when those objects need more details specified. Data dictionaries can be pulled from existing systems as a register of all data in the system and used as an input for system enhancements. They are typically created in conjunction with defining the requirements and acceptance criteria. Figure 7-7 shows a sample format of a data dictionary. There are typically many more columns in a data dictionary than are shown in Figure 7-7. Data dictionaries are further discussed and an example is provided in Section 4.10.10.3 of *Business Analysis for Practitioners: A Practice Guide*.

ID	Business Data Object	Field Name	Example Attribute 1: Data Type	Example Attribute 2: Data Type	Example Attribute 3: Data Type	Example Attribute 4: Data Type	Example Attribute 5: Data Type
BDO001	Business Object Name 1	Field Name 1	Alphanumeric				
BDO002	Business Object Name 1	Field Name 2	Graphic				
BDO003	Business Object Name 1	Field Name 3	Integer				
BDO004	Business Object Name 1	Field Name 4	Integer				
BDO005	Business Object Name 2	Field Name 5	Alphanumeric				
BDO006	Business Object Name 2	Field Name 6	Alphanumeric				

Figure 7-7. Data Dictionary Sample Format

7.2.2.3 DATA FLOW DIAGRAM

A data flow diagram is a data model that is used to describe the movement of data between external entities, data stores, and processes. External entities can be actors or systems. Data flow diagrams show the data inputs and outputs for each process.

Data flow diagrams are usually created during analysis. Entity relationship diagrams, process flows, and ecosystem maps are usually created first to identify the data objects, processes, and systems to show in a data flow diagram. Figure 7-8 shows a sample format of a data flow diagram. Data flow diagrams are further discussed and an example is provided in Section 4.10.10.2 of *Business Analysis for Practitioners: A Practice Guide*.

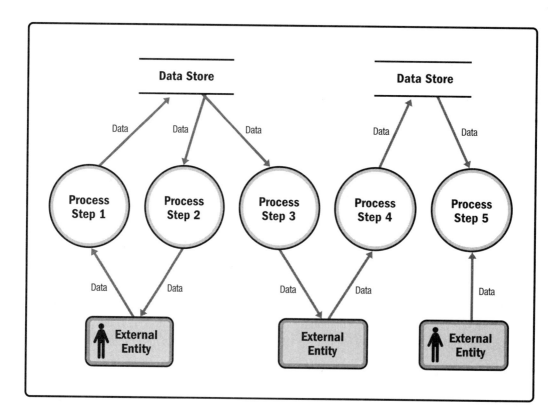

Figure 7-8. Data Flow Diagram Sample Format

7.2.2.4 DECISION TREE AND DECISION TABLE

A decision tree and decision table are rule models that show a series of decisions and the outcomes to which the decisions lead. Decision trees and tables are often used to model business rules. The two decision models are used in different ways, and both might be needed. Decision trees visually show the flow of decisions and choices that lead to an outcome and can show ordered decisions. Decision tables are useful for ensuring that the business analyst has considered all possible combinations of decision scenarios and related outcomes.

Both decision models can be employed at any point to further analyze decision logic. Decision trees are usually easier for stakeholders to review than decision tables. Both decision trees and decision tables are useful as a foundation for test case creation, with each combination of decisions and outcomes being a test case. Figure 7-9 shows a sample format of a decision tree and Figure 7-10 shows a sample format of a decision table. Decision trees and decision tables and are further discussed and examples are provided in Section 4.10.9.2 of *Business Analysis for Practitioners: A Practice Guide.*

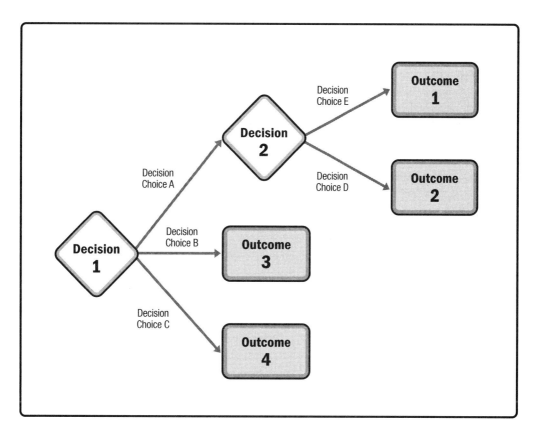

Figure 7-9. Decision Tree Sample Format

Decision Table	Rule 1	Rule 2	Rule 3	Rule 4
Conditions				
Condition 1	Decision Choice A	Decision Choice A	Decision Choice B	Decision Choice C
Condition 2	Decision Choice E	Decision Choice D	–	–
Condition 3	–	–	–	–
Outcomes				
Outcome 1	X	–	–	–
Outcome 2	–	X	–	–
Outcome 3	–	–	X	–
Outcome 4	–	–	–	X

Figure 7-10. Decision Table Sample Format

7.2.2.5 ECOSYSTEM MAP

An ecosystem map is a scope model that shows all the relevant systems, the relationships between systems, and optionally, any data objects passed between them. The systems are logical systems (business view); therefore, they may not match physical systems (implementation view) in architectural diagrams.

Ecosystem maps are most useful when they are created at the beginning of projects to understand all the systems that may be affected by or that will impact the in-scope systems. Ecosystem maps can be created for portfolios or programs to help identify potential dependencies between projects. The ecosystem map allows the business analyst to see where there are possible interface requirements or data requirements for systems directly interfacing to the solution and for those up- or downstream from the solution. Figure 7-11 shows a sample format of an ecosystem map. Ecosystem maps are further discussed and an example is provided in Section 4.10.7.2 *of Business Analysis for Practitioners: A Practice Guide.*

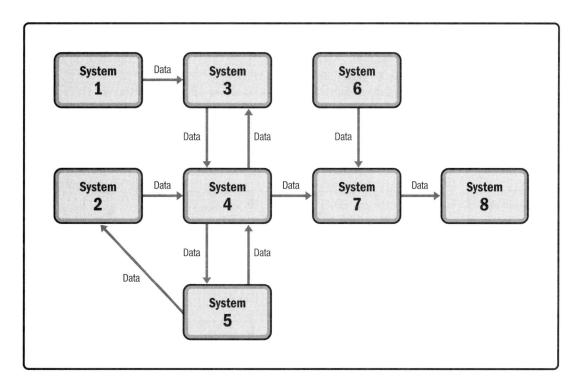

Figure 7-11. Ecosystem Map Sample Format

7.2.2.6 ENTITY RELATIONSHIP DIAGRAM

An entity relationship diagram (ERD), also called a business data diagram, is a data model that shows the business data objects or pieces of information of interest in a product and the cardinality relationship between those objects. Cardinality is the number of times that one entity occurs in relationship to the other entity in the relationship, and whether the relationship is required or optional. The data objects shown in an ERD are not meant to be exact data objects in a database, but rather a conceptual view of the data in the solution from the perspective of the business. The entity relationship diagram helps identify the data that are created in, consumed by, or output from a system. When used alongside process models, ERDs can be used to model the data of importance from a process perspective.

ERDs are typically created relatively early in analysis to understand the scope of the data to be analyzed. This model also helps identify any processes that might create, consume, or manipulate the data, as well as business rules about the data. ERDs are also a likely input for database designers and architects to use in database design. Figure 7-12 shows a sample format of an entity relationship diagram. ERDs are further discussed and an example is provided in Section 4.10.10.1 of *Business Analysis for Practitioners: A Practice Guide*.

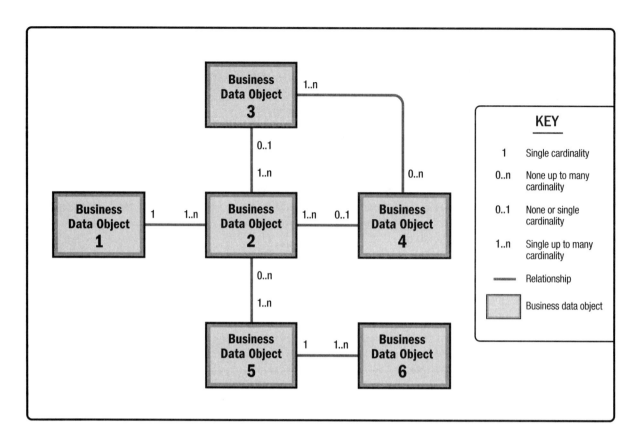

Figure 7-12. Entity Relationship Diagram Sample Format

7.2.2.7 EVENT LIST

An event list is a scope model that describes any external events that trigger solution behavior. Event lists help define the in-scope events that the solution has to react to or handle. An event response table is a related model that extends the event list to describe the system's response to any event triggers.

Event lists are created early to ensure that the scope of work is defined and might be updated as work continues and new events are identified. Event response tables are created to help identify likely use cases, user stories, or system flows. Figure 7-13 shows a sample format of an event response table where an event list would be composed of the first two columns.

Event Response Table			
ID	Event	System State	System Response
1	Event 1	System State 1	System Response to Event 1 and System State 1
2	Event 2	System State 1	System Response to Event 2 and System State 1
3	Event 3	System State 2	System Response to Event 3 and System State 2
4	Event 4	System State 2	System Response to Event 4 and System State 2
5	Event 5	System State 3	System Response to Event 5 and System State 3

Figure 7-13. Event Response Table Sample Format

7.2.2.8 FEATURE MODEL

A feature model is a scope model that visually represents all the features of a solution arranged in a tree or hierarchical structure. Most projects have features at varying levels; the top-level features are called Level 1 (L1) features, followed by Level 2 (L2) features, and so on. Feature models are helpful to show how features are grouped together and which features are subfeatures of other ones. Feature models are useful because they can easily display many features across different levels on a single page, which may represent an entire solution's feature set.

This model is typically started at the beginning of a project to show all the features that are in scope for a program or project, and is updated as additional features are identified during elicitation and analysis. In adaptive projects, features can be labeled for inclusion in different iterations to facilitate release planning. The feature model can be used in combination with a brainstorming technique to help stakeholders identify features by focusing on the groupings, similar to an affinity diagram. Affinity diagrams are described in Section 4.3.2.1. Figure 7-14 shows a sample format of a feature model. Feature models are further discussed and an example is provided in Section 4.10.7.4 of *Business Analysis for Practitioners: A Practice Guide*.

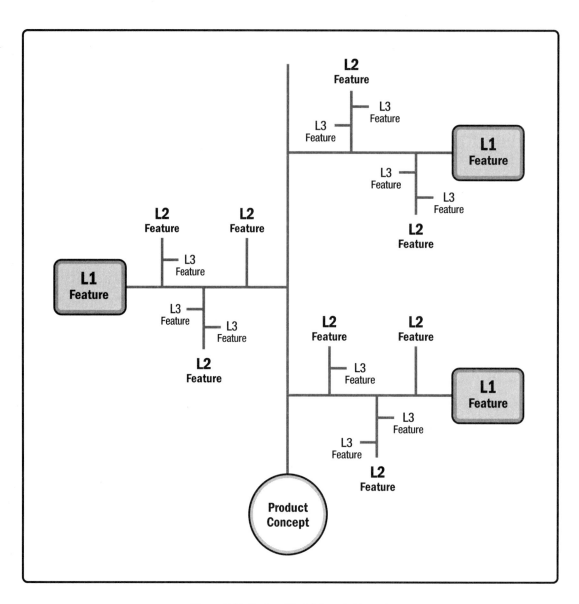

Figure 7-14. Feature Model Sample Format

7.2.2.9 GOAL MODEL AND BUSINESS OBJECTIVES MODEL

A goal model and business objectives model are scope models that organize and reflect the goals and business objectives in relation to other product information. Goal models typically show the stakeholder goals for a solution, with any supporting or conflicting goal relationships indicated. Business objectives models relate the business problems, business objectives, and top-level features. Goal models and business objectives models are typically created at the start of a new program or project or earlier to help prioritize programs and projects within a portfolio. They can be created at any point, for prioritization purposes.

In business objectives models, business problems and business objectives decompose high-level business strategies into lower-level problems and business objectives to visually represent the value of the portfolio, program, or project and how the solution will achieve the business objectives. Whether the value is identified as increasing revenue, decreasing cost, or avoiding penalties, goal models and business objectives models visually represent the value that supports feature prioritization decisions and product scope management.

Figure 7-15 shows a sample format of a business objectives model. Business objectives models are further discussed and an example is provided in Section 4.10.7.1 of *Business Analysis for Practitioners: A Practice Guide*.

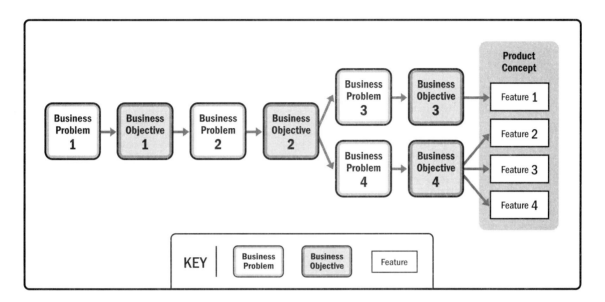

Figure 7-15. Business Objectives Model Sample Format

7.2.2.10 MODELING ELABORATION

Modeling elaboration is a technique that uses the collection of models together to further identify gaps, inconsistencies, or redundancies in product information. The requirements architecture, as defined in the analysis approach, will help determine which models are best to use together. Models can be collectively used to help complete one another. For example, a model that shows the steps people take to perform a task, like process flows, can be compared to organizational charts to ensure that all stakeholders are covered in some process flow and all people who perform steps are covered in organizational charts.

◆ **Traceability matrix.** A traceability matrix is a table that connects or traces links between items. Most commonly, business analysts use traceability matrices to trace requirements backward to features and business objectives or forward to code or other development artifacts or test cases. However, during the Create and Analyze Models process, the business analyst can repurpose the traceability matrix to analyze models to ensure that they are complete.

Common comparisons to make between models and elements of models include:

■ Features in a feature model to features in a business objectives model,

■ Process flows to features in a feature model that provide functionality,

■ Display-action-response models to steps in user interface flows or process flows,

- Data items in the data flow diagram to objects in an entity relationship diagram,

- System interface tables to systems in an ecosystem map, and

- Transitions in state tables or state diagrams to process flows.

Figure 7-16 shows a sample format of using a traceability matrix to map a few requirements objects to do modeling elaboration. For more information on a traceability matrix, see Section 8.2.2.5. Although traceability matrices can be used to systematically compare some models, models can also be similarly compared to one another less formally, even manually by looking at models side by side.

L1 Process Step	L2 Process Step	Feature	REQID	Requirement
L1 Process Step 1	L2 Process Step 1	Feature 1	REQ001	Requirement 1
L1 Process Step 1	L2 Process Step 2	Feature 1	REQ002	Requirement 2
L1 Process Step 1	L2 Process Step 3	Feature 2	REQ003	Requirement 3
L1 Process Step 2	L2 Process Step 1	Feature 3	REQ004	Requirement 4
L1 Process Step 2	L2 Process Step 2	Feature 4	REQ005	Requirement 5

Figure 7-16. Modeling Elaboration Using Traceability Sample Format

◆ **Interaction matrix.** An interaction matrix is a lightweight version of a traceability matrix that is used to figure out whether requirements are sufficiently detailed or if any entities are missing. The main difference between the two types of traceability matrices is that an interaction matrix represents a specific point in time. As a result, interaction matrices are not maintained and are simply used to evaluate requirements at any given time during a project.

In an interaction matrix, the rows are one type of product information, typically in the form of use cases, user stories, or process flows. The columns of the matrix are the names of a different type of product information, such as a data entity, business rule, or user interface. The matrix is populated by placing an X in the box where the row product information uses the column product information or entity. Figure 7-17 shows a sample format of using an interaction matrix to map a few process flows to entities.

REQID	Requirement	Entity A	Entity B	Entity C	Entity D	Entity E	Column 1
REQ001	Requirement 1	X	X				
REQ002	Requirement 2	X		X			
REQ003	Requirement 3						
REQ004	Requirement 4					X	
REQ005	Requirement 5	X					

Figure 7-17. Modeling Elaboration Using Interaction Matrix Sample Format

◆ **CRUD matrix.** CRUD, defined as create (C), read (R), update (U), and delete (D), represents the operations that can be applied to data or objects. CRUD matrices describe who or what has permission to perform each of the CRUD operations on elements, such as data or user interface screens.

7.2.2.11 ORGANIZATIONAL CHART

An organizational chart, or org chart, is a scope model that shows the reporting structure within an organization or within a part of an organization. Org charts used during analysis might vary from those used in stakeholder analysis. An org chart is used to help identify who might use or be impacted by a solution, not necessarily just those working closely with the portfolio, program, or project. For analysis purposes, org charts might describe departments across the organization, roles within those departments, or individuals in the reporting structure. Org charts are used in conjunction with other models to ensure that all stakeholders who perform process steps, interact with systems, or use data in the solution are identified. Org charts can also help when looking to identify users or groups of users that have security and permissions requirements.

An org chart is created early and updated throughout so that any missing stakeholders or stakeholder groups can be identified for elicitation purposes. Figure 7-18 shows a sample format of an organizational chart. For more information on organizational charts, see Section 5.1.2.3.

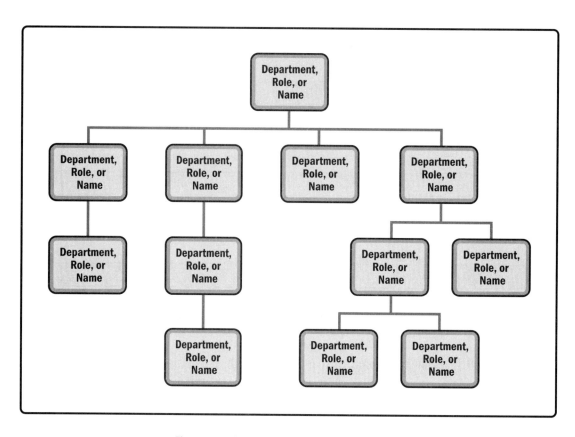

Figure 7-18. Organizational Chart Sample Format

7.2.2.12 PROCESS FLOWS

Process flows are in the process model category and are used to visually document the steps or tasks that people perform in their jobs or when they interact with a solution. Typically, process flows describe the steps that people take, although they may describe system steps and could be called system flows. Other names for process flows are swim lane diagrams, process maps, process diagrams, or process flow charts. Process flows can be organized into multiple levels, where a Level 1 (L1) process flow would show an entire end-to-end process at a high level in seven to ten steps. The steps in an L1 process flow are decomposed into the next level of processes that the user would perform and represented as Level 2 (L2) process flows. Process flows might be created as both as-is and to-be representations of the business processes so that the changes or enhancements to current solutions can be shown visually. The process flows might be accompanied by additional details to ensure that stakeholders can understand what occurs with each step.

Value stream maps are a variation of process flows. In addition to information in a traditional process flow, a value stream map shows any delays, queues, or handoffs that occur during the process. The purpose of a value stream map is to identify any time spent in the process that does not add value so it can be streamlined.

Activity diagrams are another version of process flows that can be used for general workflow modeling, but commonly are used to visually show the complex flow of use cases. They are similar to process flows in syntax, but they commonly show user and system interactions in one diagram and mirror the textual description of use cases.

Sequence diagrams are another model that describes how user or system processes interact with one another across any involved users or systems and the order in which the processes or steps are performed. Sequence diagrams are most useful for communicating with technical teams about the flow of information between systems, the delegation of functionality to where it will be performed, and the flow of control from step to step. They are particularly helpful in determining which business objects are needed by showing where the information flows.

Process flows can be created to show how programs or projects can improve processes before projects start and are also created after a project has begun, and continue to be created as product information is progressively elaborated. Figure 7-19 shows a process flow sample format indicative of the level of detail in an L2 process. Process flows are further discussed and an example is provided in Section 4.10.8.1 of *Business Analysis for Practitioners: A Practice Guide.*

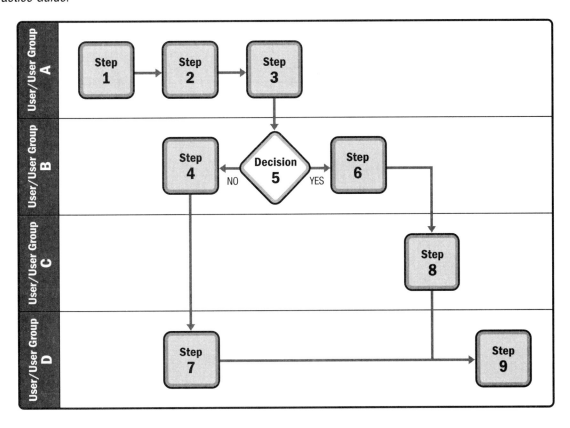

Figure 7-19. Process Flow Sample Format

7.2.2.13 PROTOTYPES, WIREFRAMES, AND DISPLAY-ACTION-RESPONSE MODELS

Prototypes, wireframes, and display-action-response models are all interface models. A prototype is a representation of the expected solution before it is built. Prototypes can be low fidelity, such as a sketch of a screen layout, or high fidelity, such as an interactive user interface. A wireframe is a type of prototype, specifically a mockup of a user interface design, used to show what a screen should look like. A wireframe can be low fidelity, like a sketch, or high fidelity, like an actual representation of what the final user interface should look like. A display-action-response model uses a tabular format to describe page elements and the functions attached to each. A display-action-response model is always used in conjunction with a prototype or wireframe to connect the user interface element requirements to a visual representation.

User interface design might be completed by a user experience expert or user interface analyst. However, business analysis is used to determine how the user interfaces should display and behave in different states of the solution, work together, and interact with underlying business logic.

Prototypes and wireframes, particularly low-fidelity versions, might be created just before the screens are constructed, or all of them could be specified in the middle of an analysis phase. Display-action-response models are generally created at the point that functional requirements or acceptance criteria are being specified. Figure 7-20 shows a sample format of a wireframe and Figure 7-21 shows a sample format of a display-action-response model. For more information on prototypes and how they can be used in context outside of user interface analysis, see Section 6.3.2.8. Wireframes and display-action-response models are further discussed and an example of each is provided in Section 4.10.11.4 of *Business Analysis for Practitioners: A Practice Guide.*

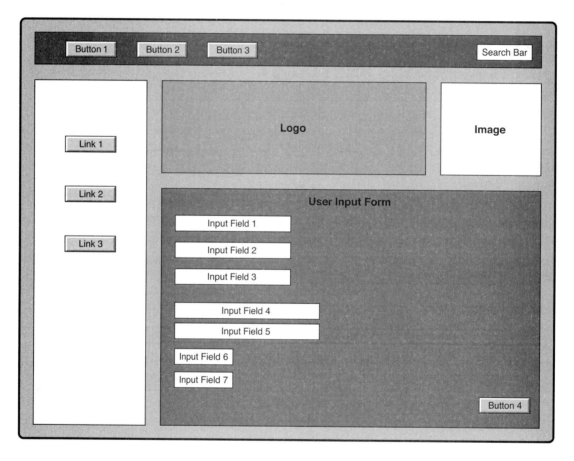

Figure 7-20. Wireframe Sample Format

UI Element: Element Name		
UI Element Description		
ID	Unique ID for the element on the wireframe	
Description	Description of the element	
UI Element Displays		
Precondition	**Display**	
Precondition 1	Display of the element under precondition 1	
Precondition 2	Display of the element under precondition 2	
UI Element Behaviors		
Precondition	**Action**	**Response**
Precondition 1	User action 1	System response under precondition 1
Precondition 2	User action 1	System response under precondition 2
Precondition 1	User action 2	System response under precondition 1
Precondition 2	User action 2	System response under precondition 2

Figure 7-21. Display-Action-Response Model Sample Format

7.2.2.14 REPORT TABLE

A report table is an interface model that describes detailed requirements for a single report. Report tables contain both information about the report as a whole, such as the report name or decisions made from the report, and field-level information, such as which data fields are displayed and any calculations. A report table typically accompanies a prototype of a report to show implementation teams what the report should look like. See Section 7.2.2.13 for more information on how prototypes are used during analysis.

Report tables are usually created any time after an initial list of reports for a solution has been identified and prioritized. Report tables are created for the highest-priority reports first. Figure 7-22 shows a sample format of a report table. Report tables are further discussed and an example is provided in Section 4.10.11.1 of *Business Analysis for Practitioners: A Practice Guide*.

Element	Description
Unique ID	Unique identifier of the report table
Name	Unique and simple report name
Description	A short summary of the report for context
Decisions Made from Report	The business decisions that are made using the information in the report
Objective	The business objectives supported by this report
Priority	The priority to implement this report
Functional Area	The business processes or areas that use the report
Related Reports	List of any other reports that have similar data
Report Owner	Business user(s) who own approval of the report requirements
Report Users	Business user(s) who run or use the report to make decisions
Trigger	What triggers the report to run
Frequency	How often the report is generated and accessed
Latency	How quickly the report is delivered to users in relation to being requested
Transaction Volume	How many transactions are pushed into the repository feeding the report
Data Volume	On average, how much data are expected to be read each time the report is accessed
Security	Security on the report or fields that varies from security specified on the fields in the data dictionary
Persistence	Expected saving of report settings between report sessions
Visual Format	How the report is visually displayed
Delivery Format	How the report is delivered to users for viewing, and any related functionality
Interactivity	Functionality within a report that allows the user to change views or other aspects of the data being displayed
Drilldowns	Links to other related reports or layers of this report with expanded data
Filtered By	The data fields that are used to filter out certain sets of data in the report
Grouped By	Logical groupings of data into separate sections within the report by data
Sorted By	The data fields that are used to sort the data in the report
User Input Parameters	Fields that the user can define to generate the report (different than filtering, grouping, and sorting)
Group Calculation	Data fields that are aggregated and to which a calculation is applied
Calculated Fields	Individual fields that have a calculation applied outside of the data prior to being displayed in the report
Displayed Fields	All fields displayed in the report

Top-Level Elements applies to rows Unique ID through Drilldowns. *Field Elements* applies to rows Filtered By through Displayed Fields.

Figure 7-22. Report Table Sample Format

7.2.2.15 STATE TABLE AND STATE DIAGRAM

The state table and state diagram are data models that show the valid states of an object and any allowed transitions between those states. Objects can be business data items or any piece of information of interest when analyzing a solution. Both models describe all the states within a solution that a single object can hold, as well as how the object transitions between states. State tables model all states as both a column and a row in a table that allows a business analyst to systematically consider each potential state transition (from row to column) to determine if the transition should be allowed or is not capable of being transitioned to from other states. State diagrams, on the other hand, visually depict the states and transitions, but only show valid transitions for the object.

State tables and state diagrams are especially useful for solutions involving workflows, and can help with the discovery of business rules that relate to an object moving from one state to another. State tables are most commonly used for analysis to ensure that all transitions are covered, while state diagrams are easier for stakeholders to visualize the valid transition flow. Figure 7-23 shows a sample format of a state table and Figure 7-24 shows a sample format of a state diagram. State tables and state diagrams are further discussed and an example of each is provided in Section 4.10.10.4 of *Business Analysis for Practitioners: A Practice Guide*.

		Target State						
	State A	**State B**	**State C**	**State D**	**State E**	**State F**	**State G**	**State ...**
State A	no	Transition from A to B	no	no	no	no	no	
State B	no	no	Transition from B to C	Transition from B to D	Transition from B to E	no	no	
State C	no	Transition from C to B	no	Transition from C to D	no	no	Transition from C to G	
State D	no	no	no	no	no	no	no	
State E	no	no	no	no	no	Transition from E to F	Transition from E to G	
State F	no	no	no	no	no	no	Transition from F to G	
State G	no	no	no	no	no	no	no	
State ...								

Figure 7-23. State Table Sample Format

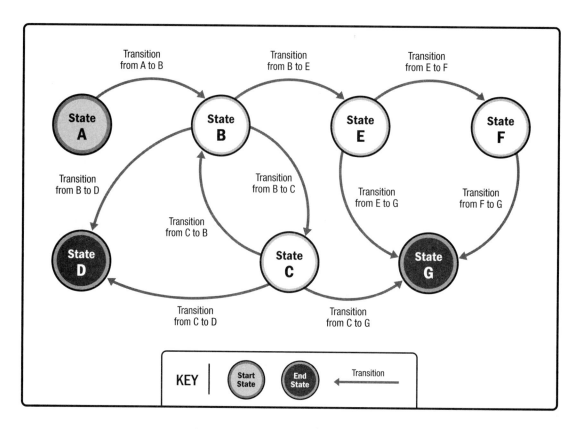

Figure 7-24. State Diagram Sample Format

7.2.2.16 STORY MAPPING

Story mapping is a technique used to sequence user stories, based upon their business value and the order in which their users typically perform them, so that teams can arrive at a shared understanding of what will be built. Story maps help break capabilities down into user stories and can be used to identify gaps in the users' capabilities.

Story maps include two foundational parts: the backbone and the walking skeleton. The backbone is the minimum set of capabilities that absolutely have to be in the first release for the solution to serve its purpose. That set of capabilities is sometimes called the minimum viable product (MVP). The capabilities are often described as features, epics, or user stories. The walking skeleton is the full set of end-to-end functionality that the stakeholders require for the solution to be accepted or considered functional. This set is usually described by a set of user stories and is sometimes called the minimum marketable features (MMF). Individual additional user stories are added below related user stories in the walking skeleton to make up the vertical groupings. The stories are ranked in order of highest business value at the top to lowest business value at the bottom. Figure 7-25 shows a sample format of a story map. For more information on how story mapping is also used to prioritize user stories to help ensure value is being delivered, see Section 7.7.2.6.

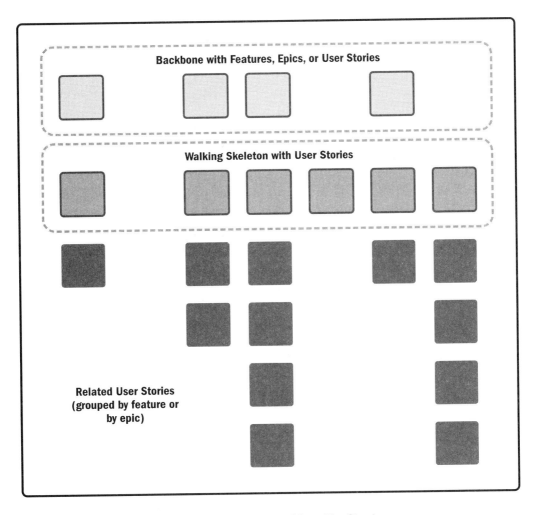

Backbone with Features, Epics, or User Stories

Walking Skeleton with User Stories

**Related User Stories
(grouped by feature or
by epic)**

Figure 7-25. Sample Format of Story Map Structure

7.2.2.17 SYSTEM INTERFACE TABLE

A system interface table is an interface model that captures all the detailed level requirements for a single system interface. System interface tables are created for each system that interfaces to the solution system. System interface tables include information such as the data fields passed from one system to another, the frequency and volume of the data passed, and any validation rules needed to ensure that the data are passed and stored correctly.

System interface tables are usually created after the ecosystem map and context diagram have been created to identify the interfaces. Their format is conducive to representing interface-related requirements and acceptance criteria. Figure 7-26 shows a sample format of a system interface table. System interface tables are further discussed and an example is provided in Section 4.10.11.2 of *Business Analysis for Practitioners: A Practice Guide.*

System Interface	
Source	System information is flowing from
Target	System information is flowing to
ID	Unique identifier
Description	Short description about the nature of the interface
Frequency	How often the information needs to be passed (real-time, once per day, monthly, etc.)
Volume	Total units in an interval (number/unit)
Security Constraints	Refers to any security or privacy needs on the business data object (encrypting fields in the data)
Error Handling	Reference to a process flow to describe how errors are handled

Interface Objects			
Object	**Field**	**Data Dictionary ID**	**Validation Rule**
Business Data Object	Field within business data object	Reference to data dictionary that defines business data object	Specific rules on validating data; leave blank if the data dictionary business rules suffice

Figure 7-26. System Interface Table Sample Format

7.2.2.18 USE CASE DIAGRAM

A use case diagram is a scope model that shows all the in-scope use cases for a solution. Creating use case diagrams involves identifying a list of both the users of the solution and the possible scenarios of how each user will use the solution. The use case diagram relates the users to relevant use cases and identifies which ones are in or out of scope for a given solution. For more information on use cases, see Section 7.3.2.8.

Use case diagrams are created early in a portfolio, program, or project and updated as use cases change or are added or cut from scope based on prioritization. Figure 7-27 shows a sample format of a use case diagram. Use case diagrams are further discussed and an example is provided in Section 4.10.7.5 of *Business Analysis for Practitioners: A Practice Guide*.

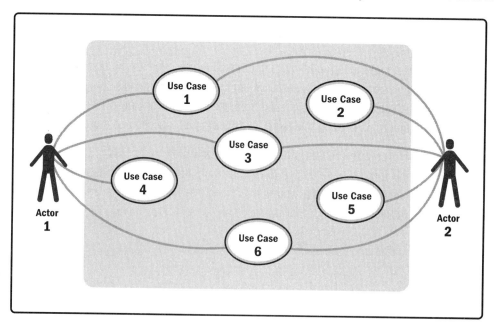

Figure 7-27. Use Case Diagram Sample Format

7.2.2.19 USER INTERFACE FLOW

A user interface flow is an interface model that displays specific user interfaces and commonly used screens within a functional design and plots out how to navigate between them. They can accompany process flows or use cases to help visually show the users' interactions with the system for a scenario.

User interface flows are typically created after process flows and use cases to ensure that the navigation of the user interface in the system makes sense and is correct. Figure 7-28 shows a sample format of a user interface flow. User interface flows are further discussed and an example is provided in Section 4.10.11.3 of *Business Analysis for Practitioners: A Practice Guide*.

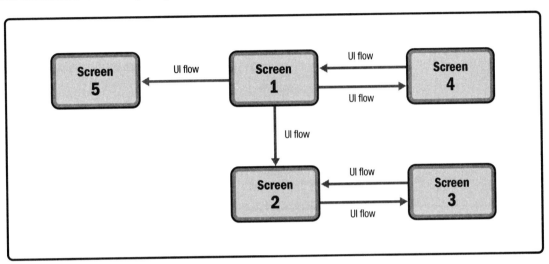

Figure 7-28. User Interface (UI) Flow Sample Format

7.2.3 CREATE AND ANALYZE MODELS: OUTPUTS

7.2.3.1 ANALYSIS MODELS

Analysis models are visual representations of product information. The analysis models might be draft or fully completed models. They might be high-fidelity, semantically correct representations or low-fidelity sketches. Throughout the course of a portfolio, program, or project, it is likely that models from every category will be created, but not all types of models will be needed. Analysis models reflect the total sum of all the models created, even though they might not be created at the same time. Analysis models show the solution from multiple facets and allow the business analyst to identify gaps in the models or requirements.

7.2.4 CREATE AND ANALYZE MODELS: TAILORING CONSIDERATIONS

Adaptive and predictive tailoring considerations for Create and Analyze Models are described in Table 7-3.

Table 7-3. Adaptive and Predictive Tailoring for Create and Analyze Models

Aspects to Be Tailored	Typical Adaptive Considerations	Typical Predictive Considerations
Name	Not a formally named process; performed as part of Backlog Refinement or Elaboration	Create and Analyze Models
Approach	Scope models and high-level process models are created and analyzed as part of scoping efforts, before a project starts or in an early iteration. Process, rule, data, and interface models are created and analyzed as needed to support identifying or elaborating user stories. All models can be refined as needed at any point in any iteration. The entire team might whiteboard the models together.	Models are created and analyzed early during an analysis phase. Scope models are typically created first and other models later as product information is elaborated. Models are fairly well refined and approved before design work begins.
Deliverables	Models might not follow formal syntax, might not be fully fleshed out, might be informally created as hand-drawn sketches, or can be created and stored in a tool.	Models might follow formal syntax and be complete. They are often maintained in a modeling tool.

7.2.5 CREATE AND ANALYZE MODELS—COLLABORATION POINT

Any of the analysis models might be created or analyzed with any project team member. In particular, the design and implementation team members might provide detailed knowledge that is helpful in creating data and interface models. Design teams may also be recipients of models to provide context to their work and can also alert the product team to current business or technical constraints and opportunities while modeling is conducted.

7.3 DEFINE AND ELABORATE REQUIREMENTS

Define and Elaborate Requirements is the process of refining and documenting requirements and other types of product information at the appropriate level of detail, format, and level of formality required for various audiences. The key benefits of this process are that it (a) helps clarify details about the product information so the team can work from it effectively, and (b) stores the product information in a manner that can be accessed and processed by all stakeholders. The inputs, tools and techniques, and outputs of the process are depicted in Figure 7-29. Figure 7-30 depicts the data flow diagram for the process.

Inputs

.1 Analysis approach
.2 Analysis models
.3 Confirmed elicitation results
.4 Relationships and dependencies
.5 Stakeholder engagement and communication approach

Tools & Techniques

.1 Business rules catalog
.2 Definition of ready
.3 Glossary
.4 Product backlog
.5 Requirements management tool
.6 Story elaboration
.7 Story slicing
.8 Use case
.9 User story

Outputs

.1 Requirements and other product information

Figure 7-29. Define and Elaborate Requirements: Inputs, Tools and Techniques, and Outputs

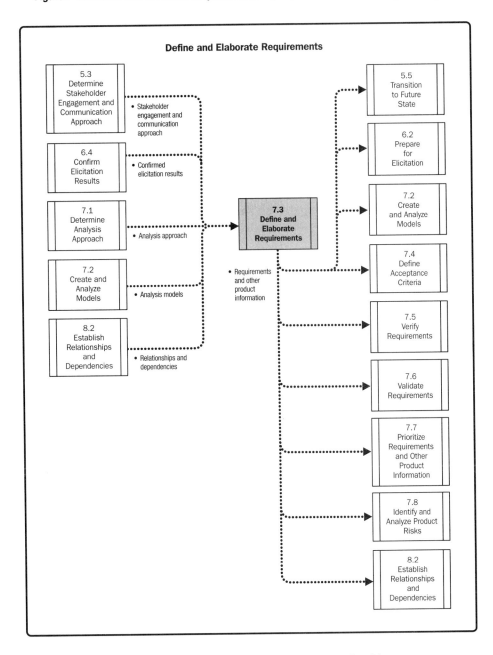

Figure 7-30. Define and Elaborate Requirements: Data Flow Diagram

The process to define and elaborate requirements is complex, thorough, and often the one that business analysts are best known for performing. This process entails understanding and analyzing information discovered during elicitation, model analysis, and relationship and dependency analysis to identify and write the requirements. This process is performed at different times to identify business, stakeholder, solution, and transition requirements on portfolios, programs, and projects. Typically, there is more definition and elaboration performed on programs and projects than on portfolios. In an adaptive approach, this process may be performed to define and elaborate user stories as the format for any of those requirement types. The analysis performed in this process also enables the definition of the requirements' attribute values. In all cases, this process also leads to the creation of the supporting product information, including assumptions, constraints, dependencies, related issues, and product risks.

The Define and Elaborate Requirements process is performed iteratively. Identifying and specifying requirements of any type can highlight relationships, dependencies, or gaps in the information that requires additional elicitation or analysis on models. Similarly, other processes might be performed concurrently with this process, such as Verify Requirements (Section 7.5), Validate Requirements (Section 7.6), Prioritize Requirements and Other Product Information (Section 7.7), and Identify and Analyze Product Risks (Section 7.8). It also might be appropriate to define acceptance criteria at the same time as defining user stories or requirements, so Define Acceptance Criteria (Section 7.4) could be performed in conjunction with this process.

Performing the Define and Elaborate Requirements process, often repeatedly, eventually leads to a reasonably complete set of requirements at whatever level is needed for the project life cycle. In some cases, this analysis results in fleshed-out user stories, and other times, it results in fully detailed functional requirements.

Defining and elaborating requirements includes defining all types of product information, not just requirements. This product information commonly includes the following:

◆ **Assumptions.** Any factors about the business problems, business objectives, requirements, design, or solution that are considered true without proof or demonstration. At any point, assumptions could become false, so they should be tracked to accommodate the impact of disproving them. Assumptions may also be proven to be true, in which case they are no longer assumptions and can be removed from the list.

◆ **Constraints.** Limiting factors that affect the execution of a portfolio, program, project, or process. In business analysis, constraints are factors that affect the development or implementation of the solution. Business rules are one type of constraint.

◆ **Dependencies.** Any product information that requirements are contingent on, supported by, or controlled by. They are further described in Section 8.2.

◆ **Issues.** Topics in question or under discussion about the requirements or other product information. Issues are documented and tracked through to their resolution, which is often required before requirements are complete.

◆ **Product risks.** Uncertain events or conditions that, if they occur, have positive or negative effects on the product. See Section 7.8 for more information on risk analysis. Risk analysis activities might be performed in conjunction with this process.

The total culmination of all product information forms what is called a requirements package. A requirements package does not have to be, and often is not, a formal document. It could be user stories and related information stored and evolving in a backlog. The package could also include requirements and related information stored in a requirements management tool or other repository. The formality and level of detail in the requirements package is defined by the project life cycle and what the stakeholders need to perform their tasks, both of which are determined during planning activities.

7.3.1 DEFINE AND ELABORATE REQUIREMENTS: INPUTS

7.3.1.1 ANALYSIS APPROACH

Described in Section 7.1.3.1. The analysis approach defines how analysis will be performed for the portfolio, program, or project. Included in the analysis approach is a decision about the types of requirements to be elaborated for the project life cycle and how the requirements and other product information will be stored. It also describes the requirements attributes that need to be captured during the Define and Elaborate Requirements process.

7.3.1.2 ANALYSIS MODELS

Described in Section 7.2.3.1. Analysis models are the cumulative set of draft or final models produced by the iterative analysis process. The analysis models are used to derive and elaborate the requirements by helping identify requirements at any level and by finding gaps, redundancies, and errors in the requirements. Additionally, some analysis models help define the attributes of requirements. Each analysis model can help derive requirements in different ways. Examples of how individual models are related to requirements are discussed in Section 4 of *Business Analysis for Practitioners: A Practice Guide*.

7.3.1.3 CONFIRMED ELICITATION RESULTS

Described in Section 6.4.3.1. Confirmed elicitation results include notes, ideas of requirements, and other outputs from the elicitation conducted. Confirmed elicitation results signify that the product team has reached a common understanding about the elicitation results and agrees to the accuracy of the information elicited. These results are a common starting point for identifying draft requirements because many were likely described by subject matter experts (SMEs) or found in elicitation source materials during the elicitation activities. However, even though elicitation results were provided by customers, SMEs, and other knowledgeable stakeholders, they are not the final requirements without additional analysis. The elicitation results are used in conjunction with the analysis models to ensure that the entire solution is fully analyzed to avoid missing, inconsistent, or conflicting requirements.

7.3.1.4 RELATIONSHIPS AND DEPENDENCIES

Described in Section 8.2.3.1. Relationships and dependencies define the links between requirements. Relationships can be parent to child, as requirements are progressively elaborated from a high level to a low level of detail, or they can be dependency relationships such as implementation, benefit, or value. Although relationships and dependencies help identify requirements or elaborate attributes, a business analyst might identify additional relationships and dependencies during this process and need to perform the process in Section 8.2 (Establish Relationships and Dependencies) concurrently.

7.3.1.5 STAKEHOLDER ENGAGEMENT AND COMMUNICATION APPROACH

Described in Section 5.3.3.1. The stakeholder engagement and communication approach summarizes all the agreements for governing how stakeholders will be engaged and communicated with across the portfolio, program, or project. This approach defines who will consume the requirements, the proposed mechanism of communication with those stakeholders, and the plan to structure and store the requirements. The approach supports efficient interaction of the business analyst with stakeholders because stakeholder expectations with regard to requirements and communication are considered and followed, although doing so often requires elicitation to be performed again.

Because this approach describes the plan for structuring and storing the requirements, it is used to decide the level of formality, level of detail, and form of the deliverables or requirements package.

7.3.2 DEFINE AND ELABORATE REQUIREMENTS: TOOLS AND TECHNIQUES

7.3.2.1 BUSINESS RULES CATALOG

A business rules catalog, a type of rule model, is a table of business rules and related attributes. Business rules are not processes or procedures; rather, they describe how to constrain or support behaviors within the operations of the business. Business rules are important to understand because they will need to be implemented or enforced by the solution. Business stakeholders may often want or need to change business rules to support business operations, so business rules provide justification for creating a highly configurable design.

The business rules catalog is created and updated at any point that business rules are identified. Figure 7-31 shows a sample format of a business rules catalog. Any given portfolio, program, or project might track different attributes about business rules, so this is just one example of a few commonly chosen attributes. Business rule catalogs can also show mappings from each rule to related processes that enforce the rule or data models that apply the rules. Business rule catalogs are further discussed and an example is provided in Section 4.10.9.1 of *Business Analysis for Practitioners: A Practice Guide.*

Business Rules Catalog Title						
BR ID	**Attribute 1**	**Attribute 2**	**Example Attribute: Business Rule Title**	**Example Attribute: Business Rule Description**	**Example Attribute: Type**	**Example Attribute: Reference**
BR01			Title of Business Rule 1	Description of Business Rule 1	Constraint	Where to find more information
BR02			Title of Business Rule 2	Description of Business Rule 2	Fact	
BR03			Title of Business Rule 3	Description of Business Rule 3	Computation	

Figure 7-31. Business Rules Catalog Sample Format

7.3.2.2 DEFINITION OF READY

The definition of ready is a series of conditions that the entire team agrees to complete before a user story is considered sufficiently understood so that work can begin to construct it. The definition of ready helps the project team know that the user story is sufficiently elaborated and ready to be brought into an iteration, designed, constructed, and delivered. For more information on the definition of done to describe when an item is complete, see Section 7.4.2.2.

7.3.2.3 GLOSSARY

The glossary is a list of all definitions for terms and acronyms about a product. Glossaries include terms that may be unfamiliar to an organization and terms that an organization defines differently from its industry. A glossary ensures that the entire team is aligned as to how specific terms will be used, any synonymous terms, and what various acronyms mean. While defining and elaborating requirements, the business analyst makes sure that all requirements use terminology as defined in the glossary and keeps the glossary up to date as new information is identified. Product teams may choose to develop one glossary that is shared across the entire portfolio, program, or project.

7.3.2.4 PRODUCT BACKLOG

The product backlog is the list of all product backlog items, typically user stories, requirements, or features, that need to be delivered for a solution. Most often, the items in a backlog are written as user stories, describing the functionality that the business or customer wants to see in the final product. The items can be requirements for the solution to be built, as well as any issues or defects that have to be resolved from previous iterations. Projects that utilize adaptive approaches use the product backlog as part of the requirements package.

The product backlog can be stored in a requirements management tool or spreadsheet, or may simply reside in a list and be tacked to a wall. The items in the product backlog are ranked in order of business value or importance to the customer and are continuously updated throughout a product's life cycle or a project's duration.

As new backlog items are added, the product backlog should be repeatedly refined. The acronym *DEEP* describes the characteristics that a product backlog needs to demonstrate to be considered well refined. *DEEP* stands for *detailed appropriately*, *estimated*, *emergent*, and *prioritized*:

◆ **Detailed appropriately.** The level of detail to describe a user story is dependent on the story's priority. The higher the priority, the more detailed the story needs to be. A product backlog is detailed appropriately when the highest-priority stories contain the most detail as compared to the lowest-priority items. Prioritizing which user stories have more detail specified will ensure that the items likely to be worked on in the next iteration are ready when needed.

◆ **Estimated.** The items in a product backlog should all be estimated. The higher-priority items should have more precise estimates than lower-priority items. Estimates might be expressed in story points or units of time to complete the work. All items should have a rough estimate at minimum to help prioritize and track progress.

◆ **Emergent.** Product backlogs are a constantly changing list of product backlog items. As inputs change, new information is discovered, or priorities change, product backlog items might be added, adjusted, removed, or reprioritized within a product backlog.

◆ **Prioritized.** All items within a product backlog should be prioritized in a rank-ordered manner, with the highest-priority items being at the top. As the priority of items changes, the backlog is reordered to reflect those changes. As items are added or removed, prioritization is adjusted as necessary to accommodate the newly added items.

For more information on backlog management, see Section 7.7.2.1. Product backlogs are further discussed in Section 4.11.10 of *Business Analysis for Practitioners: A Practice Guide*.

7.3.2.5 REQUIREMENTS MANAGEMENT TOOL

A requirements management tool allows requirements and other product information to be captured and stored in a repository. When defining and elaborating requirements, the requirements are often stored in a requirements management tool, including a status, any known attribute values, and related models. A requirements management tool might serve as the repository for the contents of a requirements package, depending on the project life cycle approach. For more information on requirements management tools, see Section 8.2.2.2.

7.3.2.6 STORY ELABORATION

Story elaboration is the process by which user stories are further detailed with additional information until they are ready for development. Story elaboration is known as backlog refinement. In adaptive approaches, user stories are at a higher level of detail than functional and nonfunctional requirements. Story elaboration is the technique used to add additional details to each story before construction of the solution. User stories are commonly treated as a promise to have a conversation about the details, rather than as rigorous requirement statements. Story elaboration can occur verbally, with very few details of the conversation being documented, as long as the knowledge is transferred to those team members who need to understand it. For more information on story elaboration, see Section 7.4.2.3.

7.3.2.7 STORY SLICING

Story slicing is a technique used to split epics or user stories from a higher level to a lower level. An epic, user story, or requirement could be split in a variety of ways, including by type of interface, user or persona, functionality, data, business rules, constraints, or any combination thereof. Whichever mechanism is used to decide how to slice the user stories, the slices are then prioritized by the value that each slice delivers. In predictive approaches, creating multiple scenarios from a broad requirement is similar to story slicing.

The reason to split stories is that sometimes stories are too big to construct in an iteration. Large stories are commonly called epics. The epics are sliced into smaller increments of value as determined by the user and are of a size that can be constructed within one iteration. Occasionally, it is necessary to reverse this thinking and take stories to a higher level of detail to ensure that the story achieves the users' goals.

There are many ways to decide how to slice stories. The different scenarios covered in one story, such as a common path and alternative paths, may each be covered by its own story, once sliced. Sometimes, parts of stories are separated out if they are more complex, riskier, or deliver higher business value than other parts. Doing so allows the implementation team to focus on those complex, high-risk, or higher-value areas separately and early.

7.3.2.8 USE CASE

A use case is a process model that uses textual narrative to describe the system-user interactions to achieve successful completion of a goal. The goal represents what the primary actor is trying to accomplish in the use case and usually is part of the use case name. Each use case contains a normal flow, which is the most common scenario of interactions between the system and user, as well as alternative and exception flows, where the scenario diverges from the normal flow. This model is frequently used to identify and elaborate requirements, especially when moving from business requirements to stakeholder requirements or solution requirements.

Use cases are typically created after process flows to provide additional details for specific steps in the process flows, particularly if there are complex interactions between users and systems. Use cases might also be created instead of process flows. They are used to identify the functional or nonfunctional requirements or acceptance criteria. Use cases can be used as the form to represent solution requirements. Figure 7-32 shows a sample format of a use case. Use cases are further discussed and an example is provided in Section 4.10.8.2 of *Business Analysis for Practitioners: A Practice Guide*.

Use Case Format	
Name	The use case name
ID	An identifier that is unique to each use case
Description	A brief sentence that states what the users wants to be able to do and what benefits they will derive
Actors	The type of user who interacts with the system to accomplish the task
Organizational benefits	The value the organization expects to receive from having the functionality described
Triggers	The event that causes the use case to start
Preconditions	Describes everything that should be in place prior to the use case starting in order for the use case to succeed
Post conditions	Everything that has changed in the environment at the end of a use case
Normal flow	The normal course of steps to move from the preconditions to the post conditions
Alternate courses	Alternate sets of steps an actor can take to achieve the goal other than what is described in the main flow
Exceptions	Errors or disruptions in the normal flow that require an actor or system to perform a different action to respond to the exception

Figure 7-32. Use Case Sample Format

7.3.2.9 USER STORY

User stories are a method to document stakeholder requirements from the users' point of view with a focus on the value or benefit achieved by the user with the completion of that story. User stories help bridge from business requirements to solution requirements.

User stories can be used to map requirements or acceptance criteria back to process models that reflect overall business user tasks. In adaptive approaches, user stories are commonly the method used to represent requirements. A user story may contain many requirements. Acceptance criteria typically capture more details about the users' needs and are further described in Section 7.4. Figure 7-33 shows a sample format of a user story and acceptance criteria. User stories are further discussed and an example is provided in Section 4.10.8.3 of *Business Analysis for Practitioners: A Practice Guide*.

User Story: <Name> <User Story ID>	
User Story	**Acceptance Criteria**
As an <actor>, *I want* to be able to <function>, *so that* I can <business reason>	*Given* <precondition(s)>, *when* <action>, *then* <post conditions>

Figure 7-33. User Story and Acceptance Criteria Sample Format

7.3.3 DEFINE AND ELABORATE REQUIREMENTS: OUTPUTS

7.3.3.1 REQUIREMENTS AND OTHER PRODUCT INFORMATION

The output of Define and Elaborate Requirements is the requirements themselves. These requirements can be of any type: business, stakeholder, solution, or transition. The requirements can be stored in any type of repository, such as a backlog, document, or a requirements management tool. In addition to requirements, other product information that is documented as part of this process includes assumptions, dependencies, constraints, issues, and risks. For more information on risks, see Section 7.8.

7.3.4 DEFINE AND ELABORATE REQUIREMENTS: TAILORING CONSIDERATIONS

Adaptive and predictive tailoring considerations for Define and Elaborate Requirements are described in Table 7-4.

Table 7-4. Adaptive and Predictive Tailoring for Define and Elaborate Requirements

Aspects to Be Tailored	Typical Adaptive Considerations	Typical Predictive Considerations
Name	User Story Definition, Story Refinement, Backlog Refinement, or Elaboration	Define and Elaborate Requirements or Specify Requirements
Approach	Requirements are represented as a combination of user stories and acceptance criteria in a product backlog. Although anyone can write a user story, the product owner decides whether and where to place the story in the backlog. User stories may be identified in a user story writing workshop, so elicitation and user story definition occur concurrently. User stories are progressively elaborated via backlog refinement sessions. User stories evolve within a product backlog because new stories can be added at any time, prioritization might change story order, and just-in-time elaboration will provide additional details.	Significant portions of elicitation might be completed before requirements are specified, though the two activities will typically be iterative with each other. Individual requirement statements, business rules, and use cases are written based on elicitation results and analysis of the models. Requirements are typically written at three levels: business, stakeholder, and solution requirements. Drafted requirements are reviewed with stakeholders and are refined or elaborated based on the feedback.
Deliverables	Deliverables are created using the principle of lightweight documentation and stored in a backlog. User stories or product backlog items need to meet the definition of ready.	Completed requirements are delivered in a document or requirements management tool.

7.3.5 DEFINE AND ELABORATE REQUIREMENTS: COLLABORATION POINT

Portfolio, program, or project managers might participate in discovering business requirements and typically own defining project requirements. Business analysts are responsible for eliciting and documenting the business requirements with other stakeholders and may be asked to support the project manager in eliciting and documenting project requirements.

7.4 DEFINE ACCEPTANCE CRITERIA

Define Acceptance Criteria is the process of obtaining agreement as to what would constitute proof that one or more aspects of a solution have been developed successfully. The key benefit of this process is that it provides complementary insights that can help refine requirements while providing the basis of a shared understanding for what is to be delivered. The inputs, tools and techniques, and outputs of the process are depicted in Figure 7-34. Figure 7-35 depicts the data flow diagram for the process.

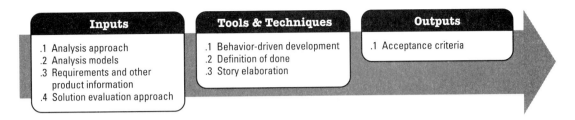

Figure 7-34. Define Acceptance Criteria: Inputs, Tools and Techniques, and Outputs

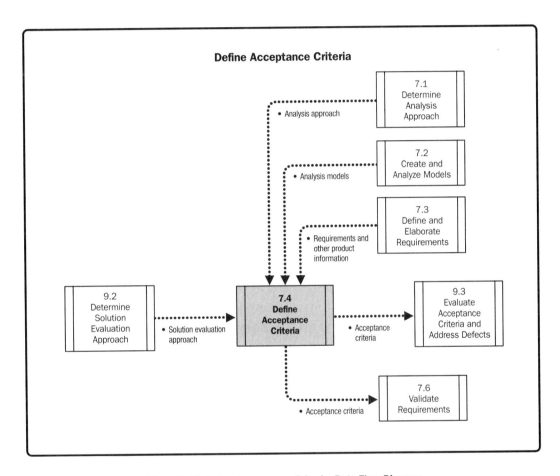

Figure 7-35. Define Acceptance Criteria: Data Flow Diagram

Acceptance criteria are the conditions that need to be met before a solution is accepted. They are used to measure whether a customer is satisfied with the solution built. Acceptance criteria form the basis of acceptance tests and are important in evaluating the solution during product review sessions, where product owners or business stakeholders decide whether to accept and release the developed solution. Determining the acceptance criteria involves reviewing requirements and analysis models with business stakeholders to identify how the business stakeholder would approve something as done.

Acceptance criteria can be created at different levels, including requirement, iteration, release, and product levels. In adaptive approaches, acceptance criteria might be written at the level of a user story, where multiple acceptance criteria need to be met for the user story to be accepted. Also in adaptive approaches, acceptance criteria are a succinct way to write requirements. Acceptance criteria can be written at the level of the overall solution or business objectives. Acceptance criteria defined as part of a portfolio or program are likely to be high level and related to the desired overarching objectives. As described in Section 6.5.3 of *Business Analysis for Practitioners: A Practice Guide*, acceptance criteria might be set based on the goals, objectives, key performance indicators, project metrics, customer metrics, sales and marketing metrics, or operational metrics.

Often, the acceptance criteria in adaptive approaches follow a behavior-driven development format, as described in Section 7.4.2.1, but they can follow any format that both the stakeholders and the developers agree upon. In all cases, acceptance criteria are used in Section 9.3 (Evaluate Acceptance Results and Address Defects) whenever it is performed, dependent on the project life cycle.

7.4.1 DEFINE ACCEPTANCE CRITERIA: INPUTS

7.4.1.1 ANALYSIS APPROACH

Described in Section 7.1.3.1. The analysis approach defines how analysis will be performed for the portfolio, program, or project. Included in the analysis approach is a decision about how and when in the project life cycle the acceptance criteria will be defined. The analysis approach describes how acceptance criteria will relate to user stories, requirements, releases, and solution definitions of acceptance and the level at which they are written.

7.4.1.2 ANALYSIS MODELS

Described in Section 7.2.3.1. Analysis models are the culmination of creating and analyzing draft or final models. The models in any state can be used to elaborate the requirements or user stories to identify acceptance criteria. This iterative derivation process is similar to using analysis models to identify requirements, as described in Section 7.3. In some cases, the acceptance criteria will be defined in analysis models. Some models, such as the business objectives model, can be used to define acceptance criteria at the product level.

7.4.1.3 REQUIREMENTS AND OTHER PRODUCT INFORMATION

Described in Section 7.3.3.1. Requirements and other product information are a starting point to define the acceptance criteria. This input is useful, whether it is used for writing acceptance criteria based on user stories, requirements, or business objectives. Stakeholders use this input to decide whether to accept or reject the solution based on how well it met the requirements.

7.4.1.4 SOLUTION EVALUATION APPROACH

Described in Section 9.2.3.1. The solution evaluation approach defines what types of metrics will be used to measure the performance of a solution. Acceptance criteria are defined to set acceptable ranges on the metrics identified.

7.4.2 DEFINE ACCEPTANCE CRITERIA: TOOLS AND TECHNIQUES

7.4.2.1 BEHAVIOR-DRIVEN DEVELOPMENT

Behavior-driven development (BDD) is an approach that suggests that the team should begin with understanding how the user will use a product (its behavior), write tests for that behavior, and then construct solutions against the tests. Behavior-driven development encourages a conversation between the user or customer who needs to be satisfied with the solution and those who are implementing the solution. The conversation often leads to examples of real-life scenarios that the team uses to build a shared understanding. This approach is a continuation of test-driven development, which suggests that writing tests first will create better products with fewer defects. While this technique is popular in adaptive approaches, it can be applied in any life cycle approach.

The behavior-driven development approach includes a commonly accepted syntax to write acceptance criteria for user stories, the given-when-then format. The given-when-then format ensures that the business stakeholders should consider the preconditions of the user in the product, the triggers, and how the product should react in these conditions. Acceptance criteria are generally written as "Given <the preconditions>, when <the user does something within the product>, then <the product reaction>." Alternatively, any format can be used for acceptance criteria as long as the criteria include the preconditions and information necessary to test the criteria, the function being tested, and the expected post conditions or results after the function is being performed.

7.4.2.2 DEFINITION OF DONE

The definition of done (DoD) is a series of conditions that the entire team agrees to complete before an item is considered sufficiently developed to be accepted by the business stakeholders. The definition of done for a user story or iteration helps the project team know that the work is complete so the team can move on to the next user story or iteration. Once an item meets the definition of done criteria, it is marked appropriately in any planning tools, such as project plans, requirements management tools, or kanban boards. Definitions of done can be created at many levels of detail. They can be closely related to acceptance criteria, including using acceptance criteria in the definition of done. They are often defined at the user story level, the iteration level, the release level, and the product level. The definition of done might include items such as:

◆ Acceptance criteria are met;

◆ Development, test, and defect standards are conformed to; and

◆ High-level nonfunctional and usability requirements are met.

Definitions of done are written early in a portfolio, program, or project. The definition of done for any given user story, iteration, release, or solution is usually similar across the product or portfolio of products, or it can be specific to a low-level entity. For example, some user stories might warrant specific definitions of done. Definitions of done can evolve over time. The definition of done, as part of acceptance criteria, is an input to evaluating a solution for release, and therefore, can be used in Section 9.4 (Obtain Solution Acceptance for Release).

7.4.2.3 STORY ELABORATION

Story elaboration is the process by which user stories are supplemented with additional information from conversations with business stakeholders, until they are sufficiently detailed for product development to begin work.

In adaptive approaches, user stories are commonly written at a higher level of detail than functional and nonfunctional requirements, so story elaboration is the technique used to add the extra details for each story so that development teams have enough information to build the solution. Adaptive life cycles explicitly define acceptance criteria with concrete examples as part of the elaboration of a user story. Together, these details establish mutual agreement between business stakeholders and those responsible for developing the solution regarding what is required and how to know that the requirement has been met.

Story elaboration is primarily used in adaptive methodologies because too much information about a user story too early in the project can hinder the development team's ability to negotiate priorities with the business and adapt to changes in the requirements. Design information and customer decisions are only added to the user story "just in time" for development to work on the user story. Story elaboration can take the form of further conversations or writing narratives around the user story, making design decisions, drafting wireframes or other analysis models, writing acceptance criteria, and documenting business rules, issues, constraints, and dependencies.

7.4.3 DEFINE ACCEPTANCE CRITERIA: OUTPUTS

7.4.3.1 ACCEPTANCE CRITERIA

Acceptance criteria are concrete and demonstrable conditions about an item that need to be met for the business stakeholders or customers to accept the item. This output can take the form of lists of acceptance criteria for each user story in an adaptive approach, or may be a list of higher-level acceptance criteria for a release or solution in a predictive approach. Regardless of the level at which they are defined, the acceptance criteria should align to the requirements and other product information because acceptance testing or evaluation of the solution will be based on the acceptance criteria. The definition of done is part of this output. An example of acceptance criteria can be found in Section 4.10.8.3 of *Business Analysis for Practitioners: A Practice Guide*.

7.4.4 DEFINE ACCEPTANCE CRITERIA: TAILORING CONSIDERATIONS

Adaptive and predictive tailoring considerations for Define Acceptance Criteria are described in Table 7-5.

Table 7-5. Adaptive and Predictive Tailoring for Define Acceptance Criteria

Aspects to Be Tailored	Typical Adaptive Considerations	Typical Predictive Considerations
Name	Define Acceptance Criteria, Backlog Refinement, or Elaboration	Define Acceptance Criteria or Define Evaluation Metrics
Approach	Written as part of user stories, typically with more than one acceptance criterion per user story. Often used to define the details from which teams develop and test solutions and are often at the level of solution requirements. They are created, reviewed, and refined throughout all iterations of a project for each user story, just in time for development.	Acceptance criteria are defined and might map to requirements, business objectives, or other success metrics. Acceptance criteria at the requirement level are defined together with requirements or after requirements are defined. They are used to help refine requirements by pointing out any lack of clarity. Acceptance criteria defined at the release or product level are defined early in a project once the goals and objectives are understood.
Deliverables	Acceptance criteria are defined and sometimes documented in a tool.	

7.4.5 DEFINE ACCEPTANCE CRITERIA: COLLABORATION POINT

Quality control team members lend assistance to business analysts to provide an understanding about how acceptance criteria will be evaluated and whether there are any standards that need to be followed when writing acceptance criteria. Quality control team members can also help write acceptance criteria.

7.5 VERIFY REQUIREMENTS

Verify Requirements is the process of checking that requirements are of sufficient quality. The key benefit of this process is that it increases the likelihood that the requirements are stated and/or understood in a way that meets the defined standards for the organization, which, in turn, enables communication of the requirements to all interested parties and contributes to the quality of the final product. The inputs, tools and techniques, and outputs of the process are depicted in Figure 7-36. Figure 7-37 depicts the data flow diagram for the process.

Inputs	Tools & Techniques	Outputs
.1 Analysis approach .2 Business analysis organizational standards .3 Compliance or regulatory standards .4 Requirements and other product information	.1 INVEST .2 Peer reviews	.1 Verified requirements and other product information

Figure 7-36. Verify Requirements: Inputs, Tools and Techniques, and Outputs

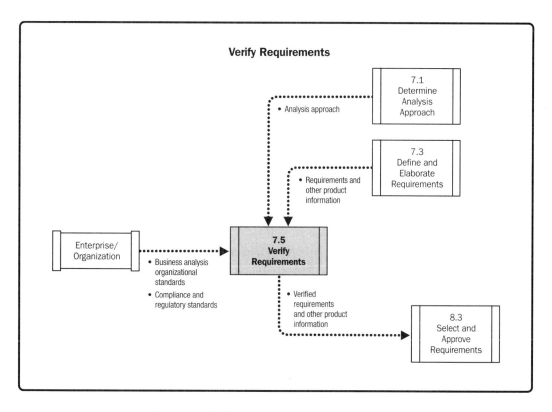

Figure 7-37. Verify Requirements: Data Flow Diagram

Verification is the process of reviewing the requirements and other product information for errors, conflicts, and adherence to quality standards. Verification also involves evaluating whether requirements and other product information comply with a regulation, specification, or imposed condition. In contrast, validation is the assurance that a product meets the needs of the customer and other identified stakeholders. Validation is covered in Section 7.6.

Verification can be conducted iteratively and can be done formally or informally, depending on the techniques used. Requirements and associated analysis models are both verified and validated.

Verification can be performed on product information at the portfolio, program, or project levels. It can be conducted on a single requirement, a single model, or a set of product information. Verification is performed to ensure that the requirements and other product information are constructed properly and that models are clear enough to be used effectively. Verification of nonfunctional requirements or acceptance criteria includes evaluating whether these items are sufficiently measurable. Verification leads to a higher likelihood of success because team members who will implement the requirements are more likely to be able to understand the verified requirements than if they were not verified.

To a certain degree, the author of the materials can do some verification. However, verification is also performed by someone else, such as a business analyst who is not on the project or other members of the project team. The person performing verification reviews the requirements and other product information against any analysis, compliance, or regulatory standards for the organization for accuracy and conformance to the applicable standards. Product information that does not pass the verification step needs to be elaborated or rewritten so that it can be deemed of sufficient quality to continue its life cycle. A measure of quality, in the absence of standards or in addition to them, at a basic level includes evaluating the information for the 3Cs: correct, complete, and consistent. Analysis models can also be verified against syntax or modeling standards.

7.5.1 VERIFY REQUIREMENTS: INPUTS

7.5.1.1 ANALYSIS APPROACH

Described in Section 7.1.3.1. The analysis approach defines how analysis will be performed for the portfolio, program, or project. Included in the analysis approach is a decision about when verification of the product information will be performed. It also describes the verification techniques and which, if any, standards should be used.

7.5.1.2 BUSINESS ANALYSIS ORGANIZATIONAL STANDARDS

Described in Section 2.3. Business analysis organizational standards describe any expected quality characteristics, formatting rules, syntax rules, and requirements structure imposed by the organization on all business analysis deliverables. These standards define what a good requirement or requirements set is and may be based on industry standards. Examples of quality characteristics include feasible, concise, measurable, testable, traceable, unambiguous, precise, consistent, correct, complete, and prioritized. Characteristics of high-quality requirements are described in more detail in Section 4.11.5.1 of *Business Analysis for Practitioners: A Practice Guide*. Analysis models may be verified against syntax or predefined modeling standards. Verification standards for predictive approaches may also define what level of requirements quality is necessary before proceeding from one phase to another.

7.5.1.3 COMPLIANCE OR REGULATORY STANDARDS

Described in Section 2.2. Compliance or regulatory standards are imposed by external organizations, commonly for reasons related to security, protecting personal information, legal considerations, or safety reasons. Most often, they are government or industry regulations. Some standards take the form of what the documentation for a project should include, while others may list actual requirements that the project has to include in its requirements set. When using external standards as an input, the reviewer needs to ensure that the requirements or documentation produced meets the standards so that the project can pass an external or internal audit.

7.5.1.4 REQUIREMENTS AND OTHER PRODUCT INFORMATION

Described in Section 7.3.3.1. Requirements and other product information accumulated throughout the portfolio, program, or project provide the information for verification. The person performing verification reviews the materials using the appropriate techniques or standards. If the reviewer is someone other than the author, the reviewer provides feedback to the author about any changes that need to be made to the requirements and other product information to make the information clearer or so that it better conforms to the chosen standards.

7.5.2 VERIFY REQUIREMENTS: TOOLS AND TECHNIQUES

7.5.2.1 INVEST

The term *INVEST* describes the characteristics that user stories need to demonstrate to be considered "good" and "ready" for development in adaptive approaches. This is the primary verification technique used in adaptive approaches. *INVEST* is an acronym for *independent, negotiable, valuable, estimable, small*, and *testable*:

◆ **Independent.** The characteristic that breaks as many dependencies between user stories as possible so that any user story can be built by itself in any order by the development team. Adhering to this characteristic facilitates planning because planning can be based purely on value and size, rather than on complex ordering of user stories.

◆ **Negotiable.** The characteristic in adaptive methodologies that ensures that too much information is not captured up front, because all user stories and the details surrounding them should be negotiable between the development team and the business stakeholders until a story is accepted for development.

◆ **Valuable.** A characteristic where each story has value to the business or the customer and the backlog is ranked based on that value.

◆ **Estimable.** The characteristic that balances against the negotiable characteristic to ensure that user stories have enough detail for the development team to provide a rough estimate of size. If the development team cannot size the story, then there is not enough information known and the business analyst needs to elaborate further.

◆ **Small.** In the adaptive sense, *small* means that the story is small enough for the development team to complete it within a single time-boxed iteration.

◆ **Testable.** The characteristic that determines whether a story can be finitely tested by a test team and if the customer understands how to accept the final requirement as done. It is usually written in the form of acceptance criteria.

These six characteristics together are a way to assess if the user stories are elaborated sufficiently enough to be taken into an iteration to be worked on. Additional details about the INVEST criteria are described in Section 4.10.8.3 of *Business Analysis for Practitioners: A Practice Guide*.

7.5.2.2 PEER REVIEWS

Peer reviews involve one or more coworkers reviewing the work completed by the business analyst. Commonly, the peer who performs the review is another business analyst, team lead, or quality control team member. Reviewers focus on reviewing the logic and readability of the requirements, along with adherence to internal organizational standards for quality characteristics, format, and syntax. Peer reviews may not always cover external standards but instead involve looking for internal consistency within the requirements to avoid contradictions, gaps, or faulty logic.

Peer reviews can be either informal or formal. Many times, business analysts will ask for an informal peer review before reviewing requirements with stakeholders to ensure that there are no glaring mistakes or issues that could be raised during stakeholder reviews and validation sessions. Formal peer reviews are typically performed prior to approval and involve either written feedback or verbal feedback during a walkthrough. Written feedback can be tracked in a problem or issue tracking repository. Three common types of peer reviews, in order of least to most formal, are as follows:

◆ **Peer desk check.** An informal peer review completed by one or multiple peers simultaneously to look over the materials. Desk checking is a way to review any logic in a set of requirements, analysis models, or other product information, and often involves working through an example to check logic. A peer reviewer walks through an analysis model or set of requirements with an objective eye to catch any issues or inconsistencies. Desk checking is also useful for checking the logic in a set of business rules. This is similar to a developer debugging code as it is written. Peer reviews are further described in Section 4.13.1 of *Business Analysis for Practitioners: A Practice Guide*.

◆ **Walkthrough.** A peer review in which the author of the materials walks the peer reviewers through the authored information. These reviews are often held using an elicitation workshop technique. Feedback is typically given verbally during the session. For more information on walkthroughs, see Section 7.6.2.4.

◆ **Inspection.** A formal and rigorous form of review in which practitioners close to the work (usually other business analysts, developers, test team members, or quality team members) inspect the work for completeness, consistency, and conformance to internal and external standards, often referring to a checklist. The inspector uses the checklist and the inspection process to review a set of requirements and provide feedback to the authoring business analyst. Inspections and suggestions for checklists are further detailed in Section 4.13.2 of *Business Analysis for Practitioners: A Practice Guide*.

7.5.3 VERIFY REQUIREMENTS: OUTPUTS

7.5.3.1 VERIFIED REQUIREMENTS AND OTHER PRODUCT INFORMATION

Verified requirements and other product information include product information that has been evaluated to ensure that it is free from errors and addresses the quality standards to which the information will be held. Verified requirements are not a guarantee that those same requirements address the business needs. The requirements also have to be validated, prioritized, and approved. When requirements and other product information are used as inputs into other processes, the inputs might include product information that has been verified.

7.5.4 VERIFY REQUIREMENTS: TAILORING CONSIDERATIONS

Adaptive and predictive tailoring considerations for Verify Requirements are described in Table 7-6.

Table 7-6. Adaptive and Predictive Tailoring for Verify Requirements

Aspects to Be Tailored	Typical Adaptive Considerations	Typical Predictive Considerations
Name	User Story Reviews, Story Elaboration, or Backlog Refinement	Verify Requirements or Requirements Reviews
Approach	User stories and acceptance criteria are checked against the INVEST criteria and any internal or external standards prior to pulling a user story into an iteration. Models can also be verified. The process is performed incrementally, just in time for each user story to be built.	Requirements and analysis models are often formally verified and completed after the requirements have been defined and elaborated. Requirements and models can be validated before, after, or while they are verified. Requirements are verified before being approved.
Deliverables	Refined user stories are updated in the backlog.	Reviewed requirements documents with feedback and sometimes audit trails of the documents.

7.5.5 VERIFY REQUIREMENTS: COLLABORATION POINT

On adaptive projects, all members of the product team can participate in reviewing user stories during backlog refinement and sprint planning. On predictive life cycle projects, business analysts might engage quality control team members to perform verification activities or other business analysts who did not create the materials.

7.6 VALIDATE REQUIREMENTS

Validate Requirements is the process of checking that the requirements meet business goals and objectives. The key benefit of this process is that it minimizes the risks of missing stakeholder expectations or delivering the wrong solution. The inputs, tools and techniques, and outputs of the process are depicted in Figure 7-38. Figure 7-39 depicts the data flow diagram for the process.

Inputs	Tools & Techniques	Outputs
.1 Acceptance criteria .2 Analysis approach .3 Business goals and objectives .4 Requirements and other product information	.1 Delphi .2 Goal model and business objectives model .3 Traceability matrix .4 Walkthroughs	.1 Validated requirements and other product information

Figure 7-38. Validate Requirements: Inputs, Tools and Techniques, and Outputs

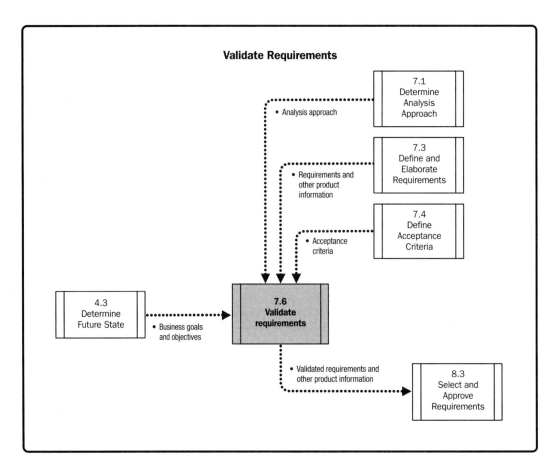

Validate Requirements

7.1 Determine Analysis Approach

7.3 Define and Elaborate Requirements

7.4 Define Acceptance Criteria

- Analysis approach

- Requirements and other product information

- Acceptance criteria

4.3 Determine Future State

- Business goals and objectives

7.6 Validate requirements

- Validated requirements and other product information

8.3 Select and Approve Requirements

Figure 7-39. Validate Requirements: Data Flow Diagram

Validation is the process of ensuring that all requirements and other product information accurately reflect the intent of the stakeholders and that each requirement aligns to one or more business requirements. While verification ensures that the product information meets the necessary standards and is well written, validation ensures that the right solution is being built.

The main goal of validating the product information is to come to a common understanding with the business stakeholders that the solution will address and support the business goals and objectives of key performance indicators (KPIs). This process is important to avoid a situation in which the solution doesn't meet the business goals and objectives because the business or customer needs were misunderstood. Validation can be performed on product information at the portfolio, program, or project levels.

Validation can be conducted iteratively or on a set of final information all at once. As business goals or objectives change, requirements may need to be updated and revalidated to reflect those changes. If any assumptions about how the requirements or solution will meet the business goals and objectives are proven false, then the requirements may need to change to meet the business goals and objectives. Validation can be conducted on a single requirement, a single model, or on a set of product information. Requirements and associated requirements models are both verified and validated.

Some requirements validation can be performed by the business analyst alone, using appropriate analysis models. This level of validation is primarily performed by mapping requirements and other product information to business objectives to identify gaps, inconsistencies, or duplication. However, most validation requires participation from stakeholders. Stakeholders have to review the requirements and other product information to ensure that the information provided is sufficient to allow the desired solution to be built. Validation can be iterative and may require additional elicitation if new items are identified that need to be elicited, modeled, analyzed, and elaborated.

7.6.1 VALIDATE REQUIREMENTS: INPUTS

7.6.1.1 ACCEPTANCE CRITERIA

Described in Section 7.4.3.1. Acceptance criteria define concrete and demonstrable conditions about an item that have to be met for the business stakeholders or customers to accept the item. An item can be a requirement, iteration, release, or solution. While performing validation activities, acceptance criteria are used to ensure that all requirements and other product information are mapped to the agreed-upon acceptance criteria. If not, the user story, iteration, release, or solution is not on track to be accepted.

Acceptance criteria can be created at different levels, including the requirement, iteration, release, and product levels. Acceptance criteria can be written at the level of the overall product or business objectives. In adaptive approaches, acceptance criteria might be written at the level of a user story, where multiple acceptance criteria need to be met for the user story to be accepted. In adaptive approaches, acceptance criteria provide a succinct way to write the requirements.

7.6.1.2 ANALYSIS APPROACH

Described in Section 7.1.3.1. The analysis approach defines how analysis will be performed for the portfolio, program, or project. Included in the analysis approach is a decision about when validation of the product information will be performed. It also describes which validation techniques are appropriate to use.

7.6.1.3 BUSINESS GOALS AND OBJECTIVES

Described in Section 4.3.3.1. Business goals and objectives define the results the business is expecting a portfolio, program, or project to deliver. Validation involves ensuring that all requirements trace back to the business goals and objectives so what is proposed to be built will actually meet the stated goals and objectives.

7.6.1.4 REQUIREMENTS AND OTHER PRODUCT INFORMATION

Described in Section 7.3.3.1. Requirements and other product information resulting from 7.3 Define and Elaborate Requirements and accumulated throughout the portfolio, program, or project provide the information for validation. The person performing validation reviews the materials and either fixes the issues or provides feedback to the author about any changes that need to be made. Often, this input will change as a result of validation because requirements or product information will be discovered to be missing, unnecessary, or incorrect. Verification and validation can occur concurrently or iteratively as more information is needed or as levels of formality for both validation and verification occur.

7.6.2 VALIDATE REQUIREMENTS: TOOLS AND TECHNIQUES

7.6.2.1 DELPHI

Delphi is a consensus-building method that consolidates anonymous input from subject matter experts (SMEs) using rounds of voting. During Validate Requirements, each SME provides feedback on whether he or she finds the requirements valid and sufficient. The team comes together to discuss the survey results and continues voting until consensus is reached. This method reduces peer pressure or groupthink in the validation process and avoids having the team give in to a voice of authority with which they might disagree. Delphi can be used on requirements or any other product information, such as features, user stories, and acceptance criteria. For more information on Delphi, see Section 8.3.2.4.

7.6.2.2 GOAL MODEL AND BUSINESS OBJECTIVES MODEL

The goal and business objectives models describe the business objectives the solution is meant to achieve, along with the high-level features for the solution. Either model can be helpful for mapping requirements or user stories through features or other models back to business objectives to ensure that requirements are in alignment with business objectives. For more information on the goal model and business objectives model, see Section 7.2.2.9.

7.6.2.3 TRACEABILITY MATRIX

A traceability matrix is a grid that allows for linkages between objects. A traceability matrix can be used to trace requirements to other types of requirements in the hierarchy—for example, from business requirements to solution requirements. It can be used to trace requirements to analysis models or to downstream items such as test cases. During Validate Requirements, a traceability matrix is primarily used to trace the requirements to analysis models and ultimately to the business objectives that each requirement supports. This analysis ensures that each business objective has coverage by the requirements and that each requirement traces directly back to support a business objective. Any requirements that cannot be traced back to business objectives are likely not valid, and can be cut from scope. For more information on the traceability matrix, see Section 8.2.2.5.

7.6.2.4 WALKTHROUGHS

Walkthroughs are used to review the requirements with the stakeholders and to receive confirmation that the requirements as stated are valid. Validated requirements accurately reflect what the stakeholders are asking the development team to build. Walkthroughs entail holding a meeting or meetings to review the requirements as a group, to ensure that there is a common understanding of the requirements and whether they are needed. Typically, a business analyst will send the requirements to the business stakeholders to review individually before the walkthrough takes place. Walkthroughs can be used to review more than just requirements, including analysis models and user stories. Walkthroughs that are specifically focused on reviewing requirements are often called requirements walkthroughs. Requirements walkthroughs are further discussed in Section 4.12.2 of *Business Analysis for Practitioners: A Practice Guide.*

7.6.3 VALIDATE REQUIREMENTS: OUTPUTS

7.6.3.1 VALIDATED REQUIREMENTS AND OTHER PRODUCT INFORMATION

Validated requirements and other product information include product information that the stakeholders agree meets the business goals and objectives. Validated requirements are not a guarantee that those same requirements are well written and address the standards to which the project will be held. The requirements also have to be verified, prioritized, and approved. When requirements and other product information are used as inputs into other processes, the inputs might include product information that has been validated.

7.6.4 VALIDATE REQUIREMENTS: TAILORING CONSIDERATIONS

Adaptive and predictive tailoring considerations for Validate Requirements are described in Table 7-7.

Table 7-7. Adaptive and Predictive Tailoring for Validate Requirements

Aspects to Be Tailored	Typical Adaptive Considerations	Typical Predictive Considerations
Name	User Story Reviews, Story Elaboration, or Backlog Refinement	Validate Requirements or Requirements Reviews
Approach	User stories and acceptance criteria are reviewed in real time with the business stakeholders or during backlog refinement and traced back to the business goals. Models are also validated. This is a continuous activity, because any user stories that are no longer valid should be removed from the product backlog immediately.	Requirements and analysis models are often formally validated. Walkthroughs can be a formal process and are completed after the requirements have been defined and elaborated. Requirements can be validated before, after, or while they are verified. Requirements are often validated before being approved.
Deliverables	Refined user stories are updated in the backlog.	Traced requirements.

7.6.5 VALIDATE REQUIREMENTS: COLLABORATION POINT

Functional managers and subject matter experts (SMEs) participate in validation activities because they will understand if the requirements meet the business goals or objectives and whether the requirements as stated present a true picture of what needs to be built.

7.7 PRIORITIZE REQUIREMENTS AND OTHER PRODUCT INFORMATION

Prioritize Requirements and Other Product Information is the process of understanding how individual pieces of product information achieve stakeholder objectives, and using that information, along with other agreed-upon prioritization factors, to facilitate ranking of the work. The key benefits of this process are that it aligns all stakeholders with how the requirements achieve the goals and objectives and determines how to allocate the requirements to iterations or releases accordingly. The inputs, tools and techniques, and outputs of the process are depicted in Figure 7-40. Figure 7-41 depicts the data flow diagram for the process.

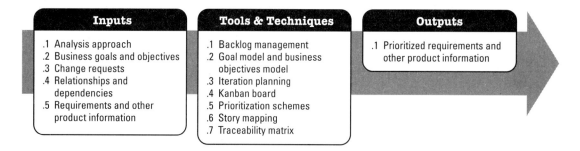

Figure 7-40. Prioritize Requirements and Other Product Information: Inputs, Tools and Techniques, and Outputs

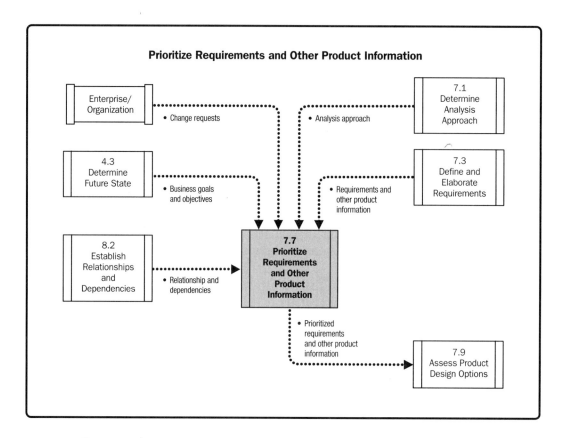

Figure 7-41. Prioritize Requirements and Other Product Information: Data Flow Diagram

Prioritizing requirements is an important step in managing product scope. Prioritization determines what should be worked on first or next so that business objectives are achieved in an order that best meets the needs of the organization. Prioritization is about focusing on what adds the most value. Product information at any level, from business needs to functional requirements, can be prioritized. Prioritization also supports the allocation of requirements to iterations or releases for release planning purposes. Requirements and other product information, such as issues or defects, are prioritized using factors such as value, cost, difficulty, regulations, and risk. Although business analysis does not typically involve estimating development costs, technical risks, and technical difficulty, these are all things that need to be analyzed to prioritize effectively.

A business analyst might recommend prioritization, but it is necessary for accountable stakeholders who have authority to prioritize requirements to be involved in this process. Business analysts help facilitate and negotiate prioritization decisions. Setting expectations about how prioritization will be performed with stakeholders early in the business analysis process helps minimize situations where stakeholders become unhappy when their requirements are prioritized to the bottom of the list. Negotiation, conflict management, and facilitation skills are used heavily during prioritization discussions.

Prioritization might happen iteratively or all at once on a portfolio, program, or project. The project life cycle influences the prioritization process and often dictates the frequency, timing, and techniques for performing prioritization. For example, the business analysis work to complete processes, use cases, or reports may be prioritized. Once product information such as requirements exists, those items are prioritized for development and testing. A project might initially require prioritization of high-level items such as business objectives, processes, or features, and later of requirements or user stories. A portfolio or program can use techniques similar to those for project prioritization, but the techniques used on portfolios and programs are applied to the prioritization of business objectives and projects or cross-project features and requirements.

Prioritization of any item at any level commonly involves two efforts and they do not have to be sequentially ordered. The first effort is when the business stakeholders, subject matter experts, or product owners prioritize requirements based on their estimated business value. The second effort is to understand the project team's estimates of effort and the risk of each requirement. The business analyst facilitates the prioritization discussions and works with the team to ensure that the high-priority requirements can be completed within the boundaries of the portfolio, program, or project.

Prioritization results are not necessarily final. Prioritization factors can change, and so can requirements. A requirement thought to be a high priority at the beginning of a project may be changed to a lower priority as the project progresses. On the other hand, a stakeholder could elevate the priority of other requirements that were originally thought to be unimportant. The project life cycle will determine how to handle changes in priority. As requirements are added to the product backlog or changes in priority result in the movement of requirements from one release or iteration to another, the changes are tracked and communicated to the appropriate stakeholders. Validation is usually complete before prioritization, but the processes could be performed simultaneously. In adaptive approaches, a list of high-level features might be prioritized initially, and later user stories can be prioritized. In predictive approaches, the full set of requirements will likely be complete and validated before prioritization.

7.7.1 PRIORITIZE REQUIREMENTS AND OTHER PRODUCT INFORMATION: INPUTS

7.7.1.1 ANALYSIS APPROACH

Described in Section 7.1.3.1. The analysis approach defines how analysis will be performed for the portfolio, program, or project. Included in the analysis approach is a decision about the approach for prioritization, including which techniques will be used, when prioritization is performed, and who will participate in and make prioritization decisions.

7.7.1.2 BUSINESS GOALS AND OBJECTIVES

Described in Section 4.3.3.1. Business goals and objectives define what results the business is expecting a portfolio, program, or project to deliver. The desired outcomes specified by the business objectives are the primary consideration in prioritizing which requirements and related work should be completed first. A key purpose of the prioritization process is ensuring that what the team builds actually meets the business goals and objectives.

7.7.1.3 CHANGE REQUESTS

Described in Section 8.4.1.3. Change requests are appeals to make a change to a requirement or other suggestions for changes to product information that are raised by the business stakeholders or project team after a set of requirements is baselined. Change requests are prioritized along with other work, including any undeveloped requirements. Sometimes a change request is of higher priority than existing work. Some change requests may require items to be removed from scope, to accommodate the change.

In adaptive approaches, there may not be a formal change request process. When a stakeholder requests a change, it is typically written in the form of a user story, and added to the backlog. In adaptive approaches, new product backlog items are prioritized against the backlog items that are already present. That reprioritization usually occurs during the planning session for the next iteration.

7.7.1.4 RELATIONSHIPS AND DEPENDENCIES

Described in Section 8.2.3.1. Relationships and dependencies define the links between requirements. Relationships can be parent to child, as requirements are progressively elaborated from a high level to a low level of detail, or they can be dependency relationships such as implementation, benefit, or value. Relationships and dependencies can affect prioritization choices.

7.7.1.5 REQUIREMENTS AND OTHER PRODUCT INFORMATION

Described in Section 7.3.3.1. Requirements and other product information include all the information about a solution and are the culmination of results from elicitation and analysis activities. The requirements and other product information accumulated throughout the portfolio, program, or project comprise the information prioritized.

7.7.2 PRIORITIZE REQUIREMENTS AND OTHER PRODUCT INFORMATION: TOOLS AND TECHNIQUES

7.7.2.1 BACKLOG MANAGEMENT

A product backlog is the list of all the work that needs to be completed to produce the solution. A backlog can contain high-level product information such as projects or features to be managed at a portfolio or program level. Backlog management is primarily used in adaptive approaches to maintain the list of backlog items to be worked on during a project.

Backlog management refers to the process by which the owner of the backlog, commonly a product owner, assists in keeping the backlog up to date. If roles are separate, the business analyst often helps the product owner refine the product backlog, which involves adding and removing backlog items, elaborating backlog items, and reprioritizing based on changing requirements or business conditions and priorities.

The product backlog needs to be organized by priority at all times. The list is ranked in order of business value or importance to the customer and sized by the development team so that the team can pull in the highest-value items that can be delivered over a duration; most commonly, it is based on a time-boxed development iteration. Dependencies and constraints are also taken into account, which might impact the order of the items in the backlog. For more information on product backlog, see Section 7.3.2.4.

7.7.2.2 GOAL MODEL AND BUSINESS OBJECTIVES MODEL

The goal model and business objectives model describe the business objectives that the solution is meant to achieve, along with the high-level features for the solution. Either model can be used as a tool to help prioritize the requirements according to how much they support or achieve the objectives. Any requirements that do not trace back to and support the business objectives can be cut from scope or assigned a low priority. Any remaining in-scope requirements are weighted by how much they help achieve the business objectives. This model can also be used to prioritize programs or projects based on the business objectives each one is expected to deliver. For example, a project might be prioritized over another project if it is expected to deliver a higher net benefit based on the business objectives. For more information on goal models and business objectives models, see Section 7.2.2.9.

7.7.2.3 ITERATION PLANNING

In adaptive approaches, iteration planning or sprint planning is the activity used to identify the subset of product backlog items that the product development team will work on for the current iteration or sprint. The entire team collaborates just before or at the beginning of the iteration to select the backlog items that should be part of an iteration backlog. Business analysis activities ensure that product backlog items are ready to be developed. The business analysis responsibilities entail choosing items for the iteration backlog that are sufficiently elaborated upon and most important in terms of delivering business value.

7.7.2.4 KANBAN BOARD

A kanban board is used in adaptive approaches to track work that is in progress by the project team. It is a visual representation of what work is in progress, whereas the product backlog is the prioritized list of all possible work. The kanban board shows the steps in a workflow, such as the project life cycle phases, and work in progress (WIP) limits for each phase. WIP limits specify how many items (typically user stories or tasks) can be in one workflow step at a time. These limits maximize the productivity of the team by ensuring that it never takes on more work than it can handle. The project team pulls items from the product backlog (usually in priority order) into the kanban board and moves them across each workflow step as each is completed, assuming there is room in the next workflow step. This technique also shows clearly what is or is not complete for any given user story. If bottlenecks emerge, the kanban board and the WIP limits become input into prioritization decisions for work in the product backlog and to manage the progress of items allocated to releases.

7.7.2.5 PRIORITIZATION SCHEMES

Prioritization schemes are different methods used to prioritize portfolio components, programs, projects, requirements, features, or any other product information. The analysis approach identifies which prioritization schemes the team has agreed to use and when. Section 4.11.6.1 of *Business Analysis for Practitioners: A Practice Guide* provides more information and examples of prioritization schemes. The following are some commonly used schemes:

◆ **Buy a feature.** A type of collaborative game used to enable a group of stakeholders to agree on prioritization by providing each stakeholder with an amount of pretend money to buy his or her choice of features, splitting the money received across features, however desired. The features are prioritized by counting the total money spent per feature by all stakeholders. The features that receive the most money from the participants are considered the most valuable and highest-prioritized features. For more information on collaborative games, see Section 6.3.2.2.

◆ **Delphi.** A consensus-building technique that conducts a survey to take anonymous input from subject matter experts (SMEs) and consolidates that input through a facilitator. Each round of input is discussed by the team to gain understanding, and then the survey is performed again. In this technique, each stakeholder provides a prioritization for the requirements set using the prioritization scheme chosen, and then the stakeholders meet together to discuss until the group agrees on the prioritization. This method is intended to reduce peer pressure or groupthink in the prioritization process or to avoid the team giving in to a voice of authority with whom they may disagree. For more information on Delphi, see Section 8.3.2.4.

◆ **Minimum viable product (MVP).** A prioritization mechanism used to define the scope of the first release of a solution to customers by identifying the fewest number of features or requirements that would constitute a solution from which the customer would obtain value. The minimum viable product may not include the items that bring the most quantifiable value to the business, but rather a set of items that accelerates time to market for solutions by focusing on releasing the fundamental pieces of a product. Additional features are added in future releases that deliver additional business value. The point of using this technique is to realize some business value faster than waiting for a full product to be built and to learn about the product early on to guide future development. Minimum marketable features (MMF) is a related prioritization mechanism in which the smallest piece of functionality that still delivers value to the customer is identified.

◆ **MoSCoW.** A technique that categorizes each requirement into one of the following groups:

  ▪ *Must have* (fundamental to solution success),

  ▪ *Should have* (important, but the solution's success does not rely on the requirement),

  ▪ *Could have* (can easily be left out without impacting the solution), or

  ▪ *Won't have* (not delivered this time around).

◆ **Multivoting.** A method also called dot voting because it can be performed by providing stakeholders with a prescribed number of colored dots and allowing them to vote by placing their dots on the requirements that they feel are the most important. All votes are aggregated and requirements are ranked by the number of dots/votes received. This method is similar to "buy a feature." Multivoting is further discussed in Section 4.11.6.1 of *Business Analysis for Practitioners: A Practice Guide.*

◆ **Purpose alignment model.** A technique that provides a framework for categorizing business options by their purpose. It supports aligning business decisions with business purposes. The purpose of each option is identified by considering how mission critical it is and how much competitive advantage each will provide to the organization. While this technique is primarily intended as a basis for making strategic or high-level product decisions, some organizations also use it to analyze and facilitate discussions about product requirements and the value each provides, which, in turn, becomes a springboard for prioritization discussions about product features and requirements. For more information on the purpose alignment model, see Section 4.3.2.9.

◆ **Timeboxing.** An estimation or planning technique that can be used during prioritization by setting a strict time limit and prioritizing only the work that the team can complete in that duration of time. Timeboxing is usually used in conjunction with a second prioritization scheme to understand the highest-prioritized requirements to pull into the time-box.

◆ **Weighted ranking.** A method that first requires decision criteria to be identified and weighted. Then each item is rated by scoring how well the option meets the criteria independent of other options. Ratings are multiplied by the weights and summed to arrive at the score for each item and the overall rankings. For more information on weighted ranking, see Section 4.4.2.8.

◆ **Weighted shortest job first (WSJF).** A method used primarily in adaptive frameworks to rank user stories based on more dimensions than just business value and effort. WSJF works by having business value, time criticality, risk reduction or opportunity enablement, and effort all sized using something similar to a Fibonacci sequence used in estimation poker. A formula is used to calculate a weighted value for each user story:

WSJF = [business value + time criticality + (risk reduction/opportunity enablement)] / effort

7.7.2.6 STORY MAPPING

Story mapping is a technique used to arrange user stories in the order they will likely be developed and released to customers. Story maps help communicate the features and solution components that the product team will be responsible for delivering. The technique supports a product team with release allocation where features or product components are assigned to different product releases. Although it can be used as a prioritization technique by itself, other prioritization techniques can be used to help prioritize the user stories in the story map. This technique is primarily used when following an adaptive delivery approach.

Releases can be shown on a story map as horizontal lines, dividing and grouping functionality based on the capacity of the development team and the release dates. Each horizontal grouping is a release, and each vertical grouping can be thought of as a functional grouping. Figure 7-42 shows a sample format of a story map, with releases labeled. For more information on story mapping, see Section 7.2.2.16.

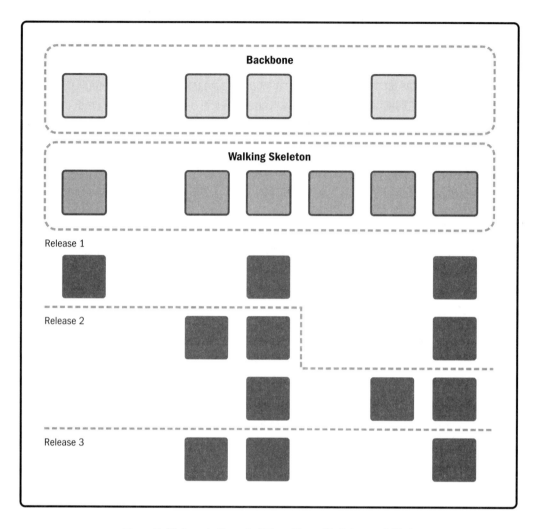

Figure 7-42. Sample Format of Story Map with Releases Added

7.7.2.7 TRACEABILITY MATRIX

The traceability matrix maps requirements backward to analysis models and business objectives and forward to business rules, designs, implementation details, and tests. For prioritization purposes, a traceability matrix can be used to help prioritize requirements using the business objectives to which they are traced. If the business objectives are quantified and ranked accordingly, then the requirements that trace to the highest-value objectives might be the highest-ranked requirements. Any requirements that are not traced to the business objectives are out of scope. For more information on the traceability matrix, see Section 8.2.2.5.

7.7.3 PRIORITIZE REQUIREMENTS AND OTHER PRODUCT INFORMATION: OUTPUTS

7.7.3.1 PRIORITIZED REQUIREMENTS AND OTHER PRODUCT INFORMATION

Prioritized requirements and other product information are a representation of which requirements and other product information the stakeholders agree are most important to address first to achieve the business goals and objectives. The result of prioritization might describe what work should be completed next, or it might be a full ordering of all work, with items allocated to iterations or releases. The prioritization output can take the form of a backlog ordered by business value and risk in adaptive approaches or a prioritization attribute set on each requirement in predictive approaches. Prioritization also indicates which items are of low priority and might be reasonable to cut from scope if change requests come in and are prioritized higher or if the team runs out of time or budget for a release. When requirements and other product information are used as input into other processes, they might include product information that has been prioritized.

7.7.4 PRIORITIZE REQUIREMENTS AND OTHER PRODUCT INFORMATION: TAILORING CONSIDERATIONS

Adaptive and predictive tailoring considerations for Prioritize Requirements and Other Product Information are described in Table 7-8.

Table 7-8. Adaptive and Predictive Tailoring for Prioritize Requirements and Other Product Information

Aspects to Be Tailored	Typical Adaptive Considerations	Typical Predictive Considerations
Name	Backlog Management, Prioritize Backlog, or Backlog Ranking	Prioritize Requirements and Other Product Information
Approach	Features or user stories are the most commonly prioritized product information, but any items in the backlog can be prioritized. Product information is continuously prioritized and reprioritized in the product backlog by the product owner or the business analyst. The product backlog is a living prioritized list of requirements, so it needs to always reflect the top priorities of the business. Prioritization techniques are used for each iteration to determine the features to be provided in the next release of the solution.	Features, requirements, and change requests are prioritized commonly after they are verified and validated and either before or after they are approved. Prioritization results are reflected on each requirement in the requirements set. Prioritization occurs before any solution construction begins. Priorities may still shift throughout the project, but incorporating such changes is more difficult than just reordering things, often requiring a change control process to be executed.
Deliverables	Prioritized backlog, ordered by business value or a combination of business value and business risk.	Each requirement in the requirements set will have a priority based on whatever prioritization scheme was chosen.

7.7.5 PRIORITIZE REQUIREMENTS AND OTHER PRODUCT INFORMATION: COLLABORATION POINT

Product team members contribute to prioritization efforts by providing the size and risk estimates for building the solution to the specified requirements. Product owners and product managers are typically two of the most influential roles in establishing priorities for the portfolio, program, or project. Product sponsors can set and approve priorities, too, and may be consulted when prioritization efforts do not result in consensus among the team.

7.8 IDENTIFY AND ANALYZE PRODUCT RISKS

Identify and Analyze Product Risks is the process of uncovering and examining assumptions and uncertainties that could positively or negatively affect success in the definition, development, and the expected results of the solution.

The key benefits of this process are that it supports proactive management of uncertainties in business analysis activities and it uncovers and proactively addresses areas of potential strengths and weaknesses in the product. The inputs, tools and techniques, and outputs of the process are depicted in Figure 7-43. Figure 7-44 depicts the data flow diagram for the process.

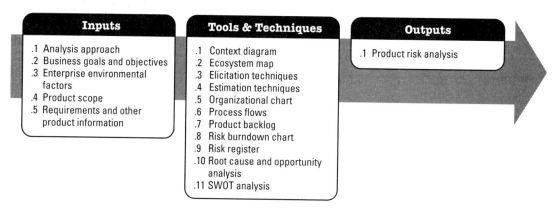

Inputs

.1 Analysis approach
.2 Business goals and objectives
.3 Enterprise environmental factors
.4 Product scope
.5 Requirements and other product information

Tools & Techniques

.1 Context diagram
.2 Ecosystem map
.3 Elicitation techniques
.4 Estimation techniques
.5 Organizational chart
.6 Process flows
.7 Product backlog
.8 Risk burndown chart
.9 Risk register
.10 Root cause and opportunity analysis
.11 SWOT analysis

Outputs

.1 Product risk analysis

Figure 7-43. Identify and Analyze Product Risks: Inputs, Tools and Techniques, and Outputs

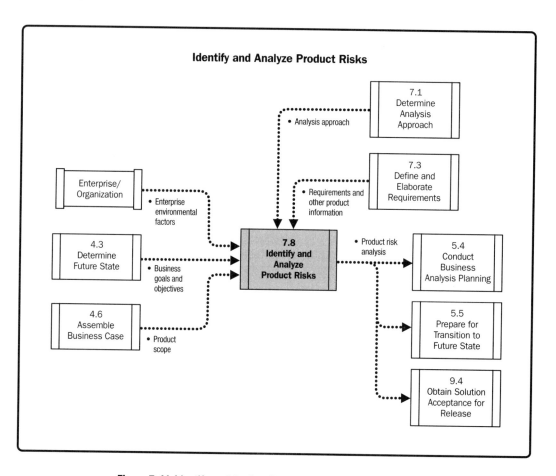

Figure 7-44. Identify and Analyze Product Risks: Data Flow Diagram

Business analysis supports the portfolio, program, or project risk management processes through the identification and analysis of risks that impact business analysis activities and/or the product, otherwise known as product risks. Product risks are uncertainties that can affect success in definition, development, and expected results of the product or solution. Product risks that have an adverse impact can lead to failures in the product if they are not addressed.

Identifying and analyzing product risks includes the following activities:

◆ **Identifying product risks.** Determining risks and documenting their characteristics, which may affect business analysis activities and/or the product.

◆ **Performing qualitative risk analysis.** Prioritizing product risks for further analysis or action by assessing and considering their probability of occurrence and impact.

◆ **Performing quantitative risk analysis.** Numerically analyzing the effect of identified product risks on the business objectives.

◆ **Planning risk responses.** Developing options and actions to address product risks. Product risk responses may include modifying or identifying additional product requirements and/or additional project activities to take advantage of opportunities or address potential failure points. Product risk management thus leads to identifying and proactively resolving gaps in requirements and other product information.

Strategies for negative risks or threats include the following:

■ *Avoid.* Eliminate the threat.

■ *Transfer.* Shift the impact of the threat to a third party.

■ *Mitigate.* Reduce the probability and/or impact of the threat.

■ *Accept.* Acknowledge the threat, but do not take any action unless the risk occurs.

Strategies for positive risks or opportunities include the following:

■ *Exploit.* Ensure that the opportunity is realized.

■ *Enhance.* Increase the probability and/or positive impacts of the opportunity.

■ *Share.* Allocate some or all of the ownership of the opportunity to a third party.

■ *Accept.* Take advantage of the opportunity if it arises, but do not actively pursue it.

◆ **Implementing risk responses.** Implementing agreed-upon risk responses.

◆ **Monitoring risks.** Monitoring the implementation of agreed-upon risk responses, tracking identified product risks, monitoring residual product risks, identifying new product risks, and evaluating risk process effectiveness.

When identifying and analyzing product risks, consideration is provided to any applicable assumptions, constraints, dependencies, or issues as follows:

◆ **Assumptions.** Factors that are considered true, real, or certain, without actual proof or demonstration. There is an element of risk with every assumption that is made. The risk is associated with the event or condition that would occur if the factor turns out not to be true, real, or certain.

◆ **Constraints.** Limiting factors that affect the execution of a portfolio, program, project, or process and may be business or technical factors. In business analysis, constraints are limiting factors that affect the development or implementation of the solution. Risks can be identified for situations if limits are reached.

◆ **Dependencies.** Logical relationships that exist between two or more entities. Risks can be identified for situations if dependencies are not met.

◆ **Issues.** Points or matters in question, in dispute, or not settled and under discussion. If a risk event occurs and the response plan is inadequate, the risk may be converted into an issue. Conversely, new risks may be introduced for unresolved issues.

Converting assumptions, constraints, dependencies, or unresolved issues into risks allows product teams to be more proactive in the management of these items, as risks tend to be analyzed in more frequent intervals.

7.8.1 IDENTIFY AND ANALYZE PRODUCT RISKS: INPUTS

7.8.1.1 ANALYSIS APPROACH

Described in Section 7.1.3.1. The analysis approach defines how analysis will be performed for the portfolio, program, or project. Included in the analysis approach is a decision about how to conduct risk analysis, including details regarding the product risk management process, the risk categories, and how risks will be documented.

7.8.1.2 BUSINESS GOALS AND OBJECTIVES

Described in Section 4.3.3.1. Business goals and objectives identify what the business is expecting a portfolio, program, or project to deliver. Product risks are evaluated and rated on whether and how much they may impact the business goals and objectives. Evaluating assumptions that were made in defining business goals and objectives might also lead to identifying additional risks.

7.8.1.3 ENTERPRISE ENVIRONMENTAL FACTORS (EEFS)

Described in Sections 2.2.1 and 2.2.2. EEFs are conditions that influence, constrain, or direct how business analysis is conducted. Analysis of EEFs can uncover product risk factors, such as when a legal or contractual restriction impacts how business analysis processes are conducted. EEFs also include stakeholder risk appetite, which may influence risk responses.

7.8.1.4 PRODUCT SCOPE

Described in Section 4.6.3.2. Product scope is defined as the features and functions that characterize a solution. Product risks are evaluated and rated on whether and how they may impact the product represented by the product scope statement.

7.8.1.5 REQUIREMENTS AND OTHER PRODUCT INFORMATION

Described in Section 7.3.3.1. Requirements and other product information include all the information about a solution and are the culmination of results from elicitation and analysis activities. Product information can be evaluated to identify product risks. For instance, assessing assumptions, constraints, dependencies, and the requirements may help uncover product risk factors. Product risk responses may trigger modifications or additions to requirements and other product information.

7.8.2 IDENTIFY AND ANALYZE PRODUCT RISKS: TOOLS AND TECHNIQUES

7.8.2.1 CONTEXT DIAGRAM

A context diagram is a scope model that shows all the direct system and human interfaces to systems within a solution. A context diagram clearly depicts the in-scope systems and any inputs or outputs, including the systems or actors providing or receiving them. These models can be used to identify product risks or failure points by analyzing the interfaces. For more information on context diagrams, see Section 7.2.2.1.

7.8.2.2 ECOSYSTEM MAP

An ecosystem map is a scope model that shows all the relevant systems, the relationships between each system, and optionally, any data objects passed between them. A business analyst would use an ecosystem map for product risk analysis in the same way that a context diagram would be used. Ecosystem maps may be used to identify product risks or potential failure points, through analyzing the interfaces and objects passed between the systems. For more information on ecosystem maps, see Section 7.2.2.5.

7.8.2.3 ELICITATION TECHNIQUES

Elicitation techniques are used to draw information from sources. Product risks are uncovered through elicitation; thus, any of the elicitation techniques can be used to identify and analyze product risks. For more information on elicitation techniques, see Section 6.3.2.

7.8.2.4 ESTIMATION TECHNIQUES

Estimation techniques are used to provide a quantitative assessment of likely amounts or outcomes. Various estimation techniques can be used to quantify the probability and impact of product risks. For more information on estimation techniques, see Section 5.4.2.3.

7.8.2.5 ORGANIZATIONAL CHART

Organizational charts are models that depict the reporting structure within an organization or within a part of an organization. These models can be used to identify risks related to stakeholder groups—for example, when there are stakeholder groups identified that may impact business analysis activities. Organizational charts can also be used to identify who should own the product risk response plans. For more information on organizational charts, see Section 5.1.2.3.

7.8.2.6 PROCESS FLOWS

Process flows visually document the steps or tasks that people perform in their jobs or when they interact with a product. These models may be used to identify product risks or potential failure points by analyzing process steps, decision points, and handoffs between different actors in a process. For more information on process flows, see Section 7.2.2.12.

7.8.2.7 PRODUCT BACKLOG

The product backlog is the list of all product backlog items, typically user stories, requirements, or features, that need to be delivered for a solution. Projects that employ adaptive approaches use the product backlog as part of the requirements package. When needed, tasks called spikes or risk spikes can be added to the product backlog to evaluate risks. The items in the product backlog are ranked in order of business value or importance to the customer and are continuously updated throughout a product's life cycle or a project's duration. For more information on the product backlog, see Section 7.3.2.4. For more information on backlog management, see Section 7.7.2.1.

7.8.2.8 RISK BURNDOWN CHART

Burndown charts are used to communicate progress over time. On adaptive projects, risk burndown charts can be used to show the status of risks across iterations. The sum of exposures (probability multiplied by impact) across all product risks is mapped for each iteration. Ideally, the burndown chart should show a downward slope when connecting the data points to indicate that product risk exposures are decreasing as iterations progress. Figure 7-45 shows a sample format of a risk burndown chart. For more information on burndown charts, see Section 5.4.2.1.

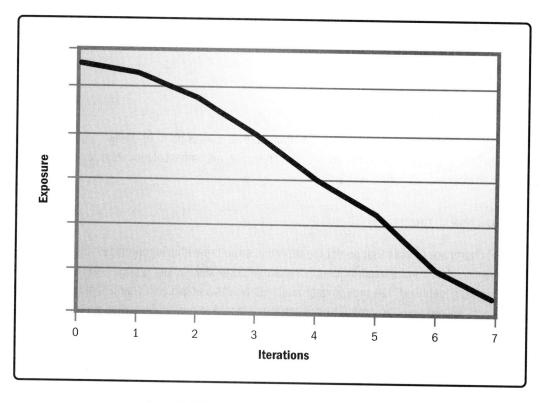

Figure 7-45. Sample Format for Risk Burndown Chart

7.8.2.9 RISK REGISTER

The risk register is a tool used to support analysis of product risks. Product risks are logged with corresponding details, which may include the following:

◆ **Risk ID.** Unique number used to identify the risk.

◆ **Risk description.** Textual description of the risk.

◆ **Date logged.** Date when the risk was identified.

◆ **Risk owner.** Person responsible for monitoring the risk.

◆ **Status.** State of the risk—for example, open or closed.

◆ **Updates.** Progress information on the risk.

◆ **Impact rating.** Numerical rating representing the severity if the risk event were to occur.

◆ **Probability rating.** Numerical rating representing the probability of the risk event occurring.

◆ **Exposure.** Impact multiplied by probability.

◆ **Trigger.** Signs that warn that the risk is about to occur or has already occurred.

◆ **Risk response.** Actions that can be taken to proactively address the risk.

◆ **Risk response owner.** Person responsible for executing the risk response.

◆ **Workaround.** Actions to be performed if the risk were to occur.

The business analyst and portfolio, program, or project manager may opt to produce a consolidated risk register. Risks can be identified during iteration or daily planning.

7.8.2.10 ROOT CAUSE AND OPPORTUNITY ANALYSIS

Root cause analysis is used to determine the basic underlying reason that causes a variance, defect, or risk. Opportunity analysis is used to study the major facets of a potential opportunity to determine the possible changes in products offered to enable its achievement. Root cause and opportunity analysis can be used to develop response plans to proactively address negative product risks or take advantage of potential opportunities. For more information on root cause and opportunity analysis, see Section 4.2.2.9.

7.8.2.11 SWOT ANALYSIS

A SWOT analysis is a technique for analyzing the (S) strengths and (W) weaknesses of an organization, project, or option, and the (O) opportunities and (T) threats that exist externally. SWOT analysis can be used to identify potential product risks in the form of positive risks (opportunities) or negative risks (threats). For more information on SWOT analysis, see Section 4.2.2.10.

7.8.3 IDENTIFY AND ANALYZE PRODUCT RISKS: OUTPUTS

7.8.3.1 PRODUCT RISK ANALYSIS

The product risk analysis includes the consolidated results from identifying and analyzing product risks. The product risk analysis may consist of:

◆ Identified product risks,

◆ List of potential responses,

◆ Relative rating or priority list of risks,

◆ Symptoms and warning signs,

◆ Risks requiring responses in the near term,

◆ Risks for additional analysis and response,

◆ Trends in qualitative analysis results,

◆ Total risk exposure, and

◆ Watch list of low-priority risks.

7.8.4 IDENTIFY AND ANALYZE PRODUCT RISKS: TAILORING CONSIDERATIONS

Adaptive and predictive tailoring considerations for Identify and Analyze Product Risks are described in Table 7-9.

Table 7-9. Adaptive and Predictive Tailoring for Identify and Analyze Product Risks

Aspects to Be Tailored	Typical Adaptive Considerations	Typical Predictive Considerations
Name	Not a formally named process	Identify and Analyze Product Risks
Approach	Risks are discussed and addressed in iteration 0, iteration planning, and/or daily stand-ups and considered when determining the value of backlog items. Assumptions, constraints, dependencies, issues, and risks may be discussed at the same time. Teams focus on short iterations that minimize risk.	Integrated with portfolio, program, or project risk management processes that are performed throughout the portfolio, program, or project, respectively. Assumptions, constraints, dependencies, issues, and risks may be discussed at the same time.
Deliverables	Risk spikes are added to the backlog.	Robust risk register. Sometimes assumptions, constraints, dependencies, issues, and risks are combined into a single register.

7.8.5 IDENTIFY AND ANALYZE PRODUCT RISKS: COLLABORATION POINT

Portfolio, program, and project managers work together on the identification, analysis, and management of product risks because collectively they are a subset of portfolio, program, or project risks. Risk response plans that modify or add requirements or project activities may have portfolio, program, or project implications; therefore, collaboration on risk activities is essential.

7.9 ASSESS PRODUCT DESIGN OPTIONS

Assess Product Design Options is the process of identifying, analyzing, and comparing solution design options based on the business goals and objectives, expected costs of implementation, feasibility, and associated risks, and using the results of this assessment to provide recommendations regarding the design options presented. The key benefit of this process is that it allows for informed recommendations of design options. The inputs, tools and techniques, and outputs of the process are depicted in Figure 7-46. Figure 7-47 depicts the data flow diagram for the process.

Figure 7-46. Assess Product Design Options: Inputs, Tools and Techniques, and Outputs

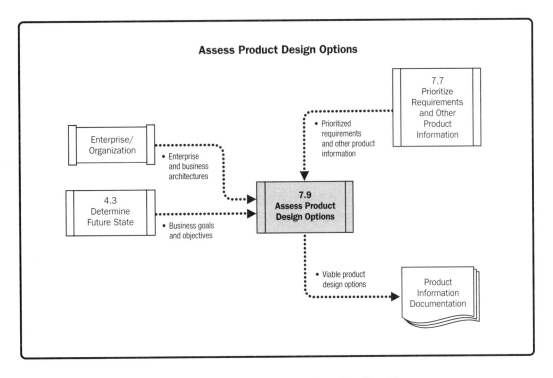

Figure 7-47. Assess Product Design Options: Data Flow Diagram

Assessing product design goes beyond what the product should do and starts to focus on how it should be built or how it should look. There are multiple options for how a solution can be built, and business analysis is used to evaluate them. This process entails understanding which design options are available and analyzing the details about how those designs would evolve into a solution. Each option's analysis results provide relevant information to articulate the pros and cons, risks, and costs of the option. Each option is compared against the others to determine which option best achieves the overall product goals and objectives and adheres to limitations, budget, and/or time constraints. Designs that are not viable are removed from consideration.

Design discussions need to take place before construction begins for any given solution or component of a solution, even if it is only a small piece of the solution. Avoiding these discussions may result in missed objectives or products that are unintuitive to use. Also, product development might take more time if the teams are trying to make up design choices as they go.

Product teams do not have to wait to assess product designs until after all the requirements are complete. This work can be completed as increments of requirements are ready for design. The requirements need to be prioritized so that the design can best address the most important requirements. If this process is performed iteratively and incrementally, the designs might change from iteration to iteration, causing some rework. In adaptive life cycles, the rework is accounted for during planning. With a predictive life cycle, requirements work is completed in its entirety before design; therefore, design changes have a much larger impact and tend to be costlier than with adaptive methods, especially if pursued as a result of discoveries made during product development.

Design can be identified and analyzed on portfolios, programs, or projects. Designs are most detailed on projects, where they are used to implement some or all of the solution. On a portfolio or program, design analysis can be done to sufficient levels of detail to ensure consistency across multiple releases or components of a solution.

7.9.1 ASSESS PRODUCT DESIGN OPTIONS: INPUTS

7.9.1.1 BUSINESS GOALS AND OBJECTIVES

Described in Section 4.3.3.1. Business goals and objectives define the results the business is expecting a portfolio, program, or project to deliver. Designs need to be aimed at achieving these goals and objectives. Poorly designed solutions that meet the requirements can keep the solution from achieving the desired goals and objectives.

7.9.1.2 ENTERPRISE AND BUSINESS ARCHITECTURES

Described in Section 4.2.1.1. Enterprise and business architectures are the aggregate of technology, business functions, organizational structures, locations, and processes of an organization. The architectures are used to ensure that the proposed designs can operate within the existing architectures or to understand how those architectures might change with proposed designs. The design options might be constrained by either architecture.

Business architecture can help identify design elements that need to be incorporated for different regions, languages, users, and organizational customs, as well as any opportunities to reuse capabilities. In some cases, a single design might not work for all components of the business architecture. Enterprise architecture can help identify any system or data limitations or reuse opportunities for consideration in choosing design options. Some designs may not be feasible with existing technologies. Some design options might need more resources than the current architecture can support.

7.9.1.3 PRIORITIZED REQUIREMENTS AND OTHER PRODUCT INFORMATION

Described in Section 7.7.3.1. Designs are created to reflect how a solution will meet the requirements. Prioritized requirements represent the stakeholders' agreement about which requirements need to be addressed first in the solution and therefore also represent which requirements are most important to account for in the designs.

Requirements sometimes contain legitimate design constraints. Some organizations have certain branding or look-and-feel requirements or capability or technical limitations that lead to design choices or limitations. However, well-written requirements avoid unnecessarily constraining or biasing design. Designs need to be created while considering known risks and should address the impact of those risks on the design. Additional risks uncovered during design also need to be analyzed.

7.9.2 ASSESS PRODUCT DESIGN OPTIONS: TOOLS AND TECHNIQUES

7.9.2.1 AFFINITY DIAGRAM

Affinity diagrams display categories and subcategories of ideas that cluster or have an affinity to one another. Affinity diagrams can be used to help identify design options by organizing user stories, features, or requirements. Similarly, design options can be organized in an affinity diagram for grouping similar designs and aiding in the decision process when trying to make a choice from among different design options. Organizing design information into categories can also facilitate brainstorming new design ideas. For more information on affinity diagrams, see Section 4.3.2.1.

7.9.2.2 BRAINSTORMING

Brainstorming is an elicitation technique that can be used to identify a list of ideas in a short period of time. Brainstorming can be used to identify design options and any risks associated with them. For more information on brainstorming, see Section 5.1.2.1.

7.9.2.3 COMPETITIVE ANALYSIS

Competitive analysis is a technique for obtaining and analyzing information about an organization's external environment. Competitive analysis is used when identifying and comparing design options to create an advantage for the product in the marketplace as compared to competitors. It is useful to understand if a proposed design is far more than what a competitor offers. For more information on competitive analysis, see Section 4.1.2.2.

7.9.2.4 FOCUS GROUPS

Focus groups bring together prequalified stakeholders and subject matter experts (SMEs) to learn about their expectations and attitudes about a proposed solution. Focus groups can be used to solicit attitudes and ideas about different design options. For more information on focus groups, see Section 6.3.2.5.

7.9.2.5 PRODUCT BACKLOG

The product backlog is the list of all product backlog items, typically user stories, requirements, or features, that need to be delivered for a solution. Product backlog items need to be factored into the design, even if the design is lightweight and not formally documented. In adaptive approaches, tasks are added to the product backlog to evaluate complex design options. These tasks are called spikes. For more information on product backlog, see Section 7.3.2.4.

7.9.2.6 REAL OPTIONS

Real options is a decision-making technique that encourages teams to delay decision making until the latest possible time. Delayed decision making provides an opportunity to obtain as much information as possible regarding the issue or item under discussion. When assessing product design options, delaying a recommendation about a possible design provides time for more information to be discovered and analyzed, answering unknowns and thereby reducing the number of uncertainties that would be present if the design choice had been made earlier. The real options technique also eliminates design options that are not feasible by considering the business objectives and goals, expected costs, and risks. For more information on real options, see Section 4.4.2.6.

7.9.2.7 VENDOR ASSESSMENT

On many projects, vendors may provide the solution that best meets the requirements. When assessing product design options, relevant vendors and their products are evaluated to understand the viability, strengths, weaknesses, and risks of each vendor solution. Performing a vendor assessment entails identifying a set of criteria by which vendors and their products will be evaluated. The criteria used to make this assessment might be a set of requirements, user stories, or features, and can be prioritized or weighted. Some of the criteria used to assess vendor offerings might be qualitative criteria—for example, measures used to evaluate the experience of working with the vendor or solution.

7.9.3 ASSESS PRODUCT DESIGN OPTIONS: OUTPUTS

7.9.3.1 VIABLE PRODUCT DESIGN OPTIONS

Design options are representations of how the solution could be constructed. Viable product design options are those that have been reviewed by stakeholders to ensure that they achieve the business goals and objectives and are feasible. Viable product design options are presented with the pros and cons of each option. Once a design is selected, construction of the solution or component of the solution can begin.

7.9.4 ASSESS PRODUCT DESIGN OPTIONS: TAILORING CONSIDERATIONS

Adaptive and predictive tailoring considerations for Assess Product Design Options are described in Table 7-10.

Table 7-10. Adaptive and Predictive Tailoring for Assess Product Design Options

Aspects to Be Tailored	Typical Adaptive Considerations	Typical Predictive Considerations
Name	Elaboration, Sizing, or Spikes	Assess Product Design Options
Approach	User stories and acceptance criteria are the basis for any design work. Design is performed iteratively as part of elaboration, sizing, or as the solution is developed. Typically, design is done just in time before development, though adaptive life cycles often do some initial overarching design early in a project to minimize major redesign efforts. Spikes are tasks used to evaluate multiple design options against one another.	Requirements are completed and are the basis for any design work, and design choices are fed to the team responsible for building the solution.
Deliverables	Designs are sketches or ideas and often are not formally documented.	Formally specified or modeled designs, completed in tools or documents.

7.9.5 ASSESS PRODUCT DESIGN OPTIONS: COLLABORATION POINT

Many product team roles assist with the assessment of design options. Architects provide expertise and recommendations and are engaged to highlight complexities and risks with the design options under discussion. Design teams contribute design ideas, sizing estimates, and any risks associated with different design options. A project sponsor provides decision authority about funding a design based on whether it sufficiently addresses the business needs and known risks; DevOps might participate by contributing infrastructure or operational considerations and risks.

8

TRACEABILITY AND MONITORING

Traceability and Monitoring includes the processes used to establish relationships and dependencies between requirements and other product information, which helps ensure that requirements are approved and managed, and that the impact of changes to them is assessed.

The Traceability and Monitoring processes are as follows:

8.1 Determine Traceability and Monitoring Approach—The process of considering how traceability will be performed on the portfolio, program, project, or product, and defining how requirement changes will be managed.

8.2 Establish Relationships and Dependencies—The process of tracing or setting linkages between and among requirements and other product information.

8.3 Select and Approve Requirements—The process of facilitating discussions with stakeholders to negotiate and confirm which requirements should be incorporated within an iteration, release, or project.

8.4 Manage Changes to Requirements and Other Product Information—The process of examining changes or defects that arise during a project by understanding the value and impact of the changes. As changes are agreed upon, information about those changes is reflected wherever necessary to support prioritization and eventual product development.

Figure 8-1 provides an overview of the Traceability and Monitoring processes. The business analysis processes are presented as discrete processes with defined interfaces, while in practice, they overlap and interact in ways that cannot be completely detailed in this guide.

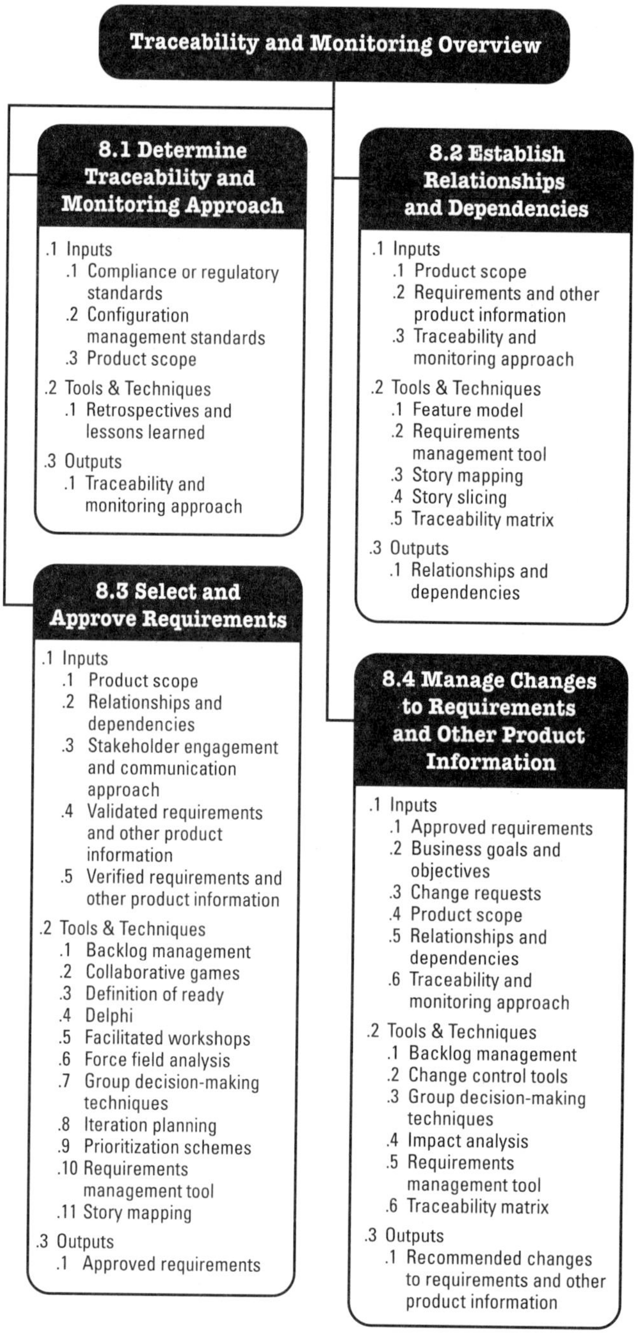

Traceability and Monitoring Overview

8.1 Determine Traceability and Monitoring Approach

.1 Inputs
　.1 Compliance or regulatory standards
　.2 Configuration management standards
　.3 Product scope

.2 Tools & Techniques
　.1 Retrospectives and lessons learned

.3 Outputs
　.1 Traceability and monitoring approach

8.2 Establish Relationships and Dependencies

.1 Inputs
　.1 Product scope
　.2 Requirements and other product information
　.3 Traceability and monitoring approach

.2 Tools & Techniques
　.1 Feature model
　.2 Requirements management tool
　.3 Story mapping
　.4 Story slicing
　.5 Traceability matrix

.3 Outputs
　.1 Relationships and dependencies

8.3 Select and Approve Requirements

.1 Inputs
　.1 Product scope
　.2 Relationships and dependencies
　.3 Stakeholder engagement and communication approach
　.4 Validated requirements and other product information
　.5 Verified requirements and other product information

.2 Tools & Techniques
　.1 Backlog management
　.2 Collaborative games
　.3 Definition of ready
　.4 Delphi
　.5 Facilitated workshops
　.6 Force field analysis
　.7 Group decision-making techniques
　.8 Iteration planning
　.9 Prioritization schemes
　.10 Requirements management tool
　.11 Story mapping

.3 Outputs
　.1 Approved requirements

8.4 Manage Changes to Requirements and Other Product Information

.1 Inputs
　.1 Approved requirements
　.2 Business goals and objectives
　.3 Change requests
　.4 Product scope
　.5 Relationships and dependencies
　.6 Traceability and monitoring approach

.2 Tools & Techniques
　.1 Backlog management
　.2 Change control tools
　.3 Group decision-making techniques
　.4 Impact analysis
　.5 Requirements management tool
　.6 Traceability matrix

.3 Outputs
　.1 Recommended changes to requirements and other product information

Figure 8-1. Traceability and Monitoring Overview

KEY CONCEPTS FOR TRACEABILITY AND MONITORING

Traceability is the ability to track information across the product life cycle by establishing linkages between objects. These linkages are also known as relationships or dependencies. Traceability is sometimes qualified as bidirectional, or forward and backward, because requirements are traced in more than one direction. For instance, backward traceability is performed from the requirements to the scope features and business goals and objectives that triggered them; forward traceability is performed from the requirements to design and test components and, ultimately, the final product. Tracing can also be performed laterally—for instance, tracing textual product information to models. For additional details on the type of information that can be traced, see Section 5.2.1 in *Business Analysis for Practitioners: A Practice Guide*.

Monitoring ensures that product information remains accurate from the point when product information has been approved through its implementation. Monitoring includes managing changes to product information and determining recommended actions to maintain the quality of the product.

The kind of thinking inherent in Traceability and Monitoring applies to all projects and all life cycles. Thinking about the relationships between requirements and their relationships to other project considerations, such as tests and releases, is critical for ensuring project consistency and completeness. Traceability principles that enable change impact analysis are the basis for confirming the fulfillment of objectives and ensuring test coverage. Traceability enables the discovery of missing and extraneous requirements. There is a need to track and monitor completed requirements, no matter what type of life cycle is used for a project or what format is used to document the requirements.

8.1 DETERMINE TRACEABILITY AND MONITORING APPROACH

Determine Traceability and Monitoring Approach is the process of considering how traceability will be performed on the portfolio, program, project, or product, and defining how requirement changes will be managed. The key benefit of this process is that it appropriately sizes the level of traceability and formality of the requirements change management process for the situation. The inputs, tools and techniques, and outputs of the process are depicted in Figure 8-2. Figure 8-3 depicts the data flow diagram for the process.

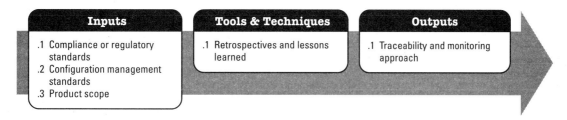

Inputs	Tools & Techniques	Outputs
.1 Compliance or regulatory standards .2 Configuration management standards .3 Product scope	.1 Retrospectives and lessons learned	.1 Traceability and monitoring approach

Figure 8-2. Determine Traceability and Monitoring Approach: Inputs, Tools and Techniques, and Outputs

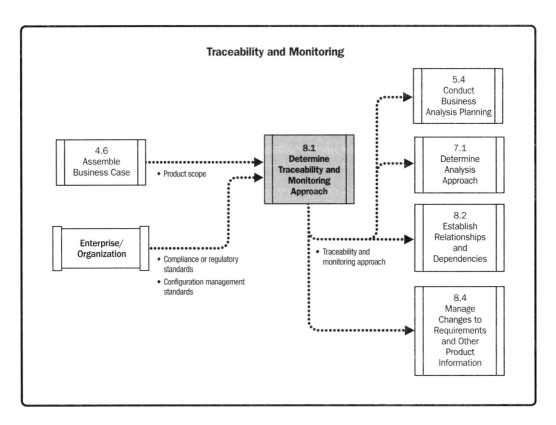

Figure 8-3. Determine Traceability and Monitoring Approach: Data Flow Diagram

The traceability and monitoring approach defines the traceability and change management processes for the portfolio, program, project, or product. Each should be structured at a level of formality that is sufficient to meet the needs of the portfolio, program, project, and product. An appropriately sized traceability and monitoring approach ensures:

◆ A traceability process that minimizes the likelihood of missing requirements in the final product;

◆ A traceability process that is not time-consuming and wasteful to maintain;

◆ A change management process that ensures that changes align with the business and/or project objectives;

◆ A change management process that makes it simple to implement necessary changes; and

◆ A traceability and change management process that aligns to organizational standards, satisfies regulatory requirements, and addresses future needs, including providing valuable information about the product over the long term, beyond the current project.

Components of the traceability and monitoring approach related to traceability may include:

◆ Types of objects to be traced;

◆ Level of detail needed in traceability;

◆ Relationships that will be established and maintained;

◆ Where relationships will be tracked (e.g., using requirements attributes, traceability matrix, or requirements management tools, etc.); and

◆ Requirement states that drive the requirements life cycle (e.g., approve, defer, reject, etc.).

Components of the traceability and monitoring approach related to change management may include:

◆ How requirements changes will be proposed;

◆ How changes will be reviewed;

◆ How change management decisions will be documented;

◆ How requirement changes will be communicated;

◆ How changes to requirements, models, traceability, and other product information will be completed and made available once a change is approved; and

◆ Roles and responsibilities for the requirements change process.

The traceability approach defines the requirements architecture that will be used to specify how requirements, models, and other product information will be related to one another, including which components of product information will be most appropriate to trace to and how they will be traced to one another. Traceability needs will vary across portfolios, programs, projects, and products; therefore, the specific items that will be traced should be clearly indicated. For a project following a predictive life cycle, the project team may trace many types of product information among other objects, whereas a project that follows an adaptive life cycle may not. Traceability decisions, regardless of the life cycle followed, should be based on the short- and long-term value attainable from creating and maintaining the traceability information. Traceability is not limited to tracing product information. Traceability may also be performed on deliverables or components of work that are not part of business analysis activities, such as product design or development. For information on what may be traced and on defining a traceability approach, see Sections 3.4.10 and 5.2.1 in *Business Analysis for Practitioners: A Practice Guide*.

The change management process defines how changes to product information will be handled across the project. The requirements change process is performed differently depending on the selected project life cycle. For a project following a predictive life cycle, the project team may use a formal change management process, whereas a project following an adaptive life cycle does not. Adaptive approaches expect that requirements will evolve over time. For information on defining requirements change processes, see Section 3.4.14 in *Business Analysis for Practitioners: A Practice Guide*.

8.1.1 DETERMINE TRACEABILITY AND MONITORING APPROACH: INPUTS

8.1.1.1 COMPLIANCE OR REGULATORY STANDARDS

Described in Section 2.2. Compliance or regulatory standards are a type of enterprise environmental factor imposed by external organizations commonly for reasons related to security, protecting personal information, legal considerations, or safety reasons. Because the traceability and monitoring approach needs to adhere to compliance and regulatory standards, the tailoring options may be constrained. Compliance and regulatory standards often mandate more formal approaches to traceability and monitoring.

8.1.1.2 CONFIGURATION MANAGEMENT STANDARDS

Described in Section 2.3.2. Configuration management is a collection of formal documented processes, templates, and documentation used to apply governance to changes to the solution or subcomponent under development. Configuration management ensures that the product being built conforms to its approved requirements. The traceability and monitoring approach should adhere to the configuration management standards in place within the organization. When such standards are not developed or in place, the team needs to determine what the configuration management process will be for all aspects of the program or project, including the business analysis work. Configuration management for business analysis ensures that the requirements and requirements-related product information, such as models, traceability matrix, and issues list, are stored where they can be easily accessed by project stakeholders, safeguarded from loss, and where access to previous versions is available, when needed. A business analyst may achieve these objectives with a configuration management system (CMS), a requirements management repository, or with a wiki platform.

8.1.1.3 PRODUCT SCOPE

Described in Section 4.6.3.2. The product scope is defined as the features and functions that characterize a solution. The product scope is used to understand the level of product complexity used to determine an appropriate size for the traceability and change management approach.

8.1.2 DETERMINE TRACEABILITY AND MONITORING APPROACH: TOOLS AND TECHNIQUES

8.1.2.1 RETROSPECTIVES AND LESSONS LEARNED

Retrospectives and lessons learned provide past performance information to the product team for use in improving future performance and, ultimately, the end product. When determining how best to approach traceability and monitoring, product teams can rely upon acquired knowledge and learning to determine which traceability and monitoring approach to follow. Retrospectives and lessons learned, combined with experience and expert judgment, are the basis for tailoring the traceability and change management processes to fit the portfolio, program, or project and the needs of the organization. For more information on retrospectives and lessons learned, see Section 5.7.2.4.

8.1.3 DETERMINE TRACEABILITY AND MONITORING APPROACH: OUTPUTS

8.1.3.1 TRACEABILITY AND MONITORING APPROACH

The traceability and monitoring approach defines how traceability and change management activities will be performed throughout the portfolio, program, or project. The traceability components of the approach include types of objects to trace, types of relationships, the level of tracing detail required, and information about where tracing information will be tracked. The monitoring components of the approach include how changes are proposed and reviewed, how decisions are documented and communicated, and how changes are made to existing product information. Both approaches describe the roles and responsibilities and how the information is stored.

8.1.4 DETERMINE TRACEABILITY AND MONITORING APPROACH: TAILORING CONSIDERATIONS

Adaptive and predictive tailoring considerations for Determine Traceability and Monitoring Approach are described in Table 8-1.

Table 8-1. Adaptive and Predictive Tailoring for Determine Traceability and Monitoring Approach

Aspects to Be Tailored	Typical Adaptive Considerations	Typical Predictive Considerations
Name	Not a formally named process	Determine Traceability and Monitoring Approach
Approach	May be planned at a high level in iteration 0. Tracing and managing changes to product information are often not considered, as these processes are already built into adaptive approaches. Traceability performed via story splitting or story mapping and change management is performed via backlog management.	A high-level traceability and monitoring approach is defined early, during planning. The traceability and monitoring approach is refined throughout the portfolio, program or project. Often, large components of product information and deliverables are traced. A change management process often exists, but the level of formality is dependent on multiple factors, including organizational maturity, size and the complexity of the initiative.
Deliverables	Not a separate deliverable.	Detailed traceability and monitoring approach might reside in a business analysis plan.

8.1.5 DETERMINE TRACEABILITY AND MONITORING APPROACH: COLLABORATION POINT

Portfolio, program, and project managers may contribute to the development of the traceability and monitoring approach to ensure that it is appropriately sized and does not incur unnecessary cost or risk by being over- or underperformed for the needs of the product and portfolio, program, or project. The project manager will be interested in ensuring that the approach for traceability and monitoring is aligned with the tasks, resources, and level of effort specified for this work in the project management plan.

8.2 ESTABLISH RELATIONSHIPS AND DEPENDENCIES

Establish Relationships and Dependencies is the process of tracing or setting linkages between and among requirements and other product information. The key benefits of this process are that it helps in checking that each requirement adds business value and meets the customer's expectations, and it supports monitoring and controlling of product scope. The inputs, tools and techniques, and outputs of the process are depicted in Figure 8-4. Figure 8-5 depicts the data flow diagram for the process.

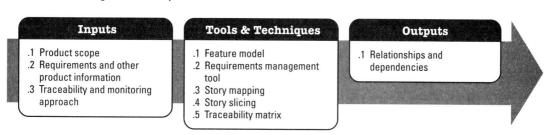

Inputs	Tools & Techniques	Outputs
.1 Product scope .2 Requirements and other product information .3 Traceability and monitoring approach	.1 Feature model .2 Requirements management tool .3 Story mapping .4 Story slicing .5 Traceability matrix	.1 Relationships and dependencies

Figure 8-4. Establish Relationships and Dependencies: Inputs, Tools and Techniques, and Outputs

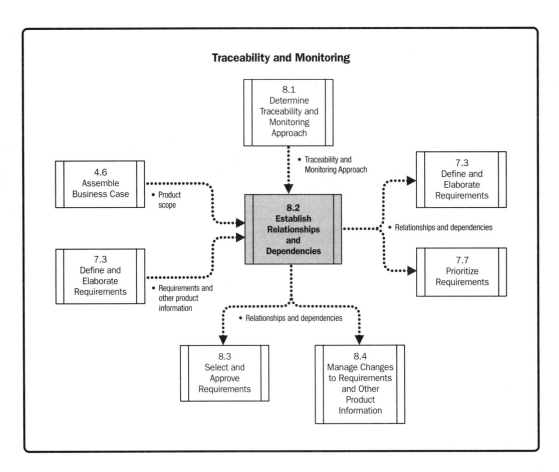

Figure 8-5. Establish Relationships and Dependencies: Data Flow Diagram

As product information is progressively elaborated and additional details surface, relationships and dependencies are created and progressively elaborated. Product information is traced to help provide different and complete views of the product scope. The linkages among different components of product information help do the following:

◆ **Ensure that product information adds business value and meets customer expectations.** Tracing each component of product information to the business need, goals, and objectives helps ensure its relevancy.

◆ **Manage scope.** Non-value-added product information is highlighted through product information that cannot be traced back to the product scope and business goals and objectives.

◆ **Minimize the probability of missing requirements.** Forward traceability helps ensure that product information is not dropped as product information is elaborated, built, tested, and implemented.

◆ **Perform impact analysis.** While analyzing changes to product information, the linkages provide a comprehensive view of the related components that may also require changes.

◆ **Make release decisions.** Implementation, benefit or value relationships, and dependencies between product information may inform certain release decisions.

Because requirements are often related to other requirements, sometimes a requirement is not able to be satisfied in a solution without including the other requirements to which it is related. Some examples of relationships between requirements are as follows:

◆ **Subsets.** A requirement may be a subset of another requirement. Figure 8-6 displays requirements 1, 2, and 3, each as a subset of requirement A. For example, requirements 1, 2, and 3 could represent different nuances of a process where A represents common elements across the subsets. Requirements 1, 2, and 3 could also represent the different components of the parent process A.

◆ **Implementation dependency.** Some requirements are dependent on the implementation of other requirements before they can be implemented. For instance, if requirement A is dependent on requirement B, then A cannot be implemented until B is implemented.

◆ **Benefit or value dependency.** Sometimes the benefit of a requirement is unable to be realized unless another requirement is implemented first. For instance, requirement A can be implemented, but the benefit from doing so may not be achieved until requirement C is also implemented. This relationship may sound similar to implementation dependency, but it is not about whether A can be implemented; rather, it is whether the value from A can be recognized.

Relationships and dependencies are further discussed in Section 5.3 of *Business Analysis for Practitioners: A Practice Guide.*

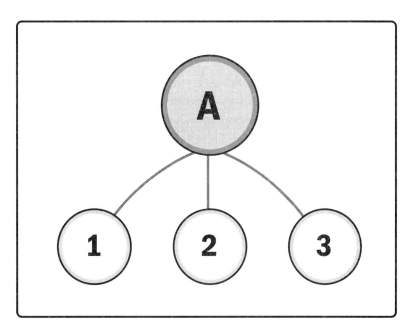

Figure 8-6. Show Requirements 1, 2, and 3, Each as a Subset of Requirement A

Predictive projects provide a better case for formal traceability than adaptive projects; however, the project life cycle is not the only factor that determines the optimal amount of traceability. Other factors include whether the business is highly regulated, organizational standards, product complexity, the risk of product errors, and the degree to which the traceability results are actually used.

8.2.1 ESTABLISH RELATIONSHIPS AND DEPENDENCIES: INPUTS

8.2.1.1 PRODUCT SCOPE

Described in Section 4.6.3.2. The product scope is defined as the features and functions that characterize a solution. Product information is traced to the features and functions that make up the definition of product scope. When there are components of product information that are unable to trace back to the features and functions defined in product scope, the value of including them should be questioned. If it is determined that the product information should be included, then the product scope may need to be reevaluated.

8.2.1.2 REQUIREMENTS AND OTHER PRODUCT INFORMATION

Described in Section 7.3.3.1. Requirements and other product information include all information about a solution and are the culmination of results from elicitation and analysis activities. Relationships and dependencies are established between the requirements and other product information resulting from elicitation and analysis.

8.2.1.3 TRACEABILITY AND MONITORING APPROACH

Described in Section 8.1.3.1. The traceability and monitoring approach defines the decisions made by the team about how traceability will be performed on the portfolio, program, or project. The traceability and monitoring approach may include details about the objects that will be traced, to what level traceability will be performed, and where relationships will be tracked or maintained. As the portfolio, program, or project progresses, more objects are created, increasing the opportunities to establish linkages among these objects. The product team will monitor the approach as it is followed to ensure that the traceability work is adding value. Too much traceability will become time-consuming to maintain, and if the team abandons the traceability work, information will become outdated. While preplanning is performed to ensure that the right traceability approach is established for the portfolio, program, or project, the traceability and monitoring approach can be revised as the team assesses the value throughout the course of its work.

8.2.2 ESTABLISH RELATIONSHIPS AND DEPENDENCIES: TOOLS AND TECHNIQUES

8.2.2.1 FEATURE MODEL

A feature model is a scope model that visually represents all the features of a solution arranged in a tree or hierarchical structure. The feature model shows relationships between features and which features are subfeatures of other ones. The feature model helps teams establish and communicate relationships between different features. For more information on feature models, see Section 7.2.2.8.

8.2.2.2 REQUIREMENTS MANAGEMENT TOOL

Requirements management tools allow requirements and other product information to be captured and stored in a repository. These tools often have functionality to:

◆ Maintain audit trails and perform version control to assist with change management,

◆ Facilitate review and approval processes through workflow functionality,

◆ Generate visual models and interactive prototypes,

- Support team collaboration,

- Integrate with office productivity software for easy imports and exports,

- Track and report on requirements status, and

- Assist in performing detailed traceability based on trace links established in the tool.

Requirements management tools catered to adaptive projects may include additional functionality to create and manage product and iteration backlogs, and product burndown charts. A requirements management tool does not help define high-quality product information, but can assist with the process of storing, managing, and maintaining product information. Selecting the right tool and tool adoption can sometimes be challenging. Requirements management tools should be evaluated on how well they meet the organization's needs to increase the probability of tool adoption. Traceability support is a common feature in most requirements management tools today.

8.2.2.3 STORY MAPPING

Story mapping is a technique used to sequence user stories, based upon their business value and the order in which their users typically perform them, so that teams can arrive at a shared understanding of what will be built. Horizontally, the story map shows what will be delivered within an iteration, and vertically the story map depicts higher-level groupings or categories of user stories. User stories may be grouped by different categories such as functionality, themes, or application. Story mapping can be used to establish relationships between user stories to iterations and the higher-level categories. For more information on story mapping, see Section 7.2.2.16.

8.2.2.4 STORY SLICING

Story slicing is a technique used to split requirements or user stories from a higher level to a lower level. Story slicing is a means of establishing relationships between requirements as lower-level requirements or user stories are subsets of higher-level requirements or epics. For more information on story slicing, see Section 7.3.2.7.

8.2.2.5 TRACEABILITY MATRIX

A traceability matrix is a grid that links product requirements from their origin to the deliverables that satisfy them. The matrix can support linkages among many different types of objects, providing a mechanism for tracking product information through the project and product life cycles. A traceability matrix can be used to establish relationships among product information, deliverables, and project work to ensure that each relates back to business objectives. Establishing these linkages manages scope creep by ensuring that only relevant product information is incorporated into the solution. Traceability matrices are further discussed in Section 5.2.3 of *Business Analysis for Practitioners: A Practice Guide*.

On projects using an adaptive project life cycle, the product team may choose to develop an interaction matrix. An interaction matrix is a lightweight version of a traceability matrix that is used to determine whether requirements are sufficiently detailed or if any entities are missing. The main difference between these two types of traceability matrices is that an interaction matrix is a temporary artifact that represents a snapshot in time, whereas a traceability matrix is typically maintained throughout a portfolio, program, or project. For more information on interaction matrices, see Section 7.2.2.10.

8.2.3 ESTABLISH RELATIONSHIPS AND DEPENDENCIES: OUTPUTS

8.2.3.1 RELATIONSHIPS AND DEPENDENCIES

Relationships and dependencies are the linkages established among objects, such as components of product information, deliverables, and project work. Relationships and dependencies are established to help ensure that product information adds business value and meets customer expectations, manages scope, decreases the probability of missing requirements, performs impact analysis, and makes release decisions.

8.2.4 ESTABLISH RELATIONSHIPS AND DEPENDENCIES: TAILORING CONSIDERATIONS

Adaptive and predictive tailoring considerations for Establish Relationships and Dependencies are described in Table 8-2.

Table 8-2. Adaptive and Predictive Tailoring for Establish Relationships and Dependencies

Aspects to Be Tailored	Typical Adaptive Considerations	Typical Predictive Considerations
Name	Backlog Refinement	Establish Relationships and Dependencies or Trace Requirements
Approach	Typically establishes linkages between user stories and acceptance criteria. Might trace to objectives. Epics or user stories may be traced to features and acceptance tests. Any components of product information might trace forward to design and test and ultimately to the solution. Performed iteratively via story slicing or story mapping as new items are added to the product backlog. May be forms of direct tracing such as attaching a visual model to a story or linking user stories and acceptance criteria.	Minimal to extensive tracing, bidirectional between all components of product information, and deliverables that may contain product information. Established throughout the product life cycle. As more product information is defined, more detailed traceability is performed. Performed after an analysis phase of a project to trace forward to design and test and ultimately, the final solution.
Deliverables	Feature model, story map, interaction matrix, or linked product information like stories and acceptance criteria that may be stored in a requirements management tool.	Small to large traceability matrices. Regulatory environments often dictate formal traceability. Traceability information may be stored in a requirements management tool.

8.2.5 ESTABLISH RELATIONSHIPS AND DEPENDENCIES: COLLABORATION POINT

Joint review of the relationships and dependencies with project team members is needed as these relationships may impact release decisions. On predictive projects, tracing may be performed between business analysis deliverables and deliverables produced by other project team members, such as project requirements and design, development, and test components. Business analysis work to define product information may be performed by different people; therefore, collaboration is required to understand the relationships between the different components of product information.

8.3 SELECT AND APPROVE REQUIREMENTS

Select and Approve Requirements is the process of facilitating discussions with stakeholders to negotiate and confirm which requirements should be incorporated within an iteration, release, or project. The key benefit of this process is that it provides authorization to consider how and when to build all or part of a solution to develop or modify a product. The inputs, tools and techniques, and outputs of the process are depicted in Figure 8-7. Figure 8-8 depicts the data flow diagram for the process.

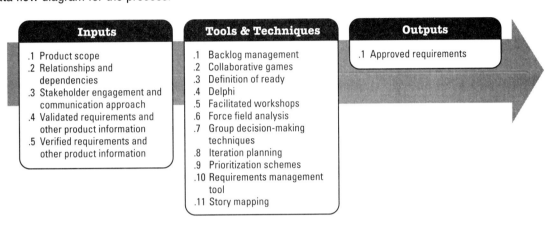

Inputs	Tools & Techniques	Outputs
.1 Product scope .2 Relationships and dependencies .3 Stakeholder engagement and communication approach .4 Validated requirements and other product information .5 Verified requirements and other product information	.1 Backlog management .2 Collaborative games .3 Definition of ready .4 Delphi .5 Facilitated workshops .6 Force field analysis .7 Group decision-making techniques .8 Iteration planning .9 Prioritization schemes .10 Requirements management tool .11 Story mapping	.1 Approved requirements

Figure 8-7. Select and Approve Requirements: Inputs, Tools and Techniques, and Outputs

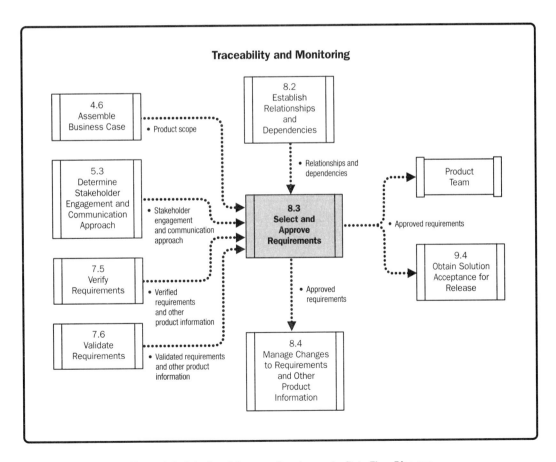

Figure 8-8. Select and Approve Requirements: Data Flow Diagram

Approving requirements is performed to obtain agreement that the requirements accurately depict what the product team is being asked to build. Requirements that are approved establish the requirements baseline. The requirements baseline is the boundary that contains all the approved requirements for the solution, project, project phase, iteration, increment, release, or any other part of a project or solution. On projects that use a predictive life cycle, once the baseline has been established, changes can only be made by performing the change management procedures defined for the project. On projects using an adaptive life cycle, requirements are effectively baselined when they are identified as planned work to be addressed in the next or subsequent iteration, and can only change if the team agrees to make the change or the product owner decides to abnormally terminate the user story, task, or perhaps the entire iteration. When user stories or tasks are terminated, they can be moved back onto the product backlog for future consideration or marked as no longer needed.

Organizations and projects vary in how requirements are approved. Some organizations require a formal sign-off on a requirements package, such as a business requirements document. In other organizations or for specific types of projects, the approval of requirements may be informal, requiring only verbal approval. On adaptive projects, approved requirements could be represented by a list of backlog items ready for development or the results of iteration planning, where decisions on the list of backlog items to be addressed in the current or next iteration are made.

Obtaining approval of requirements and other product information requires those authorized to select and approve requirements to reach consensus that the requirements are correct and complete. Conflicting requirements are not uncommon. Often, consensus is achieved through negotiation. Business analysis includes facilitating discussions among stakeholders to work through different viewpoints and conflicts in the requirements and to negotiate an agreed-upon outcome and, ultimately, approval.

Approvals should be tracked and, in situations where stakeholders are hesitant to approve, concerns should be understood and addressed. Additional authorization of work hinges on the approval of the requirements; therefore, if consensus is not possible among the immediate team, the authority levels governing the requirements approval process set forth in the stakeholder engagement approach are followed.

8.3.1 SELECT AND APPROVE REQUIREMENTS: INPUTS

8.3.1.1 PRODUCT SCOPE

Described in Section 4.6.3.2. Product scope is defined as the features and functions that characterize a solution. Requirements approval is performed to confirm with stakeholders that the defined product information is correct and within the established scope parameters.

8.3.1.2 RELATIONSHIPS AND DEPENDENCIES

Described in Section 8.2.3.1. Relationships and dependencies define the links between requirements. Relationships can be parent to child, as requirements are progressively elaborated from a high level to a low level of detail, or they can be dependency relationships such as implementation, benefit, or value. Relationships and dependencies may indicate which requirements may need to be selected and approved together.

8.3.1.3 STAKEHOLDER ENGAGEMENT AND COMMUNICATION APPROACH

Described in Section 5.3.3.1. The stakeholder engagement and communication approach summarizes all the agreements for governing how stakeholders will be engaged and communicated with across the portfolio, program, or project. It contains the decisions about the role responsibilities and authority levels governing the requirements approval process. The approach identifies who has responsibility for reviewing, approving, rejecting, and proposing changes to requirements.

8.3.1.4 VALIDATED REQUIREMENTS AND OTHER PRODUCT INFORMATION

Described in Section 7.6.3.1. Validated requirements and other product information is product information that the stakeholders agree meets the business goals and objectives. Although verification and validation do not have to be sequenced, commonly the requirements and supporting product information are both verified and validated prior to being presented to stakeholders for review and approval.

8.3.1.5 VERIFIED REQUIREMENTS AND OTHER PRODUCT INFORMATION

Described in Section 7.5.3.1. Verified requirements and other product information are product information that has been evaluated to ensure that it is free from errors and adheres to the quality standards to which the information will be held. Although verification and validation do not have to be sequenced, commonly the requirements and supporting product information are both verified and validated prior to being presented to stakeholders for review and approval.

8.3.2 SELECT AND APPROVE REQUIREMENTS: TOOLS AND TECHNIQUES

8.3.2.1 BACKLOG MANAGEMENT

Backlog management is a technique used in adaptive approaches to maintain the requirements list. The list is ranked in order of business value or importance to the customer and sized by the development team so that the team can work on the highest-value items that it can deliver over the specified duration. The prioritization of the backlog can be interpreted as approval. For more information on backlog management, see Section 7.7.2.1.

8.3.2.2 COLLABORATIVE GAMES

Collaborative games are a collection of elicitation techniques that foster collaboration, innovation, and creativity to obtain the goal of the elicitation activity. Collaborative games can be used to work through requirements-related conflicts and help teams work toward consensus on requirements. For more information on collaborative games, see Section 6.3.2.2.

8.3.2.3 DEFINITION OF READY

The definition of ready is a series of conditions that the entire team agrees to complete before a user story is considered sufficiently understood so that work can begin to construct it. The definition of ready can be used in place of approval in adaptive life cycles to help the project team know that the user story is sufficiently elaborated and ready to be brought into an iteration for the development team to work on. For more information on the definition of ready, see Section 7.3.2.2.

8.3.2.4 DELPHI

Delphi is a consensus-building technique. Experts on the subject participate in this technique anonymously. A facilitator uses a questionnaire to elicit ideas about the important points related to the subject. The responses are summarized and are then recirculated to the experts for further comments. Additional rounds are repeated to solicit comments from the experts again, until the results start to converge. Consensus may be reached in a few rounds of this process. The Delphi technique helps reduce bias in the data and prevents any one person from having undue influence on the outcome. Delphi can be used to gain consensus on anything, including requirements approval, requirements validity, estimation, prioritization, and design option preferences. Delphi is further discussed in Section 4.15.1 of *Business Analysis for Practitioners: A Practice Guide.*

8.3.2.5 FACILITATED WORKSHOPS

Facilitated workshops use a structured meeting led by a skilled, neutral facilitator and a carefully selected group of stakeholders to collaborate and work toward a stated objective. Facilitated workshops can be used to bring product teams together to select and approve requirements, or resolve requirements conflicts that are hindering the team from reaching consensus. Workshops are considered a primary technique for reconciling stakeholder differences. For more information on facilitated workshops, see Section 6.3.2.4.

8.3.2.6 FORCE FIELD ANALYSIS

Force field analysis is a decision-making technique that can be used to help product teams analyze whether there is sufficient support to pursue a change. A description of the change is placed in the middle of the model. The team identifies the forces for or against the proposed change. Forces that support the change are listed on the left and the forces that are impediments are listed on the right. Each of the forces is provided a weight based on how significant the force is and how easy it will be to influence it. Positive forces are conditions that need to be strengthened and negative forces are those that need to be weakened or eliminated. Scores are tallied to determine whether there is enough organizational support to pursue the change. When support is lacking, the team discusses whether there are factors that can be used to influence the situation. When negative forces outweigh positive forces or when negative forces cannot be influenced enough to develop sufficient organizational support for the change, the change should be avoided. Figure 8-9 shows a sample format of a force field analysis model.

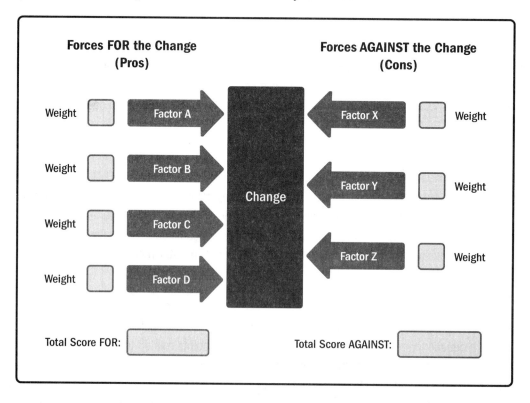

Figure 8-9. Force Field Analysis Sample Format

8.3.2.7 GROUP DECISION-MAKING TECHNIQUES

Group decision-making techniques are techniques that can be used in a group setting to bring participants to a final decision on an issue or topic under discussion. Some techniques help the team reach consensus, while other techniques have the objective of reaching a decision that does not necessarily reflect agreement by everyone. During business analysis planning, the team should establish how decisions will be made across the business analysis effort to avoid misunderstandings or conflict later on when performing the work. A few decision-making techniques include the following:

◆ **Autocratic.** One individual makes the decision for the group.

◆ **Delphi.** Reduces bias and prevents any one person from imposing undue influence on the team. Delphi reaches a decision through consensus. For more information on Delphi, see Section 8.3.2.4.

◆ **Force field analysis.** Reaches a decision by exploring the forces that are for or against a change and assessing which is greatest. For more information on force field analysis, see Section 8.3.2.6.

◆ **Majority.** Reaches a decision when support is obtained from more than 50% of the members of the group.

◆ **Plurality.** Obtains a decision by taking the most common answer received from among the decision makers.

◆ **Unanimity.** Reaches a decision by everyone agreeing on a single course of action.

Group decision-making techniques can be used in conjunction with other techniques to solve requirements-related conflicts.

8.3.2.8 ITERATION PLANNING

In adaptive approaches, iteration planning, or sprint planning, is the activity used to identify the subset of product backlog items from the product backlog that the development team will work on for the current iteration or sprint. Because the results of iteration planning provide the backlog items that will be considered the planned work for the current or next iteration, these items can be interpreted as approved. For more information on iteration planning, see Section 7.7.2.3.

8.3.2.9 PRIORITIZATION SCHEMES

Prioritization schemes are different methods used to prioritize requirements, features, or other product information. Prioritization schemes can also be used to resolve requirements-related conflicts. The stakeholder engagement and communication approach defines which prioritization schemes to use and when. For more information on prioritization schemes, see Section 7.7.2.5.

8.3.2.10 REQUIREMENTS MANAGEMENT TOOL

Requirements management tools allow requirements and other product information to be captured and stored in a repository. Requirements management tools often include workflow functionality to facilitate review and approval processes. Requirements management tools catered to adaptive projects may include functionality to create and manage product and iteration backlogs. For more information on requirements management tools, see Section 8.2.2.2.

8.3.2.11 STORY MAPPING

Story mapping is a technique used to sequence user stories, based upon their business value and the order in which their users typically perform them, so that teams can arrive at a shared understanding of what will be built. Story mapping can be used to perform release allocation in which features or solution components are assigned to different product releases. For more information on story mapping, see Section 7.2.2.16.

8.3.3 SELECT AND APPROVE REQUIREMENTS: OUTPUTS

8.3.3.1 APPROVED REQUIREMENTS

Approved requirements are requirements that are:

◆ Verified, in that the requirements are of sufficient quality; and

◆ Validated, in that the requirements meet business needs.

Approved requirements are an indication that those with the authority to approve requirements have agreed that the requirements as stated are what the product development team should build. On projects using an adaptive life cycle, approved requirements can be represented by a prioritized backlog ready for development or stories chosen from the product backlog as the planned work for the next or subsequent iteration.

On predictive projects, requirements, once reviewed, are approved by decision makers and the approved set of requirements establishes the requirements baseline. The process to approve requirements may involve written approval or sign-off or could involve verbal acceptance. During planning, the product team determines the approval process, including the roles that should participate.

8.3.4 SELECT AND APPROVE REQUIREMENTS: TAILORING CONSIDERATIONS

Adaptive and predictive tailoring considerations for Select and Approve Requirements are described in Table 8-3.

Table 8-3. Adaptive and Predictive Tailoring for Select and Approve Requirements

Aspects to Be Tailored	Typical Adaptive Considerations	Typical Predictive Considerations
Name	Backlog Refinement or Iteration Planning	Select and Approve Requirements
Approach	The product owner's prioritization of the backlog can be interpreted as approval. Definition of ready may also be used in place of approval. Prioritization of backlog occurs continuously until a set of items is moved into an iteration. Requirements management tools may be used to create and manage product and iteration backlogs.	Approval is obtained after verification and validation, but before design. May require sign-off of a document—for example, a requirements package, such as a business requirements document (BRD). In some cases, verbal approval may suffice. A requirements management tool may be used to facilitate review and approval processes.
Deliverables	Prioritized backlog ready for development, or decision on content to be built in an iteration or sprint, or designation of what gets pulled next from "to do" to "doing" on a kanban board.	Baselined requirements package and approvals may be stored in a repository, such as a requirements management tool.

8.3.5 SELECT AND APPROVE REQUIREMENTS: COLLABORATION POINT

On adaptive projects, team collaboration helps prepare the backlog and guide the team to make a decision on what can be accomplished in each iteration. The product owner is a key contributor to defining scope for an iteration. On predictive projects, approvals are milestones that should be communicated to the project team, as their work may depend on the results of the approval decisions. The project manager is dependent on the approved product requirements to confirm scope, determine the project requirements, and refine estimates on the work required to deliver the solution. Approved requirements are typically a major milestone in the predictive life cycle that a project manager would track in the project plan.

8.4 MANAGE CHANGES TO REQUIREMENTS AND OTHER PRODUCT INFORMATION

Manage Changes to Requirements and Other Product Information is the process of examining changes or defects that arise during a project by understanding the value and impact of the changes. As changes are agreed upon, information about those changes is reflected wherever necessary to support prioritization and eventual product development. The key benefits of this process include facilitating the incorporation of important solution changes for projects, limiting unnecessary changes, and providing understanding of how change will impact the end product. The inputs, tools and techniques, and outputs of the process are depicted in Figure 8-10. Figure 8-11 depicts the data flow diagram for the process.

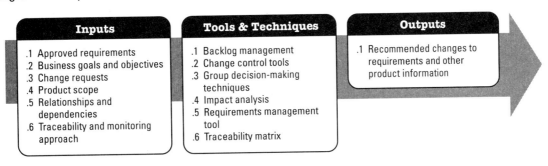

Inputs	Tools & Techniques	Outputs
.1 Approved requirements .2 Business goals and objectives .3 Change requests .4 Product scope .5 Relationships and dependencies .6 Traceability and monitoring approach	.1 Backlog management .2 Change control tools .3 Group decision-making techniques .4 Impact analysis .5 Requirements management tool .6 Traceability matrix	.1 Recommended changes to requirements and other product information

Figure 8-10. Manage Changes to Requirements and Other Product Information: Inputs, Tools and Techniques, and Outputs

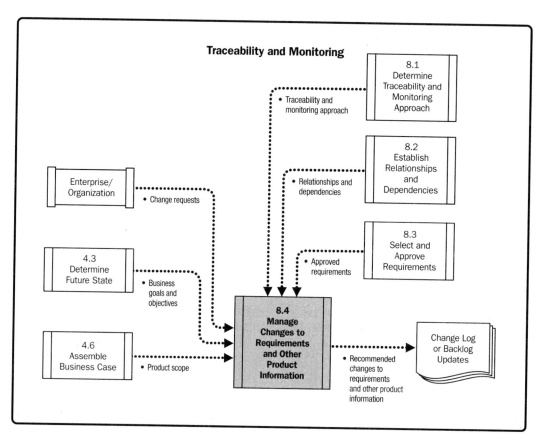

Figure 8-11. Manage Changes to Requirements and Other Product Information: Data Flow Diagram

Managing changes to requirements and other product information entails maintaining the integrity of the requirements and the associated deliverables and work products and ensuring that each new requirement aligns with the business need and business objectives. The key benefit of a requirements change process is that it provides a process to manage changes to approved requirements while minimizing product and project risks associated with uncontrolled and unapproved change. Negative impacts to the product and project often arise from making changes without taking into consideration any dependencies, and how the change will affect the overall product and project, including expected business value.

On adaptive projects, change is ongoing. The team utilizes emergent learning, where stakeholders discover their requirements as portions of the solution are delivered over time. Adaptive methods expect that requirements will change as stakeholders learn what they want as they see the solution evolve. On adaptive projects, a prioritization process is used to determine if and when a change is considered for inclusion in the product. For more information on prioritization, see Section 7.7.

On predictive projects, a change is a modification that is requested after requirements have been baselined. Changes may arise at any point, but changes are harder and more expensive to accommodate in a predictive life cycle. Changes are reviewed as requested by a governing body for the impact on the in-process work and approved requirements. If the value of pursuing the change is deemed greater than the impact on cost, time, and resources, the change is more likely to be approved.

The following courses of actions are possible after the proposed change is evaluated:

◆ **Change approved.** Necessary updates to the impacted business analysis deliverables are made. Planned and in-process business analysis activities are adjusted when they are impacted. In an adaptive life cycle, there is no concept of "approved," because any proposed change can be added to the backlog.

◆ **Change deferred.** The decision to defer making the change is documented, along with a rationale for the decision. When the change is provided with a proposed date for a future product release, it is noted and reflected in the appropriate plans to ensure that the change is addressed at the requested future date. In adaptive life cycles, this is equivalent to the proposed change being assigned a lower ranking in the product backlog.

◆ **Change rejected.** The decision to reject the proposed change is documented, along with the rationale for the decision. Unlike the action for a deferred change, there are no future date reminders established in the plans, because this work will not occur. In adaptive life cycles, this means not adding the item to the backlog or removing the item from the backlog.

◆ **More information required.** Despite best efforts to ensure that the impact analysis is thoroughly constructed, sometimes the change control board (CCB) or approval team requests more information. Conditions in the business may have changed since the project was first approved, or the CCB may now be considering different solutions or working from new data that were unavailable previously. This, in turn, involves another round of elicitation and analysis, an update to the impact analysis, and a resubmittal to the authoritative body considering the change. In adaptive life cycles, backlog items are elaborated just enough to prioritize the product backlog, then, if they are chosen for an iteration, items are elaborated further to obtain the necessary details required for development. The idea that a change will require more information is inevitable as the process of elaboration is factored into the approach.

The applied level of change management depends upon many factors, such as the application area, the organizational culture, the organizational process assets, the complexity of the specific project and end result, contractual requirements, the project life cycle, and the context and environment in which the project is performed. The degree of formality and the amount of documentation needed for the change control process depends upon the organizational policies and processes or external regulations.

8.4.1 MANAGE CHANGES TO REQUIREMENTS AND OTHER PRODUCT INFORMATION: INPUTS

8.4.1.1 APPROVED REQUIREMENTS

Described in Section 8.3.3.1. Approved requirements are requirements that are verified, validated, and deemed an accurate representation of what the product development team should build. In predictive life cycles, change requests are evaluated against the approved requirements to conduct an impact analysis.

8.4.1.2 BUSINESS GOALS AND OBJECTIVES

Described in Section 4.3.3.1. Business goals and objectives specify stated targets that the business is seeking to achieve. New or revised requirements or product information is evaluated to ensure that these requirements are aligned with and supporting the attainment of the stated goals and objectives.

8.4.1.3 CHANGE REQUESTS

Change requests are appeals to make a change to a requirement or other suggestions for changes to product information raised by the business stakeholders or project team after a set of requirements is baselined. Change requests may arise from many sources, such as new regulations, internal or external constraints, missed requirements, or stakeholder recommendations after seeing part or all of the solution in development or completed. If an impact analysis has been performed, evaluated acceptance results may be looked at in conjunction with the change request. Not all change requests impact product requirements, but when they do, business analysis is required to analyze the impacts of the proposed change.

In adaptive approaches, there is no formal change request process. When a stakeholder requests a change, it is written in the form of a user story and added to the backlog. These are typically not referred to as change requests. A prioritization process is used to evaluate product backlog items against existing backlog items to determine which items will be included in the next iteration. The prioritization process works to ensure that the team focuses development efforts on the stories deemed of highest importance and value. For more information on prioritizing change requests, see Section 7.7.1.3.

8.4.1.4 PRODUCT SCOPE

Described in Section 4.6.3.2. Product scope is defined as the features and functions that characterize a solution. In adaptive life cycles, additional features are added to the product backlog and prioritized based on an assessment of the benefits or value; therefore, product scope evolves over time. In predictive life cycles, new or revised product information is evaluated against the product scope to assess the size of the change and impacts. When a proposed change is determined to be outside of the defined product scope, decision makers will need to consider whether a modification to the product scope is viable.

8.4.1.5 RELATIONSHIPS AND DEPENDENCIES

Described in Section 8.2.3.1. Relationships and dependencies are the linkages established between objects, such as components of product information, deliverables, and project work. In adaptive life cycles, this information is used when prioritizing the backlog, as a newly added backlog item may have linkages to other items in the backlog and these may be grouped and prioritized together. In predictive approaches, relationships and dependencies can be used to identify other impacted backlog items to size up the impact of making a change. In a predictive life cycle, relationships and dependencies decrease the probability of missing requirements, support impact analysis, and help the team maintain scope.

8.4.1.6 TRACEABILITY AND MONITORING APPROACH

Described in Section 8.1.3.1. The traceability and monitoring approach defines how traceability and change management activities will be performed throughout the portfolio, program, or project. The approach includes information on who can propose and approve changes and how those changes are proposed and evaluated.

8.4.2 MANAGE CHANGES TO REQUIREMENTS AND OTHER PRODUCT INFORMATION: TOOLS AND TECHNIQUES

8.4.2.1 BACKLOG MANAGEMENT

Backlog management is a technique used in adaptive approaches to maintain the list of backlog items to be worked on during a project. The list is ranked in order of business value or importance to the customer and sized by the development team so that the highest-value items are selected and delivered in the next development cycle. Proposed changes or new stories are added to the bottom of the backlog, where they sit until the next time the backlog is reprioritized. In adaptive life cycles, backlog management is the technique used to manage changes. For more information on backlog management, see Section 7.7.2.1.

8.4.2.2 CHANGE CONTROL TOOLS

On projects following a predictive life cycle, change control tools can be manual or automated and are used to manage change requests and the resulting decisions. These tools may already be in place within the organization. When a change control tool is being introduced on a project, the needs of all stakeholders involved in the change control process should be considered. Two examples of change control tools are the following:

◆ **Configuration management system (CMS).** Configuration management helps ensure that the solution being built conforms to its approved product information. It provides a process for verifying this conformance, documenting changes, and reporting the status of each change throughout the project life cycle. It includes documentation, a tracking process, and defined approval levels necessary for authorizing changes. It enables managing changes to aspects of a solution in the context of the entire product, as well as the context of other products on which it depends or that depend upon it.

◆ **Version control system (VCS).** A VCS tracks the history of revisions of any type of work product. A VCS is like a baseline in that the original work product is established, and changes to that work product are tracked. A VCS falls under the umbrella of a CMS and is one of the many functions that comprise configuration management.

Change control tools are further discussed in Section 5.8.2 of *Business Analysis for Practitioners: A Practice Guide*.

8.4.2.3 GROUP DECISION-MAKING TECHNIQUES

Group decision-making techniques are techniques that can be used in a group setting to bring participants to a final decision on an issue or topic under discussion. Group decision-making techniques can be used in conjunction with other techniques to decide whether proposed changes should be acted on. For more information on group decision-making techniques, see Section 8.3.2.7.

8.4.2.4 IMPACT ANALYSIS

Impact analysis is a technique used to evaluate a change in relation to how it will affect related elements. When a change to product information is proposed, an impact analysis is performed to evaluate the proposed change in relation to how it will affect components of the portfolio, program, project, and product, including requirements and other product information. Impact analysis includes identifying the risks associated with the change, the work required to incorporate the change, and the schedule and cost implications. A key benefit of completing an impact analysis is that it allows for changes within the project to be considered in an integrated fashion, thereby minimizing project and product risk. Impact analysis is further discussed in Section 5.8.3 of *Business Analysis for Practitioners: A Practice Guide.*

8.4.2.5 REQUIREMENTS MANAGEMENT TOOL

Requirements management tools allow requirements and other product information to be captured and stored in a repository. Requirements management tools often include functionality to maintain audit trails and perform version control to assist with change control. Workflow functionality can facilitate review and approval processes for changes. Traceability information stored in requirements management tools assists with impact analysis. Requirements management tools configured to adaptive projects may include functionality to create and manage product and iteration backlogs. For more information on requirements management tools, see Section 8.2.2.2.

8.4.2.6 TRACEABILITY MATRIX

The traceability matrix contains information on the relationships and dependencies between requirements and other product information. The components of product information that are impacted by the change can be easily identified within a traceability matrix. The affected relationships are easily recognized and can be used to quickly and roughly quantify the size and complexity of the change. As described in Section 8.2, in adaptive approaches, formal traceability matrices are rarely used or named as such, but the concept of tracing to understand impacts to things that are already built still applies. For more information on traceability matrices, see Section 8.2.2.5.

8.4.3 MANAGE CHANGES TO REQUIREMENTS AND OTHER PRODUCT INFORMATION: OUTPUTS

8.4.3.1 RECOMMENDED CHANGES TO REQUIREMENTS AND OTHER PRODUCT INFORMATION

Recommended changes to requirements and other product information describe the course of action that is proposed after analyzing all the impacts associated with making a proposed change, including impacts to product and project scope, product usage, value, risk, schedule, and cost. The possible courses of action include approving the change, deferring the change, rejecting the change, or requesting additional information before making a decision about the change.

8.4.4 MANAGE CHANGES TO REQUIREMENTS AND OTHER PRODUCT INFORMATION: TAILORING CONSIDERATIONS

Adaptive and predictive tailoring considerations for Manage Changes to Requirements and Other Product Information are described in Table 8-4.

Table 8-4. Adaptive and Predictive Tailoring for Manage Changes to Requirements and Other Product Information

Aspects to Be Tailored	Typical Adaptive Considerations	Typical Predictive Considerations
Name	Backlog Refinement	Manage Changes to Requirements and Other Product Information or Change Control
Approach	No formal change management procedures. Change is expected and embraced. Change can occur anytime, outside an iteration. Additional details can be added to stories within an iteration if the team agrees to it. New stories are added to the product backlog and change is prioritized through refining the backlog or iteration planning.	Change control begins after requirements are approved. Formalized change management process is followed, including roles and process steps. New product information is captured in a change request. Change is often treated like a mini-project, with elicitation, analysis, assessment of value, and requirements approval.
Deliverables	Scaled impact analysis is conducted. Determination where the change should be prioritized within the backlog.	Impact analysis with recommended course of action. Revised requirements documentation and updated or new models.

8.4.5 MANAGE CHANGES TO REQUIREMENTS AND OTHER PRODUCT INFORMATION: COLLABORATION POINT

Functional managers may be the source of changes, as they may be some of the first from the business side to become aware of business changes, including new regulations or changes in the competitive environment that may prompt a need for change. Subject matter experts (SMEs) provide information needed to understand the change and participate in elicitation activities as requested.

9

SOLUTION EVALUATION

Solution Evaluation includes the processes to validate a full solution or a segment of a solution that is about to be or has already been implemented. Evaluation determines how well a solution meets the business needs expressed by stakeholders, including delivering value to the customer.

The Solution Evaluation processes are as follows:

9.1 Evaluate Solution Performance—The process of evaluating a solution to determine whether the implemented solution or solution component is delivering the business value as intended.

9.2 Determine Solution Evaluation Approach—The process of determining which aspects of the organization and/or solution will be evaluated, how performance will be measured, when performance will be measured, and by whom.

9.3 Evaluate Acceptance Results and Address Defects—The process of deciding what to do with the results from a comparison of the defined acceptance criteria against the solution.

9.4 Obtain Solution Acceptance for Release—The process of facilitating a decision on whether to release a partial or full solution into production and eventually to an operational team, as well as transitioning knowledge and existing information about the product, its risks, known issues, and any workarounds that may have arisen in response to those issues.

Figure 9-1 provides an overview of the Solution Evaluation processes. The business analysis processes are presented as discrete processes with defined interfaces, although, in practice, they overlap and interact in ways that cannot be completely detailed in this guide.

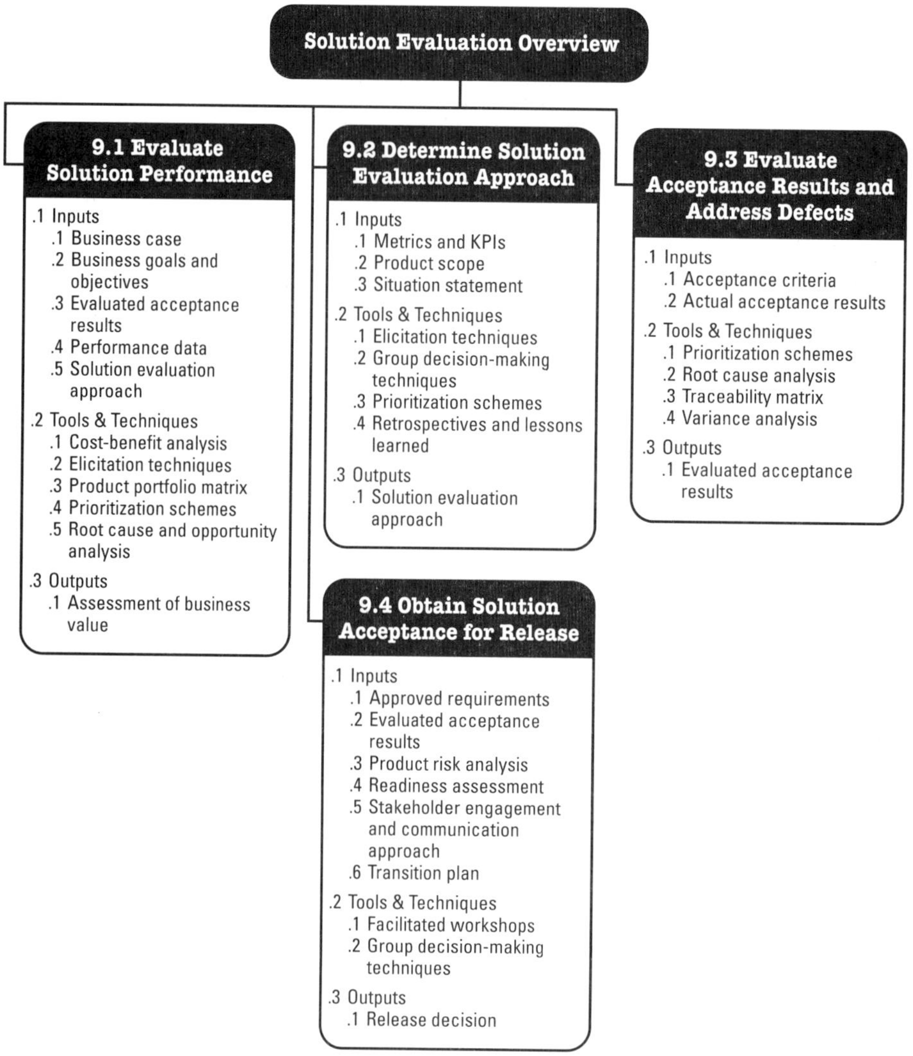

Figure 9-1. Solution Evaluation Overview

KEY CONCEPTS FOR SOLUTION EVALUATION

Solution Evaluation activities are performed to assess whether or not a solution has achieved the desired business results. Solution evaluation practices apply to anything that needs to be evaluated, from a discrete usage scenario to a broad business outcome. Solution Evaluation consists of the work done to analyze measurements obtained for the solution by comparing the actual results of acceptance testing to the expected or desired values, as defined by the acceptance criteria. Over the long term, these activities evaluate whether the expected business value of a solution has been achieved.

Analyzing the results from surveys, focus groups, or the results of exploratory testing of functionality are examples of qualitative or coarsely quantitative evaluation activities. Other evaluation activities involve obtaining more precise quantitative measurements, such as directly looking at data from a solution. Nonfunctional characteristics of a solution are often evaluated with measurements as well. For example, performance standards in service-level agreements can be measured for actual compliance. Comparing estimated and actual costs and benefits may also be part of Solution Evaluation. For solutions involving manufacturing, evaluations may include comparisons between actual and expected production outputs or conformance to tolerances for a product. For solutions involving software, analyzing comparisons between expected and actual values of data manipulated by the high-level functionality of the solution may be part of evaluation.

Evaluation activities may occur:

◆ At any point when a go/no-go or release decision needs to be made for a solution or a substantive segment of it;

◆ During a short-term period after a solution or segment is put into operation, such as after a warranty period; or

◆ Well after a solution is put into operation, to obtain a long-term perspective about whether the business goals and objectives for the solution were met and whether the value expected continues to be delivered.

Solution Evaluation often requires early preparation, so that what is needed to perform this work is in place later when evaluation is conducted. Preparation for evaluating a solution includes defining and confirming the expected business value, identifying and defining what kind of performance data will be used to evaluate whether value has been achieved, confirming that performance data will actually be available, and obtaining baseline or control data when necessary. Definition of specific evaluation criteria, such as the expected or desired range of values for the selected metrics, supports analysis activities beyond Solution Evaluation; therefore, determining specific evaluation criteria is considered part of Section 7.4 on Define Acceptance Criteria.

For portfolios, programs, and projects, the following can be stated with regard to Solution Evaluation:

◆ Evaluation of an implemented solution may be used to identify new or changed requirements, which may lead to solution refinement or new solutions.

◆ Solution Evaluation can provide input into go/no-go business and technical decisions when releasing an entire solution or a segment of it.

◆ Evaluation may identify a point of diminishing returns, such as the point where additional value that could be obtained from a solution does not justify the additional effort needed to achieve that value. In this case, Solution Evaluation gives teams the ability to "end early" even if there is still additional functionality that could be built, allowing funds to be reallocated to work on higher-priority projects that can bring additional business value.

◆ Assessed limitations of the solution might be the basis for recommendations for a wide variety of follow-up activities, ranging from actions to improve the performance of the solution to recommendations for replacing it or phasing it out.

◆ Solution evaluations provide a basis for portfolio and program management to make decisions about new products and product enhancements.

Complicating factors for evaluating a solution are as follows:

◆ Some of the benefits and value of the solution may seem to be intangible, and therefore, not possible to measure. For intangible benefits, it may be necessary to define measurements that provide indirect evidence that the benefits have been achieved.

◆ Some of the information needed to evaluate the solution may not be needed for the solution itself. Obtaining and using such data may add to the costs of developing the solution.

◆ Some aspects of a solution that reflect the benefits and value may not be measurable until well after a solution is released. In these situations, the operational business area responsible for the product or perhaps an enterprise organizational area may take responsibility for identifying and measuring leading indicators.

These factors are yet other reasons for thinking about Solution Evaluation as part of initial product development efforts. For more information on Solution Evaluation, see Section 6.3 of *Business Analysis for Practitioners: A Practice Guide.*

9.1 EVALUATE SOLUTION PERFORMANCE

Evaluate Solution Performance is the process of evaluating a solution to determine whether the implemented solution or solution component is delivering the business value as intended. The key benefit of this process is that the analysis provides tangible data to determine whether the solution that the business has invested in is achieving the expected business results and serves as an input to decisions about future initiatives. The inputs, tools and techniques, and outputs for this process are shown in Figure 9-2. Figure 9-3 depicts the data flow diagram for the process.

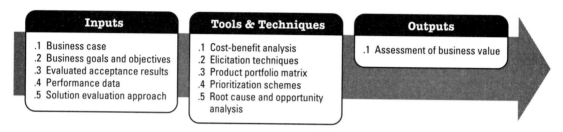

Inputs	Tools & Techniques	Outputs
.1 Business case .2 Business goals and objectives .3 Evaluated acceptance results .4 Performance data .5 Solution evaluation approach	.1 Cost-benefit analysis .2 Elicitation techniques .3 Product portfolio matrix .4 Prioritization schemes .5 Root cause and opportunity analysis	.1 Assessment of business value

Figure 9-2. Evaluate Solution Performance: Inputs, Tools and Techniques, and Outputs

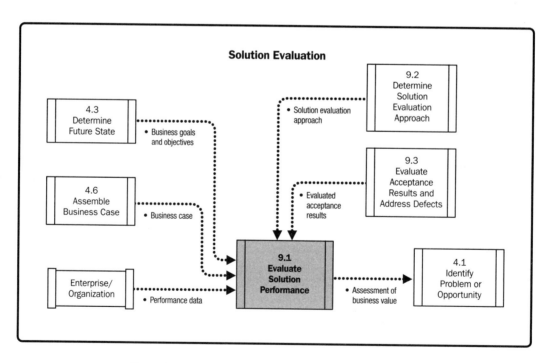

Figure 9-3. Evaluate Solution Performance: Data Flow Diagram

Evaluating solution performance involves determining whether a solution or solution component that has been put into operation is delivering the desired business value. The actual business value of a solution is measured in terms of the business goals or objectives. Business analysis also assesses the underlying reasons behind the results obtained.

Evaluation of solution performance typically occurs after a solution has been released. Therefore, it is more likely that the evaluation of solution performance will occur during portfolio or program activities rather than project activities. The extent to which business value has been achieved and the reasons for the achievement are significant factors to consider when making product decisions within a portfolio or program. However, Evaluate Solution Performance not only supports product decisions within a program or portfolio, but also may be used during a project at any time when solution evaluation can provide insights.

Data to evaluate the business value are often measured by and obtained from the business area that takes ownership of the solution or by instrumentation that has been built into the product. Business analysis techniques are used to analyze variations between desired and actual results as part of assessing the business value of the solution. Because many measurements of business value need to take place after a solution is released and often need to be measured over the long term to detect trends, there needs to be organizational commitment to invest in making the measurements and to invest in building or purchasing the capabilities to measure business value when those capabilities would not otherwise be available. When such investments are not possible, organizations need to consider less costly next-best-alternative ways to measure business value. Proxies for business value might be used in these situations.

The relevant business goals and objectives, evaluated acceptance results from a previous release, performance data, and baseline data, when available, are analyzed to determine whether value has been delivered, as well as the reasons for better-than-expected results or the root causes of any problems. Among the typical reasons for missed business value are:

◆ Technical causes,

◆ Business practices or constraints,

◆ Resistance to the product or the way it is intended to be used, and

◆ Opportunistic workarounds devised by those who use the product to get around real or perceived solution limitations.

The assessment of the performance of a product becomes input into recommendations for improving the long-term performance of the solutions and for portfolio and program management decisions about further enhancements to the product, decisions about new products, and decisions to replace or discontinue products.

9.1.1 EVALUATE SOLUTION PERFORMANCE: INPUTS

9.1.1.1 BUSINESS CASE

Described in Section 4.6.3.1. The business case describes pertinent information to determine whether the initiative is worth the required investment. It is an authoritative source where expected benefits have been stated.

9.1.1.2 BUSINESS GOALS AND OBJECTIVES

Described in Section 4.3.3.1. Business goals and objectives specify stated targets that the business is seeking to achieve. They provide the context for evaluating solution performance, because they are a measurable description of the expected business value. Examples of business objectives include increased throughput in the manufacture of a product by x%, reduction in costs by y%, and increased sales volume by $$z$.

Many products support business goals and objectives that can be associated with one or more key performance indicators (KPIs), which are target performance levels that are usually defined by an organization's executives. For organizations that already define and measure KPIs, it may sometimes be possible to use one or more of these KPIs to evaluate the solution, taking advantage of existing measurement capabilities.

9.1.1.3 EVALUATED ACCEPTANCE RESULTS

Described in Section 9.3.3.1. Evaluated acceptance results are comparisons between the acceptance criteria and the actual results, and the root cause for variances between them. The evaluated acceptance results from when the solution was released describe the state of the product, and specifically any proficiencies or deficiencies it may have, which might have altered the expected business value. A product that exceeds expectations can provide a basis for future opportunities. A product that does not meet expectations may have defects, which will necessitate analysis of the cost to address the defects and the business impact of addressing them or accepting them.

9.1.1.4 PERFORMANCE DATA

Performance data are a quantified output of a product. Examples of outputs that might be measured include throughput in the manufacture of a product, volume of some output generated by the product, reduction in costs, productivity achieved in using a service, number of users adopting a solution, amount of revenue generated, sales volume, number of individuals reached in a marketing campaign, and levels of customer satisfaction.

Performance data are used to determine the actual business value of a product by assessing the performance data before and after a release. Any performance data from a prior version of a product or manual process represent a baseline. For example, if business value is measured in terms of increased sales volume, then the quantified business value is the difference in sales volume before (the baseline) and after release of the solution.

If there is no baseline of performance data, then either the performance data after a release can represent the business value or estimates of the original baseline can be made. Ideally, performance data are measured for the stated business goals and objectives. However, when that is not possible, proxies for those objectives might be used to determine business value. For example, proxy performance data could include measurements that describe the effectiveness or quality of the product, such as the average duration of a task while using the product, response time for solutions involving software, or counts of errors made while performing a task.

Performance data are generally measured by and obtained from the business area that takes ownership of the solution or by instrumentation built into the solution. Performance data also can be measured using capabilities externally available to the solution, such as the results from surveys or focus groups conducted after a solution has been released.

9.1.1.5 SOLUTION EVALUATION APPROACH

Described in Section 9.2.3.1. The solution evaluation approach provides the agreements made about how solution evaluation activities will be performed. The solution evaluation approach identifies which types of metrics will be used to evaluate whether the expected business value has been achieved. It explains how solution performance will be evaluated. Because solutions can be evaluated long after their release, the original solution evaluation approach may need to be updated over time based on the current state.

9.1.2 EVALUATE SOLUTION PERFORMANCE: TOOLS AND TECHNIQUES

9.1.2.1 COST-BENEFIT ANALYSIS

Cost-benefit analysis is a financial analysis tool used to determine the benefits provided by a project or solution against its costs. Considering the results of an actual versus expected cost-benefit analysis is one way to assess the business value of the solution. Conducting a cost-benefit analysis can help determine whether recommendations made as part of the evaluation of solution performance are likely to be cost-effective. For more information on cost-benefit analysis, see Section 4.4.2.2.

9.1.2.2 ELICITATION TECHNIQUES

Elicitation techniques are used to draw out information from sources. Facilitated workshops, focus groups, interviews, and observation are among the elicitation techniques often used to uncover root causes for identifying the differences between the expected and actual business value of a solution and making recommendations to address those variances:

◆ **Facilitated workshops.** Use a structured meeting led by a skilled, neutral facilitator and a carefully selected group of stakeholders to collaborate and work toward a stated objective. Facilitated workshops may be conducted with decision makers to collaboratively work together to identify the root cause and any variances. For more information on facilitated workshops, see Section 6.3.2.4.

◆ **Focus groups.** Provide an opportunity to obtain feedback directly from customers and/or end users. Focus groups can be used to learn about which deficiencies in business value are important or of concern to stakeholders. For more information on focus groups, see Section 6.3.2.5.

◆ **Interviews.** May be conducted with individual stakeholders and users to gain insights about root causes in situations where expected and actual business value differs widely. The privacy and confidentiality of an individual interview may reveal considerations that might not otherwise be expressed in a facilitated workshop or focus group. For more information on interviews, see Section 6.3.2.6.

◆ **Observation.** An elicitation technique that provides a direct way of eliciting information about how a process is performed or a product is used by viewing individuals in their own environment performing their jobs or tasks. For some products, direct observation of users actually performing their jobs or tasks may uncover workarounds that they use to compensate for product gaps. These workarounds may have had unintended consequences leading to missed business value. Such workarounds could be missed when using interviews and other verbal communication techniques, because it may not occur to users who are familiar with using the product for a long time to mention how they compensate for a lack—or perceived lack—of functionality. For more information on observation, see Section 6.3.2.7.

For more information on elicitation techniques, see Section 6.3.2.

9.1.2.3 PRODUCT PORTFOLIO MATRIX

A product portfolio matrix, also known as a growth-share matrix, is a market analysis quadrant diagram used by some organizations to qualitatively analyze their products or product lines. One axis reflects market growth (or demand for a product) from low to high, while the other reflects the market share of the organization from low to high. The matrix provides a quick visual way to evaluate which products are meeting or exceeding performance expectations in the marketplace, and as a result, can contribute to evaluating the performance of a product.

Figure 9-4 is an example of a product portfolio matrix. In this figure, assuming that the costs to produce, market, and distribute the product are not a significant factor, the products that provide the most significant benefits to the organization would be found in the upper left quadrant, because these are the products where the organization has a high market share in a market with a high growth rate. Those in the upper right quadrant are regarded as having good potential because, although they have a low market share, they are in a market that is continuing to grow. Those in the lower left quadrant, with a high market share in a low growth market, are considered a dependable income stream.

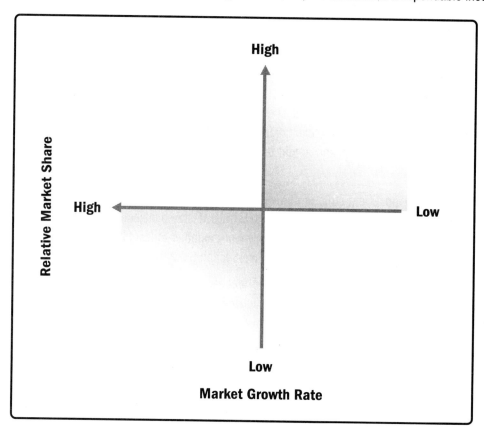

Figure 9-4 Evaluate Solution Performance: Product Portfolio Matrix

9.1.2.4 PRIORITIZATION SCHEMES

Prioritization schemes are different methods used to prioritize requirements, features, or other product information. For the purposes of evaluating solution performance, prioritization schemes can be used to rank the value of the benefits obtained from the solution as well as the severity of any challenges it creates. Doing so can provide a way to consider whether the benefits outweigh the challenges and vice versa. For more information on prioritization schemes, see Section 7.7.2.5.

9.1.2.5 ROOT CAUSE AND OPPORTUNITY ANALYSIS

Root cause analysis is used to determine the basic underlying reason that causes a variance, defect, or risk. Opportunity analysis is used to study the major facets of a potential opportunity to determine the possible changes in products offered to enable its achievement. When used to evaluate solution performance, root cause and opportunity analysis can help uncover the reasons why the actual business value either did not meet or possibly exceeded expectations and where there may be further product improvement opportunities. The results of root cause and opportunity analysis can be used when making decisions about new products and whether to enhance, retire, or discontinue existing products. For more information on root cause and opportunity analysis, see Section 4.2.2.9.

9.1.3 EVALUATE SOLUTION PERFORMANCE: OUTPUTS

9.1.3.1 ASSESSMENT OF BUSINESS VALUE

The assessment of business value is the result from comparing expected business value from a solution against the actual value that has been realized. If the desired business value was not achieved, the assessment includes the reasons why.

The assessment is used to make decisions about whether to develop a new product or to enhance, retire, or discontinue an existing product. The work done to implement any recommendations will need to be prioritized as part of the ongoing planning activities the organization performs for portfolio or program management. For more information on assessing business value, see Section 6.10.3 of *Business Analysis for Practitioners: A Practice Guide*.

9.1.4 EVALUATE SOLUTION PERFORMANCE: TAILORING CONSIDERATIONS

Adaptive and predictive tailoring considerations for Evaluate Solution Performance are described in Table 9-1.

Table 9-1. Adaptive and Predictive Tailoring for Evaluate Solution Performance

Aspects to Be Tailored	Typical Adaptive Considerations	Typical Predictive Considerations
Name	Evaluate Solution Performance	
Approach	After a solution is launched, performance data are used to compare business value to what was expected. Subjective and objective evidence is collected. Root causes are identified for deviations from what was expected. Recommendations may be made to address reducing the deviations. Root causes become input into decisions to enhance, maintain, replace, or discontinue the product.	
Deliverables	Assessment results can be formally documented or not.	

9.1.5 EVALUATE SOLUTION PERFORMANCE: COLLABORATION POINT

Several roles may contribute to evaluating solution performance. Functional managers may provide insights on how the product is performing that might not be obvious solely by looking at metrics, and DevOps (which some organizations use to coordinate activities and improve collaboration between development and operational areas) may provide insights on how product performance is trending during the warranty period. Subject matter experts (SMEs) may be responsible for conducting the evaluation or may help surface the reasons behind the results obtained. Once the performance data are acquired, portfolio, program, and project managers use the results when making strategic and tactical decisions.

9.2 DETERMINE SOLUTION EVALUATION APPROACH

Determine Solution Evaluation Approach is the process of determining which aspects of the organization and/or solution will be evaluated, how performance will be measured, when performance will be measured, and by whom. The key benefit of this process is that performance indicators and metrics are selected or defined so they can be collected, reported on, and evaluated to support the continual improvement of the organization and/or product. The inputs, tools and techniques, and outputs for this process are shown in Figure 9-5. Figure 9-6 depicts the data flow diagram for the process.

Inputs	Tools & Techniques	Outputs
.1 Metrics and KPIs .2 Product scope .3 Situation statement	.1 Elicitation techniques .2 Group decision-making techniques .3 Prioritization schemes .4 Retrospectives and lessons learned	.1 Solution evaluation approach

Figure 9-5. Determine Solution Evaluation Approach: Inputs, Tools and Techniques, and Outputs

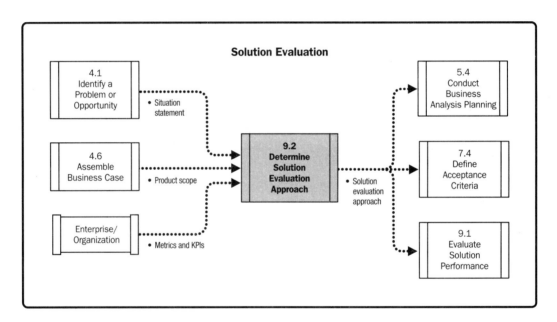

Figure 9-6. Determine Solution Evaluation Approach: Data Flow Diagram

Determining an approach for Solution Evaluation involves conducting research, discussions, and analysis to identify how and when to evaluate a product. Determining the solution evaluation approach should include:

◆ Planning when and how often solution evaluation activities should be performed. Solution evaluation may occur during solution development for some components of a solution, just before a release, soon after a release, or long after a release;

◆ Planning which evaluation techniques will be used. Not all techniques need to be decided before analysis begins, but by thinking ahead, it is more likely that business analysts will be prepared to use a variety of techniques;

The PMI Guide to Business Analysis

- Planning how the evaluation results will be analyzed and reported;

- Planning how the progress of solution evaluation and its outputs will be communicated to stakeholders and other interested parties, including what level of formality is appropriate; and

- Planning which metrics will be used to evaluate performance and how they tie to the business goals and objectives.

A metric is a set of quantifiable measures used to evaluate a solution or business. When performing solution evaluation, a metric defines how solution performance can be quantified. Many metrics can be used to compare the tangible properties of the solution, such as throughput, productivity, or efficiency. There are two common types of metrics defined by the solution evaluation approach:

- Metrics that will be used to evaluate the solution or its components for acceptance during or shortly after development. Acceptance criteria are defined to set acceptable ranges on these metrics. For information about acceptance criteria, see Section 7.4.3.1; and

- Metrics likely to be used later to determine if the business value was delivered. Because solution performance is not evaluated until after a solution is released, the choice of metrics or how they are measured might change over time.

When determining the solution evaluation approach, the team needs to consider the following about metrics:

- What type of performance data will be collected for the metrics, when, and how frequently?

- Who is responsible for collecting and reporting the performance data?

- Are there built-in collection and reporting mechanisms already available for these metrics? If not, what additional capabilities are needed? Who is going to cover the costs of developing them?

Information about the problem or opportunity that the solution will address and the product scope provide a basis for deciding which types of metrics could help the organization assess the product's performance. There may be industry or organizational standards that have defined benchmarks that can be used to compare a solution with general expectations for it.

The solution evaluation approach should be defined as early as possible in the product development life cycle because some of the metrics identified in it may require capturing additional information, above and beyond what the product itself requires. Without early definition, there is a risk that necessary information will be expensive or impossible to obtain. When considering new metrics, the cost of capturing actual measurements and reporting on them is an important factor. When the proposed metrics appear too costly or time-consuming to justify their use, less costly, next-best alternatives may be considered.

9.2.1 DETERMINE SOLUTION EVALUATION APPROACH: INPUTS

9.2.1.1 METRICS AND KPIs

A metric is a set of quantifiable measures used to evaluate a solution or business. In solution evaluation, a metric defines how solution performance can be quantified. Many types of metrics could be used to evaluate a solution. Business objectives are a type of metric that describe the desired business value of a product. Key performance indicators (KPIs) are a related type of metric, usually defined by an organization's executives, used to evaluate an organization's progress toward meeting its objectives or goals. Other, more granular metrics that also trace back to business objectives can be used to evaluate the interim success of a solution during or after development. Defining a solution evaluation approach involves choosing which metrics to use to evaluate a solution under development as part of its acceptance criteria or a previously released solution as part of its performance. When choosing, consideration can be given to metrics that are already available within the organization.

9.2.1.2 PRODUCT SCOPE

Described in Section 4.6.3.2. Product scope is defined as the features and functions that characterize a solution. The product scope and the business goals and objectives on which a solution is based provide suggestions as to what types of information should be collected and measured for evaluation purposes.

9.2.1.3 SITUATION STATEMENT

Described in Section 4.1.3.2. A situation statement describes the problem or opportunity and its effect on the organization. The wording of the situation statement may suggest ways to measure whether or not the problem or opportunity has been addressed. The situation statement might also be used to determine how, when, and how frequently a solution should be evaluated.

9.2.2 DETERMINE SOLUTION EVALUATION APPROACH: TOOLS AND TECHNIQUES

9.2.2.1 ELICITATION TECHNIQUES

Elicitation techniques are used to draw information from sources. Elicitation techniques can be used to identify existing metrics or potential new metrics for determining solution acceptance or evaluating whether business value has been delivered. Elicitation techniques are also helpful to identify ideas about how a solution can be evaluated.

A few common elicitation techniques that can support determining the solution evaluation approach are document analysis, facilitated workshops, and interviews:

◆ **Document analysis.** An elicitation technique used to analyze existing documentation to identify relevant product information. A team may be able to gain ideas for likely metrics from documentation that inventories the kind of information that is currently collected or that will be available once the solution is in place. The team may also be able to reuse all or part of a documented solution evaluation approach. For more information on document analysis, see Section 6.3.2.3.

◆ **Facilitated workshop.** A structured meeting led by a skilled, neutral facilitator and a carefully selected group of stakeholders to collaborate and work toward a stated objective. The structure of a facilitated workshop promotes an efficient and focused meeting for proposing metrics. For more information on facilitated workshops, see Section 6.3.2.4.

◆ **Interviews.** Used to elicit information about the solution evaluation approach. They can be scheduled with various stakeholders who possess key information for determining the approach. When necessary, individual interviews can provide each stakeholder with an opportunity to speak candidly about the ability of the organization to capture proposed metrics. For more information on interviews, see Section 6.3.2.6.

For more information on elicitation techniques, see Section 6.3.2.

9.2.2.2 GROUP DECISION-MAKING TECHNIQUES

Group decision-making techniques are methods that can be used in a group setting to bring participants to a final decision on an issue or topic under discussion. Decision-making techniques are used to reach consensus about the solution evaluation approach. For example, teams need to reach decisions about which metrics to collect, the value of information against costs to obtain it, which of the proposed metrics to use, and the frequency of collecting metrics.

For more information on group decision-making techniques, see Section 8.3.2.7.

9.2.2.3 PRIORITIZATION SCHEMES

Prioritization schemes are different methods used to prioritize requirements, features, or any other product information. When developing the solution evaluation approach, the interest in obtaining information needs to be balanced against the cost of obtaining and communicating that information. The balance is achieved through decision making and may require prioritizing among the proposed metrics.

Prioritization schemes such as MoSCoW can help decide which metrics must, should, could, and won't be collected, as can weighted rankings. For more information on prioritization schemes, see Section 7.7.2.5.

9.2.2.4 RETROSPECTIVES AND LESSONS LEARNED

Retrospectives and lessons learned leverage past experiences to plan for the future. As part of devising a solution evaluation approach, retrospectives and lessons learned can be used to learn about the ease of collecting and analyzing different types of metrics and the effectiveness of different evaluation techniques. For more information on retrospectives and lessons learned, see Section 5.7.2.4.

9.2.3 DETERMINE SOLUTION EVALUATION APPROACH: OUTPUTS

9.2.3.1 SOLUTION EVALUATION APPROACH

The solution evaluation approach describes when and how a solution will be evaluated, the types of metrics that will support evaluation, the feasibility of collecting and communicating the actual performance data for these metrics, and who is responsible for conducting the evaluation and communicating results. For information about what to include in a solution evaluation approach, see Section 3.4.15 of *Business Analysis for Practitioners: A Practice Guide*.

9.2.4 DETERMINE SOLUTION EVALUATION APPROACH: TAILORING CONSIDERATIONS

Adaptive and predictive tailoring considerations for Determine Solution Evaluation Approach are described in Table 9-2.

Table 9-2. Adaptive and Predictive Tailoring for Solution Evaluation Approach

Aspects to Be Tailored	Typical Adaptive Considerations	Typical Predictive Considerations
Name	Not a formally named process	Determine Solution Evaluation Approach
Approach	Considered part of initial planning and taken into account when defining acceptance criteria, creating a definition of done, and during coordination with quality assurance. The decisions may be documented informally or discussed among the team.	The approach for Solution Evaluation is defined as part of planning and prior to defining acceptance criteria.
Deliverables	Not a separate deliverable.	The solution evaluation approach becomes a component of the business analysis plan.

9.2.5 DETERMINE SOLUTION EVALUATION APPROACH: COLLABORATION POINT

Many roles can participate in determining the solution evaluation approach. Any manager whose area could be responsible for collecting, monitoring, evaluating, or funding the costs to obtain the performance data could participate in determining and approving the approach. Risk compliance and legal areas may provide requirements as to what needs to be measured, for how long, and for what length of time performance data need to be retained. Project sponsors also need to be included because they hold different insights as funders and may have different priorities in terms of what they are willing to spend for Solution Evaluation. Operational leads may provide ideas for metrics and assess the ability of their operational areas to measure them and provide insights into the costs associated with collecting them.

9.3 EVALUATE ACCEPTANCE RESULTS AND ADDRESS DEFECTS

Evaluate Acceptance Results and Address Defects is the process of deciding what to do with the results from a comparison of the defined acceptance criteria against the solution. The key benefit of this process is that it allows for informed decision making about whether to release all or part of a solution and whether to undertake changes, fixes, or enhancements to the product. The inputs, tools and techniques, and outputs for this process are shown in Figure 9-7. Figure 9-8 depicts the data flow diagram for the process.

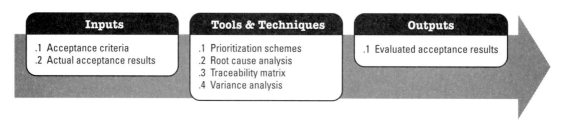

Inputs	Tools & Techniques	Outputs
.1 Acceptance criteria .2 Actual acceptance results	.1 Prioritization schemes .2 Root cause analysis .3 Traceability matrix .4 Variance analysis	.1 Evaluated acceptance results

Figure 9-7. Evaluate Acceptance Results and Address Defects: Inputs, Tools and Techniques, and Outputs

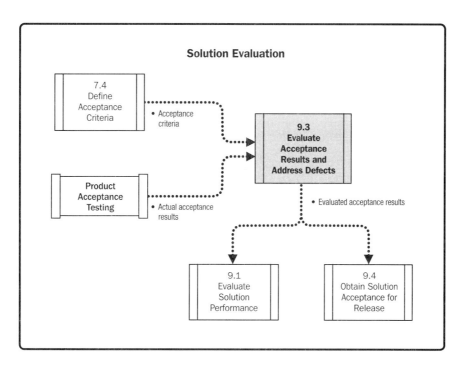

Figure 9-8. Evaluate Acceptance Results and Address Defects: Data Flow Diagram

This process compares the acceptance criteria and the actual results of acceptance testing to provide recommendations on how to deal with situations where aspects of a solution do not meet the acceptance criteria specified for it. It covers acceptance testing at any level of granularity, from something as big as an entire solution release to something as small as one business scenario (composed of one or more user stories). It focuses on the actual results from comparing acceptance testing to their acceptance criteria, rather than on the tests themselves. This distinction supports common practice in the industry, where organizations distinguish between roles that conduct business analysis and roles that perform testing. The pass/fail aspect of comparing actual results from acceptance testing to testing criteria is typically a task within the testing discipline. Business analysis is then needed to consider the magnitude and severity of the defects, to determine their root cause, to identify risks associated with them, and to identify and recommend ways to address them. As part of those recommendations, business analysis can consider the business impacts and costs incurred by repairing or working around the defects, along with potential business impacts and costs of deploying the solution without addressing the defects.

The test results that are part of evaluating acceptance criteria and addressing defects may come from:

◆ Exploratory tests and user acceptance tests,

◆ Day-in-the-life (DITL) tests,

◆ Preproduction or simulated production testing,

◆ Tests of functionality within a scenario, and

◆ Tests of nonfunctional requirements.

For more information about testing approaches, see Section 6.6 of *Business Analysis for Practitioners: A Practice Guide.*

In organizations that conduct some form of ongoing monitoring and acceptance testing for quality, such as in manufacturing or construction, differences between actual results and acceptance criteria can be evaluated to look for trends and patterns in terms of increases or decreases in unacceptable results. For solutions that involve software, where an organization has adopted automated regression testing, it may be possible to spot trends and patterns in out-of-tolerance results.

The evaluation process includes determining the root cause of any variance or defect. It may include an analysis of the cost to address the defect and the business impact of addressing it or accepting it. Recommendations for how to address the defect can also be made and may include:

◆ Potential workarounds to business practices or product usage that will not interfere with other product functionality or cause the product to behave in unintended ways;

◆ Possible modifications to the product, which could require a change request;

◆ Potential adjustments to how or which results are measured;

◆ Identifying a need to investigate the technical causes of the defect; and

◆ Communications to customers and users to clarify how the product is expected to be used.

Activities to evaluate acceptance results and address defects generally occur at any point at which a go/no-go or release decision needs to be made for a solution or a component of it. However, they may also occur while working with product defects discovered after the solution is put into operation.

9.3.1 EVALUATE ACCEPTANCE RESULTS AND ADDRESS DEFECTS: INPUTS

9.3.1.1 ACCEPTANCE CRITERIA

Described in Section 7.4.3.1. Acceptance criteria are concrete and demonstrable conditions that have to be met for the business stakeholders or customers to accept the item. They may take the form of lists of acceptance criteria for each user story in an adaptive approach or a list of higher-level acceptance criteria for a release or solution in a predictive approach. Acceptance criteria are a key input because they indicate the conditions against which the solution is being tested.

9.3.1.2 ACTUAL ACCEPTANCE RESULTS

Actual acceptance results contain the pass/fail results from comparing test results against the acceptance criteria, often provided by a quality control team. In business analysis, the actual acceptance results are then analyzed to determine the reasons for any differences between the test results and acceptance criteria and to recommend how to address the defects. For organizations that conduct regression testing, regression test results may be valuable to analyze as well, as they may reveal situations where new or enhanced functionality impacts existing functionality.

9.3.2 EVALUATE ACCEPTANCE RESULTS AND ADDRESS DEFECTS: TOOLS AND TECHNIQUES

9.3.2.1 PRIORITIZATION SCHEMES

Prioritization schemes are different methods used to prioritize requirements, features, or any other product information. As part of addressing defects, prioritization schemes can be used to rank each defect based on its severity and how likely a user is to encounter it, as well as on the impact of not fixing the defect. For more information on prioritization schemes, see Section 7.7.2.5.

9.3.2.2 ROOT CAUSE ANALYSIS

Root cause analysis techniques are used to determine the reason for a variance or a defect. Root cause analysis techniques can be used to discover the reasons why actual results did not meet the acceptance criteria. These root cause reasons will also figure into decisions about whether or not to move forward to obtain solution acceptance for a release. For more information on root cause analysis techniques, see Section 4.2.2.9. For an example of how root cause analysis can be applied to evaluating acceptance criteria and addressing defects, see Section 6.10.3 of *Business Analysis for Practitioners: A Practice Guide*.

9.3.2.3 TRACEABILITY MATRIX

A traceability matrix is a grid that links product requirements from their origin to the deliverables that satisfy them. A traceability matrix can be used to establish relationships among product information, deliverables, and project work to ensure that each relates back to business objectives. As part of evaluating acceptance results, a traceability matrix can be used as a tool to assess the business impact of not addressing variations from acceptance criteria and defects; for example, there could be a significant business impact from not addressing defects associated with features that trace to a high-priority objective. For more information on traceability matrices, see Section 8.2.2.5.

9.3.2.4 VARIANCE ANALYSIS

Variance is a quantifiable deviation, departure, or divergence from a known baseline or expected value. Variance analysis is a technique for determining the cause and degree of difference between the baseline and actual performance. Irrespective of product life cycle, when there are significant differences between the acceptance criteria and actual results from testing, variance analysis may be applied to consider causes of the differences. For more information on variance analysis, see Section 5.7.2.6.

9.3.3 EVALUATE ACCEPTANCE RESULTS AND ADDRESS DEFECTS: OUTPUTS

9.3.3.1 EVALUATED ACCEPTANCE RESULTS

Evaluated acceptance results provide a summarized comparison between the acceptance criteria and the actual acceptance results, along with the root cause for variances or defects, the analysis of the cost to address the defect, and the business impact of addressing it or accepting it. Some organizations will track the evaluated acceptance results and recommendations in logs. When evaluated acceptance results are communicated, recommendations about ways to address the defect may be included. For organizations that make it a practice to maintain documentation about their products and projects, another type of evaluated acceptance result can be obtained by comparing approved requirements to as-built documentation.

9.3.4 EVALUATE ACCEPTANCE RESULTS AND ADDRESS DEFECTS: TAILORING CONSIDERATIONS

Adaptive and predictive tailoring considerations for Evaluate Acceptance Results and Address Defects are described in Table 9-3.

Table 9-3. Adaptive and Predictive Tailoring for Evaluate Acceptance Results and Address Defects

Aspects to Be Tailored	Typical Adaptive Considerations	Typical Predictive Considerations
Name	Not a formally named process; performed as part of the work to demonstrate and obtain feedback on the solution	Evaluate Acceptance Results and Address Defects
Approach	Typically covers a slice of product capabilities at a time, along with the acceptance criteria associated with those capabilities. Demonstrate what was developed during the most recent iteration, obtain feedback from decision makers, and add defects that need to be addressed to the backlog for prioritization. When conducted for a specific user story, if the demonstration does not prove conformance to the acceptance criteria, the entire story can be rejected and returned to the backlog to be reprioritized.	Performed on a segment of the product that is to be delivered as part of a release or the entire product. Use evaluated acceptance results and the acceptance criteria as a starting point to determine root cause for variances or defects. Consider the costs to address the defects and the business impacts of addressing or accepting them. Provide recommendations for how to address the defects.
Deliverables	Additions of defects to the backlog.	Documentation of evaluated acceptance results, along with any associated change requests.

9.3.5 EVALUATE ACCEPTANCE RESULTS AND ADDRESS DEFECTS: COLLABORATION POINT

Many roles collaborate with the business analyst when evaluating acceptance results and determining how to address identified defects. Developers, designers, quality control analysts, and subject matter experts (SMEs) from the business or operational areas may have insights on reasons for a variance between actual results and the expected results. Any role involved in identification, prioritization, or adjudication of change requests, such as an individual on a change control team, might take leadership for addressing defects in consultation with those responsible for business analysis.

9.4 OBTAIN SOLUTION ACCEPTANCE FOR RELEASE

Obtain Solution Acceptance for Release is the process of facilitating a decision on whether to release a partial or full solution into production and eventually to an operational team, as well as transitioning knowledge and existing information about the product, its risks, known issues, and any workarounds that may have arisen in response to those issues. The key benefit of this process is the creation of an agreed-upon break between building a solution and releasing a solution for acceptance by the stakeholders. The inputs, tools and techniques, and outputs for this process are shown in Figure 9-9. Figure 9-10 depicts the data flow diagram for the process.

Figure 9-9. Obtain Solution Acceptance for Release: Inputs, Tools and Techniques, and Outputs

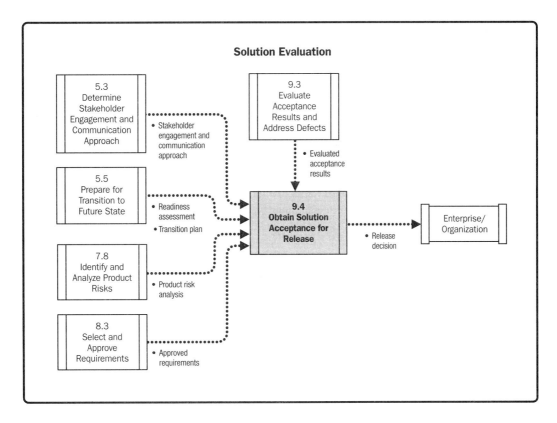

Figure 9-10. Obtain Solution Acceptance for Release: Data Flow Diagram

Obtaining solution acceptance for a release provides the stakeholders who are accountable for the product with an opportunity to decide whether it should be released in whole, in part, or not at all.

For solution acceptance, the term *release* may refer to releasing a solution or a segment of a solution into a production environment while its development team is still responsible for it. It can also refer to releasing a solution or a segment of it to the operational area that will take responsibility for it.

Release decisions are typically based upon:

◆ Acceptability of the solution, as evidenced by the evaluated acceptance results;

◆ Confirmation that the organization is ready for the release;

◆ Confirmation that the transition activities to prepare for the release have been completed to the degree necessary, including the coordination of this solution release with any other releases that are happening concurrently; and

◆ Acceptance of any remaining product risks and workarounds.

A decision to release a solution to its operational area requires confirmation of the completion of any warranty period that may have been established. A warranty period is an interval of time during which the product development team is responsible for addressing any defects found after the solution is released for production.

Depending on organizational norms, obtaining a release decision may include obtaining sign-off. For an iterative or adaptive project life cycle, informal sign-off generally occurs at the end of each sprint or iteration, with formal sign-off, when required, occurring prior to each release of the solution to the production environment. For a predictive project life cycle, sign-off usually occurs at the end of the project life cycle, either immediately prior to release to production or post release after the warranty period is complete.

9.4.1 OBTAIN SOLUTION ACCEPTANCE FOR RELEASE: INPUTS

9.4.1.1 APPROVED REQUIREMENTS

Described in Section 8.3.3.1. Approved requirements are requirements that are verified, validated, and deemed an accurate representation of what the product development team should build. Approved requirements provide the baseline for comparisons made in release decisions between what was approved for the solution and what was actually implemented in the product.

9.4.1.2 EVALUATED ACCEPTANCE RESULTS

Described in Section 9.3.3.1. Evaluated acceptance results provide a summarized comparison between the acceptance criteria and the actual results, along with the root cause for variances or defects, the analysis of the cost to address the defect, and the business impact of addressing it or accepting it. For solutions developed using an adaptive life cycle, the definition of done is also part of these results.

Evaluated acceptance results provide concrete evidence of whether or not the solution has met or exceeded expectations. Any recommendations within evaluated acceptance results for how to deal with the discrepancies may impact when and whether a solution is accepted for release.

9.4.1.3 PRODUCT RISK ANALYSIS

Described in Section 7.8.3.1. The product risk analysis includes the consolidated results from identifying and analyzing product risks. The product risk analysis consists of the recommended responses to manage and control potential threats and strategies to take advantage of potential opportunities related to the product. This context is required when seeking solution acceptance for a release to determine the degree to which the product risks have been addressed. Product risks not addressed within the duration of the project may be transferred to operational teams to manage going forward.

9.4.1.4 READINESS ASSESSMENT

Described in Section 5.5.3.1. A readiness assessment is an evaluation of how well an organization is prepared for a change. It provides an evaluation of the ability of an organization to transition to the future state enabled by the solution. It also identifies risks to achieving readiness for the transition, and may also propose responses for how to address those risks. Consideration of whether any unaddressed readiness risks remain and whether the organization is truly ready for the release at the proposed point in time will figure into release decisions.

9.4.1.5 STAKEHOLDER ENGAGEMENT AND COMMUNICATION APPROACH

Described in Section 5.3.3.1. The stakeholder engagement and communication approach summarizes all the agreements for governing how stakeholders will be engaged and communicated with across the portfolio, program, or project. The stakeholder engagement and communication approach includes information about which roles are accountable for the release decision and how the release decision will be made.

9.4.1.6 TRANSITION PLAN

Described in Section 5.5.3.2. A transition plan is based on the readiness assessment as well as the transition strategy. It covers development of all the communication, rollout, training and user documentation procedure updates, business recovery updates, and other collateral and final production tasks needed to successfully cut over and adapt to the future state. It provides the information needed to coordinate and ensure that the release of the solution will occur at a time when the business can accept the changes and that any interruptions caused by the transition itself are not in conflict with other in-process programs and project work.

At a minimum, a transition plan would include a checklist of transition activities with "no later than" completion dates. When formalized, a transition plan would have a schedule developed in collaboration with and managed by those responsible for project management and operations. On projects using an adaptive delivery approach, rather than developing a formal transition plan, transition planning may manifest itself in setting up a reserved block of time or specific iteration to work through transition details, coordinating this time with the operational area that will own the product. For solutions involving software, this effort often includes time to clean up "technical debt," the tactical workarounds within the solution that could result in a product that would be difficult to maintain or enhance over time. A very important part of obtaining solution acceptance involves confirming that the transition activities have been completed.

9.4.2 OBTAIN SOLUTION ACCEPTANCE FOR RELEASE: TOOLS AND TECHNIQUES

9.4.2.1 FACILITATED WORKSHOPS

Facilitated workshops use a structured meeting led by a skilled, neutral facilitator and a carefully selected group of stakeholders to collaborate and work toward a stated objective. Whenever possible, release decisions should be made during a facilitated workshop to allow all stakeholders to hear the rationale for the decisions made. The individuals who evaluated the acceptance criteria should attend and contribute to decision making. It can be helpful to provide summarized information in tabular or visual form (i.e., charts/graphs/pictorial) whenever possible, to help decision makers render their decisions. Summarizing the evaluated acceptance results, along with the remaining product and readiness risks, incomplete transition activities, and any gaps between approved requirements and what the solution will deliver, provides decision makers with the necessary information to render a decision more quickly. For more information on facilitated workshops, see Section 6.3.2.4.

9.4.2.2 GROUP DECISION-MAKING TECHNIQUES

Group decision-making techniques are used in a group setting to bring participants to a final decision on an issue or topic under discussion. To make the release decision, group decision making is conducted using an agreed-upon model for reaching a decision. The decision model should be identified as part of the stakeholder engagement and communication approach. For more information on group decision-making techniques, see Section 8.3.2.7.

9.4.3 OBTAIN SOLUTION ACCEPTANCE FOR RELEASE: OUTPUTS

9.4.3.1 RELEASE DECISION

A release decision may permit the release or partial release of the solution, delay it, or disapprove and prevent it. A release decision often includes a sign-off. The formality of the sign-off depends upon the type of project, the type of product, the project life cycle, the scale of the release, and corporate and regulatory constraints. Organizations with informal sign-off practices need to obtain sign-off in the manner that is acceptable to the organization. For more information on the format of a sign-off and typical situations where a formal sign-off is required, see Section 6.9 in *Business Analysis for Practitioners: A Practice Guide*.

9.4.4 OBTAIN SOLUTION ACCEPTANCE FOR RELEASE: TAILORING CONSIDERATIONS

Adaptive and predictive tailoring considerations for Obtain Solution Acceptance for Release are described in Table 9-4.

Table 9-4. Adaptive and Predictive Tailoring for Obtain Solution Acceptance for Release

Aspects to Be Tailored	Typical Adaptive Considerations	Typical Predictive Considerations
Name	Not a formally named process; performed as part of Demonstration and Feedback. For large-scale implementations, there may be a formal process to obtain solution acceptance for release	Obtain Solution Acceptance for Release
Approach	Often, verbal approval alone is obtained with the product owner, as part of demonstration and feedback, that a solution or solution segment meets the definition of done and can be released to production. For a full solution release using an adaptive life cycle, the approach may match what is done in a predictive life cycle. Some large organizations are moving to a DevOps approach, to coordinate activities and improve collaboration between development and operational areas. DevOps may also use automated practices to support release management, such as continuous integration and automated regression testing. These approaches can streamline the way organizations push releases to production and can make a release almost seamless with its approval.	A formal meeting to review inputs and render a decision on an entire solution or a substantial segment of a solution, as part of a phased release. This formal meeting to make the release decision may be part of an overall release management approach, which coordinates the release of all products.
Deliverables	Release decision with whatever level of formality of documentation is required.	

9.4.5 OBTAIN SOLUTION ACCEPTANCE FOR RELEASE: COLLABORATION POINT

Business analysts collaborate with several roles when obtaining solution acceptance for a release. For formal solution acceptance approaches, a release management organization might be responsible for coordinating all release-related activities, including obtaining solution acceptance. In many organizations, someone in a project management role is typically accountable to obtain the sign-off. Operational managers may confirm that all business transition considerations have been sufficiently addressed and that they are comfortable with the solution and any workarounds associated with it. Quality control may be consulted to confirm that all product testing concerns have been sufficiently addressed, and architects and designers may be consulted to confirm that technical product concerns have been sufficiently addressed. For informal solution acceptance, project teams may make the release decision part of a demo and feedback process in collaboration with other product team members in participation.

REFERENCES

[1] Project Management Institute. 2016. *PMI's Pulse of the Profession® In-Depth Report: Requirements Management: A Core Competency for Project and Program Success.* Newtown Square, PA: Author.

[2] Project Management Institute. 2017. *PMI Pulse Report: Success Rates Rise—Transforming the High Cost of Low Performance.* Newtown Square, PA: Author.

[3] Project Management Institute. 2017. *Business Analysis: Leading Organizations to Better Outcomes.* Newtown Square, PA: Author.

[4] Project Management Institute. 2017. *The Standard for Business Analysis.* Newtown Square, PA: Author.

[5] Project Management Institute. 2017. *A Guide to the Project Management Body of Knowledge (PMBOK® Guide)* – Sixth Edition. Newtown Square, PA: Author.

[6] Project Management Institute. 2017. *The Standard for Program Management* – Fourth Edition. Newtown Square, PA: Author.

[7] Project Management Institute. 2017. *The Standard for Portfolio Management* – Fourth Edition. Newtown Square, PA: Author.

[8] Project Management Institute. In Review. *The Standard for Organizational Project Management.* Newtown Square, PA: Author.

[9] Project Management Institute. 2015. *Business Analysis for Practitioners: A Practice Guide.* Newtown Square, PA: Author.

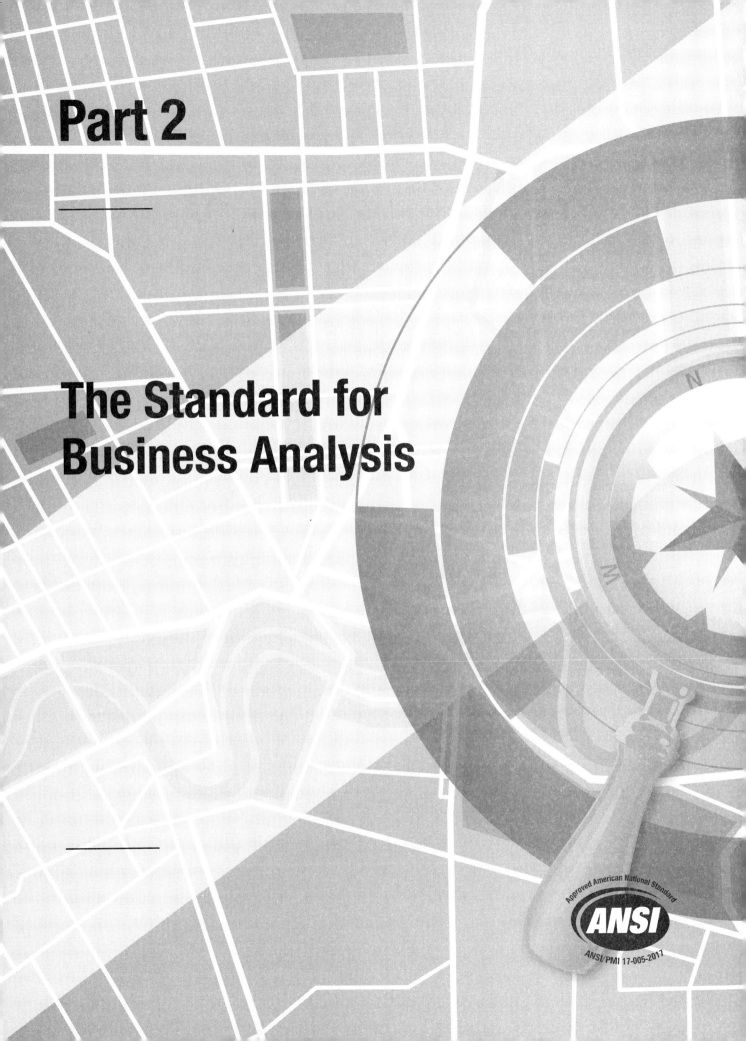

Part 2

The Standard for
Business Analysis

ANSI/PMI 17-005-2017

1

INTRODUCTION

This standard covers the foundational concepts of business analysis and how business analysis supports organizational strategy, governance, portfolio management, program management, project management, and the project environment, as well as business analysis's contribution to achieving business outcomes. These relationships are explained throughout the guide and standard through the use of Business Analysis Process Groups, Knowledge Areas, processes, mapping tables, collaboration points, and other tools. It also includes information on the role of the business analyst, differing project life cycles, and diverse stakeholders. This standard describes the processes used to perform business analysis within programs and projects and to support portfolio management.

Section 1 provides key concepts and contextual information about business analysis. Sections 2 through 7 provide definitions for each of the six Process Groups; describe all of the business analysis processes within those groups; and identify the key benefits, inputs, and outputs for each.

This standard serves as the foundation and framework for *The PMI Guide to Business Analysis* [2], referred to herein as the guide. The guide expands on the information in this standard by providing a more in-depth discussion of the context, environment, and influences on business analysis. In addition, the guide provides descriptions of the inputs and outputs; identifies tools and techniques used to perform each process; and discusses key concepts, emerging trends, and opportunities for collaboration between business analysts and those with whom they collaborate within each Knowledge Area.

1.1 WHAT IS A STANDARD?

A standard is established by an authority, by custom, or by general consent as a model or example. This standard provides a foundational reference for anyone performing business analysis in support of portfolios, programs, projects, and operations. *The Standard for Business Analysis* is a global standard that has been developed using a process based on the concepts of consensus, openness, due process, and balance, and it is meant to define good practices for most portfolios, programs, or projects most of the time.

1.2 FRAMEWORK FOR THIS STANDARD

This standard describes the nature of business analysis processes in terms of the integration among processes, their interactions, and the purposes they serve. The processes included in this standard define the activities and outcomes of business analysis, regardless of the job title or role of those performing the work. This standard acknowledges that some business analysis work is performed outside the confines of a project in support of portfolio and program management and is a blend of business analysis activities that support the formulation of organizational strategy and its fulfillment through successful project delivery. The business analysis activities presented in this standard are applicable for all project life cycles, from predictive to adaptive and the various approaches in between. The activities are applicable across industries and all types of organizations (e.g., for-profit, nonprofit, and government organizations, etc.).

1.3 BUSINESS ANALYSIS AND REQUIREMENTS

In this standard and guide, the term *business* represents the area of the organization that possesses the problem or opportunity to be investigated. The investigation and subsequent analysis is performed using business analysis.

Business analysis is the application of knowledge, skills, tools, and techniques to:

◆ Determine problems and opportunities;

◆ Identify business needs and recommend viable solutions to meet those needs and support strategic decision making;

◆ Elicit, analyze, specify, communicate, and manage requirements and other product information; and

◆ Define benefits and approaches for measuring and realizing value, and analyzing those results.

In short, business analysis is the set of activities performed to support the delivery of solutions that align to business objectives and provide continuous value to the organization.

A requirement is defined as a condition or capability that is necessary to be present in a product, service, or result to satisfy a business need. Whether they are expressed as requirement statements, use cases, user stories, backlog items, or visual models, a clear understanding of requirements is essential for developing solutions that meet the business needs. Sometimes requirements are unstated because stakeholders are unaware of what is really needed until they use a solution or view a prototype. Although unstated, these needs are still requirements. This highlights the importance of using a variety of elicitation techniques to draw forth sufficient information to develop the solution, reducing the likelihood that stakeholders have expectations that have not been verbalized.

1.4 THE BENEFITS OF BUSINESS ANALYSIS

PMI research conducted as part of the *2017 Pulse of the Profession® In-Depth Report Success Rates Rise: Transforming the High Cost of Low Performance* [3] revealed that requirements-related issues continue to remain a primary cause of project failure (39% in 2017, which was up from 37% in 2014 and 32% in 2013). Research also indicates that when business analysis is poorly sized, performed inadequately, or sparsely considered, there is a direct impact to a team's ability to deliver to the commitments made. As a result of the direct impact that business analysis has on program and project success, there is substantial interest across organizations to fully understand the best usage of business analysis, which will enable successful portfolio, program, project, and business outcomes.

The same PMI research validates that when business analysis is properly accounted for and executed on programs and projects, the following benefits are achieved:

◆ Requirements are well defined;

◆ Projects are more likely to be delivered on time, within scope, and within budget; and

◆ High-quality solutions are implemented that result in achieving customer satisfaction.

When business analysis is performed well, program and project outcomes are more likely to be aligned with each other and with organizational strategies. Also, stakeholder participation and engagement increase, making it easier for the product team to obtain buy-in on the requirements, design, and ultimately, the final solution. Business analysis enables the development of high-quality solutions that deliver value to organizations. With sufficient business analysis, unnecessary legal and regulatory risks can be mitigated as program or project noncompliance issues are reduced. As repeatable business analysis processes are used, organizations can develop improved business analysis skills and competencies that are reusable to support future portfolios, programs, and projects.

1.5 HOW BUSINESS ANALYSIS SUPPORTS PORTFOLIO, PROGRAM, AND PROJECT MANAGEMENT

Portfolio management is the centralized management of one or more groupings of projects, programs, subsidiary portfolios, and operations to achieve strategic objectives. Programs focus on achieving a specific set of expected benefits as determined by organizational strategy and objectives, whereas projects are largely concerned with creating specific deliverables that support specific organizational objectives. Projects may or may not be part of a program. Business analysis supports portfolio, program, and project management. Business analysis competencies increase alignment between the higher-level strategies and outcomes of programs and enable portfolio, program, and project management practices and processes.

Business analysis begins with defining a situation and a complete understanding of the problem or opportunity that the organization wishes to address; this work is considered pre-project. The results of pre-project activities provide information to understand the value a given project provides to the portfolio and program. When organizations lack portfolio and program management practices, the definition of the problem or opportunity should be performed at the onset of the project. Business analysis activities support portfolio management by helping to align programs and projects to organizational strategy. In portfolio, program, and project management, business analysis also involves the elicitation and analysis necessary to define the product scope, requirements, models, and other product information necessary to build a common understanding of the solution and clearly communicate product features to those responsible for developing the end product.

The business analysis processes performed as part of the Defining and Aligning Process Group produce analysis results and other outputs leveraged by portfolio management. All other business analysis activities performed outside of the Defining and Aligning Process Group help define the solution and support the work of program and project management. Business Analysis Process Groups are explained in more detail in Section 1.12 on Business Analysis Process Groups.

Table 1-1 compares business analysis with project, program, and portfolio management.

Table 1-1. Comparative Overview of Business Analysis with Project, Program, and Portfolio Management

	Business Analysis	Project Management	Program Management	Portfolio Management
Definition	The set of activities performed to support the delivery of solutions that align to business objectives and provide continuous value to the organization.	The application of knowledge, skills, tools, and techniques to project activities to meet the project requirements.	The application of knowledge, skills, and principles to a program to achieve the program objectives and obtain benefits and control not available by managing program components individually.	The centralized management of one or more portfolios to achieve strategic objectives.
Focus	**Solution:** Something that is produced to deliver measurable business value to meet the business need and expectations of stakeholders (e.g., new products and enhancements to products).	**Project:** A temporary endeavor undertaken to create a unique product, service, or result.	**Program:** A group of related projects, subsidiary programs, and program activities that are managed in a coordinated way to obtain benefits not available from managing them individually.	**Portfolio:** A collection of projects, programs, subsidiary portfolios, and operations managed as a group to achieve strategic objectives.
Scope Definition	**Product scope:** The features and functions that characterize a solution.	**Project scope:** The work performed to deliver a product, service, or result with the specified features and functions.	**Program scope:** The scope that encompasses program components and the interactions and synergy between them.	**Portfolio scope:** The organizational scope that changes with the strategic objectives of the organization.
Roles	Those who identify business needs, and recommend and describe solutions through the definition of product requirements.	Those who manage the project team to meet the project objectives.	Those who ensure that program benefits are delivered as expected by coordinating the activities of a program's components.	Those who coordinate portfolio management staff, or program and project staff that may have reporting responsibilities into the aggregate portfolio.
Success	Measured by a solution's ability to deliver its intended benefits to an organization, degree of customer satisfaction, and achievement of business objectives.	Measured by product and project quality, timelines, budget compliance, and degree of customer satisfaction.	Measured by program's ability to deliver its intended benefits to an organization, and by the program's efficiency and effectiveness in delivering those benefits.	Measured in terms of the aggregate investment performance and benefit realization of the portfolio.

1.6 THE ROLE OF THE BUSINESS ANALYST

Those who perform business analysis are commonly called business analysts, but there are business analysis professionals with other job titles who also perform business analysis activities. Some business analysis professionals are specialized and therefore have a title that reflects that area of their competency; strategic business analyst, data analyst, process analyst, or systems analyst are a few examples of these roles. How an organization uses business analysis resources; where these resources functionally report; and the type of industry, type of project, and type of project life cycle being used are some of the factors that influence how organizations title those who have the responsibility for business analysis.

There are also many roles where business analysis is performed as a part of the role but is not necessarily the only responsibility. Enterprise and business architects; portfolio, program, and project managers; and operational analysts are a few examples. The business analysis processes, tools, and techniques presented in the guide and this standard are relevant to these individuals, too. Because there are many titles and variations of business analysis roles in use, the guide and this standard use the phrase *business analysis professional* over *business analyst*. When the term *business analyst* is used, it is done for the sake of brevity and should always be considered a reference to anyone performing business analysis, regardless of the title a person holds or the percentage of job function spent on the work. The objective of this guide and standard is to establish an understanding about business analysis and not job titles.

This standard establishes an understanding of business analysis by presenting 35 business analysis processes to explain the work and discussing these in context to the Process Groups and Knowledge Areas to which each relates.

1.7 THE DIFFERENCE BETWEEN PROJECT MANAGERS AND BUSINESS ANALYSTS

Project managers and business analysts serve in critical leadership roles on programs and projects. When these roles partner and collaborate effectively, a project has a greater chance of being successful. While collaboration is key, many projects and organizations struggle with or confuse project manager and business analyst responsibilities. These struggles are compounded when the project manager and business analyst report into different functional units, or when these roles are from different organizations as is often the case when there is a client-supplier relationship.

This standard describes the work of business analysis, regardless of the role performing it. For organizations and projects that separate business analysis responsibilities from project management responsibilities, *The PMI Guide to Business Analysis* provides additional details to identify the areas of perceived overlap and clarify the areas of confusion that exist between project managers and business analysts. While several of the business analysis processes identified in this standard appear to have the same process names as those in *A Guide to the Project Management Body of Knowledge (PMBOK® Guide)* [4], they are not the same. For example, the *PMBOK® Guide* – Sixth Edition includes Section 4.1 on Develop Project Charter, and this standard includes the process performed to support this work, that is, Section 3.1 on Support Charter Development.

Project managers are responsible for the successful delivery of the *project*, while business analysts are responsible for successful delivery of the *product*. Therefore, the processes presented and discussed in this standard are product focused. Sometimes, project management and business analysis activities overlap, which is why project managers and business analysts work closely together. Products, or enhancements to products, are delivered by employing project life cycles. For example, project managers are responsible for stakeholders remaining engaged across the project, and business analysts are responsible for stakeholders remaining engaged throughout the business analysis processes. The processes identified in this standard are intended to reduce the confusion and perceived overlap between these two roles.

1.8 PRODUCT AND PROJECT LIFE CYCLES

A product life cycle is a series of phases that represent the evolution of a product from concept through delivery, growth, maturity, maintenance, and retirement. The number of intermediary phases that a product goes through is dependent on the longevity of the product life cycle. Projects may be implemented to evolve products, but projects are not required for this evolution. It may take multiple projects to evolve a product through the product life cycle, and in some cases, a product may evolve in the same phase.

A product life cycle may consist of multiple project life cycles. A needs assessment conducted within the product life cycle provides strategic alignment and justification for the investment of a new project. After the project is complete, an evaluation of the product is performed within the product life cycle to determine if a new project is needed to evolve the product. Business analysis focuses on the entire product life cycle, including the many projects that advance the product.

A project life cycle is the series of phases through which a project passes from its initiation to its closure. The phases can be sequential or they may overlap. The names, number, and duration of the project phases are influenced by a number of factors, including the management and control needs of the organization(s) involved in the project, the nature of the project itself, its area of application, and the complexity or volatility of the product information. The phase or phases associated with the development of features and capabilities can be unitary or composed of multiple iterations. Iterations are generally time-bounded, with a start and end or control point. At the control point, the project charter, business case, and other project baselines are reexamined based on the current environment. The project's risk exposure and evaluation of project execution compared to its performance measurement baseline are used to determine if the project should be changed, terminated, or continued as planned.

The project life cycle is influenced by many internal and external factors, including but not limited to the unique aspects of the organization, industry, or technology employed. While every project has a clear start and end, the specific deliverables and work that take place vary widely depending on the project. The life cycle provides the basic framework for managing the project, regardless of the specific work involved.

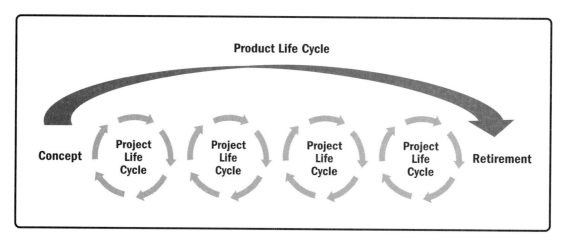

Figure 1-1. Relationship Between Product and Project Life Cycles

Figure 1-1 illustrates the relationship between product and project life cycles, showing that a product life cycle is comprised of one or more project life cycles. While the diagram is not intended to model life cycle phases, keep in mind that each project life cycle may contain activities related to a part of the product life cycle, for example, product development, product maintenance, and eventually, product retirement.

Project life cycles can range along a continuum from predictive life cycles at one end to adaptive life cycles at the other. In a predictive life cycle, the project deliverables are defined at the beginning of the project, and any changes to the scope are managed. In an adaptive life cycle such as an agile approach, the deliverables are developed over multiple iterations where a detailed scope is defined and approved at the beginning of each iteration.

1.9 HOW ITERATIVE AND ADAPTIVE LIFE CYCLES AFFECT BUSINESS ANALYSIS ROLES

Over the past 20 years, the emergence of iterative and adaptive project life cycles has introduced new ways to address product complexity and the ever-increasing pace of change by delivering segments of solutions to stakeholders for early and frequent feedback.

Adopting these project life cycles alters the notion that an individual assigned to a project performs only the role that is his or her specialty. Whether dealing with iterative or scrum projects with time-boxed iterations or sprints or working with projects using the Kanban approach, with continuous flow and work-in-progress limits, the team commits to demonstrating completed features and capabilities to the stakeholders at the end of each delivery. In situations where a project team using a scrum approach confronts a negative risk that the selected features and capabilities cannot be completed within the time-box, all team members will pitch in to make sure the work gets done, even if that means doing work not usually associated with their roles. For teams using a Kanban approach with continuous flow and work-in-progress limits, if the amount of work that needs to be completed exceeds the capacity of the individuals who normally perform that work, one option is for all team members to pitch in; the other is for the flow to be interrupted until the individuals who normally perform that work can take on more work. This means that individuals assigned to iterative or adaptive projects are either part of cross-functional teams or are considered specialty resources. On cross-functional teams, every team member can typically play more than one role. Specialty resources possess a particular skill, such as business analysis, which they provide to the team by serving as practitioners, mentors, or subject matter experts. With the help of other team members who can advise or mentor them, specialty resources also take on other roles that are less familiar to them to complete the work to which the team is committed.

Additionally, for adaptive approaches such as scrum and Kanban, from the perspective of business analysis, the entire team is responsible for the work of eliciting and analyzing requirements, whether or not the team has an individual who holds the role of business analyst. One or more people on the team should have sufficient business analysis skills to help the team identify and refine the requirements, so that the team can develop a solution that will satisfy those requirements.

1.10 TAILORING THE BUSINESS ANALYSIS PLAN AND PROJECT DOCUMENTS

Business analysis involves selecting the appropriate processes, inputs, and outputs represented in this standard for use on a specific portfolio, program, or project. Likewise, tools and techniques can be selected from *The PMI Guide to Business Analysis*. This selection activity is known as tailoring business analysis. Tailoring is necessary because each organization, portfolio, program, and project is unique; therefore, not every process, tool, or technique is required for every business analysis effort. The format of inputs and outputs listed within each process may also be tailored. For example, in the guide, the output of the Define and Elaborate Requirements process is requirements and other product information. Requirements and other product information can be presented in the form of a requirements document, a collection of user stories, or another format deemed suitable for the situation. The inputs themselves can also be tailored, in that the inputs listed for each process are required at minimum to perform that process; however, if there are other helpful inputs available, they should be used. For example, a product roadmap may be beneficial when prioritizing product information, but is not listed as an input because a product roadmap may not always be available when prioritizing product information.

Because this standard is adapted to support the characteristics of a portfolio, program, or project, it is important to note that organizational process assets, enterprise environmental factors, expert judgment, and the business analysis plan are commonly used as inputs into all business analysis processes and will therefore not be repeated as inputs for each process discussed within the guide.

The business analysis deliverables that are produced from a process—and the degree of formality with which each is detailed and maintained—will depend on the selected project life cycle and other project characteristics, for example, size of the project, complexity of the solution, and industry in which the solution will be used. During business analysis planning, the business analyst identifies the types of deliverables expected to be produced and considers the maintenance, storage, and access needs for each.

1.11 KNOWLEDGE AREAS

Knowledge Areas are fields or areas of specialization that are commonly employed when performing business analysis. A Knowledge Area is a set of processes associated with a particular function. In this standard, the Knowledge Areas contain the set of processes that the work of business analysis comprises. Although they are related, the processes do not prescribe a sequence or order. This standard covers the following Business Analysis Knowledge Areas:

- ◆ **Needs Assessment.** Analyzing current business problems or opportunities to understand what is necessary to attain the desired future state.

- ◆ **Stakeholder Engagement.** Identifying and analyzing those who have an interest in the outcome of the solution to determine how to collaborate and communicate with them.

- ◆ **Elicitation.** Planning and preparing for elicitation, conducting elicitation, and confirming elicitation results to obtain information from sources.

- ◆ **Analysis.** Examining, breaking down, synthesizing, and clarifying information to further understand it, complete it, and improve it.

- ◆ **Traceability and Monitoring.** Tracing, approving, and assessing changes to product information to manage it throughout the business analysis effort.

- ◆ **Solution Evaluation.** Validating a full solution, or a segment of a solution, that is about to be or has already been implemented to determine how well a solution meets the business needs and delivers value to the organization.

Figure 1-2 illustrates the relationships that exist among the six Business Analysis Knowledge Areas. The processes in the Stakeholder Engagement Knowledge Area are used throughout all business analysis efforts and interact with all the other Business Analysis Knowledge Areas. The processes in the Elicitation, Analysis, and Traceability and Monitoring Knowledge Areas tend to be used concurrently. The results obtained by using the processes in the Needs Assessment Knowledge Area are the basis for work conducted using the processes in Elicitation, Analysis, and Traceability and Monitoring. The processes in Elicitation, Analysis, and Traceability and Monitoring produce results that are analyzed with the processes in the Solution Evaluation Knowledge Area, which, in turn, may trigger additional usage of the processes in the Needs Assessment Knowledge Area.

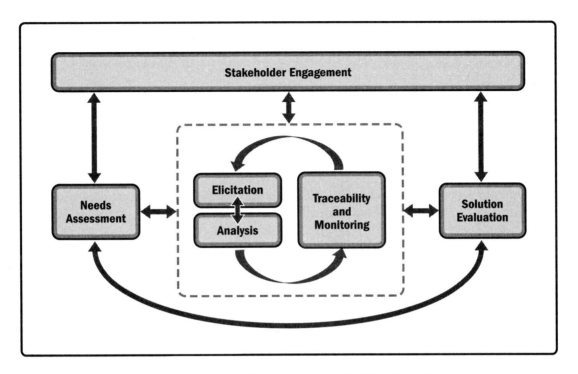

Figure 1-2. Relationships Among Business Analysis Knowledge Areas

1.12 BUSINESS ANALYSIS PROCESS GROUPS

Within this standard, the nature of business analysis is described through 35 processes distributed across the six Business Analysis Process Groups. Each Process Group is independent of the application area or industry in which it is performed. Processes are not one-time events, and processes can overlap throughout the project and product life cycles.

The six Business Analysis Process Groups presented in this standard are defined as follows:

◆ **Defining and Aligning Process Group.** The processes performed to investigate and evaluate the viability of initiating a new product or changes to or retirement of an existing product as well as defining scope and aligning products, portfolios, programs, and projects to the overall organizational strategy.

◆ **Initiating Process Group.** The process performed to define the portfolio, program, or project objectives and apply resources to a portfolio component, program, project, or project phase.

◆ **Planning Process Group.** The processes performed to determine an optimal approach for performing business analysis activities, including how they are adapted for the chosen project life cycle, and to analyze the internal and external stakeholders who will interact and influence the overall definition of the solution.

◆ **Executing Process Group.** The processes performed to elicit, analyze, model, define, verify, validate, prioritize, and approve all types of product information, ranging from backlogs to user stories and requirements to constraints.

◆ **Monitoring and Controlling Process Group.** The processes performed on an ongoing basis to assess the impact of proposed product changes within a portfolio, program, or project to assess business analysis performance and to promote ongoing communication and engagement with stakeholders.

◆ **Releasing Process Group.** The process performed to determine whether all or part of a solution should be released and to obtain acceptance that all or part of a solution is ready to be transitioned to an operational team that will take ongoing responsibility for it.

Figure 1-3 depicts the six Business Analysis Process Groups within the product and project life cycles. This figure demonstrates that processes within the Business Analysis Process Groups can be performed within the context of a project and beyond by supporting the activities in portfolio or program management. The left side of Figure 1-3 shows the Business Analysis Process Groups that are used before a project initiates, but still within the product life cycle. The center section shows the Business Analysis Process Groups that are used during one or more iterations of a project. The right side of the figure shows the Business Analysis Process Groups that are used after a project but still within a product life cycle.

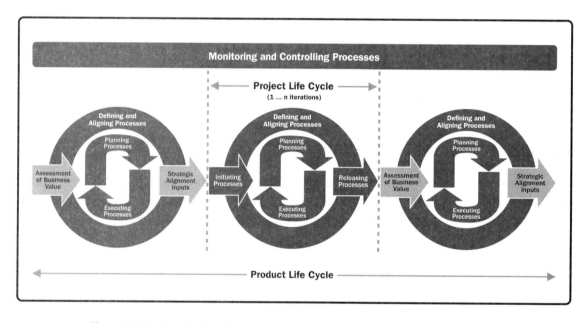

Figure 1-3. Business Analysis Process Groups Within the Product and Project Life Cycles

The output of one process may become an input to another process, a project deliverable, or supporting information, leveraged by portfolio and program management. The definitions of each process, which follow the more detailed descriptions of each Business Analysis Process Group, include a list of typical inputs and outputs.

Process Groups are not project phases or product life cycle phases. When the project or product life cycle is divided into phases, Process Groups may interact within each phase. In fact, it is possible that all Process Groups could be conducted within a phase, as illustrated in Figure 1-3. As projects are separated into distinct phases or subcomponents, such as concept development, feasibility study, design, prototype, build, test, and so forth, all of the Process Groups are normally repeated for each phase until the completion criteria for that phase have been satisfied.

Individual processes are often iterated several times throughout the product life cycle and even within a project. They may require that decisions or deliverables produced early on be revisited and revised. The timing and duration of the iterations and interactions among processes will vary based on the selected project life cycle. The processes presented in this standard provide a comprehensive picture of the activities that business analysis comprises and are transferable to all delivery methods, from predictive to adaptive and variations in between.

There are patterns for how the Process Groups are used in support of different project delivery methods:

◆ **Predictive life cycles.** For predictive life cycles, typically most of the Business Analysis Initiating, Planning, and Executing Process Group activities are conducted earlier in a project, in the front end, along with any defining and aligning that has not been completed prior to project approval. For predictive life cycles, the Business Analysis Releasing Process Group activities are conducted near the end of a project.

◆ **Adaptive life cycles.** For adaptive life cycles, all of the Process Groups are focused on the segment of product features or functionality that the team has committed to deliver in each iteration. Each iteration incrementally delivers a segment of a product for early feedback. The feedback from that delivery can impact the commitment priorities for the next iteration. Each iteration is not a mini-predictive life cycle, but rather encompasses whatever level of business analysis effort is necessary for the team to make its commitment. Consequently, the Business Analysis Execution Process Group activities are exercised the most during each iteration. Some teams working with an adaptive life cycle use some of the time within an iteration to look ahead and start Business Analysis Execution Process Group activities for product backlog items that are likely to be delivered in the next one or two iterations.

The following figures show a typical level of effort expended during each Business Analysis Process Group over the course of a project. Figure 1-4 depicts the level of effort for a project following a predictive life cycle and Figure 1-5 provides the level of effort for a project following an adaptive life cycle.

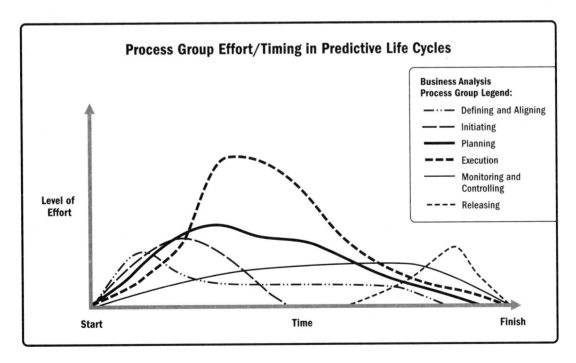

Figure 1-4. Business Analysis Process Group Interactions for Predictive Life Cycles

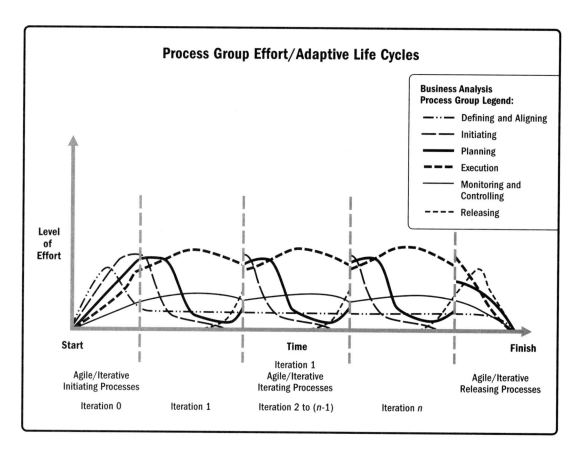

Figure 1-5. Business Analysis Process Group Interactions for Adaptive Life Cycles

Table 1-2 reflects the mapping of the 35 business analysis processes that are within the six Business Analysis Process Groups and the six Knowledge Areas. Within this standard, processes are numbered according to the sequence in which they appear within each Process Group.

The business analysis processes are shown in the Process Group where most of the activity takes place. For example, when a process that normally takes place in the Planning Process Group is revisited in the Executing Process Group, it is not considered a new process. The iterative nature of business analysis means that processes from any Process Group may be used throughout the product life cycle. For example, when managing stakeholder engagement in the Monitoring and Controlling Process Group, it may be necessary to adjust how best to engage stakeholders after gaining some experience working with them, thereby resulting in a need to revisit the Stakeholder Engagement and Communication Approach process.

Table 1-2. Business Analysis Process Group/Knowledge Area Mapping

Knowledge Areas	Business Analysis Process Groups [A]					
	Defining and Aligning Process Group (2)	Initiating Process Group (3)	Planning Process Group (4)	Executing Process Group (5)	Monitoring and Controlling Process Group (6)	Releasing Process Group (7)
4. Needs Assessment	4.1 Identify Problem or Opportunity (2.1) 4.2 Assess Current State (2.2) 4.3 Determine Future State (2.3) 4.4 Determine Viable Options and Provide Recommendation (2.4) 4.5 Facilitate Product Roadmap Development (2.5) 4.6 Assemble Business Case (2.6)	4.7 Support Charter Development (3.1)				
5. Stakeholder Engagement	5.1 Identify Stakeholders (2.7)		5.2 Conduct Stakeholder Analysis (4.1) 5.3 Determine Stakeholder Engagement and Communication Approach (4.2) 5.4 Conduct Business Analysis Planning (4.3)	5.5 Prepare for Transition to Future State (5.1)	5.6 Manage Stakeholder Engagement and Communication (6.1) 5.7 Assess Business Analysis Performance (6.2)	
6. Elicitation			6.1 Determine Elicitation Approach (4.4)	6.2 Prepare for Elicitation (5.2) 6.3 Conduct Elicitation (5.3) 6.4 Confirm Elicitation Results (5.4)		
7. Analysis			7.1 Determine Analysis Approach (4.5)	7.2 Create and Analyze Models (5.5) 7.3 Define and Elaborate Requirements (5.6) 7.4 Define Acceptance Criteria (5.7) 7.5 Verify Requirements (5.8) 7.6 Validate Requirements (5.9) 7.7 Prioritize Requirements and Other Product Information (5.10) 7.8 Identify and Analyze Product Risks (5.11) 7.9 Assess Product Design Options (5.12)		
8. Traceability and Monitoring			8.1 Determine Traceability and Monitoring Approach (4.6)	8.2 Establish Relationships and Dependencies (5.13) 8.3 Select and Approve Requirements (5.14)	8.4 Manage Changes to Requirements and Other Product Information (6.3)	
9. Solution Evaluation	9.1 Evaluate Solution Performance (2.8)		9.2 Determine Solution Evaluation Approach (4.7)	9.3 Evaluate Acceptance Results and Address Defects (5.15)		9.4 Obtain Solution Acceptance for Release (7.1)

[A] The section number preceding each process name identifies the location of the process in the guide. The section number in parentheses following the process name identifies the location of the process in the standard.

2

DEFINING AND ALIGNING PROCESS GROUP

The Defining and Aligning Process Group consists of the processes performed to investigate and evaluate the viability of initiating a new product, making changes to an existing product, or retiring a product; it also includes defining scope and aligning products, portfolios, programs, and projects to the overall organizational strategy. Within the Defining and Aligning Process Group, analysis is conducted to investigate a current business problem or opportunity of significance to the business. An assessment of the current internal and external environments and current capabilities of the organization is performed to identify any organizational capability gaps that might impede the business from achieving its strategic goals and objectives. The culmination of the analysis conducted within the Defining and Aligning processes is applied to formulate a set of viable solution options, any one of which, if pursued, would enable the organization to address the business need and support the organization's strategy and objectives.

A critical part of the work performed within the Defining and Aligning Process Group is to support creating the business case. The business case provides justification to pursue a solution and some form of enterprise change to address the business need. The results of the analysis performed in the Defining and Aligning Process Group provide essential information used by the business to initiate portfolio components, programs, and projects to realize strategy, satisfy business objectives, and increase the value delivered by existing or new portfolios. These activities typically involve supporting the business with the development of the business case by leveraging the knowledge gained when defining the business need and analyzing the current and desired future state. Business case assessment, approval, and funding activities are performed prior to the initiation of the resulting portfolio component, program, or project.

Much of the business analysis work performed within the Defining and Aligning Process Group is leveraged within portfolio and program management. When reviewing portfolios, portfolio components are evaluated to check that performance is as expected and continues to support the organization's strategy and objectives. Programs are typically reviewed to confirm that they reflect the current and most accurate profile of the intended outcomes, that outcomes are in line with business strategy, and that any documents associated with the program, such as its business case, charter, roadmap, risk strategy, and benefits realization plan, are up to date. A concept may be approved for a limited time with limited funding to develop a business case for further evaluation. The business case is then revisited during the portfolio and program review processes. Additionally, this analysis serves as input into the development of the charter and as the foundation by which scope is established for a portfolio component, program, program phase, project, or project phase. A business case may need to be revised after an initiative has started. Business case modifications occurring at this point will result in business case reviews at the portfolio, program, and project levels. Revisions may be initiated for many reasons, including changes to product risks and scope. Adjustments to the portfolio are considered to optimize value as necessary.

The Defining and Aligning Process Group also includes a process, Evaluate Solution Performance, which assesses the business value of a product or a segment of a product. Like all processes, there is no implied sequence for when Evaluate Solution Performance is conducted. This process not only supports the other processes within the Defining and Aligning Process Group, but also may be used at any time when solution evaluation can provide insights. When an

---

evaluation reveals that a gap exists between the expected value and the current value, there may be a problem or opportunity that begins the Defining and Aligning cycle of problem/opportunity identification all over again.

Table 2-1 depicts the relationship among the processes that are within the Business Analysis Defining and Aligning Process Group and portfolio management.

Table 2-1. Relationship Between the Business Analysis Defining and Aligning Process Group and Portfolio Management

Business Analysis Process Group	Business Analysis Process[A]	Portfolio Management Performance Domain
Defining and Aligning	4.1 Identify Problem or Opportunity (2.1) 4.2 Assess Current State (2.2) 4.3 Determine Future State (2.3) 4.4 Determine Viable Options and Provide Recommendation (2.4) 4.5 Facilitate Product Roadmap Development (2.5) 4.6 Assemble Business Case (2.6) 9.1 Evaluate Solution Performance (2.8)	Strategic Management
	4.2 Assess Current State (2.2) 4.3 Determine Future State (2.3)	Capacity and Capability Management
	5.1 Identify Stakeholders (2.7)	Portfolio Stakeholder Engagement
	4.6 Assemble Business Case (2.6) 9.1 Evaluate Solution Performance (2.8)	Value Management

[A] For the business analysis processes, the numbers in parentheses refer to the section numbers for the processes that appear in *The Standard for Business Analysis*; the other numbers refer to the sections in *The PMI Guide to Business Analysis*.

Table 2-2 shows the relationship between the Defining and Aligning Process Group in business analysis and the Initiating Process Group in project management. The key connection point is the work to identify stakeholders. This activity is important prior to project initiation to obtain a sense of which stakeholders can help in defining the business need and identifying associated risks; this work is revisited by project managers during project initiation to obtain a sense of the stakeholders who will be involved in the project. Organizational or project needs may determine how stakeholder identification and management is best performed. Because business analysis and project management both rely on the results of stakeholder identification, there should be a high level of collaboration between roles.

Table 2-2. Relationship of Business Analysis Defining and Aligning Process Group to Project Management

Business Analysis Process Group	Business Analysis Process[A]	Project Management Process	Project Management Process Group
Defining and Aligning	5.1 Identify Stakeholders (2.7)	13.1 Identify Stakeholders	Initiating

[A] For the business analysis processes, the numbers in parentheses refer to the section numbers for the processes that appear in *The Standard for Business Analysis*; the other numbers refer to the sections in *The PMI Guide to Business Analysis*.

The PMI Guide to Business Analysis

2.1 IDENTIFY PROBLEM OR OPPORTUNITY

Identify Problem or Opportunity is the process of identifying the problem to be solved or the opportunity to be pursued. The key benefit of this process is the formation of a clear understanding of the situation that the organization is considering to address. If the problem or opportunity is not thoroughly understood, the organization may pursue a solution that does not address the business need. The inputs and outputs for this process are shown in Figure 2-1.

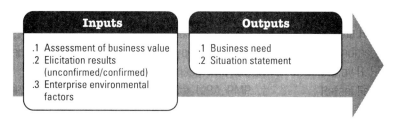

Figure 2-1. Identify Problem or Opportunity: Inputs and Outputs

2.2 ASSESS CURRENT STATE

Assess Current State is the process of examining the current environment under analysis to understand important factors that are internal or external to the organization, which may be the cause or reason for a problem or opportunity. The key benefit of this process is that it provides a sufficient understanding of the existing state of the organization, providing context for determining which elements of the current state will remain unchanged and which changes are necessary to achieve the future state. The inputs and outputs for this process are shown in Figure 2-2.

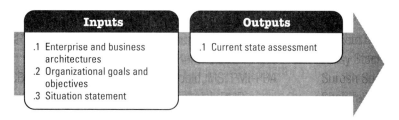

Figure 2-2. Assess Current State: Inputs and Outputs

2.3 DETERMINE FUTURE STATE

Determine Future State is the process of determining gaps in existing capabilities and a set of proposed changes necessary to attain a desired future state that addresses the problem or opportunity under analysis. The key benefit of this process is the resulting identification of a set of capabilities required for the organization to be able to transform from the current state to the desired future state and satisfy the business need. The inputs and outputs for this process are shown in Figure 2-3.

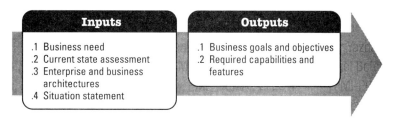

Figure 2-3. Determine Future State: Inputs and Outputs

2.4 DETERMINE VIABLE OPTIONS AND PROVIDE RECOMMENDATION

Determine Viable Options and Provide Recommendation is the process of applying various analysis techniques to examine possible solutions for meeting the business goals and objectives and to determine which of the options is considered the best possible one for the organization to pursue. The key benefits of this process are that it validates the feasibility of proposed solutions and promotes the best course of action for executives and decision makers to meet the business goals and objectives. The inputs and outputs for this process are shown in Figure 2-4.

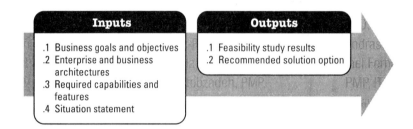

Inputs
.1 Business goals and objectives
.2 Enterprise and business architectures
.3 Required capabilities and features
.4 Situation statement

Outputs
.1 Feasibility study results
.2 Recommended solution option

Figure 2-4. Determine Viable Options and Provide Recommendation: Inputs and Outputs

2.5 FACILITATE PRODUCT ROADMAP DEVELOPMENT

Facilitate Product Roadmap Development is the process of supporting the development of a product roadmap that outlines, at a high level, which aspects of a product are planned for delivery over the course of a portfolio, program, or one or more project iterations or releases, and the potential sequence for the delivery of these aspects. The key benefit of this process is that it creates shared expectations among stakeholders for the deliverables and the potential order in which they will be delivered. The inputs and outputs for this process are shown in Figure 2-5.

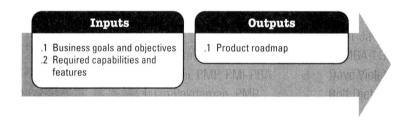

Inputs
.1 Business goals and objectives
.2 Required capabilities and features

Outputs
.1 Product roadmap

Figure 2-5. Facilitate Product Roadmap Development: Inputs and Outputs

2.6 ASSEMBLE BUSINESS CASE

Assemble Business Case is the process of synthesizing well-researched and analyzed information to support the selection of the best portfolio components, programs, or projects to address the business goals and objectives. The key benefit of this process is that it helps organizations scrutinize programs and projects in a consistent manner, enabling the decision makers to determine whether a program and/or project is worth the required investment. The inputs and outputs for this process are shown in Figure 2-6.

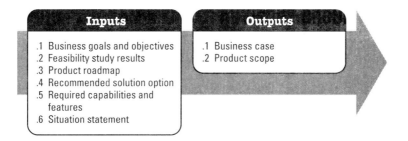

Figure 2-6. Assemble Business Case: Inputs and Outputs

2.7 IDENTIFY STAKEHOLDERS

Identify Stakeholders is the process of identifying the individuals, groups, or organizations that may impact, are impacted, or are perceived to be impacted by the area under assessment. The key benefit of this process is that it helps determine whose interests should be taken into account throughout the business analysis–related activities. The inputs and outputs for this process are shown in Figure 2-7.

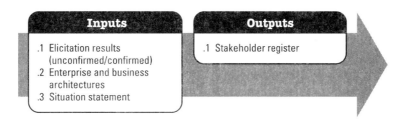

Figure 2-7. Identify Stakeholders: Inputs and Outputs

2.8 EVALUATE SOLUTION PERFORMANCE

Evaluate Solution Performance is the process of evaluating a solution to determine whether the implemented solution or solution component is delivering the business value as intended. The key benefit of this process is that the analysis provides tangible data to determine whether the solution that the business has invested in is achieving the expected business results and serves as an input to decisions about future initiatives. The inputs and outputs for this process are shown in Figure 2-8.

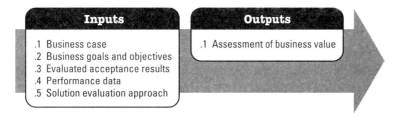

Figure 2-8. Evaluate Solution Performance: Inputs and Outputs

3

INITIATING PROCESS GROUP

The Initiating Process Group consists of the one business analysis process performed to define the portfolio, program, or project objectives and apply resources to a portfolio component, program, project, or project phase. Once a portfolio component, program, or project is approved, the business case is translated into a charter. Analysis performed within the Defining and Aligning Process Group is leveraged to support charter development. The Initiating process is performed within a portfolio or at the start of a program, project, or phase to keep the focus on the business need that the initiative addresses.

The key purpose of the Initiating Process Group is to align the expectations of stakeholders with the portfolio, program, or project purpose; to provide visibility of the scope and objectives; and to demonstrate how stakeholder participation in the initiative and business analysis activities is critical to meet their expectations. This process within the Initiating Process Group helps set the objective of the portfolio, program, or project, and defines what needs to be accomplished to address the business need.

Table 3-1 depicts the relationship between the process within the Business Analysis Initiating Process Group and project management.

Table 3-1. Relationship Between the Business Analysis Initiating Process Group and Project Management

Business Analysis Process Group	Business Analysis Process[A]	Project Management Process	Project Management Process Group
Initiating	4.7 Support Charter Development (3.1)	4.1 Develop Project Charter	Initiating

[A] For the business analysis processes, the numbers in parentheses refer to the section numbers for the processes that appear in *The Standard for Business Analysis*; the other numbers refer to the sections in *The PMI Guide to Business Analysis*.

3.1 SUPPORT CHARTER DEVELOPMENT

Support Charter Development is the process of collaborating on charter development with the sponsoring entity and stakeholder resources using the business analysis knowledge, experience, and product information acquired during needs assessment and business case development efforts. The key benefit of this process is that it enables a smooth transition from the business case to charter development and provides stakeholders with a foundational understanding of the portfolio, program, or project objectives, including product scope and requirements. The inputs and outputs for this process are shown in Figure 3-1.

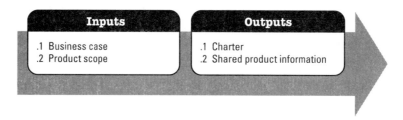

Figure 3-1. Support Charter Development: Inputs and Outputs

4

—

PLANNING

The Planning Process Group consists of the processes performed to determine an optimal approach for performing business analysis activities, including how they are adapted for the chosen project life cycle, and to analyze the internal and external stakeholders who will interact and influence the overall definition of the solution so that:

◆ Business analysis activities and deliverables are defined and agreed upon;

◆ Processes that will be used for engaging stakeholders, eliciting, analyzing, tracing, monitoring, and evaluating are acceptable to key stakeholders; and

◆ Key stakeholders are aware of and support the activities and time commitments required to complete the business analysis effort.

In the same way that the outputs of the project management planning processes are consolidated to form the project management plan, the outputs of business analysis planning processes are consolidated to form the business analysis plan. Business analysis planning makes it possible to understand the scope of the work, stakeholders' expectations and their risk appetite, dependencies between activities, and the appropriate amount and level of business analysis required for the situation to avoid unrealistic expectations by those involved in the requirements-related activities. Business analysis planning activities work in conjunction with portfolio, program, and project management planning activities; therefore, collaboration is a key consideration so that content is neither duplicated nor contradictory.

There is no single approach to business analysis planning that works for every situation; ultimately, the project life cycle, context, complexity, and project characteristics, among other considerations, need to be understood to appropriately choose and size the planning activities for the situation.

Significant changes occurring throughout the project life cycle, lessons learned, or retrospectives trigger the need to revisit one or more of the planning processes. This progressive detailing of the approach is called progressive elaboration, indicating that planning and execution are iterative and ongoing activities.

Table 4-1 depicts the relationship between the processes within the Business Analysis Planning Process Group and project management.

Table 4-1. Relationship Between the Business Analysis Planning Process Group and Project Management

Business Analysis Process Group	Business Analysis Process[A]	Project Management Process	Project Management Process Group
Planning	5.2 Conduct Stakeholder Analysis (4.1)	13.1 Identify Stakeholders	Initiating
	5.3 Determine Stakeholder Engagement and Communication Approach (4.2)	10.1 Plan Communications Management 13.2 Plan Stakeholder Engagement	Planning
	5.4 Conduct Business Analysis Planning (4.3)	4.2 Develop Project Management Plan 5.4 Create WBS 6.2 Define Activities 6.3 Sequence Activities 6.4 Estimate Activity Durations 6.5 Develop Schedule 7.2 Estimate Costs 7.3 Determine Budget 9.2 Estimate Activity Resources	Planning
	6.1 Determine Elicitation Approach (4.4) 7.1 Determine Analysis Approach (4.5) 8.1 Determine Traceability and Monitoring Approach (4.6) 9.2 Determine Solution Evaluation Approach (4.7)	5.1 Plan Scope Management 11.1 Plan Risk Management	Planning

[A] For the business analysis processes, the numbers in parentheses refer to the section numbers for the processes that appear in *The Standard for Business Analysis*; the other numbers refer to the sections in *The PMI Guide to Business Analysis*.

4.1 CONDUCT STAKEHOLDER ANALYSIS

Conduct Stakeholder Analysis is the process of researching and analyzing quantitative and qualitative information about the individuals, groups, or organizations that may impact, are impacted, or are perceived to be impacted by the area under assessment. The key benefit of this process is that it provides important insights about stakeholders that can be used when choosing elicitation and analysis techniques, selecting which stakeholders are appropriate to involve at different times in the business analysis efforts, and determining the best communication and collaboration methods to use. The inputs and outputs of this process are depicted in Figure 4-1.

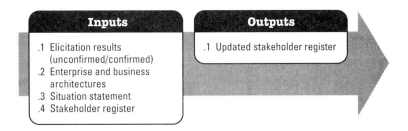

Figure 4-1. Conduct Stakeholder Analysis: Inputs and Outputs

4.2 DETERMINE STAKEHOLDER ENGAGEMENT AND COMMUNICATION APPROACH

Determine Stakeholder Engagement and Communication Approach is the process of developing appropriate methods to effectively engage and communicate with stakeholders throughout the product life cycle, based on an analysis of their needs, interests, and roles within the business analysis process. The key benefit of this process is that it provides a clear, actionable approach to engage stakeholders throughout business analysis and requirements-related activities, so that stakeholders receive the right information through the best communication methods and frequency to satisfy the needs of the initiative and meet stakeholder expectations. The inputs and outputs of this process are depicted in Figure 4-2.

Figure 4-2. Determine Stakeholder Engagement and Communication Approach: Inputs and Outputs

4.3 CONDUCT BUSINESS ANALYSIS PLANNING

Conduct Business Analysis Planning is the process performed to obtain shared agreement regarding the business analysis activities the team will be performing and the assignment of roles, responsibilities, and skill sets for the tasks required to successfully complete the business analysis work. The results of this process are assembled into a business analysis plan that may be formally documented and approved, or may be less formal depending on how the team operates. Whether the plan is formally documented or not, the results from all of the planning processes should be considered in the overall approach. Failing to make planning decisions can result in a less than optimal approach when performing the business analysis work. The key benefit of this process is that it sets expectations by encouraging discussion and agreement on how the business analysis work will be undertaken and avoids confusion regarding roles and responsibilities during execution. The inputs and outputs for this process are shown in Figure 4-3.

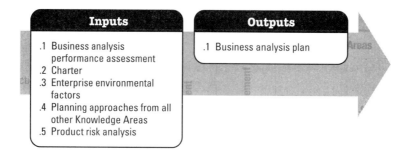

Figure 4-3. Conduct Business Analysis Planning: Inputs and Outputs

4.4 DETERMINE ELICITATION APPROACH

Determine Elicitation Approach is the process of thinking through how elicitation activities will be conducted, which stakeholders will be involved, which techniques may be used, and the order in which the elicitation activities are best performed. The key benefits of this process are efficient use of stakeholder time, effective stakeholder collaboration, and an organized approach to elicitation. The inputs and outputs of this process are depicted in Figure 4-4.

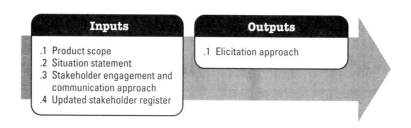

Figure 4-4. Determine Elicitation Approach: Inputs and Outputs

4.5 DETERMINE ANALYSIS APPROACH

Determine Analysis Approach is the process of thinking ahead about how analysis will be performed, including what will be analyzed; which models will be most beneficial to produce; and how requirements and other product information will be verified, validated, and prioritized. The key benefit of this process is that it supports a shared understanding of the business analysis work to be performed to develop the solution. The inputs and outputs of this process are depicted in Figure 4-5.

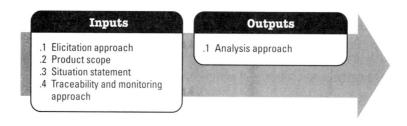

Figure 4-5. Determine Analysis Approach: Inputs and Outputs

4.6 DETERMINE TRACEABILITY AND MONITORING APPROACH

Determine Traceability and Monitoring Approach is the process of considering how traceability will be performed on the portfolio, program, project, or product, and defining how requirement changes will be managed. The key benefit of this process is that it appropriately sizes the level of traceability and formality of the requirements change management process for the situation. The inputs and outputs of this process are depicted in Figure 4-6.

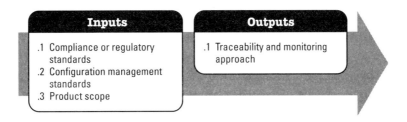

Figure 4-6. Determine Traceability and Monitoring Approach: Inputs and Outputs

4.7 DETERMINE SOLUTION EVALUATION APPROACH

Determine Solution Evaluation Approach is the process of determining which aspects of the organization and/or solution will be evaluated, how performance will be measured, when performance will be measured, and by whom. The key benefit of this process is that performance indicators and metrics are selected or defined so they can be collected, reported on, and evaluated to support the continual improvement of the organization and/or product. The inputs and outputs of this process are depicted in Figure 4-7.

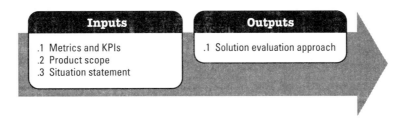

Figure 4-7. Determine Solution Evaluation Approach: Inputs and Outputs

5

EXECUTING

The Executing Process Group involves coordinating with stakeholders and using available product information to perform the appropriate business analysis activities. These processes are performed to identify, analyze, and evaluate the components of portfolios, programs, and projects. A significant amount of the work performed in this Process Group is to elicit, model, prioritize, define, verify, and approve all types of product information, ranging from backlogs to user stories and requirements to constraints. This work includes analyzing product risks, defining and evaluating acceptance criteria, and evaluating solution options.

During the product life cycle, program, or project execution, it may be necessary to revisit business problems, goals, and objectives; other portfolio components; and the business analysis plan. Additionally, analysis could trigger change requests to previously understood and approved information. Changes to any of these could reveal additional product information and could cause cascading changes to elicitation activities being performed, stakeholders being engaged, analyzed product information details and priorities, any existing approvals, acceptance criteria, and solution options. A large portion of the business analysis budget and effort will be expended in performing the Executing Process Group processes.

Table 5-1 depicts the relationship between the processes within the Business Analysis Executing Process Group and project management.

Table 5-1. Relationship Between the Business Analysis Executing Process Group and Project Management

Business Analysis Process Group	Business Analysis Process[A]	Project Management Process	Project Management Process Group
Executing	5.5 Prepare for Transition to Future State (5.1)	13.2 Plan Stakeholder Engagement	Planning
	6.2 Prepare for Elicitation (5.2) 6.3 Conduct Elicitation (5.3) 7.2 Create and Analyze Models (5.5) 7.3 Define and Elaborate Requirements (5.6) 7.5 Verify Requirements (5.8) 7.7 Prioritize Requirements and Other Product Information (5.10) 8.2 Establish Relationships and Dependencies (5.13)	5.2 Collect Requirements	Planning
	8.2 Establish Relationships and Dependencies (5.13)	6.3 Sequence Activities	Planning
	6.4 Confirm Elicitation Results (5.4) 7.5 Verify Requirements (5.8) 7.6 Validate Requirements (5.9)	5.5 Validate Scope	Monitoring and Controlling
	7.4 Define Acceptance Criteria (5.7)	8.1 Plan Quality Management	Planning
	7.7 Prioritize Requirements and Other Product Information (5.10) 7.9 Assess Product Design Options (5.12)	5.3 Define Scope	Planning
	7.8 Identify and Analyze Product Risks (5.11)	11.2 Identify Risks 11.3 Perform Qualitative Risk Analysis 11.4 Perform Quantitative Risk Analysis 11.5 Plan Risk Responses	Planning
	7.8 Identify and Analyze Product Risks (5.11)	11.6 Implement Risk Responses	Executing
	7.8 Identify and Analyze Product Risks (5.11)	11.7 Monitor Risks	Monitoring and Controlling
	8.3 Select and Approve Requirements (5.14)	5.3 Define Scope 6.5 Develop Schedule	Planning
	8.3 Select and Approve Requirements (5.14)	5.6 Control Scope	Monitoring and Controlling
	9.3 Evaluate Acceptance Results and Address Defects (5.15)	8.3 Control Quality	Monitoring and Controlling

[A] For the business analysis processes, the numbers in parentheses refer to the section numbers for the processes that appear in *The Standard for Business Analysis*; the other numbers refer to the sections in *The PMI Guide to Business Analysis*.

5.1 PREPARE FOR TRANSITION TO FUTURE STATE

Prepare for Transition to Future State is the process of determining whether the organization is ready for a transition and how the organization will move from the current to the future state to integrate the solution or partial solution into the organization's operations. The key benefits of this process are that the organization can successfully adopt the changes resulting from the implementation of the new solution or solution component, and that any product or program component or overall program benefit anticipated for the solution can be sustained after it is put into operation. The inputs and outputs of this process are depicted in Figure 5-1.

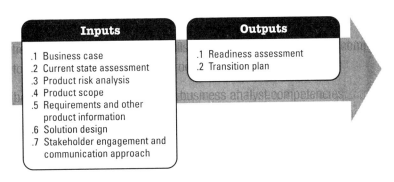

Inputs
.1 Business case
.2 Current state assessment
.3 Product risk analysis
.4 Product scope
.5 Requirements and other product information
.6 Solution design
.7 Stakeholder engagement and communication approach

Outputs
.1 Readiness assessment
.2 Transition plan

Figure 5-1. Prepare for Transition to Future State: Inputs and Outputs

5.2 PREPARE FOR ELICITATION

Prepare for Elicitation is the process of organizing and scheduling resources and preparing necessary materials for an individual elicitation activity. The key benefits of this process are that the elicitation activities are organized and effectively performed and participants understand up front why they are involved and what is required of them. The inputs and outputs of this process are depicted in Figure 5-2.

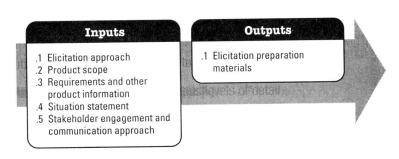

Inputs
.1 Elicitation approach
.2 Product scope
.3 Requirements and other product information
.4 Situation statement
.5 Stakeholder engagement and communication approach

Outputs
.1 Elicitation preparation materials

Figure 5-2. Prepare for Elicitation: Inputs and Outputs

5.3 CONDUCT ELICITATION

Conduct Elicitation is the process of applying various elicitation techniques to draw out information from stakeholders and other sources. The key benefit of this process is that it obtains information from the appropriate sources to sufficiently define and elaborate requirements and other product information. The inputs and outputs of this process are depicted in Figure 5-3.

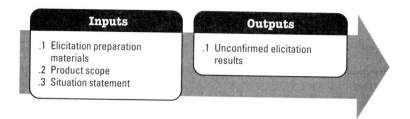

Figure 5-3. Conduct Elicitation: Inputs and Outputs

5.4 CONFIRM ELICITATION RESULTS

Confirm Elicitation Results is the process of performing follow-up activities on the elicitation results, determining an appropriate level of formality to use, reviewing with stakeholders for accuracy and completeness, and comparing to historical information. The key benefit of this process is that it validates that stakeholders and the elicitation results were understood during elicitation. The inputs and outputs for this process are shown in Figure 5-4.

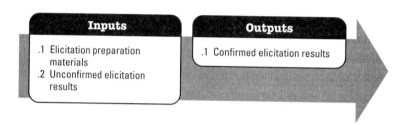

Figure 5-4. Confirm Elicitation Results: Inputs and Outputs

5.5 CREATE AND ANALYZE MODELS

Create and Analyze Models is the process of creating structured representations, such as diagrams, tables, or structured text, of any product information to facilitate further analysis by identifying gaps in information or uncovering extraneous information. The key benefit of this process is that it helps convey information in an organized manner that provides clarity and helps achieve correctness and completeness. The inputs and outputs for this process are shown in Figure 5-5.

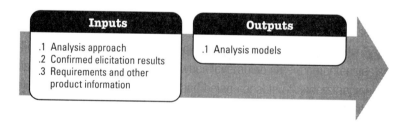

Figure 5-5. Create and Analyze Models: Inputs and Outputs

5.6 DEFINE AND ELABORATE REQUIREMENTS

Define and Elaborate Requirements is the process of refining and documenting requirements and other types of product information at the appropriate level of detail, format, and level of formality required for various audiences. The key benefits of this process are that it (a) helps clarify details about the product information so the team can work from it effectively, and (b) stores the product information in a manner that can be accessed and processed by all stakeholders. The inputs and outputs for this process are shown in Figure 5-6.

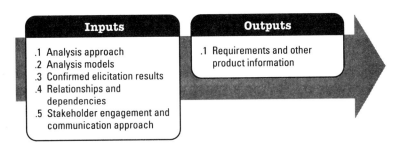

Inputs

.1 Analysis approach
.2 Analysis models
.3 Confirmed elicitation results
.4 Relationships and dependencies
.5 Stakeholder engagement and communication approach

Outputs

.1 Requirements and other product information

Figure 5-6. Define and Elaborate Requirements: Inputs and Outputs

5.7 DEFINE ACCEPTANCE CRITERIA

Define Acceptance Criteria is the process of obtaining agreement as to what would constitute proof that one or more aspects of a solution have been developed successfully. The key benefit of this process is that it provides complementary insights that can help refine requirements while providing the basis of a shared understanding for what is to be delivered. The inputs and outputs for this process are shown in Figure 5-7.

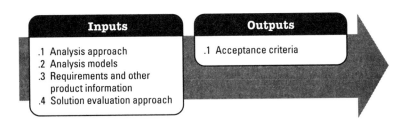

Inputs

.1 Analysis approach
.2 Analysis models
.3 Requirements and other product information
.4 Solution evaluation approach

Outputs

.1 Acceptance criteria

Figure 5-7. Define Acceptance Criteria: Inputs and Outputs

5.8 VERIFY REQUIREMENTS

Verify Requirements is the process of checking that requirements are of sufficient quality. The key benefit of this process is that it increases the likelihood that the requirements are stated and/or understood in a way that meets the defined standards for the organization, which in turn enables communication of the requirements to all interested parties and contributes to the quality of the final product. The inputs and outputs for this process are shown in Figure 5-8.

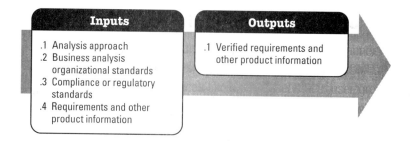

Figure 5-8. Verify Requirements: Inputs and Outputs

5.9 VALIDATE REQUIREMENTS

Validate Requirements is the process of checking that the requirements meet business goals and objectives. The key benefit of this process is that it minimizes the risks of missing stakeholder expectations or delivering the wrong solution. The inputs and outputs for this process are shown in Figure 5-9.

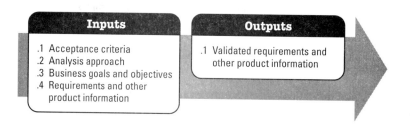

Figure 5-9. Validate Requirements: Inputs and Outputs

5.10 PRIORITIZE REQUIREMENTS AND OTHER PRODUCT INFORMATION

Prioritize Requirements and Other Product Information is the process of understanding how individual pieces of product information achieve stakeholder objectives, and using that information, along with other agreed-upon prioritization factors, to facilitate ranking of the work. The key benefits of this process are that it aligns all stakeholders with how the requirements achieve the goals and objectives and determines how to allocate the requirements to iterations or releases accordingly. The inputs and outputs for this process are shown in Figure 5-10.

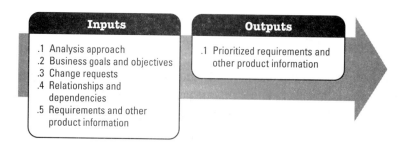

Figure 5-10. Prioritize Requirements and Other Product Information: Inputs and Outputs

5.11 IDENTIFY AND ANALYZE PRODUCT RISKS

Identify and Analyze Product Risks is the process of uncovering and examining assumptions and uncertainties that could positively or negatively affect success in the definition, development, and the expected results of the solution. The key benefits of this process are that it supports proactive management of uncertainties in business analysis activities and it uncovers and proactively addresses areas of potential strengths and weaknesses in the product. The inputs and outputs for this process are shown in Figure 5-11.

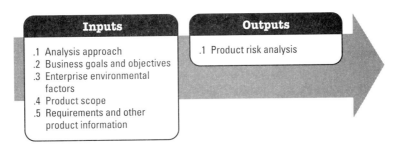

Inputs
.1 Analysis approach
.2 Business goals and objectives
.3 Enterprise environmental factors
.4 Product scope
.5 Requirements and other product information

Outputs
.1 Product risk analysis

Figure 5-11. Identify and Analyze Product Risks: Inputs and Outputs

5.12 ASSESS PRODUCT DESIGN OPTIONS

Assess Product Design Options is the process of identifying, analyzing, and comparing solution design options based on the business goals and objectives, expected costs of implementation, feasibility, and associated risks, and using the results of this assessment to provide recommendations regarding the design options presented. The key benefit of this process is that it allows for informed recommendations of design options. The inputs and outputs for this process are shown in Figure 5-12.

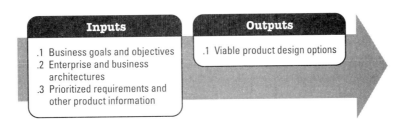

Inputs
.1 Business goals and objectives
.2 Enterprise and business architectures
.3 Prioritized requirements and other product information

Outputs
.1 Viable product design options

Figure 5-12. Assess Product Design Options: Inputs and Outputs

5.13 ESTABLISH RELATIONSHIPS AND DEPENDENCIES

Establish Relationships and Dependencies is the process of tracing or setting linkages between and among requirements and other product information. The key benefits of this process are that it helps in checking that each requirement adds business value and meets the customer's expectations, and it supports monitoring and controlling of product scope. The inputs and outputs of this process are depicted in Figure 5-13.

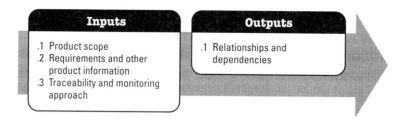

Figure 5-13. Establish Relationships and Dependencies: Inputs and Outputs

5.14 SELECT AND APPROVE REQUIREMENTS

Select and Approve Requirements is the process of facilitating discussions with stakeholders to negotiate and confirm which requirements should be incorporated within an iteration, release, or project. The key benefit of this process is that it provides authorization to consider how and when to build all or part of a solution to develop or modify a product. The inputs and outputs for this process are shown in Figure 5-14.

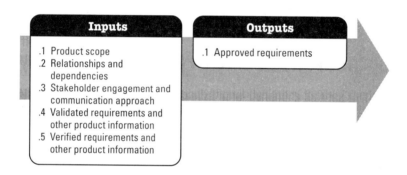

Figure 5-14. Select and Approve Requirements: Inputs and Outputs

5.15 EVALUATE ACCEPTANCE RESULTS AND ADDRESS DEFECTS

Evaluate Acceptance Results and Address Defects is the process of deciding what to do with the results from a comparison of the defined acceptance criteria against the solution. The key benefit of this process is that it allows for informed decision making about whether to release all or part of a solution and whether to undertake changes, fixes, or enhancements to the product. The inputs and outputs for this process are shown in Figure 5-15.

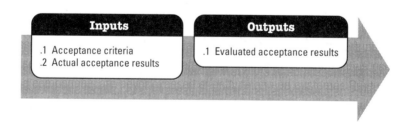

Figure 5-15. Evaluate Acceptance Results and Address Defects: Inputs and Outputs

6

MONITORING AND CONTROLLING

The Monitoring and Controlling Process Group consists of those processes performed on a continuing basis to:

◆ Promote ongoing and appropriate levels of communication and engagement with stakeholders;

◆ Assess the impact of proposed product changes within portfolios, programs, and projects; and

◆ Improve business analysis performance by assessing how well business analysis activities are being performed.

From a business analysis perspective, Monitoring and Controlling focuses on tracking and reviewing the product and business analysis work used to define the solution. It is complementary to Monitoring and Controlling from a project management perspective, which focuses on tracking, reviewing, and regulation of the project.

A significant amount of the work performed in the Monitoring and Controlling Process Group involves using outputs from the Executing Process Group to assess changes to requirements, other product information, and the business analysis plan itself. The Monitoring and Controlling Process Group includes evaluating whether there are any cascading impacts to requirements and other product information, and involves determining whether proposed changes are aligned with the achievement of the business goals and objectives. These proposed changes may trigger additional elicitation, analysis, and evaluation activities. While the team is performing processes from other Process Groups, these processes are key to enabling resources to work well with one another, confirming that all stakeholders are involved at the necessary level and verifying that communications among all participants are working properly. These processes are performed to check that the methods used in other Business Analysis Process Groups are working well individually as well as together, when applicable. When problems are found in or between processes, this process supports making changes to them, so that their interactions are more effective and efficient. Continuous business analysis performance improvement is essential for improving project and organizational outcomes.

Table 6-1 depicts the relationship between the processes within the Business Analysis Monitoring and Controlling Process Group and project management.

Table 6-1. Relationship Between the Business Analysis Monitoring and Controlling Process Group and Project Management

Business Analysis Process Group	Business Analysis Process[A]	Project Management Process	Project Management Process Group
Monitoring and Controlling	5.6 Manage Stakeholder Engagement and Communication (6.1)	10.2 Manage Communications 13.3 Manage Stakeholder Engagement	Executing
	5.6 Manage Stakeholder Engagement and Communication (6.1)	10.3 Monitor Communications 13.4 Monitor Stakeholder Engagement	Monitoring and Controlling
	5.7 Assess Business Analysis Performance (6.2)	8.3 Control Quality	Monitoring and Controlling
	8.4 Manage Changes to Requirements and Other Product Information (6.3)	4.6 Perform Integrated Change Control 5.6 Control Scope	Monitoring and Controlling

[A] For the business analysis processes, the numbers in parentheses refer to the section numbers for the processes that appear in *The Standard for Business Analysis*; the other numbers refer to the sections in *The PMI Guide to Business Analysis*.

6.1 MANAGE STAKEHOLDER ENGAGEMENT AND COMMUNICATION

Manage Stakeholder Engagement and Communication is the process of fostering appropriate involvement in business analysis processes, keeping stakeholders appropriately informed about ongoing business analysis efforts, and sharing product information with stakeholders as it evolves. The key benefits of this process are that it promotes continuous stakeholder participation in the business analysis process and in defining the solution, and maintains ongoing communication with stakeholders. The inputs and outputs of this process are depicted in Figure 6-1.

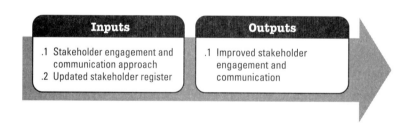

Inputs	Outputs
.1 Stakeholder engagement and communication approach .2 Updated stakeholder register	.1 Improved stakeholder engagement and communication

Figure 6-1. Manage Stakeholder Engagement and Communication: Inputs and Outputs

6.2 ASSESS BUSINESS ANALYSIS PERFORMANCE

Assess Business Analysis Performance is the process of considering the effectiveness of the business analysis practices in use across the organization, typically in the context of considering the ongoing deliverables and results of a portfolio component, program, or project. Practices that are working well at the project level can be elevated to best practices and standards for use by the organization across future projects. The key benefit of this process is that it provides the opportunity to adjust business analysis practices to meet the needs of a project, its team, and ultimately, the organization. The inputs and outputs for this process are shown in Figure 6-2.

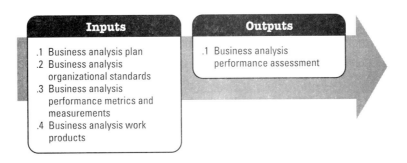

Figure 6-2. Assess Business Analysis Performance: Inputs and Outputs

6.3 MANAGE CHANGES TO REQUIREMENTS AND OTHER PRODUCT INFORMATION

Manage Changes to Requirements and Other Product Information is the process of examining changes or defects that arise during a project by understanding the value and impact of the changes. As changes are agreed upon, information about those changes is reflected wherever necessary to support prioritization and eventual product development. The key benefits of this process include facilitating the incorporation of important solution changes for projects, limiting unnecessary changes, and providing understanding of how changes will impact the end product. The inputs and outputs for this process are shown in Figure 6-3.

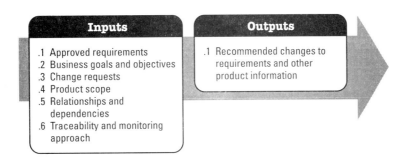

Figure 6-3. Manage Changes to Requirements and Other Product Information: Inputs and Outputs

7

RELEASING

The Releasing Process Group consists of one process that is performed at points within a project when a potentially releasable solution or a segment of that solution is delivered for feedback or review. This process is also performed when a released solution is evaluated for transition from ownership by the area that developed it to the area that will put it into operation. It is used to:

◆ Determine whether all or part of the solution should be released, and

◆ Obtain agreement that all or part of a solution is now ready to be transitioned to an operational team under the ownership of the business area that will have ongoing responsibility for it.

The Releasing Process Group provides information to support decision making about the solution and sometimes includes the work to facilitate the decision-making process. This is complementary to the Closing Process Group from a project management perspective, which verifies that the work to build the solution or a segment of the solution has been completed and contractual obligations have been met, and includes participating in the actual releasing decision itself. A significant amount of the business analysis work performed in the Releasing Process Group involves researching and assembling evidence that indicates whether or not the solution is ready to be released to production or handed over from the area that developed it to the area that will put it into operation. Evidence may include evaluating actual product performance or evaluating test results and feedback from product users or testers.

Table 7-1 depicts the relationship between the process within the Business Analysis Releasing Process Group and project management.

Table 7-1. Relationship Between the Business Analysis Releasing Process Group and Project Management

Business Analysis Process Group	Business Analysis Process[A]	Project Management Process	Project Management Process Group
Releasing	9.4 Obtain Solution Acceptance for Release (7.1)	4.7 Close Project or Phase	Closing

[A] For the business analysis processes, the numbers in parentheses refer to the section numbers for the processes that appear in *The Standard for Business Analysis*; the other numbers refer to the sections in *The PMI Guide to Business Analysis*.

7.1 OBTAIN SOLUTION ACCEPTANCE FOR RELEASE

Obtain Solution Acceptance for Release is the process of facilitating a decision on whether to release a partial or full solution into production and eventually to an operational team, as well as transitioning knowledge and existing information about the product, its risks, known issues, and any workarounds that may have arisen in response to those issues. The key benefit of this process is the creation of an agreed-upon break between building a solution and releasing a solution for acceptance by the stakeholders. The inputs and outputs for this process are shown in Figure 7-1.

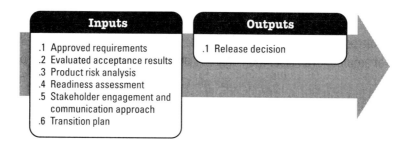

Inputs	Outputs
.1 Approved requirements .2 Evaluated acceptance results .3 Product risk analysis .4 Readiness assessment .5 Stakeholder engagement and communication approach .6 Transition plan	.1 Release decision

Figure 7-1. Obtain Solution Acceptance for Release: Inputs and Outputs

REFERENCES

[1]   Project Management Institute. 2015. *Business Analysis for Practitioners: A Practice Guide.* Newtown Square, PA: Author.

[2]   Project Management Institute. 2017. *The PMI Guide to Business Analysis.* Newtown Square, PA: Author.

[3]   Project Management Institute. 2017. *PMI's Pulse of the Profession®: Success Rates Rise—Transforming the High Cost of Low Performance.* Newtown Square, PA: Author.

[4]   Project Management Institute. 2017. *A Guide to the Project Management Body of Knowledge (PMBOK® Guide) – Sixth Edition.* Newtown Square, PA: Author.

Part 3

Appendixes, Glossary, and Index

APPENDIX X1
CONTRIBUTORS AND REVIEWERS OF
THE PMI GUIDE TO BUSINESS ANALYSIS

This appendix lists, within groupings, those individuals who have contributed to the development and production of *The PMI Guide to Business Analysis.*

The Project Management Institute is grateful to all of these individuals for their support and acknowledges their contributions to the project management profession.

X1.1 *THE PMI GUIDE TO BUSINESS ANALYSIS* CORE COMMITTEE

The following individuals served as members, were contributors of text or concepts, and served as leaders within the Project Core Committee:

Laura Paton, PMP, PMI-PBA, Chair
Joy Beatty, PMI-PBA, CBAP
David P. Bieg, PMI-PBA
Susan M. Burk
Cheryl G. Lee, PMP, PMI-PBA
Kristin L. Vitello, Standards Project Specialist

X1.2 REVIEWERS:

X1.2.1 SME REVIEW

In addition to the members of the Committee, the following individuals provided their review and recommendations on drafts of the standard:

Steve Blais, PMP, PMI-PBA

Greta Blash, PMP, PMI-PBA

Steve Blash

Shika Carter, PgMP, PMP

Sergio Luis Conte, PhD, PMI-PBA

Victoria Cupet, CBAP, PMI-PBA

Marcos Antonio Da Silva, PMP, PMI-PBA

Kaisheng Duan, PgMP, PMI-PBA

Christopher Edwards

Flavia Guarnieri, PMP, PMI-PBA

Dave Hatter, PMP, PMI-PBA

Maciej P. Kaniewski, PMP, PMI-PBA

Gladys S.W. Lam

Elizabeth Larson, PMP, PMI-PBA

Richard Larson, PMP, PMI-PBA

Peter Lefterov

Kent J. McDonald

Elizabeth Moore, PMP, CBAP

Amy E. Paolo, CBAP

Sheryl Pass, PMP, PMI-PBA

Ronald G. Ross

Thomas Slahetka, MBA, CBAP

Cynthia Sneed, MBA, PMI-PBA

Joyce Statz, PhD, PMP, ECBA

Angela Wick, PMP, PMI-PBA

Laura C. Wright, PMP, CBAP

Rolf Dieter Zschau, PMP, PMI-PBA

X1.2.2 FINAL EXPOSURE DRAFT REVIEW (STANDARD PORTION)

In addition to the members of the Committee, the following individuals provided recommendations for improving the Exposure Draft of *The PMI Guide to Business Analysis* (standard portion):

Habeeb Abdulla, PMP, PMI-RMP

Bill Allbee, PMP

Lavanya Arul, PMP, PMI-PBA

Nadeem Azmi

Nabeel Eltyeb Babiker, PMP, P3O

Mary Baker

Ganesan Balaji, PgMP, PMP

Deborah Bellew, PMP, PMI-PBA

Greta Blash, PMI-PBA, PMI-ACP

Farid F. Bouges, PhD, PfMP, PMP

Sonja G. Brown, PMP

Armando Camino, MBA, PMP

Donna M. Capella

Balasubramanian Chandrasekaran, PMP, Prosci Certified

Satish Chhiba

Anthony Clarke, CBAP, PMI-PBA

Corinn M. Claydon

Jennifer B. Colucci, PMP

Adriana Conte, PMP, PMI-PBA

David Cousins

Tim Coventry, BEd, CBAP

Josh Cruz

Graziella DAmico

Farshid Damirchilo, MSc, PMP

Doripp Dgpgri

Vahid Dokhtzeynal, PMP, PMI-RMP

Josee Dufour, PMP

Francine J. Duncan, PMP, SIEEE

Arnold N. Eddula, PfMP, PMI-PBA

Havillah Preethi Eddula, MS, PMI-PBA

Wael K. Elmetwaly, PMP, PMI-ACP

Patrice M. Fanning, PMI-PBA

Asher Fawad, PMP

Diane E. Foster, PMP

Tammy Fowler, PMI-PBA, CBAP

Nestor C. Gabarda Jr., ECE, PMP

Hisham Sami Ghulam, PMP PMI-PBA

Theofanis Giotis, PhDc, PMP

Kalyani Govindan, PMP

Jorge Lamadrid Guerrero, PMP, PMI-PBA

Gunawan, PMP, PMI-RMP

Hironori Hayashi, PMP, PMI-PBA

Bruce A. Hayes, PMP, PMI-ACP

Gheorghe Hriscu, PMP, CGEIT

Seyed Ibrahim, MBA, PMP

Lemya Musa M. Idris, PMP, PMI-PBA

Shuichi Ikeda

Nikolaos Ioannou, CPRE-FL&AP, PRINCE2

Ana C. Johnson, MBA, PMP

Hariprasad Kulakkottu Variyam, PMP

Taeyoung Kim, PMP

Shaun D. Kimpton, CBAP

Henry Kondo, PfMP, PMP

Rouzbeh Kotobzadeh, PMP, PMI-PBA

Rakesh Kumar, MBA, PMP

Thomas M. Kurihara

Trent D. Leopold, MS, PMI-PBA

Michael J. Licholat, PMP

Winnie Liem, PMP, ITIL

Ediwanto Liga, PMP

Tong Liu, PhD, PMP

Casey Loo, PMP, PMI-PBA

Hugo K. M. Lourenço, PMP, PMI-PBA

Mordaka Maciej, PMP, PMI-ACP

Marwan M. Malibari, MBA, KPI-P

Sanjay Mandhan, MBA, PMP

Gaitan Marius Titi, Eng, PMP

Puian Masudi Far, PhDc, PMP

Mohammad Mohammad

Venkatramvasi Mohanvasi, PMP

Arash Momeni, MBA, PMP

Syed Ahsan Mustaqeem, PE, PMP

Marlys Norby, PMP, NCMA FELLOW

Habeeb Omar, PfMP, PgMP

Mozhgan Pakdaman, PMP, PMI-RMP

Panagiotis Papaporfyriou, PMP, PMI-ACP

Crispin ("Kik") Piney, BSc, PfMP

Jelena Radovanovic, MscEE, PMP

Chandrasekar Ramakrishnan

Sandy B. Ritchey

Rafael Fernando Ronces Rosas, PMP, ITIL

Robert M. Roque, PMP

John A. Rush IV, MBA, PMP

Mohammad Sabbouh, PMP, PMI-PBA

Madhavi Sanakkayala, MS, PMI-PBA

O. Patanjali Sastry

Kyra Smith, PgMP

Terrell J. Smith, PMP, PMI-PBA

María Specht, MSc, PMP

Joyce Statz, PhD, PMP

Ernesto Stefani

Betsy Stockdale, PMI-PBA

Suresh Supramaniam, PMP, CMBB

Shoji Tajima, PMP, ITC

Tetsuya Tani, PMP

Suresh Thiagarajan

Sal J. Thompson, MBA, PMP

Micol Trezza, MBA, PMP

Carmen Valle, MBA, PMP

Vijaya Nath Veepuri, PMP

Dave Violette, MPM, PMP

Michael Mitra Wagan, PMP

Lars Wendestam, MSc, PMP

Simon Wild

Loni L. Wong, MBA, PMP

Tao Xu

Amir Yazdani

Rafael Beteli Silva Zanon, PMP, PMI-PBA

Cristina Zerpa, MC, PMP

Rolf Dieter Zschau, PMP, PMI-PBA

X1.2.3 FINAL EXPOSURE DRAFT REVIEW (GUIDE PORTION)

In addition to the members of the Committee, the following individuals provided recommendations for improving the Exposure Draft of the *The PMI Guide to Business Analysis* (guide portion):

Habeeb Abdulla, PMP, RMP
Adekunle P. Adeniyi, PMP, PMI-PBA
Bill Allbee, PMP
Guillermo J. Anton, MSc, PMP
Sridhar Arjula
Jeremy Aschenbrenner
Deborah Bellew, PMP, PMI-PBA
Farid F. Bouges, PhD, PfMP, PMP
Armando Camino, MBA, PMP
Balasubramanian Chandrasekaran, PMP, Prosci Certified
Satish Chhiba
Sergio Luis Conte, PhD
Tim Coventry, BEd, CBAP
Graziella DAmico
Farshid Damirchilo, MSc, PMP
Lorenzo De Lorenzo, PMI-PBA
Ivana Dilparic
Vahid Dokhtzeynal, PMP, PMI-RMP
Francine J. Duncan, PMP, SIEEE
Arnold N. Eddula, PfMP, PMI-PBA
Havillah Preethi Eddula, MS, PMI-PBA
Hazem Elbadry, PMP, C-KPI
Kishore Erukulapati
Patrice M. Fanning, PMI-PBA
Nestor C. Gabarda Jr., ECE, PMP

Theofanis Giotis, PhDc, PMP
Hironori Hayashi, PMP, PMI-PBA
Katy M. Hennings, PMP
Gheorghe Hriscu, PMP, CGEIT
Lemya Musa M. Idris, PMP, PMI-PBA
Shuichi Ikeda
Rouzbeh Kotobzadeh, PMP, PMI-PBA
Thomas M. Kurihara
Jorge Lamadrid Guerrero, PMP, PMI-PBA
Trent D. Leopold, MS, PMI-PBA
Tong Liu, PhD, PMP
Casey Loo, PMP, PMI-PBA
Abhijit A. Maity, PMP, PMI-PBA
Francis V Manning, MBA, PMP
Gaitan Marius Titi, Eng, PMP
Venkatramvasi Mohanvasi, PMP
Arash Momeni, MBA, PMP
Daud Nasir, PMP, LSSBB
Mufaro Mary Nyachoto, PMI-PBA, CAPM
Habeeb Omar, PfMP, PgMP
Stefano Orfei, PMP, PMI-PBA
Mozhgan Pakdaman, PMP, PMI-RMP

Panagiotis Papaporfyriou, PMP, PMI-ACP
Crispin ("Kik") Piney, BSc, PfMP
Sriramasundararajan Rajagopalan, PhD, PMP
Chandrasekar Ramakrishnan
Rafael Fernando Ronces Rosas, PMP, ITIL
Madhavi Sanakkayala, MS, PMI-PBA
Saad Sheikh, PMI-RMP, PMI-ACP
Chihiro Shimiz, CBAP
Joyce Statz, PhD, PMP
Tetsuya Tani, PMP
Gerhard J. Tekes, PMP, PMI-RMP
Sunil Telkar, PMP, PGXPM
Suresh Thiagarajan
Laurent Thomas, PMP, PMI-ACP
Sal J. Thompson, MBA, PMP
Micol Trezza, MBA, PMP
Carmen Valle, MBA, PMP
Vijaya Nath Veepuri, PMP
Jean-Jacques Verhaeghe, MBA-LS, PMP
Dave Violette, MPM, PMP
Rolf Dieter Zschau, PMP, PMI-PBA

X1.3 PMI STANDARDS PROGRAM MEMBER ADVISORY GROUP (MAG)

The following individuals served as members of the PMI Standards Program Member Advisory Group during development of the *The PMI Guide to Business Analysis*:

Maria Cristina Barbero, PMP, PMI-ACP
Brian Grafsgaard, PMP, PgMP
Hagit Landman, PMP, PMI-SP
Yvan Petit, PhD, PMP
Chris Stevens, PhD
Dave Violette, MPM, PMP
John Zlockie, MBA, PMP, PMI Standards Manager

X1.4 CONSENSUS BODY REVIEW

The following individuals served as members of the PMI Standards Program Consensus Body:

Nigel Blampied, PE, PMP
Chris Cartwright, MPM
John L. Dettbarn, Jr., DSc, PE
Charles T. Follin, PMP
Laurence Goldsmith, MBA, PMP
Dana J Goulston, PMP
Brian Grafsgaard, PMP, PgMP
Dorothy L. Kangas, PMP
Timothy A. MacFadyen, MBA, MPM

Harold "Mike" Mosley, Jr., PE, PMP
Nanette Patton, MSBA, PMP
Yvan Petit, PhD, PMP
Crispin ("Kik") Piney, BSc, PfMP
Michael Reed, PfMP, PMP
David W. Ross, PgMP, PMP
Paul E. Shaltry, PMP
Chris Stevens, PhD
Dave Violette, MPM, PMP

X1.5 PRODUCTION STAFF

Special mention is due to the following employees of PMI:

Donn Greenberg, Manager, Publications
Andrew Levin, PMP, Project Manager
Dylan Mcquire, Communication Specialist
Kim Shinners, Publications Production Associate
Roberta Storer, Product Editor
Barbara Walsh, Publications Production Supervisor

APPENDIX X2
TOOLS AND TECHNIQUES

There are 110 individual tools and techniques in *The PMI Guide to Business Analysis*. Some are mentioned once and some appear many times across multiple processes within the guide. Information in this guide, including which techniques to use, need to be tailored to the needs of the environment, organization, or situation. Not every tool or technique in this guide is necessarily required for every business analysis effort nor is the listing of tools and techniques in this guide exhaustive.

Where appropriate, tools and techniques have been grouped by their purpose. The group name describes the intent of what needs to be done and the tools and techniques in the group represent different methods to accomplish the intent. For example, prioritization schemes is a tools and techniques group with the intent on prioritizing portfolio components, programs, projects, requirements, features, or any other product information. Multivoting, timeboxing, and weighted ranking are among the techniques that can be used to prioritize.

To assist practitioners in identifying where specific tools and techniques are used, this appendix identifies each tool and technique, the group to which it belongs (if appropriate), and the process(es) where it is listed in *The PMI Guide to Business Analysis*. The process in which a tool or technique is described is in boldface type. For other processes where the tool or technique is listed, it references the process where it is fully described and may provide additional verbiage on how a tool or technique is used in that particular process. A reference to the section number where the tool or technique is described in *Business Analysis for Practitioners: A Practice Guide* is provided when applicable. The *Business Analysis for Practitioners: A Practice Guide* may be consulted for examples and additional information on how to use the tool or perform the technique.

X2.1 TOOLS AND TECHNIQUES GROUPS

The following tools and techniques groups are used throughout *The PMI Guide to Business Analysis*:

◆ **Change control tools.** Used to assist with change and/or configuration management.

◆ **Elicitation techniques.** Used to draw information from various sources.

◆ **Estimation techniques.** Used to provide a quantitative assessment of likely amounts or outcomes.

◆ **Group decision-making techniques.** Used in a group setting to bring participants to a final decision on an issue or topic under discussion.

- ◆ **Modeling elaboration.** Used to further identify gaps, inconsistencies, or redundancies in product information.

- ◆ **Peer reviews.** Used to examine business analysis work for logic, readability, and adherence to internal organizational standards for quality characteristics, format, and syntax.

- ◆ **Planning techniques.** Used to plan business analysis work.

- ◆ **Prioritization schemes.** Used to prioritize portfolio components, programs, projects, requirements, features, or any other product information.

- ◆ **Root cause and opportunity analysis.** Root cause analysis is used to determine the basic underlying reason that causes a variance, defect, or risk. Opportunity analysis is used to study the major facets of a potential opportunity to determine the possible changes in products offered to enable its achievement.

- ◆ **Valuation techniques.** Used to quantify the return or value that an option will provide.

- ◆ **Stakeholder maps.** Used for analyzing how stakeholders relate to one another and the solution under analysis.

There are 59 ungrouped tools and techniques. Table X2-1 contains a list of the tools and techniques, identifies them by Knowledge Area, and provides the referenced sections in *The PMI Guide to Business Analysis* and *Business Analysis for Practitioners: A Practice Guide*.

Table X2-1. Categorization and Index of Tools and Techniques

Tool or Technique	Section in *Business Analysis for Practitioners: A Practice Guide*	Section in *The PMI Guide to Business Analysis*	Knowledge Areas					
			Needs Assessment	Stakeholder Engagement	Elicitation	Analysis	Traceability and Monitoring	Solution Evaluation
Change Control Tools								
Configuration management system (CMS)	5.8.2.1	8.4.2.2					**8.4**	
Version control system (VCS)	5.8.2.2	8.4.2.2					**8.4**	
Elicitation Techniques								
Brainstorming	3.3.1.1	5.1.2.1	4.2, 4.3, 4.4	**5.1**, 5.3, 5.5, 5.6, 5.7	6.1, 6.3	7.1, 7.8, 7.9		9.1, 9.2
Collaborative games	N/A	6.3.2.2	4.2, 4.3, 4.4	5.3, 5.5, 5.6, 5.7	**6.3**	7.7, 7.8	8.3	9.1, 9.2
Product box	N/A	6.3.2.2	4.2, 4.3, 4.4	5.3, 5.5, 5.6, 5.7	6.3	7.7, 7.8	8.3	9.1, 9.2
Speedboat	N/A	6.3.2.2	4.2, 4.3, 4.4	5.3, 5.5, 5.6, 5.7	6.3	7.7, 7.8	8.3	9.1, 9.2
Spider web	N/A	6.3.2.2	4.2, 4.3, 4.4	5.3, 5.5, 5.6, 5.7	6.3	7.7, 7.8	8.3	9.1, 9.2
Document analysis	4.5.5.2	6.3.2.3	4.1, 4.2, 4.3, 4.4, 4.6, 4.7	5.3, 5.5, 5.6, 5.7	6.2, **6.3**, 6.4	7.1, 7.8		9.1, 9.2
Facilitated workshops	4.5.5.3	6.3.2.4	4.2, 4.3, 4.4, 4.5, 4.6, 4.7	5.3, 5.5, 5.6, 5.7	**6.3**	7.8	8.3	9.1, 9.2, 9.4
Focus groups	4.5.5.4	6.3.2.5	4.2, 4.3, 4.4	5.3, 5.5, 5.6, 5.7	**6.3**	7.8, 7.9		9.1, 9.2
Interviews	4.5.5.5	6.3.2.6	4.1, 4.2, 4.3, 4.4, 4.7	5.1, 5.3, 5.5, 5.6, 5.7	6.1, 6.2, **6.3**, 6.4	7.8		9.1, 9.2
Observation	4.5.5.6	6.3.2.7	4.2, 4.3, 4.4	5.3, 5.5, 5.6, 5.7	**6.3**, 6.4	7.8		9.1, 9.2

Tool or Technique	Section in *Business Analysis for Practitioners: A Practice Guide*	Section in *The PMI Guide to Business Analysis*	Knowledge Areas					
			Needs Assessment	Stakeholder Engagement	Elicitation	Analysis	Traceability and Monitoring	Solution Evaluation
Elicitation Techniques *(Continued)*								
Prototyping	4.5.5.7	6.3.2.8	4.2, 4.3, 4.4	5.3, 5.5, 5.6, 5.7	**6.3**	7.2, 7.8		9.1, 9.2
Evolutionary prototyping	4.5.5.7	6.3.2.8	4.2, 4.3, 4.4	5.3, 5.5, 5.6, 5.7	**6.3**	7.2, 7.8		9.1, 9.2
Storyboarding	4.5.5.7	6.3.2.8	4.2, 4.3, 4.4	5.3, 5.5, 5.6, 5.7	**6.3**	7.2, 7.8		9.1, 9.2
Wireframes	4.5.5.7	6.3.2.8	4.2, 4.3, 4.4	5.3, 5.5, 5.6, 5.7	**6.3**	7.2, 7.8		9.1, 9.2
Questionnaires and surveys	4.5.5.8	6.3.2.9	4.2, 4.3, 4.4	5.1, 5.3, 5.5, 5.6, 5.7	**6.3**	7.8		9.1, 9.2
Estimation Techniques								
Affinity estimating	N/A	5.4.2.3		**5.4**		7.8		
Bottom-up estimating	N/A	5.4.2.3		**5.4**		7.8		
Delphi	4.15.1	5.4.2.3	4.4	5.4, 5.5		7.6, 7.7, 7.8	**8.3**, 8.4	9.1, 9.2, 9.3, 9.4
Estimation poker	N/A	5.4.2.3		**5.4**		7.8		
Relative estimation	N/A	5.4.2.3		**5.4**		7.8		
Wide-Band Delphi	N/A	5.4.2.3		**5.4**		7.8		
Group Decision-Making Techniques								
Delphi	4.15.1	8.3.2.4	4.4	5.4, 5.5		7.6, 7.7, 7.8	**8.3**, 8.4	9.1, 9.2, 9.3, 9.4
Force field analysis	N/A	8.3.2.6	4.4	5.5			**8.3**, 8.4	9.2, 9.4

Tool or Technique	Section in *Business Analysis for Practitioners: A Practice Guide*	Section in *The PMI Guide to Business Analysis*	Knowledge Areas					
			Needs Assessment	Stakeholder Engagement	Elicitation	Analysis	Traceability and Monitoring	Solution Evaluation
Modeling Elaboration								
CRUD matrix	N/A	7.2.2.10				**7.2**		
Traceability matrix	5.2.3	7.2.2.10, 8.2.2.5				7.2, 7.6, 7.7	**8.2**, 8.4	9.3
Interaction matrix	N/A	7.2.2.10				**7.2**, 7.6, 7.7	8.2, 8.4	9.3
Peer Reviews								
Inspection	4.13.2	7.5.2.2				**7.5**		
Peer desk check	4.13.1	7.5.2.2				**7.5**		
Walkthroughs	4.12.2	7.5.2.2, 7.6.2.4			6.4	7.5, **7.6**		
Planning Techniques								
Product backlog	4.11.10	7.3.2.4, 7.7.2.1		5.4		**7.3**, 7.8, 7.9		
Rolling wave planning	3.4	5.4.2.4		**5.4**				
Story mapping	N/A	7.2.2.16	4.5, 4.6	5.4		**7.2**, 7.7	8.2, 8.3	
Work breakdown structure (WBS)	N/A	5.4.2.4		**5.4**				
Prioritization Schemes								
Buy a feature	N/A	7.7.2.5		5.5		**7.7**	8.3	9.1, 9.2, 9.3
Delphi	4.15.1	7.7.2.5, 8.3.2.4	4.4	5.4, 5.5		7.6, 7.7, 7.8	**8.3**, 8.4	9.1, 9.2, 9.3, 9.4
Minimum viable product (MVP)	N/A	7.7.2.5		5.5		**7.7**	8.3	9.1, 9.2, 9.3

Table X2-1. *(Continued)*

Tool or Technique	Section in *Business Analysis for Practitioners: A Practice Guide*	Section in *The PMI Guide to Business Analysis*	Needs Assessment	Stakeholder Engagement	Elicitation	Analysis	Traceability and Monitoring	Solution Evaluation
Prioritization Schemes *(Continued)*								
MoSCoW	4.11.6.1	7.7.2.5		5.5		**7.7**	8.3	9.1, 9.2, 9.3
Multivoting	4.11.6.1	7.7.2.5		5.5		**7.7**	8.3	9.1, 9.2, 9.3
Purpose alignment model	N/A	4.3.2.9, 7.7.2.5	**4.3**	5.5		7.7	8.3	9.1, 9.2, 9.3
Timeboxing	4.11.6.1	7.7.2.5		5.5		**7.7**	8.3	9.1, 9.2, 9.3
Weighted Ranking	2.5.5.1, 4.11.6.1	4.4.2.8, 7.7.2.5	**4.4**	5.5		7.7	8.3	9.1, 9.2, 9.3
Weighted shortest job first (WSJF)	N/A	7.7.2.5		5.5		**7.7**	8.3	9.1, 9.2, 9.3
Root Cause and Opportunity Analysis								
Fishbone/Ishikawa diagram	2.4.4.2	4.2.2.9	**4.2**	5.7		7.8		9.1, 9.3
Five-Whys	2.4.4.1	4.2.2.9	**4.2**	5.7		7.8		9.1, 9.3
Interrelationship diagrams	2.4.4.2	4.2.2.9	**4.2**	5.7		7.8		9.1, 9.3
Valuation Techniques								
Internal rate of return (IRR)	2.5.6.3	4.4.2.7	**4.4**					
Net present value (NPV)	2.5.6.4	4.4.2.7	**4.4**					
Payback period (PBP)	2.5.6.1	4.4.2.7	**4.4**					
Return on investment (ROI)	2.5.6.2	4.4.2.7	**4.4**					

Tool or Technique	Section in *Business Analysis for Practitioners: A Practice Guide*	Section in *The PMI Guide to Business Analysis*	Knowledge Areas					
			Needs Assessment	Stakeholder Engagement	Elicitation	Analysis	Traceability and Monitoring	Solution Evaluation
Stakeholder Maps								
Onion diagram	N/A	5.2.2.4		**5.2**, 5.3				
Stakeholder matrix	N/A	5.2.2.4		**5.2**, 5.3				
Ungrouped Tools and Techniques								
Affinity diagram	2.4.5.2	4.3.2.1	**4.3**			7.9		
Backlog management	N/A	7.7.2.1, 7.3.2.4				**7.7**	8.3, 8.4	
Behavior-driven development (BDD)	N/A	7.4.2.1				**7.4**		
Benchmarking	2.4.5.3	4.1.2.1	**4.1**, 4.3, 4.4					
Burndown charts	N/A	5.4.2.1		**5.4**, 5.7		7.8		
Business architecture techniques	N/A	4.2.2.1	**4.2**					
Business capability analysis	N/A	4.2.2.2	**4.2**					
Business rules catalog	4.10.9.1	7.3.2.1				**7.3**		
Capability framework	2.4.6	4.2.2.3	**4.2**					
Capability table	2.4.5.1	4.2.2.4	**4.2**, 4.3					
Competitive analysis	2.4.5.3	4.1.2.2	**4.1**			7.9		
Context diagram	4.10.7.3	7.2.2.1				**7.2**, 7.8		
Cost-benefit analysis	2.5.6	4.4.2.2	**4.4**					9.1

Tool or Technique	Section in *Business Analysis for Practitioners: A Practice Guide*	Section in *The PMI Guide to Business Analysis*	Needs Assessment	Stakeholder Engagement	Elicitation	Analysis	Traceability and Monitoring	Solution Evaluation
Ungrouped Tools and Techniques *(Continued)*								
Data dictionary	4.10.10.3	7.2.2.2				**7.2**		
Data flow diagram	4.10.10.2	7.2.2.3				**7.2**		
Decision tree and decision table	4.10.9.2	7.2.2.4				**7.2**		
Decomposition model	3.5.2.2	5.4.2.2	**5.4**					
Definition of done (DoD)	N/A	7.4.2.2				**7.4**		
Definition of ready	N/A	7.3.2.2				**7.3**	8.3	
Display-action-response model	4.10.11.4	7.2.2.13				**7.2**		
Ecosystem map	4.10.7.2	7.2.2.5				**7.2**, 7.8		
Entity relationship diagram (ERD)	4.10.10.1	7.2.2.6				**7.2**		
Event list	N/A	7.2.2.7				**7.2**		
Feature injection	N/A	4.4.2.4	**4.4**					
Feature model	4.10.7.4	7.2.2.8	4.3			**7.2**	8.2	
Gap analysis	2.4.7	4.3.2.6	**4.3**					
Glossary	N/A	7.3.2.3	4.2, 4.6, 4.7		6.4	**7.3**		
Goal model and business objectives model	4.10.7.1	7.2.2.9				**7.2**, 7.6, 7.7		
Impact analysis	5.8.3	8.4.2.4					**8.4**	
INVEST	4.10.8.3	7.5.2.1				**7.5**		

Tool or Technique	Section in *Business Analysis for Practitioners: A Practice Guide*	Section in *The PMI Guide to Business Analysis*	Knowledge Areas					
			Needs Assessment	Stakeholder Engagement	Elicitation	Analysis	Traceability and Monitoring	Solution Evaluation
Ungrouped Tools and Techniques *(Continued)*								
Iteration planning	N/A	7.7.2.3				**7.7**	8.3	
Job analysis	3.3.3.1	5.2.2.1		**5.2**, 5.5				
Kanban board	N/A	7.7.2.4				**7.7**		
Kano analysis	N/A	4.3.2.7	**4.3**					
Market analysis	N/A	4.1.2.5	**4.1**					
Organizational chart	3.3.1.2	5.1.2.3		**5.1**		7.2, 7.8		
Pareto diagrams	N/A	4.2.2.7	**4.2**					
Persona analysis	3.3.3.2	5.2.2.2		**5.2**, 5.3				
Process flows	4.10.8.1	7.2.2.12	4.2, 4.3	5.1, 5.5, 5.7		**7.2**, 7.8		
Product portfolio matrix	N/A	9.1.2.3						**9.1**
Product visioning	N/A	4.5.2.3	**4.5**, 4.6					
RACI model	2.3.1	5.2.2.3		**5.2**, 5.3				
Real options	N/A	4.4.2.6	**4.4**			7.9		
Report table	4.10.11.1	7.2.2.14				**7.2**		
Requirements management tool	N/A	8.2.2.2				7.3	**8.2**, 8.3, 8.4	
Retrospectives and lessons learned	3.4.6.1, 3.4.6.2	5.7.2.4		5.3, **5.7**	6.1	7.1	8.1	9.2
Risk register	N/A	7.8.2.9				**7.8**		
Solution capability matrix	N/A	4.3.2.10	**4.3**					

Tool or Technique	Section in *Business Analysis for Practitioners: A Practice Guide*	Section in *The PMI Guide to Business Analysis*	Knowledge Areas					
			Needs Assessment	Stakeholder Engagement	Elicitation	Analysis	Traceability and Monitoring	Solution Evaluation
Ungrouped Tools and Techniques *(Continued)*								
State table and state diagram	4.10.10.4	7.2.2.15				**7.2**		
Story elaboration	N/A	7.4.2.3				7.3, **7.4**		
Story slicing	N/A	7.3.2.7				**7.3**	8.2	
SWOT analysis	2.4.2	4.2.2.10	**4.2**	5.5		7.8		
System interface tables	4.10.11.2	7.2.2.17				**7.2**		
Use case	4.10.8.2	7.3.2.8				**7.3**		
Use case diagram	4.10.7.5	7.2.2.18				**7.2**		
User interface flow	4.10.11.3	7.2.2.19				**7.2**		
User story	4.10.8.3	7.3.2.9		5.5		**7.3**		
Variance analysis	N/A	5.7.2.6		**5.7**				9.3
Vendor assessment	N/A	7.9.2.7				**7.9**		

APPENDIX X3
BUSINESS ANALYST COMPETENCIES

Business analysts who possess the knowledge, skills, and personal qualities that comprise the business analyst competencies are able to perform business analysis processes effectively.

This appendix describes six categories of important business analyst competencies:

◆ Analytical skills,

◆ Expert judgment,

◆ Communication skills,

◆ Personal skills,

◆ Leadership skills, and

◆ Tool knowledge.

Although the list of competencies provided is comprehensive, it is not intended to be complete. It does serve as a checklist for business analysts to gauge and measure their personal competencies in order to highlight areas where future professional development efforts may be targeted.

X3.1 ANALYTICAL SKILLS

Analytical skills are utilized by the business analyst to:

◆ Process information of various types and at various levels of detail,

◆ Break down the information,

◆ Look at information from different viewpoints,

◆ Draw conclusions,

◆ Distinguish the relevant from irrelevant,

◆ Formulate decisions, and

◆ Solve problems.

The analytical skills category is composed of the following:

◆ Creative thinking,

◆ Conceptual and detailed thinking,

◆ Decision making,

◆ Design thinking,

◆ Numeracy,

◆ Problem solving,

◆ Research skills,

◆ Resourcefulness, and

◆ Systems thinking.

X3.1.1 CREATIVE THINKING

Creative thinking is the ability to resolve a problem or set of problems by exploring multiple and different solutions to arrive at an improved result. Creative thinking takes into account known constraints and encourages the use of a divergent thinking approach when solving problems. It is important for business analysts to be able to apply creative thinking to their work so they can help stakeholders identify requirements and solutions that will successfully address business problems and respond effectively to changing conditions.

X3.1.2 CONCEPTUAL AND DETAILED THINKING

Conceptual and detailed thinking is the ability to move between high-level and detailed thinking, for example analyzing holistically and then analyzing a specific detail of the whole. Business analysts need to be able to think both conceptually and in detail so that they can communicate effectively across different stakeholder groups, break apart large problems into component parts, roll up details to find common themes, assess the viability of different solutions, and suggest adjustments as needed.

X3.1.3 DECISION MAKING

Decision making is the ability to weigh the benefits and drawbacks associated with a set of options, choose among various options, and articulate the rationale for the choice. Decision making can involve rational reasoning, intuitive reasoning, or both. Decision making can be improved when leveraging other competencies such as systems thinking which considers the holistic view of the organization and being capable of understanding the details in conjunction with the whole. Another critical component of decision making is being able to identify when it is appropriate to postpone making a decision, which could occur when there are too many assumptions or inadequate results to work from. Decision making is a critical skill for business analysts because they are responsible for making a variety of decisions when performing business analysis in addition to supporting stakeholder decision making.

X3.1.4 DESIGN THINKING

Design thinking is an approach that uses solution-based thinking as its focus rather than problem-based thinking. Teams determine an end goal to achieve, rather than a problem to solve, and produce creative solutions to achieve the goal. Design thinking is based on the following four principles:

◆ Encourage social design activities,

◆ Allow for ambiguity rather than constraints,

◆ Assume that most design is a redesign of a previous problem's solutions, and

◆ Ensure abstract ideas are made tangible.

Design thinking can be used as a method for transforming business processes as well as achieving outputs or solutions. Design thinking could entail using business analysis techniques such as visual modeling, five-whys, prototyping, persona analysis, or others.

X3.1.5 NUMERACY

Numeracy is sometimes called mathematical literacy. Being numerate means being able to reason with numbers and other mathematical concepts and to apply these in a range of contexts and to solve a variety of problems. Numeracy is necessary for a business analyst to effectively analyze data, work with organizational leaders on quantifying business needs and objectives, and be able to judge whether or not a mathematical argument holds up at any point in their work.

X3.1.6 PROBLEM SOLVING

Problem solving is the ability to analyze an issue or difficult situation by:

◆ Understanding the problem,

◆ Identifying potential solutions,

◆ Selecting and implementing a solution to address the problem, and

◆ Monitoring the outcome to ensure that the problem was addressed satisfactorily.

An important component of problem solving is identifying the nature of the problem and tailoring the solution appropriately. For example, interpersonal conflict on the product team creates problems that require resolutions that are very different from those required to resolve technical challenges or system issues. Problem solving is a critical skill for business analysts because they encounter problems throughout the product life cycle. Often, the success or failure of the portfolio, program, or project hinges on the analyst's ability to help resolve problems successfully.

X3.1.7 RESEARCH SKILLS

Research skills are the ability to elicit useful information in a timely and effective manner. There are many different ways to elicit information, such as in-person interviews with subject matter experts (SMEs), observation, document analysis, or using more conventional information sources like internet searches, user groups, and books. Effective research leads to information that is trustworthy, clear, and useful as an input for solving a problem or making a decision. A key component of an effective researcher is being willing and eager to learn more about a given subject. Because information is always required to analyze a situation effectively and devise a path forward, research skills are critical to a business analyst's overall success.

X3.1.8 RESOURCEFULNESS

Resourcefulness is using alternative or creative means to elicit information and solve problems, especially when a clear or conventional solution is not available. Resourcefulness includes leveraging available resources and identifying when a particular method of research might not be appropriate. A business analyst is resourceful when finding different ways to deal with a situation, such as looking for creative and alternative methods to secure time with stakeholders who have minimal availability. Learning from past experience, including lessons learned and retrospective sessions, is another key component of resourcefulness. Business analysts need to be resourceful because the information they require is often not readily available, requiring alternative methods for eliciting useful inputs to the decision-making and problem-solving processes.

X3.1.9 SYSTEMS THINKING

Systems thinking is the ability to analyze information from both a holistic and detailed viewpoint. Applying systems thinking at the organizational level requires skills to recognize and analyze the organization as a system made up of component parts in the form of people, processes, and tools. Recognizing the organization by the components and the relationships between them is necessary to ensure proposed organizational changes are analyzed to understand how a change to one component can impact related items.

X3.2 EXPERT JUDGMENT

Expert judgment relates to the skills and knowledge obtained from acquiring expertise in an application area, Knowledge Area, discipline, industry, etc., as appropriate for the activity being performed. It includes the skills to apply acquired knowledge and enterprise environmental factors and organizational process assets to perform work effectively. Expert judgment is composed of enterprise/organizational knowledge, business acumen, industry knowledge, life cycle knowledge, political and cultural awareness, product knowledge, and standards.

◆ Enterprise/organizational knowledge,

◆ Business acumen,

◆ Industry knowledge,

◆ Life cycle knowledge,

◆ Political and cultural awareness,

◆ Product knowledge, and

◆ Standards.

X3.2.1 ENTERPRISE/ORGANIZATIONAL KNOWLEDGE

Enterprise/organizational knowledge is having an understanding and familiarity with the way a specific business is organized and operates, both from a high-level perspective and from a tactical standpoint. This skill also includes the ability to understand how the unique characteristics of an enterprise might constrain or enable the success of a given solution and how to effectively negotiate across different organizational levels. This skill also encompasses a working knowledge of common business functions, including finance, marketing, operations, legal, etc. Because business analysis work frequently spans across different organizational functions and impacts multiple areas of an enterprise, enterprise/organizational knowledge is a crucial skill.

X3.2.2 BUSINESS ACUMEN

Business acumen is the skill of applying business and industry knowledge with decision-making capabilities to make sound decisions. Business acumen requires an understanding about how the organization operates within the competitive environment, what drives its profitability, and the relationship of its products to strategy. A person who demonstrates business acumen understands the bigger picture and is capable of using that knowledge to critically think through a situation.

X3.2.3 INDUSTRY KNOWLEDGE

Industry knowledge is expertise in and familiarity with the industry in which an organization is participating, and includes knowledge about an organization's competitors, industry trends and challenges, applicable business models, and so forth. Industry knowledge is beneficial because it helps the business analyst relate to and build credibility with stakeholders, identify outside economic forces that could provide context for the current situation, and inform decision making regarding organizational solutions designed to take advantage of market opportunities or minimize market threats.

X3.2.4 LIFE CYCLE KNOWLEDGE

Life cycle knowledge includes familiarity with the different frameworks that a given industry uses to identify phases of product development, from envisioning and planning through construction, iteration, and end-of-life. Life cycle knowledge also includes an in-depth understanding of the frameworks that the organization subscribes to, as well as the business analyst's role in each phase. It is crucial that business analysts know what is expected of them in each phase of the product or software development life cycle so that they can perform the responsibilities of their role effectively. Working knowledge of other frameworks is helpful as well, in order to identify areas of opportunity for organizational improvement.

X3.2.5 POLITICAL AND CULTURAL AWARENESS

Political awareness involves being conscious of organizational dynamics as they relate to organizational levels, hierarchy, and the way power is distributed throughout an organization. Cultural awareness involves being conscious of the organization's culture and values, as well as being sensitive to the cultural mores of colleagues, especially when operating within an organization that has multinational employees. Political awareness is important because politics can influence the success of an organization both positively and negatively: positively when organizational power can be leveraged to enable a solution, or negatively when a solution is found to be at odds with the interests of one or more powerful actors in the organization. It is important for the business analyst to understand the dynamics at play and be able to navigate them to have the best possible outcome for the product and the organization. Cultural awareness is critical because its presence creates trust and compassion among coworkers, while its absence creates misunderstanding and inhibits effective communication and engagement.

X3.2.6 PRODUCT KNOWLEDGE

Product knowledge is understanding the different offerings that an organization provides to its customers, their strengths and weaknesses compared to the organization's competitors, and the opportunities and threats that exist for those offerings. It also includes knowledge of the internal workings of an organization used to facilitate business operations, even if those components are never exposed directly to an end customer. Product knowledge is required to ensure that organizations focus on the problems that will provide the most value when addressed and pursue solutions that will increase the organization's ability to compete in the marketplace.

X3.2.7 STANDARDS

A business analyst should recognize and be aware of the various governance structures in place within and external to the organization, including project management governance, quality governance, and external regulatory or legal guidelines. These structures are taken into account as constraints when designing business solutions, and are incorporated into business analysis activities. Equally important are industry standards that help the organization evolve its practices and align with common practices in use within the external business analysis community.

X3.3 COMMUNICATION SKILLS

Communication skills are composed of a collection of skills utilized to provide, receive, or elicit information from various sources. Because of the number of relationships and interactions business analysts need to manage and the amount of information that has to be exchanged, these skills are some of the most critical ones for the business analyst to master. The communication skills category is composed of:

◆ Active listening,

◆ Communication tailoring,

◆ Facilitation,

◆ Nonverbal and verbal communication,

◆ Visual communication skills,

◆ Professional writing, and

◆ Relationship building.

X3.3.1 ACTIVE LISTENING

Active listening is being attentive and participatory when engaging with another individual. It includes comprehension-checking skills such as repeating what the speaker said in the listener's own words and nonverbal cues to show the speaker that the listener is paying attention. It also includes asking for clarification, expansion, or explanation when needed. Active listening is critical for business analysts when eliciting information from stakeholders and working with other members of the team because it aids comprehension and facilitates communication.

X3.3.2 COMMUNICATION TAILORING

Communication tailoring is selecting the appropriate method and style of communication to use in a given situation based on factors such as audience (role, internal versus external, individual versus group, etc.) and available communication methods (email, phone, instant message, teleconference, in-person meeting, etc.). Communication tailoring is important because business analysts consistently need to communicate across multiple levels of an organization and with both internal and external stakeholders. The business analyst makes decisions about the best communication methods to use based on project and stakeholder characteristics.

X3.3.3 FACILITATION

Facilitation is the collection of activities involved in directing and coordinating work among groups of people. Facilitation skills for a business analyst involves facilitating work within the business analysis approach such as facilitating decision making and organizational change as well as facilitating activities supporting elicitation including scheduling and planning meetings, inviting appropriate members, preparing agendas and meeting materials, maintaining control of a meeting, encouraging useful discussion and comprehensive engagement, and ensuring proper capture of information and tracking of issues and action items.

X3.3.5 NONVERBAL COMMUNICATION

Nonverbal communication refers to the ability to use unspoken communication methods to communicate. A commonly used unspoken communication method is body language. Business analysts are more effective in understanding the stakeholders they interact with when they develop their skills to recognize and understand body language. This skill is important in the context of facilitating effective elicitation sessions and interviewing stakeholders because nonverbal cues provide useful information about the mood and feelings of stakeholders and their thoughts toward the subject being discussed.

X3.3.6 VERBAL COMMUNICATION

Verbal communication refers to being an effective speaker in all professional contexts, from a one-on-one elicitation session to a presentation in front of executives. In all situations, business analysts should be able to communicate complex ideas concisely, clearly, and in a manner tailored to the audience. In cross-cultural contexts, verbal communication styles should take into account the language proficiency of the other party. Verbal communication is a key skill in any role, but is especially important for business analysts, who often need to communicate with diverse stakeholder groups to work through complex topics.

X3.3.7 VISUAL COMMUNICATION SKILLS

Visual communication involves the ability to communicate through the use of models and visual representations and involves knowing when best to use these representations over the spoken or written words. Business analysts are often faced with complex information that makes for a difficult exchange of ideas and understanding. Effective visual communication skills are demonstrated when a business analyst applies visual models to assist with the facilitation of complex logic or concepts.

X3.3.8 PROFESSIONAL WRITING

Professional writing refers to the ability to communicate complex ideas clearly and succinctly using written language. It includes proficiency both in the mechanics of writing (grammar, spelling, sentence structure, etc.) and in choosing the appropriate writing style (technical versus business writing, formal versus informal, etc.). Though clear writing is important when writing requirements, professional writing proficiency is also required for email, instant messaging, and other more informal modes of writing, such as status reporting. Informal written communication is increasingly being used to facilitate communication across organizations, making good writing skills even more important.

X3.3.9 RELATIONSHIP BUILDING

Relationship-building skills include interpersonal skills, empathy, and other social skills required to be an effective member of a team or a group. Being willing to make sacrifices for the good of the team, showing appreciation and gratitude, using appropriate humor to make people feel comfortable, letting other people speak in group settings without interrupting them, and finding constructive ways to offer criticism and feedback are just a few ways that business analysts can successfully build lasting professional relationships. Relationship building is crucial for business analysts because they are a key member of a product team and depend on others, just as others depend on them. Much of the work the business analyst completes is achieved through the input and support of others; therefore, business analysts need to be proactive in building relationships.

X3.4 PERSONAL SKILLS

Personal skills are the set of skills and quality attributes that identify the personal attributes of an individual. The skills and qualities listed are commonly used by stakeholders, project team members, and peers to critique a business analyst on a personal level. When a business analyst is viewed as being strong in any or all of these skills and attributes, the business analyst is able to build credibility. The personal skills category is composed of:

- ◆ Adaptability,
- ◆ Ethics,
- ◆ Learner,
- ◆ Multitasking,
- ◆ Objectivity,
- ◆ Self-awareness,
- ◆ Time management, and
- ◆ Work ethic.

X3.4.1 ADAPTABILITY

Adaptability is adjusting one's way of working or how one approaches a problem or situation to fit the circumstances. For a business analyst, it means choosing the appropriate tools or techniques based on the type of problem that is being addressed, being able to understand things quickly and react to changing circumstances, embracing change, and being able to admit when an approach is not working. Adaptability is critical for business analysts because they work in unpredictable environments with lots of moving parts. Being able to adjust quickly to change improves the chances of finding a successful approach to problems. Demonstrating comfort with change helps reduce the anxieties of stakeholders who have difficulty with changing circumstances.

X3.4.2 ETHICS

Ethical behavior is acting with integrity in business dealings and displaying professional behavior that is honest. Behaving ethically can result in being recognized by peers as a trustworthy and reliable team member. Most organizations have a code of conduct or similar guideline that outlines key components of ethical behavior as it relates to the organization. A business analyst is expected to understand and explicitly follow an organization's code of conduct. It is important for a business analyst to behave ethically because doing so creates trust and facilitates good working relationships with team members and stakeholders. Business analysts applying for a professional certification, for example, the PMI Professional in Business Analysis (PMI-PBA)®, are required to acknowledge and agree to a professional code of ethics.

X3.4.3 LEARNER

Being a learner involves a constant willingness to learn new skills, discover improved ways of doing things, and generally being curious. Although part of being a learner involves continuing education through industry organizations and other structured means, unstructured or self-led education also plays an important role. It is necessary for business analysts to be open to learning new things and applying new skills to assimilate improvements into their work, and to remain informed of any trends impacting the industry and profession.

X3.4.4 MULTITASKING

Participating in more than one product team, navigating competing stakeholder interests, and meeting multiple deadlines are all part of multitasking. This skill also includes the ability to prioritize tasks to ensure that the most important tasks are completed first. Business analysts are often juggling multiple tasks and are accountable to many different stakeholders, making it crucial for them to be able to multitask effectively. Knowing when to multitask is equally important, because taking on too much work could result in ineffectiveness. The quality of deliverables and work performed should not be jeopardized by multitasking; business analysts should continue to deliver high-quality results whether the task being performed is conducted singularly or through multitasking.

X3.4.5 OBJECTIVITY

Being objective means listening to and encouraging the presentation of multiple perspectives on a given issue, weighing the merits of each perspective dispassionately and without bias, and avoiding taking sides prematurely. It also means being intellectually honest with oneself and having the capacity to realize that one's personal viewpoint might not always be correct. Business analysts are often asked for guidance on the appropriate solution for a given problem. In these scenarios, being able to weigh the merits and drawbacks of each path objectively is important, not only in making the most sensible choice but also in earning trust from team members.

X3.4.6 SELF-AWARENESS

Being self-aware is the capacity for understanding, controlling, and being able to express emotions. This is also known as emotional intelligence. Self-awareness also involves being able to identify how one's actions might be perceived by others. For a business analyst, having self-awareness is important for dealing with the inevitable stresses of the job. The ability to identify and control emotions is beneficial because business analysts are sometimes tasked with playing the neutral facilitator between stakeholders to work through conflict.

X3.4.7 TIME MANAGEMENT

Time management skills enable business analysts to stay organized, be productive, and plan effectively. Skilled time managers have a good sense of everything they need to work on, can estimate how long each task will take, are able to effectively break large tasks down into component parts, and understand sequencing in order to prioritize the most important work first. They use past experience and time management techniques to estimate when tasks will be complete, and confidently commit to those estimates. Staying productive, applying effective prioritization, and managing time in order to meet deadlines helps a business analyst work effectively.

X3.4.8 WORK ETHIC

Having a good work ethic means completing assigned work on time and being motivated and driven to do what needs to be done, with minimal supervision. This is often referred to as being a "self-starter." Business analysts who possess a strong work ethic help motivate peer business analysts and other product team members. Their passion and excitement for the work being performed can become infectious, but when a good work ethic is not demonstrated, it can breed complacency across the team.

X3.5 LEADERSHIP SKILLS

Leadership involves focusing the efforts of a group of people toward a common goal and enabling them to work as a team. Business analysts leverage leadership skills to lead disparate groups of stakeholders through various forms of elicitation, to sort through stakeholder differences, to help the business reach decisions on requirements and priorities, and ultimately to gain buy-in to transition a solution into the business environment. The leadership category is composed of:

◆ Change agent skills,

◆ Negotiation skills,

◆ Personal development skills, and

◆ Skills to enable one to become a trusted advisor.

X3.5.1 CHANGE AGENT

A change agent is someone who acts as a catalyst for organizational innovation. A change agent has the vision to recognize where and when change is needed and is able to influence actions that bring those changes to fruition. Business analysts are great candidates for change agents because their role entails understanding business and enterprise architectures, the business need, different stakeholder perspectives, transition requirements, and the issues that relate to organizational change, all of which provides them with the knowledge to recognize where and when organizational change can be most beneficial.

X3.5.2 NEGOTIATION

Negotiation skills refer to the set of behaviors that allow a business analyst to navigate conflict and disagreement effectively. Negotiation involves recognizing when there is a potential for conflict and being able to manage and deescalate conflicts that arise in order to mitigate negative impacts and facilitate agreement or consensus. Negotiation skills are critical for business analysts, who are often forced to facilitate through difficult prioritization choices and requirements conflicts from different stakeholder groups.

X3.5.3 PERSONAL DEVELOPMENT

Personal development refers to all actions related to improving the skills of business analysts. Senior business analysts can help improve the performance of less experienced peers by providing coaching, mentoring, peer review, and teaching services. Senior resources may be paired with less experienced business analysts on activities to provide on-the-job experience. Communities of practice enable business analysts to learn from one another within an organization, and local PMI chapter involvement allows business analysts to learn from one another in a professional community. All business analysts, regardless of skill level, should seek out professional development opportunities to keep informed of the changing trends in the profession.

X3.5.4 TRUSTED ADVISOR

Being a trusted advisor means stakeholders have enough confidence in an individual that the stakeholder can speak freely and candidly. It also means that stakeholders trust and respect the individual enough to feel comfortable confiding in him or her when they need help or want advice. Being a trusted advisor is not a competency or skill, but to attain this label of distinction one must possess the traits and skills stakeholders look for in advisors such as honesty and trustworthiness. Stakeholders may consider someone a trusted advisor based on observable actions; for example, how someone builds and cares for relationships, puts the interests of others first, takes ownership of difficult situations, or works beyond their role for the betterment of the team. Being seen as a trusted advisor is imperative for business analysts so they can present information openly and honestly and can obtain the trust of stakeholders who often need to share sensitive or controversial information.

X3.6 TOOL KNOWLEDGE

Tool knowledge is composed of various categories of tools that, when mastered, enable practitioners to work effectively at their jobs. Business analysts use several different software and hardware tools to help them interact with stakeholders and get work done. The tool knowledge category is composed of:

◆ Communication and collaboration tools,

◆ Desktop tools,

◆ Reporting and analysis tools,

◆ Requirements management tools, and

◆ Modeling tools.

X3.6.1 COMMUNICATION AND COLLABORATION TOOLS

Communication and collaboration tools help business analysts disseminate critical information to stakeholders, work with project participants regardless of location, keep track of versioning, and coordinate information among different groups. Common examples of communication and collaboration tools include email, instant messaging, screen sharing, videoconferencing, and file sharing tools. Business analysts need to be able to effectively utilize the communication and collaboration tools selected for the project, regardless of their level of business analysis experience, as all business analysts have a need to communicate and collaborate across the product team.

X3.6.2 DESKTOP TOOLS

Desktop tools help business analysts manage their time and work productively. Tools such as standard office software, work timers, note-taking programs, issue trackers, and audio recording pens fall within this category. Having working knowledge of the desktop tools that suit an individual's working style and environment can help make that individual more productive and effective on projects.

X3.6.3 REPORTING AND ANALYSIS TOOLS

Reporting and analysis tools help business analysts make sense of the ever-increasing amount of data available in today's business environment. Being able to dissect and analyze data leads to smarter, more informed, and more effective decision making, so knowledge of reporting and analysis tools is critical for business analysts operating in almost any industry. These tools are of significant value for business analysts who have responsibility for summarizing results and reporting trends to senior-level managers.

X3.6.4 REQUIREMENTS MANAGEMENT TOOLS

Requirements management tools are tools that facilitate the requirements management process. They enable functions beyond standard office software, for example:

◆ Effective capture and storage of requirements and associated attributes;

◆ Supporting changes to requirements and other product information, including automating impact analysis;

◆ Tracking relationships between requirements and other product information;

◆ Enabling requirements reuse;

◆ Facilitating collaboration, including verification, validation, and sign-off processes;

◆ Supporting prototyping and simulation; and

◆ Providing automatic versioning and support for historical reporting.

Because requirements management is one of the most important components of business analysis, it is critical for the business analyst to obtain mastery of the requirements management tool in use by the organization.

X3.6.5 MODELING TOOLS

Modeling tools help create the visualizations that business analysts use during elicitation, analysis, and requirements management and development. These tools facilitate the creation of artifacts such as screen mockups, rough sketches, process models, system diagrams, storyboards, and prototypes. Modeling and visualization have proven to be effective techniques for eliciting and managing product requirements. Modeling tools range from the simple to the sophisticated and it is beneficial for business analysts to be proficient in their use whenever an organization has the will and means to use them.

BIBLIOGRAPHY

Active TPC benchmarks. n.d. *TPC*. Available at http://www.tpc.org/information/benchmarks.asp

Agile Alliance. 2015. Backlog grooming. *Agile Alliance*. Available at https://www.agilealliance.org/glossary/backlog-grooming

Alexander, I., & Beus-Dukic, L. 2009. *Discovering requirements: How to specify products and services*. Chichester, England: Wiley.

Ambler, S. W. n.d. Agile requirements best practices. *Agile modeling*. Available at http://agilemodeling.com/essays/agileRequirementsBestPractices.htm#QuestionTraceability

Ambler, S. W. n.d. The practices of agile modeling. *Agile modeling*. Available at http://agilemodeling.com/practices.htm

Ambler, S. W. n.d. The principles of agile modeling. *Agile modeling*. Available at http://agilemodeling.com/principles.htm

Blais, S. 2011. *Business analysis: Best practices for success.* New York, NY: ILL.

Cadle, J., Turner, P., & Paul, D. 2010. *Business analysis techniques: 72 essential tools for success.* Swindon, England: British Informatics Society Limited.

Carkenord, B. A. 2008. *Seven steps to mastering business analysis.* Fort Lauderdale, FL: J. Ross Publishing.

Cohn, M. 2014, February 25. Making the decision to abnormally terminate a sprint. *Mountain Goat Software*. Available at https://www.mountaingoatsoftware.com/blog/making-the-decision-to-abnormally-terminate-a-sprint

Cohn, M. 2015, May 26. Product backlog refinement (grooming). *Mountain Goat Software*. Available at https://www.mountaingoatsoftware.com/blog/product-backlog-refinement-grooming

Cooke, J. L. 2013. *The power of the agile business analyst: 30 surprising ways a business analyst can add value to your agile development team.* Ely, England: IT Governance Publishing.

The Disciplined Agile (DA) Framework. n.d. *DisciplinedAgileDelivery.com*. Available at http://www.disciplinedagiledelivery.com/disciplineddevops/

Eclipse Foundation n.d.. *OpenUP*. Available at http://epf.eclipse.org/wikis/openup/

GameStorming. 2017. Available at http://gamestorming.com/

Gigante, A. 2013, August 28. Creating an agile road map using story mapping. *Scrum Alliance*. Available at https://www.scrumalliance.org/community/articles/2013/august/creating-an-agile-roadmap-using-story-mapping

Gottesdiener, E. 2002. *Requirements by collaboration: Workshops for defining needs.* Boston, MA: Addison-Wesley Professional.

Gottsdiener, E., & Gorman, M. 2012. *Discover to deliver: Agile product planning and analysis.* Acton, MA: EBG Consulting.

Gottesdiener, E., & Gorman, M. n.d. It's in the driver's seat. *PM Times.* Available at https://www.projecttimes.com/articles/it-s-time-to-put-value-in-the-driver-s-seat.html

Griffiths, M. 2012. *PMI-ACP Exam Prep, Premier Edition: A course in a book for passing the PMI Agile Certified Practitioner (PMI-ACP) Exam.* Minnetonka, MN: RMC Publications.

Hohman, L. 2017. Innovation games: Creating breakthrough products through collaborative play. *Innovation games.* Available at http://www.innovationgames.com

Hooks, I. F., & Farry, K. A. 2001. *Customer-centered products: Creating successful products through smart requirements management.* New York, NY: AMACOM.

Hubbard, D. W. 2014. *How to measure anything: Finding the value of "intangibles" in business.* Hoboken, NJ: John Wiley & Sons.

iSixSigma. n.d. Competently use capability analysis. *iSixSigma.* Available at https://www.isixsigma.com/tools-templates/capability-indices-process-capability/competently-use-capability-analysis/

Larson, E., & Larson, R. 2013. *The practitioner's guide to requirements management* (2nd ed.). Minneapolis, MN: Watermark Learning.

Leffingwell, D. 2011. *Agile software requirements: Lean requirements practices for teams, programs, and the enterprise.* Upper Saddle River, NJ: Addison-Wesley.

MailChimp. 2017, February 1. Email marketing benchmarks. *MailChimp.* Available at https://mailchimp.com/resources/research/email-marketing-benchmarks/

Marr, B. 2012. *Key performance indicators (KPI): The 75 measures every manager needs to know.* Saddle River, NJ: FT Publishing/Pearson.

Matts, C., & Adzic, G. 2011, December 14. Feature injection: Three steps to success. *InfoQ.* Available at https://www.infoq.com/articles/feature-injection-success

Matts, C., & Maassen, O. 2007, June 8. "Real options" underlie agile practices. *InfoQ.* Available at https://www.infoq.com/articles/real-options-enhance-agility

MindTools Content Team. n.d. Force field analysis: Analyzing the pressures for and against change. *MindTools.* Available at https://www.mindtools.com/pages/article/newTED_06.htm

Nickolaisen, N. 2009, August 20. Breaking the project management triangle. *InformIT.* Available at http://www.informit.com/articles/article.aspx?p=1384195&seqNum=2

Pichler, R. 2009, January 1. The product vision. *Scrum Alliance.* Available at https://www.scrumalliance.org/community/articles/2009/january/the-product-vision

Pichler, R. 2014, April 15. Building a project users want: From idea to backlog with the vision board. *Mountain Goat Software.* Available at https://www.mountaingoatsoftware.com/blog/building-a-product-users-want-from-idea-to-backlog-with-the-vision-board

Pichler, R. 2016, July 20. 10 tips for creating an agile project roadmap. *Romanpichler.com.* Available at http://www .romanpichler.com/blog/10-tips-creating-agile-product-roadmap/

Project Management Institute. 2013a. *The standard for portfolio management* – Third Edition. Newtown Square, PA: Author.

Project Management Institute. 2013b. *The standard for program management* – Third Edition. Newtown Square, PA: Author.

Project Management Institute. 2014a. *Business analysis for practitioners: A practice guide.* Newtown Square, PA: Author.

Project Management Institute. 2014b. *A guide to the project management body of knowledge* – Fourth Edition. Newtown Square, PA: Author.

Project Management Institute. 2014c. *PMI pulse of the profession® report on requirements management.* Newtown Square, PA: Author.

Project Management Institute. 2016. *PMI pulse of the profession® report: High cost of low performance: How will you improve business results?* Newtown Square, PA: Author. Available at http://www.pmi.org/-/media/pmi/documents/ public/pdf/learning/thought-leadership/pulse/pulse-of-the-profession-2016.pdf

Readiness Roadmap. n.d. Available at http://www.readinessroadmap.org/

Rico, D. 2012, August 24. Business value of agile methods: Using ROI and real options. *ProjectManagement.com.* Available at https://www.projectmanagement.com/videos/285280/Business-Value-of-Agile-Methods-Using-ROI- and-Real-Options

Rubin, K. S. 2013. *Essential scrum: A practical guide to the most popular agile process.* Upper Saddle River, NJ: Pearson Education.

Scaled Agile Inc. 2017, June 21. Iteration planning. *SAFe®.* Available at http://www.scaledagileframework.com/ iteration-planning/

Schibi O., & Lee, C. 2015. *Effective PM and BA role collaboration: Delivering business value through projects and programs successfully.* Plantation, FL: J. Ross Publishing.

Seilvel. 2017. Requirements management tools evaluation. *Seilevel.* Available at https://www.seilevel.com/ business-analyst-resources/requirements-tools-reviews/

Spencer, K. F. 2015, October 25. 4 L's. *Tasty Cupcakes.* Available at http://tastycupcakes.org/2015/10/4-ls/

Tasty Cupcakes. n.d. Available at http://tastycupcakes.org/category/agile/

Veethil, S. T. 2013, May 3. Risk management in agile. *Scrum Alliance.* Available at https://www.scrumalliance.org/ community/articles/2013/2013-may/risk-management-in-agile

Wiegers, K. n.d. Getting the most from a requirements management tool. *Jama Software.* Available at http://www .jamasoftware.com/wp-content/uploads/documents/Jama-Getting-Most-Out-of-Requirements-Management-Tools.pdf

Wiegers, K., & Beatty, J. 2013. *Software requirements* (3rd ed.). Redmond, WA: Microsoft Press.

GLOSSARY

1. INCLUSIONS AND EXCLUSIONS

This glossary includes terms that are:

◆ Unique or nearly unique to business analysis (e.g., business requirements document, business analysis plan, modeling elaboration).

◆ Not unique to business analysis, but used differently or with a narrower meaning in business analysis than in general everyday usage (e.g., acceptance criteria, business inspection).

This glossary generally does not include:

◆ Application area-specific terms.

◆ Terms used in business analysis that do not differ in any material way from everyday use (e.g., competency, culture).

◆ Compound terms whose meaning is clear from the meanings of the component parts.

◆ Variants when the meaning of the variant is clear from the base term.

◆ Terms that are used only once and are not critical to understanding the point of the sentence (e.g., terms in a list of examples would not be defined in the Glossary).

2. COMMON ACRONYMS

BA	business analyst
BRD	business requirements document
BDD	behavior-driven development
BPMN	business process modeling notation
CCB	change control board
CMS	configuration management system
CRUD	create, read, update, delete
DEEP	detailed appropriately, estimated, emergent, and prioritized
DevOps	development and operations

DITL	day in the life testing
DoD	definition of done
EEFs	Enterprise Environmental Factors
ERD	entity relationship diagram
IRR	Internal Rate of Return
INVEST	independent, negotiable, valuable, estimable, small, and testable
KPI	key performance indicator
MMF	minimum marketable features
MVP	minimum viable product
MoSCoW	must haves, should haves, could haves, and won't haves
NPV	net present value
OD/CM	organizational development/change management
OPAs	organizational process assets
PBP	payback period
PM	project manager
PMBOK	Project Management Body of Knowledge
QA	quality assurance
QC	quality control
RACI	responsible, accountable, consult, and inform
ROI	return on investment
RML	requirements modeling language
SME	subject matter expert
SWOT	strengths, weaknesses, opportunities, and threats
SysML	system modeling language
UI	user interface
UML	unified modeling language
VCS	version control system
WBS	work breakdown structure
WIP	work in progress
WSJF	weighted shortest job first

3. DEFINITIONS

The words within this glossary are defined in the context of business analysis. Many of the words defined here have different dictionary definitions and, in some cases, different meaning when considered in the context of project, program, or portfolio management. This glossary is best used to understand how terms are being used throughout this standard and guide and to further understand how terms are commonly used when discussing business analysis work.

Acceptance Criteria. A set of conditions that are met before deliverables are accepted. In business analysis, acceptance criteria are built to evaluate the product requirements and solution.

Active Listening. The act of listening completely with all senses so as to pick up all of the information that is being communicated. Active listening entails paraphrasing or reciting back what is heard to ensure accurate understanding of what has been stated.

Activity. A distinct, scheduled portion of work performed during the course of a project.

Activity Diagram. A type of process model that visually shows the complex flow of use cases. Activity diagrams are similar to process flows in syntax, however they commonly show user and system interactions in one diagram and mirror the textual description of use cases. See also *process flow*.

Actor. People or other systems that interact with a solution.

Actual Acceptance Result. Contains the pass/fail results from comparing test results against the acceptance criteria.

Adaptability. The skill of being flexible and willing to adjust how one performs work or goes about approaching a situation as change and new information is encountered.

Adaptive Life Cycle. A project life cycle that is iterative and incremental.

Affinity Diagram. A technique that allows large numbers of ideas to be classified into groups for review and analysis.

Agile Approach. An example of an adaptive project life cycle.

Analogous Estimating. A technique for estimating the duration or cost of an activity or a project using historical data from a similar activity or project.

Analysis. The process of examining, breaking down, and synthesizing information to further understand, complete, and improve it.

Analysis Approach. Describes how analysis will be performed; how to verify, validate, and prioritize requirements and other product information; how risks will be identified and analyzed; how design options will be assessed; and what techniques and templates are expected to be used to perform analysis.

Analysis Knowledge Area. Includes the processes for examining, breaking down, synthesizing, and clarifying information to further understand it, complete it, and improve it.

Analysis Model. A visual representation of product information. See also *product information*.

Analytical Resource. A person on the product team who performs business analysis.

Analytical Skills. A set of skills in business analysis that are used to process information of various types and at various levels of detail for the purpose of determining the relevant information from the irrelevant, drawing conclusions, building models, formulating decisions, and specifying requirements.

Approved Requirement. A requirement that is verified and validated and has been deemed an accurate reflection of what the product development team should build.

Architecture. A method to describe an organization by mapping its essential characteristics, such as people, locations, processes, applications, data, and technology.

As-Built Documentation. Analysis and design documentation that has been updated to correspond to a released product.

Assemble Business Case. The process of synthesizing well-researched and analyzed information to support the selection of the best portfolio components, programs, or projects to address the business goals and objectives.

Assess Business Analysis Performance. The process of considering the effectiveness of the business analysis practices in use across the organization, typically in the context of considering the ongoing deliverables and results of a portfolio component, program, or project.

Assess Current State. The process of examining the current environment under analysis to understand important factors that are internal or external to the organization, which may be the cause or reason for a problem or opportunity.

Assess Product Design Options. The process of identifying, analyzing, and comparing solution design options based on the business goals and objectives, expected costs of implementation, feasibility, and associated risks and using the results of this assessment to provide recommendations regarding the design options presented.

Assessment of Business Value. The result of comparing expected business value for a solution against actual value that has been realized.

Assumption. A factor in the planning process that is considered to be true, real, or certain, without proof or demonstration.

Autocratic Decision Making. An approach for making decisions where one individual makes the decision for the group.

Automated Regression Testing. Tool-supported validation used after changes are made to a software system to ensure those changes did not unintentionally alter the system in some other way.

Backbone. A foundational part of a story map representing the minimum set of capabilities that absolutely are required to be in the first release for the solution to serve its purpose. That set of capabilities or user stories is sometimes called the minimum viable product. See also *story mapping*.

Backlog. A listing of product requirements and deliverables to be completed, often written as user stories, and prioritized by the business to manage and organize the project's work.

Backlog Management. See *backlog refinement*.

Backlog Refinement. A process used on agile projects where the product team works with the product owner to gain more in-depth understanding about the user stories in the backlog list. The portion of the backlog which is refined at any point in time is typically considered ready to use as an input for sprint planning meetings, which are used to determine which user stories to cover in the next iteration.

Backsliding. A circumstance in a burndown chart where the remaining quantity of what is being tracked increases over time.

Backward Traceability. A technique that establishes the relationship of a requirement to the scope, business goals, or business objectives from which it originated.

Baseline. The approved version of a work product that can be changed using formal change control procedures and is used as the basis for comparison to actual results.

Behavior-Driven Development (BDD). An approach that suggests the team begins with understanding how the user will use a product (its behavior), writes tests for that behavior, and then constructs solutions against the tests.

Benchmarking. The comparison of actual or planned practices, such as processes and operations, to those of comparable organizations to identify best practices, generate ideas for improvement, and provide a basis for measuring performance.

Benefit. The gains and assets realized by the organization and other stakeholders as the result of outcomes delivered by the solution.

Bottom-Up Estimating. A method of estimating duration or cost by aggregating the estimates of the lower-level components of the work breakdown structure (WBS).

Brainstorming. In business analysis, brainstorming is an elicitation technique that is performed in a group setting and led by a facilitator to engage stakeholders to quickly identify a list of ideas for a specific topic in a relatively short time period.

Burndown Chart. A graphical representation that counts the remaining quantity of some trackable aspect over time. Burndown charts that track the number of remaining backlog items are used on projects using an adaptive life cycle.

Business. In business analysis, the area of an organization that is experiencing a problem or possessing an opportunity along with the desire and interest in and willingness to sponsor changes to address the need.

Business Acumen. The skill of applying business and industry knowledge with decision-making capabilities to make sound decisions.

Business Analysis. The set of activities performed to support delivery of solutions that align to business objectives and provide continuous value to the organization.

Business Analysis Approach. A description of how business analysis processes will be conducted for a portfolio component, program, or project. When following a formal delivery process, the business analysis approaches from each Knowledge Area are included in the business analysis plan. See *business analysis plan*.

Business Analysis Center of Excellence. An organizational structure created whereby business analysts are managed centrally or are provided mentorship centrally for the purpose of improving the business analysis discipline across the organization. Also called a center of business analysis practice.

Business Analysis Deliverables. Any unique and verifiable result, produced throughout the course of performing business analysis activities, which is provided to team members and stakeholders to perform future work, decision making, or complete a process, phase, or initiative.

Business Analysis Documentation. The set of business analysis information produced as an output of the business analysis work conducted on a portfolio, program, or project. Such output may be comprised of business analysis deliverables, business analysis work products, or a combination thereof.

Business Analysis Methodology. A system of practices, techniques, tools, procedures, and rules used by those who work in the business analysis discipline.

Business Analysis Organizational Standard. Part of organizational process assets, these standards may include expectations for how business analysis is conducted and which tools are used to support business analysis efforts.

Business Analysis Performance Assessment. An evaluation of what has been learned about the effectiveness of the business analysis processes and of the business analysis techniques that have been used.

Business Analysis Performance Metrics. A qualitative or quantitative measure of or inference about the effectiveness of business analysis practices.

Business Analysis Plan. A summary of the choices and process decisions made in the business analysis approaches, including the identification of the business analysis tasks that will be performed, the deliverables that will be produced, and the roles required to perform the work.

Business Analysis Tailoring. The need to adjust which business analysis activities should be performed for projects of varying characteristics.

Business Analyst (BA). Any resource who is performing the work of business analysis.

Business Architecture. A collection of the business functions, organizational structures, and locations, and processes of an organization, including documents and depictions of those elements. It is usually a subset of the enterprise architecture and is extended with the applications, information, and supporting technology to form a complete blueprint of an organization.

Business Architecture Technique. An organizational framework available to model business architecture, providing different approaches for analyzing various aspects of the business.

Business Capability Analysis. A technique used to analyze performance in terms of processes, people skills, and other resources used by an organization to perform its work. Historical data obtained from analyzing current capabilities are used to understand trends and determine what measures will be helpful guidelines for determining whether a capability is performing as it should be in the current state.

Business Case. A documented economic feasibility study used to establish validity of the benefits to be delivered by a portfolio component, program, or project.

Business Data Diagram. See *entity relationship diagram*.

Business Data Object. For business analysis, a business data object is a grouping of facts that together describe a person, place, thing, or concept of interest to a business. The term *business data object* is sometimes used interchangeably with *business entity*. It can also refer to the physical data storage of such groupings.

Business Goal. A broad-based translation of a corporate goal into what the business specifically is seeking to achieve. Business goals should align to the organizational goals.

Business Need. The impetus for a change in an organization based on an existing problem or opportunity. The business need provides the rationale for initiating a portfolio component, program, or project.

Business Objective. Measurable representation of the goals the business is seeking to achieve. Business objectives are specific and should align to the organizational objectives.

Business Objectives Model. A business analysis model that relates the business problems, business objectives, and top-level features.

Business Requirement. A requirement that describes a higher-level need of the organization, such as a business issue or opportunity, the rationale for why an initiative is being undertaken, and a measurable representation of a goal the business is seeking to achieve.

Business Rule. A constraint about how the organization wants to operate. These constraints are usually enforced by data and/or processes and are under the jurisdiction of the business.

Business Rules Catalog. A business analysis model that details all of the business rules and their related attributes.

Business Value. The net quantifiable benefit derived from a business endeavor. The benefit may be tangible, intangible, or both. In business analysis, business value is considered the return, in the form of time, money, goods, or intangibles for something exchanged.

Buy a Feature. A type of collaborative game used to enable a group of stakeholders to agree on prioritization by giving each stakeholder an amount of pretend money to buy their choice of features, splitting the money received across features however desired.

Capability. The ability to add value or achieve objectives in an organization through a function, process, service, or other proficiency.

Capability Framework. A collection of an organization's capabilities, organized into manageable pieces, similar to business architecture.

Capability Table. A table that displays the capabilities needed to solve a problem or seize an opportunity. This tool can show the relationship between a situation, its root causes, and the capabilities needed to address the situation.

Cardinality. An indication of the quantity of one business data object which is associated with a related business data object. Current usage of the term also includes whether the relationship between the two objects is required or optional.

Cause and Effect Diagram. A decomposition technique that helps trace an undesirable effect back to its root cause.

Change Agent. A person who acts as a catalyst for organizational innovation possessing the vision to recognize where and when a change is needed and influencing to bring the change to fruition.

Change Control. A process whereby modifications to documents, deliverables, or baselines associated with the project are identified, documented, approved, or rejected.

Change Control Board (CCB). A formally chartered group responsible for reviewing, evaluating, approving, delaying, or rejecting changes to the project, and for recording and communicating such decisions.

Change Control Tools. Manual or automated tools to assist with change and/or configuration management. At a minimum, the tools should support the activities of the change control board (CCB).

Change Request. A formal proposal to modify a document, deliverable, or baseline.

Charter. See *portfolio charter, program charter,* or *project charter.*

Collaborative Games. A collection of elicitation techniques that foster collaboration, innovation, and creativity to achieve the goal of the elicitation activity.

Communication and Collaboration Tool. A category of tools used in business analysis to effectively work with stakeholders and share and manage information.

Communication Skills. A collection of skills in business analysis utilized to provide, receive, or elicit information from various sources.

Communications Management Plan. A component of the project, program, or portfolio management plan that describes how, when, and by whom information will be administered and disseminated.

Communication Tailoring. Selecting the appropriate method and style of communication to use in a given situation based on factors such as audience (role, internal versus external, individual versus group, etc.) and available communication methods (email, phone, instant message, teleconference, in-person meeting, etc.).

Competitive Analysis. A technique for obtaining and analyzing information about an organization's external environment.

Compliance Standard. See *regulatory standard.*

Conduct Business Analysis Planning. The process performed to obtain shared agreement regarding the business analysis activities the team will be performing and the assignment of roles, responsibilities, and skill sets for the tasks required to successfully complete the business analysis work.

Conceptual and Detailed Thinking. The ability to move between analyzing at a high-level view of a problem space and a specific detail or set of details that comprise one aspect of the problem space.

Conduct Elicitation. The process of applying various elicitation techniques to draw out information from stakeholders and other sources.

Conduct Stakeholder Analysis. The process of researching and analyzing quantitative and qualitative information about the individuals, groups, or organizations that may impact, are impacted, or are perceived to be impacted by the area under assessment.

Configuration Management. A collection of formal documented processes, templates, and documentation used to apply governance to changes to the solution, or subcomponent being developed.

Configuration Management Standard. The criteria established for what constitutes compliance with configuration management procedures and their associated systems and tools.

Configuration Management System (CMS). A collection of procedures used to track project artifacts and monitor and control changes to these artifacts.

Confirm Elicitation Results. The process of performing follow-up activities on the elicitation results, determining an appropriate level of formality to use, reviewing with stakeholders, and comparing to historical information.

Confirmed Elicitation Results. Consist of the business analysis information obtained from completed elicitation activities. Confirmed elicitation results signify that the product team has reached a common understanding and agrees to the accuracy of the information elicited.

Constraint. A factor that limits the options for managing a project, program, portfolio, or process.

Context Diagram. A visual depiction of the product scope showing a business system (process, equipment, computer system, etc.) and how people and other systems (actors) interact with it.

Control Point. A designated event scheduled for the conclusion of a segment of work in order to evaluate progress against plans and the project charter and business case to determine if the project should be changed, terminated, or continued as planned. Examples of control points are stage gates or phase gates. The evaluation which occurs at the end of a sprint, iteration, or release can also be considered a control point.

Cost-Benefit Analysis. A financial analysis tool used to determine the benefits provided by a portfolio component, program, or project against its costs.

Cost-Effectiveness Feasibility. The high-level economic feasibility of a potential portfolio component, program, or project, taking into account both financial benefits and costs.

Create and Analyze Models. The process of creating structured representations, such as diagrams, tables, or structured text, of any product information, to facilitate further analysis by identifying gaps in information or uncovering extraneous information.

Creative Thinking. The ability to resolve a problem or set of problems by exploring multiple and different solutions to arrive at an improved future result.

Cross-Functional Team. A team where each team member can play more than one role.

CRUD Matrix. CRUD, defined as (C) create, (R) read, (U) update, and (D) delete, represents the operations that can be applied to data or objects. CRUD matrices describe who or what has permission to perform each of the CRUD operations on elements, such as data or user interfaces.

Cultural Awareness. Being conscious of the cultural norms and values of others.

Current State Assessment. An understanding of the current mode of operations, or the as-is state of the organization.

Customer. Internal or external stakeholders who benefit from the development of a solution.

Data Dictionary. A business analysis model that catalogs the attributes of specific data objects.

Data Flow Diagram. A business analysis model that combines processes, systems, and data to show how data flows through a solution.

Data Model. A visual representation of the business data objects of interest to a business and the relationships between them. See also *business data object.*

Data Store. A source of business information, often represented visually on a data flow diagram.

Day in the Life Testing (DITL). A semiformal activity conducted by someone with in-depth business knowledge. The results obtained from DITL testing enable validation or evaluation of whether a solution provides the functionality for a typical day of usage by a role that interacts with the solution.

Decision by Consensus. An approach for making group decisions based upon general agreement for the decision by the group. Before making decisions by consensus, the group should first define what it means for it to reach general agreement. Among popular choices for consensus are convergence of individual decisions to one group decision or majority support for a decision with other individuals not seriously opposed to it. See also *Delphi.*

Decision by Sponsor. An approach for making decisions where the decision is made by the sponsor, with or without input from a group. See also *autocratic decision making.*

Decision by Weighted Analysis. An approach for making decisions using decision criteria identified by and assigned relative weights by those involved in making the decision. Each option involved in the decision is rated by scoring how well the option meets the criteria independent of other options. Ratings are multiplied by the weights and summed to arrive at the score for each option. The summed scores represent the overall rankings of the options.

Decision Making. The ability to weigh the benefits and drawbacks associated with a set of options, choose among various options, and articulate the rationale for the choice.

Decision Table. A business analysis model that helps identify business rules associated with any complex branching logic in a solution by considering all combinations of choices.

Decision Tree. A business analysis model that shows business rules associated with any complex branching logic in a solution.

Decomposition Model. A model that is used to divide and subdivide a high-level concept into lower-level concepts, for example dividing the project scope and project deliverables into smaller, more manageable parts for the purpose of analysis. Also known as decomposition diagrams.

DEEP. Describes the characteristics that a product backlog needs to demonstrate to be considered well refined. DEEP is an acronym that stands for detailed appropriately, estimated, emergent, and prioritized.

Define Acceptance Criteria. The process of obtaining agreement as to what would constitute proof that one or more aspects of a solution have been developed successfully.

Define and Elaborate Requirements. The process of refining and documenting requirements and other types of product information at the appropriate level of detail, format, and level of formality required for various audiences.

Defining and Aligning Process Group. The business analysis processes performed to investigate and evaluate the viability of initiating a new product or changes to or retirement of an existing product as well as defining scope and aligning products, portfolios, programs, and projects to the overall organizational strategy.

Definition of Done (DoD). A series of conditions that the entire team agrees to complete before an item is considered sufficiently developed to be accepted by the business stakeholders.

Definition of Ready. A series of conditions that the entire team agrees to complete before a user story is considered sufficiently understood for work to begin to construct it.

Deliverable. Any unique and verifiable product, result, or capability to perform a service that is produced to complete a process, phase, or project.

Delphi. A consensus-building method that consolidates anonymous input from subject matter experts (SMEs) using rounds of voting. See also *wide-band Delphi*.

Dependency. A logical relationship that exists between two or more entities.

Dependency Analysis. A technique that is used to discover dependent relationships.

Design Option. A representation of how a solution could be constructed.

Design Thinking. An approach that uses solution-based thinking rather than problem-based thinking to produce creative solutions to achieve goals.

Desktop Tool. A category of tools used in a personal workspace, for example on a laptop or on a personal device, for the purpose of aiding organization and productivity.

Determine Analysis Approach. The process of thinking ahead about how analysis will be performed including what will be analyzed; which models will be most beneficial to produce, and how requirements and other product information will be verified, validated, and prioritized.

Determine Elicitation Approach. The process of thinking through how elicitation activities will be conducted, which stakeholders will be involved, which elicitation techniques may be used, and the order in which the elicitation activities will be best performed.

Determine Future State. The process of determining gaps in existing capabilities and a set of proposed changes necessary to attain a desired future state that addresses the problem or opportunity under analysis.

Determine Solution Evaluation Approach. The process of determining what aspects of the organization and/or solution will be evaluated, how performance will be measured, when performance will be measured, and by whom.

Determine Stakeholder Engagement and Communication Approach. The process of developing appropriate methods to effectively engage and communicate with stakeholders throughout the product life cycle, based on the analysis of their needs, interests, and roles within the business analysis process.

Determine Traceability and Monitoring Approach. The process of considering how traceability will be performed on the portfolio, program, project, or product, and defining how requirement changes will be managed.

Determine Viable Options and Provide Recommendation. The process of applying various analysis techniques to examine possible solutions for meeting the business goals and objectives and to determine which of the options is considered the best possible one for the organization to pursue.

DevOps (Development and Operations). A concept or an organizational unit that promotes collaboration between development, quality control, and operations (IT and business operations). It supports rapidly releasing a solution by operationalizing it in small segments, each of which provides additional functionality to its users.

Display-Action-Response Model. A business analysis model that dissects a user interface mockup into its display and behavior requirements at the page element level.

Document Analysis. An elicitation technique used to analyze existing documentation to identify relevant product information.

Domain. A discipline or area of study. See also *performance domain*.

Ecosystem Map. A scope model that shows the relevant systems, the relationships between systems, and optionally any data objects passed between them.

Elaboration. A term used on adaptive projects to describe the process of detailing product information over time.

Elicitation. The activity of drawing out information from stakeholders and other sources.

Elicitation Approach. An informal device used by a business analyst to prepare for elicitation work. It defines important information about the elicitation process, such as how elicitation will be performed, what information to elicit, where to find that information, how to obtain the information, and when to conduct the elicitation activities.

Elicitation Knowledge Area. The processes for planning and preparing for elicitation, conducting elicitation and confirming elicitation results to obtain information from sources.

Elicitation Plan. See *elicitation approach*.

Elicitation Preparation Materials. The items that are created to increase the probability of meeting elicitation activity objectives, while maximizing time spent with elicitation participants.

Elicitation Result. The business analysis information obtained from a completed elicitation activity.

Elicitation Session. A session or activity conducted to obtain information from participants.

Emergent Learning. A process where stakeholders discover their requirements as portions of the solution are delivered over time.

Emotional Intelligence. See *self-awareness*.

Enterprise and Organizational Knowledge. An understanding and familiarity with the way a specific business is organized and operates, from both a high-level and tactical standpoint.

Enterprise Architecture. A collection of the business and technology components needed to operate an enterprise. The business architecture is usually a subset of the enterprise architecture and is extended with the applications, information, and supporting technology to form a complete blueprint of an organization.

Enterprise Environmental Factors (EEFs). Conditions, not under the immediate control of the team, that influence, constrain, or direct the project, program, or portfolio.

Entity Relationship Diagram (ERD). A business analysis model that shows the business data objects or pieces of information of interest and the relationships between those objects, including the cardinality of those relationships.

Epic. A large user story that is too big to construct in an iteration. See also *user story*.

Establish Relationships and Dependencies. The process of tracing or setting linkages between and among requirements and other product information.

Estimate. A quantitative assessment of the likely amount or outcome of a variable, such as costs, resources, effort, or durations.

Estimation Poker. A collaborative relative estimation technique in which there is an agreed-upon scale used for the relative estimates. See also *relative estimation*.

Ethics. Acting with integrity and displaying behavior that is honest.

Evaluate Acceptance Results and Address Defects. The process of deciding what to do with the results from a comparison of the defined acceptance criteria against the solution.

Evaluate Solution Performance. The process of evaluating a solution to determine whether the implemented solution or solution component is delivering the business value as intended.

Evaluated Acceptance Results. The comparison between the acceptance criteria and the actual results, along with the root cause for variances or defects, the analysis of the cost to address the defect, and the business impact of addressing it or accepting it.

Evaluation. See *solution evaluation*.

Event. For business analysis, an event is an action of interest to a business, for which there is often a planned response.

Event List. A scope model that describes any external events that trigger solution behavior.

Event Trigger. See *trigger*.

Evolutionary Prototype. A prototype that is the actual finished solution in process. See also *prototypes*.

Executing Process Group. The business analysis processes performed to elicit, analyze, model, define, verify, validate, prioritize, and approve all types of product information, ranging from backlogs to user stories and requirements to constraints. In project management, it consists of the processes performed to complete the work defined in the project management plan to satisfy the project requirements.

Expert Judgment. Judgment based upon expertise in an application area, Knowledge Area, discipline, industry, etc., as appropriate for the activity being performed. Such expertise may be provided by any group or person with specialized education, knowledge, skill, experience, or training.

Exploratory Testing. An unscripted, free-form validation or evaluation activity conducted by someone with in-depth business or testing knowledge to validate the solution and discover product errors.

External Entity. A source or receiver of business information that is outside of the scope of the system under study.

External Event. An action that is triggered outside of the boundary of the system under study where there is an expectation that the planned response to that action is within scope.

Facilitate Product Roadmap Development. The process of supporting the development of a product roadmap that outlines, at a high level, which aspects of a product are planned for delivery over a course of the portfolio, program, or one or more project iterations or releases, and the potential sequence for the delivery of these aspects.

Facilitated Workshops. In business analysis, facilitated workshops use a structured meeting led by a skilled, neutral facilitator and a carefully selected group of stakeholders to collaborate and work toward a stated objective. Requirements workshops bring together a carefully selected group of stakeholders to collaborate, explore, and evaluate product requirements.

Facilitation. The collection of activities involved in directing and coordinating work among groups of people.

Feasibility Analysis. A study that produces a potential recommendation to address business needs. It examines feasibility using one or more of the following variables: operational, technology/system, cost-effectiveness, and timeliness of the potential solution.

Feasibility Assessment. See *feasibility analysis*.

Feasibility Study Results. The summarized outcomes obtained from the completion of the feasibility analysis.

Feature. A set of related requirements typically described in short phrases.

Feature Injection. A framework and set of principles used to improve and expedite how a product team develops and analyzes product requirements.

Feature Model. A scope model that visually represents all the features of a solution arranged in a tree or hierarchical structure.

Fibonacci Sequence. A numeric sequence in which each succeeding number is the sum of the two previous numbers, such as 0, 1, 1, 2, 3, 5, 8, 13, 21 etc.

Fishbone Diagram. A version of a cause-and-effect diagram that depicts a problem and its root causes in a visual manner. It uses a fish image, listing the problem at the head, with causes and subcauses of the problem represented as bones of the fish. See also *cause and effect diagram*.

Five Whys. A technique for conducting root cause analysis suggesting anyone trying to understand a problem needs to ask why it is occurring up to five times to thoroughly understand its causes.

Focus Group. An elicitation technique that brings together prequalified stakeholders and subject matter experts to learn about their expectations and attitudes about a proposed product, service, or result.

Force Field Analysis. A decision-making technique that can be used to help product teams analyze whether there is sufficient support to pursue a change.

Formality. For business analysis, formality is the degree of conformance to a precise detailed format of documentation and to following established procedures which a group or organization may require for business analysis work products and activities.

Forward Traceability. A technique that establishes the relationship of a requirement to the design or code which implements it or to tests which verify that it has been satisfied.

Functional Requirement. A requirement that describes the behavior of a product.

Future State. Desired mode of operations once a solution is implemented.

Gap Analysis. A technique for understanding the gap between current capabilities and needed capabilities. Filling the gap is what comprises a solution recommendation.

Glossary. In business analysis, a glossary is used to list terms, definitions, and acronyms. Glossaries typically include the list of terms the organization most commonly defines differently from its industry or across its own organization as well as terms that are unfamiliar.

Goal. Something that an organization seeks to accomplish or achieve.

Goal Model. A business analysis model that shows the stakeholder goals for a solution with any supporting or conflicting goal relationships indicated.

Ground Rule. An expectation regarding acceptable behavior for team members.

Growth Share Matrix. See *product portfolio matrix*.

High Fidelity. A high-quality reproduction of something that is identical to, or indistinguishable from, the thing or functionality or concept which it replicates.

High-Fidelity Prototype. A method of prototyping that creates a functioning representation of the final finished solution to the user. High-fidelity prototyping is performed using a programming language or a pseudo language of the solution to be demonstrated.

Identify and Analyze Product Risks. The process of uncovering and examining assumptions and uncertainties that could positively or negatively affect success in the definition, development, and the expected results of the solution.

Identify Problem or Opportunity. The process of identifying the problem to be solved or the opportunity to be pursued.

Identify Stakeholders. The process of identifying the individuals, groups, or organizations that may impact, are impacted, or are perceived to be impacted by the area under assessment. In project management, stakeholders are identified based on involvement and influence on the project where in business analysis the focus is on their relationship to the solution.

Impact Analysis. A technique for evaluating a change in relation to how it will affect other requirements, the product, the program, and the project.

Industry Knowledge. Expertise in and familiarity with the industry in which an organization is participating and includes knowledge about an organization's competitors, industry trends and challenges, applicable business models, etc.

Initiating Process Group. The business analysis processes performed to define the portfolio, program, or project objectives and apply resources to a portfolio component, program, project, or project phase. In project management, this Process Group is similar as it includes the processes for defining a new project or new phase of an existing project by obtaining the authorization to do so.

Input. Any item that is required by a process before that process proceeds. May be an output from a predecessor process.

Inspection. In business analysis, a formal and rigorous form of review in which practitioners close to the work (usually other business analysts, developers, test team members, or quality team members) examine the work for completeness, consistency, and conformance to internal and external standards, usually by means of a checklist. See also *peer review*.

Interaction Matrix. A lightweight version of a traceability matrix that is used to figure out whether requirements are sufficiently detailed or if any entities are missing. See also *requirements traceability matrix* and *CRUD matrix*.

Interface Model. A model that shows how the solution interacts with other systems and users.

Internal Rate of Return (IRR). The projected annual yield of an investment, incorporating both initial and ongoing costs into an estimated percentage growth rate a given project is expected to have.

Interpersonal Skills. Skills used to establish and maintain relationships with other people.

Interrelationship Diagram. A special type of cause-and-effect diagram that depicts related causes and effects for a given situation. Interrelationship diagrams help to uncover the most significant causes and effects involved in a situation. See also *cause and effect diagram*.

Interview. A formal or informal approach to elicit information from stakeholders by asking questions and documenting the responses provided by the interviewees.

Intuitive Reasoning. Using instinct to drive decision making.

INVEST. The characteristics that user stories need to demonstrate to be considered "good" and "ready" for development in adaptive approaches. An acronym that is commonly considered to stand for the following characteristics: independent, negotiable, valuable, estimable, small, and testable.

Ishikawa Diagram. See *fishbone diagram* and *cause and effect diagram*.

Issue. A current condition or situation that may have an impact on the project objectives.

Iteration. On adaptive projects, an iteration is a development cycle that begins with an iteration planning session and ends with retrospectives. Iterations typically span 1-4 weeks.

Iteration 0. On adaptive projects, iteration 0 is the iteration where the initial planning for all iterations occur. In some approaches it might be called sprint 0.

Iteration Backlog. The subset of the product backlog that was chosen during iteration planning to be delivered during a specific iteration. Also known as a sprint backlog. See also *backlog* and *iteration planning*.

Iteration Planning. In adaptive approaches, iteration planning or sprint planning is the activity to identify the subset of work items that the product development team will work on for the current iteration or sprint.

Iterative Life Cycle. A project life cycle where the project scope is generally determined early in the project life cycle, but time and cost estimates are routinely modified as the project team's understanding of the product increases. Iterations develop the product through a series of repeated cycles, while increments successively add to the functionality of the product.

Job Analysis. A technique used to identify job requirements and the competencies needed to perform effectively in a specific job.

Kanban. An adaptive life cycle in which items are pulled from a backlog and started when other product backlog items are completed. Kanban also establishes work-in-progress limits to constrain the number of product backlog items that can be in progress at any point in time.

Kanban Board. A tool used within the continuous improvement method of Kanban to visually depict workflow and capacity and assist team members in seeing the work that is planned, in process, or completed. The kanban board is a variation of the original kanban cards.

Kano Analysis. A technique used to model and analyze product features by considering the features from the viewpoint of the customer.

Key Performance Indicator (KPI). Metrics usually defined by an organization's executives that are used to evaluate an organization's progress toward meeting the targets or end-states stated in their objectives or goals.

Key Stakeholder. A stakeholder who is identified as having a significant stake in a portfolio, program, or project, and who can hold key responsibilities such as approving requirements or approving changes to product scope.

Knowledge Area. A set of processes associated with a particular function.

Leadership. The actions and efforts of a group of people toward a common goal, which enables them to work as a team.

Leadership Skills. A category of skills in business analysis consisting of the skills to direct a group of people to work together toward a common goal.

Learner. A person who possesses a willingness to learn new skills, discover improved ways of doing things, and staying curious.

Lessons Learned. The knowledge gained during a project, which shows how project events were addressed or should be addressed in the future for the purpose of improving future performance.

Life Cycle Knowledge. Having familiarity with the different frameworks that a given industry uses to identify phases of product development, from envisioning and planning through construction, iteration, and end-of-life.

Logical Relationship. A dependency between two activities or between an activity and a milestone.

Logical System. Conceptual, business, or theoretical entities that represent how people think about subdividing parts of a solution.

Low Fidelity. A rough representation of something that enables someone to better understand the thing or functionality or concept which it illustrates.

Low-Fidelity Prototype. A method of prototyping that provides fixed sketches, diagrams, and notes to provide a visual representation of what a user interface will look like. Static prototypes do not demonstrate the operation of the system to the user; however, they are sometimes used to demonstrate navigation.

Low-Fidelity Wireframe. A method of prototyping or creating a mockup of web pages or screens that is sometimes used to demonstrate navigation. While some low-fidelity wireframes are created using electronic drawing tools, others are created using automated tools that support the evolution of the wireframe into a high-fidelity prototype.

Maintainability. The ease with which a product can be kept in good working order, including the ability to make appropriate modifications.

Manage Changes to Requirements and Other Product Information. The process of examining changes or defects that arise during a project by understanding the value and impact of the changes. As changes are agreed upon, information about those changes is reflected wherever necessary to support prioritization and eventual product development.

Manage Stakeholder Engagement and Communication. The process of fostering appropriate involvement in business analysis processes, keeping stakeholders appropriately informed about ongoing business analysis efforts, and sharing product information with stakeholders as it evolves.

Market Analysis. A technique used to obtain and analyze market characteristics and conditions for the market area an organization is operating in and overlaying this information with an organization's own plans and projections for growth.

Maturity Model. A standard that describes typical behaviors for a practice or set of practices as a series of levels, where each level represents increased levels of competence, independence, and perhaps even wisdom. A maturity model is used to assess individuals or organizations. Examples include the Capability Maturity Model and the Data Management Maturity Model.

Measure. The quantity of some element at a point in time or during a specific time duration, such as the number of work months spent on a project during a specific time period, the number of defects uncovered, or the number of customers responding to a survey stating that they were extremely satisfied.

Methodology. A system of practices, techniques, tools, procedures, and rules used by those who work in a discipline.

Metric. A set of quantifiable measures used to evaluate a solution or business.

Minimum Marketable Features (MMF). A prioritization mechanism in which the smallest piece of functionality that still delivers value to the customer is identified.

Minimum Viable Product (MVP). A prioritization mechanism to define the scope of the first release of a solution to customers by identifying the fewest number of features or requirements that would constitute a solution that the customer would obtain value from.

Model. A visual representation of information, both abstract and specific, which operates under a set of guidelines to efficiently arrange and convey a lot of information in an efficient manner.

Modeling Elaboration. A technique that uses the collection of models together to further identify gaps, inconsistencies, or redundancies in product information.

Modeling Language. A set of models and their syntax. Examples include Business Process Modeling Notation (BPMN), Requirements Modeling Language (RML), System Modeling Language (SysML), and Unified Modeling Language (UML).

Modeling Tools. A category of tools used in business analysis to develop visual representations of information for the purpose of communicating and analyzing information in a clear, efficient manner.

Monitoring. The process of collecting performance data, producing performance measures, and reporting and disseminating performance information.

Monitoring and Controlling Process Group. The processes performed on an ongoing basis to assess the impact of proposed product changes within a portfolio, program, or project to assess business analysis performance and to promote ongoing communication and engagement with stakeholders. In project management, the Monitoring and Controlling Process Group involves the tracking, reviewing, and reporting of progress to meet the performance objectives defined in the project management plan.

MoSCoW. A technique used for establishing requirement priorities where participants divide the requirements into four categories of must haves, should haves, could haves, and won't haves.

Multitasking. Being capable of performing more than one task at a time.

Multivoting Process. A technique used to facilitate decision making among a group of stakeholders. Multivoting processes can be used to prioritize requirements, determine the most favorable solution, or to identify the most favorable response to a problem.

Narrative. A story. In business analysis, narratives are written when developing personas.

Needs Assessment Knowledge Area. Includes the processes for analyzing current business problems or opportunities to understand what is necessary to attain the desired future state.

Negotiation. The process and activities used to resolve disputes through consultations between involved parties. Those who possess skills in negotiation are able to navigate conflict and disagreements, effectively bringing opposing viewpoints to a common ground.

Net Present Value (NPV). The future value of expected benefits expressed in the value those benefits have at the time of investment. NPV takes into account current and future costs and benefits, inflation, and the yield that could be obtained through investing in financial instruments as opposed to a portfolio component, program, or project.

Nonfunctional Requirement. A requirement that expresses an environmental condition or quality required for the product to be effective.

Nonverbal Communication. The ability to use unspoken communication methods to interact with stakeholders.

Normal Flow. Within the context of use case analysis, the normal flow is the set of steps that are followed through the use case scenario when everything goes as planned or expected.

Numeracy. The ability of being able to reason with numbers and other mathematical concepts and to apply these in a range of contexts and to solve a variety of problems. It is sometimes called *mathematical literacy*.

Objective. Something toward which work is to be directed, a strategic position to be attained, a purpose to be achieved, a result to be obtained, a product to be produced, or a service to be performed. In business analysis, objectives are quantifiable outcomes that are desired from a solution.

Objectivity. Listening to and encouraging the presentation of multiple perspectives on a given issue, weighing the merits of each perspective dispassionately and without bias, and avoiding taking sides prematurely.

Observation. An elicitation technique that provides a direct way of obtaining information about how a process is performed or a product is used by viewing individuals in their own environment performing their jobs or tasks and carrying out processes.

Obtain Solution Acceptance for Release. The process of facilitating a decision on whether to release a partial or full solution into production and eventually to an operational team, as well as transitioning knowledge and existing information about the product, its risks, known issues, and any workarounds that may have arisen in response to those issues.

Onion Diagram. A technique that can be used to model relationships between different aspects of a subject. In business analysis, an onion diagram can be created to depict the relationships existing between stakeholders and the solution.

Operational Feasibility. The extent to which a proposed solution meets operational needs and requirements related to a specific situation. It also includes factors such as sustainability, maintainability, supportability, and reliability.

Opportunity. A risk that would have a positive effect on one or more project objectives.

Opportunity Analysis. A study of the major facets of a potential opportunity to determine the viability of successfully launching a new solution.

Organizational Chart. A model that depicts the reporting structure within an organization or within a part of an organization.

Organizational Development/Change Management (OD/CM). Complementary approaches for improving the performance of an organization by catalyzing improvements in the actions of and interactions between individuals or teams.

Organizational Goal. A broad-based translation of a corporate goal into an expression that is actionable and measurable. Goals are typically longer in scope than objectives.

Organizational Objective. An accomplishment that an organization wants to achieve to help enable a goal. An organizational goal is specific and tends to be of shorter duration than a goal, often 1 year or less.

Organizational Process Assets (OPAs). Plans, processes, policies, procedures, and knowledge bases specific to and used by the performing organization.

Organizational System. A system composed of organizational components that are identifiable elements within an organization and provide a particular function or group of related functions. See also *system.*

Organizational Standard. See *business analysis organizational standard.*

Outcome. An end result or consequence of a process or actions.

Output. A product, result, or service generated by a process. May be an input to a successor process.

Pareto Diagram. A histogram, ordered by frequency of occurrence, that shows how many results were generated by each identified cause.

Participant. One who participates in a group activity, such as focus groups or facilitated workshops.

Payback Period (PBP). The time needed to recover an investment, usually in months or years.

Peer Desk Check. An informal peer review completed by one or multiple peers simultaneously to look over the materials. See also *peer review*.

Peer Review. Involves a review process where a coworker examines work completed by a business analyst. Commonly, the peer performing the review is another business analyst, manager, or quality control team member. See also *peer desk check*, *inspections*, and *walkthrough*.

Performance Data. A quantified output of a product.

Performance Domain. A complementary grouping of related areas of activity or function that uniquely characterize and differentiate the activities within it from the others within the full scope of some overall area of study. Portfolio Stakeholder Engagement is an example of one of several Portfolio Management Performance Domains within the full scope of portfolio management work.

Performance Measurement Baseline. Integrated scope, schedule, and cost baselines used for comparison to manage, measure, and control project execution.

Persona. An archetype user representing a set of similar end users described with their goals, motivations, and representative personal characteristics.

Persona Analysis. A technique that can be used to analyze a class of users or process workers to understand their needs or solution design and behavior requirements.

Personal Development. The efforts and actions taken to improve skills and knowledge.

Personal Skills. In business analysis, the set of skills and attributes that identify the personal qualities of an individual and enable them to build credibility with others.

Phase. See *project phase*.

Physical System. Entities such as systems or software that exist as part of a solution. They can be installed, implemented, touched, or seen.

Planning Approach. Decisions regarding how business analysis is to be conducted.

Planning Process Group. The business analysis processes performed to determine an optimal approach for performing business analysis activities, including how they are adapted for the chosen project life cycle, and to analyze the internal and external stakeholders who will interact and influence the overall definition of the solution. In project management, it consists of the processes required to establish the scope of the project, refine the objectives, and define the course of action required to attain the objectives that the project was undertaken to achieve.

Policy. A structured pattern of actions adopted by an organization such that the organization's policy can be explained as a set of basic principles that govern the organization's conduct.

Political Awareness. Being conscious of the human dynamics within a work environment as they relate to organizational levels, hierarchy, and the way power is distributed throughout.

Portfolio. Projects, programs, subsidiary portfolios, and operations managed as a group to achieve strategic objectives.

Portfolio Charter. A document issued by a sponsor that authorizes and specifies the portfolio structure and links the portfolio to the organization's strategic objectives.

Portfolio Component. A discrete element of a portfolio that is a program, project, or other work.

Portfolio Management. The centralized management of one or more portfolios to achieve strategic objectives.

Portfolio Risk Management. Portfolio activities related to actively identifying, monitoring, analyzing, accepting, mitigating, avoiding, or retiring portfolio risk.

Practice. The manner in which work is performed, which is less formal than a methodology, is not required, and is typically based on preferences or recommended conventions or approaches.

Predictive Life Cycle. A form of project life cycle in which the project scope, time, and cost are determined in the early phases of the life cycle.

Prepare for Elicitation. The process of organizing and scheduling resources and preparing necessary materials for an individual elicitation activity.

Prepare for Transition to Future State. The process of determining whether the organization is ready for a transition and how the organization will move from the current to the future state to integrate the solution or partial solution into the organization's operations.

Preproduction Testing. Testing a solution in a separate environment that is identical or nearly identical to the production environment, so that adverse interactions with other products in the production environment can be observed and addressed before the solution is released to production.

Prioritize Requirements and Other Product Information. The process of understanding how individual pieces of product information achieve stakeholder objectives, and using that information, along with other agreed-upon prioritization factors, to facilitate ranking of the work.

Prioritization Scheme. Different methods used to prioritize portfolio components, programs, projects, requirements, features, or any other product information.

Prioritized Requirements and Other Product Information. A representation of the requirements and other product information that stakeholders agree are most important to address first to achieve the business goals and objectives. See also *product information*.

Problem. An internal or external environmental area of an organization that is causing detriment to the organization, for example, lost revenue, dissatisfied customers, delays in launching new products, or noncompliance with government regulations.

Problem Solving. The ability to analyze an issue or difficult situation by performing sufficient analysis to understand the problem, identify possible options to address the situation, select and implement an effective solution, and monitor the outcomes to ensure the problem was sufficiently addressed.

Procedure. An established method of accomplishing a consistent performance or result. A procedure typically can be described as the sequence of steps that will be used to execute a process.

Process. A systematic series of activities directed toward causing an end result such that one or more inputs will be acted upon to create one or more outputs.

Process Flow. A business analysis model that visually shows the steps taken in a process by a human user as it interacts with a solution. A set of steps taken by a system can be shown in a similar model, called a system flow.

Process Model. See *process flow.*

Process Worker. The stakeholder who physically works with or within the business process that is under analysis or the user who works specifically with a system that is part of the business process. Not all process workers are users.

Product. An artifact that is produced, is quantifiable, and can be either an end item in itself or a component item. Additional words for products are materials and goods. See also *deliverable* and *service.*

Product Backlog. See *backlog.*

Product Backlog Item. A work item or item of value to the customer that has to be prioritized and completed.

Product Box. An elicitation technique that uses game play to focus on the features of a product that are important to the customer. See also *collaborative games.*

Product Document. Any documentation produced to support business analysis processes.

Product Information. All elements needed to produce a solution successfully. Product information can include one or more of the following: business, stakeholder, solution or transition requirements, models, assumptions, dependencies, constraints, issues, and risks.

Product Knowledge. Having an understanding about the different product offerings an organization provides to its customers, the strengths and weaknesses of each compared against competitor offerings, and the opportunities and threats existing for those offerings.

Product Life Cycle. The series of phases that represent the evolution of a product, from concept through delivery, growth, maturity, and to retirement.

Product Manager. An individual responsible for achieving customer and market success for a product.

Product Owner. An individual with decision-making authority for prioritizing what to include or exclude from one or more specific products.

Product Portfolio Matrix. A market analysis quadrant diagram that is used to qualitatively analyze products or product lines. One axis reflects market growth (or demand for a product) from low to high, while the other reflects the market share of the organization from low to high. The matrix provides a quick visual way to evaluate which products are meeting or exceeding performance expectations in the marketplace. Also known as a growth share matrix.

Product Quality Assurance. See *product quality control.*

Product Quality Control. The process of determining whether or not a delivered product meets or exceeds acceptance criteria. Referred to as product quality assurance (QA) in some organizations.

Product Requirement. Something that can be met by a solution and addresses a need of a business, person, or group of people. These type of requirement is part of the business analysis effort. See also *requirement, business requirement, stakeholder requirement, solution requirement, functional requirement, nonfunctional requirement,* and *transition requirement.*

Product Risk. An uncertainty that can affect success in definition, development, and expected results of the product or solution.

Product Risk Analysis. The consolidated results from identifying and analyzing product risks.

Product Roadmap. A high-level view of the features and functionality to include in a product, along with the sequence in which they will be built or delivered.

Product Scope. The features and functions that characterize a product, service, or result.

Product Stakeholder. An individual, group, or organization that may affect, be affected by, or perceive to be affected by the solution.

Product Vision. An explanation of the product, intended customers, and how needs will be met. The product vision is developed to help product teams envision what it is that needs to be built.

Product Visioning. A category of techniques a product team can use to obtain a shared understanding about the product and set the high-level direction for its development.

Professional Writing. The ability to communicate complex ideas clearly and succinctly using written language and demonstrating proficiency in the mechanics of writing and in the selection of the appropriate writing style.

Program. Related projects, subsidiary programs, and program activities managed in a coordinated manner to obtain benefits not available from managing them individually.

Program Charter. A document issued by a sponsor that authorizes the program management team to use organizational resources to execute the program and links the program to the organization's strategic objectives.

Program Management. The application of knowledge, skills, and principles to a program to achieve the program objectives and to obtain benefits and control not available by managing program components individually.

Program Risk Management. Program activities related to actively identifying, monitoring, analyzing, accepting, mitigating, avoiding, or retiring program risk.

Project. A temporary endeavor undertaken to create a unique product, service, or result.

Project Benefit. An outcome of an action, behavior, or product that provides value to the sponsoring organization as well as to the intended beneficiaries of the project.

Project Charter. A document issued by the project initiator or sponsor that formally authorizes the existence of a project and provides the project manager with the authority to apply organizational resources to project activities.

Project Life Cycle. The series of phases that a project passes through from its start to its completion.

Project Management. The application of knowledge, skills, tools, and techniques to project activities to meet the project requirements.

Project Management Plan. The document that describes how the project will be executed, monitored and controlled, and closed.

Project Manager (PM). The person assigned by the performing organization to lead the team that is responsible for achieving the project objectives.

Project Phase. A collection of logically related project activities that culminates in the completion of one or more deliverables.

Project Risk Management. The processes of conducting risk management planning, identification, analysis, response planning, response implementation, and monitoring risk on a project.

Project Schedule. An output of a schedule model that presents linked activities with planned dates, durations, milestones, and resources.

Project Scope. The work performed to deliver a product, service, or result with the specified features and functions.

Project Team. A set of individuals who support the project manager in performing the work of the project to achieve its objectives.

Proof of Concept (PoC). Also known as a prototype. See *prototype*.

Prototype. A representation of the expected solution before it is built.

Prototyping. A method of obtaining early feedback on requirements by providing a working model of the expected solution before actually building it.

Purpose Alignment Model. A technique that can be used to help facilitate discussions about priorities by placing product features on a matrix according to their criticality and market differentiation.

Quality Assurance (QA). The process of examining the effectiveness of quality control.

Quality Control (QC). See *product quality control*.

Questionnaire and Survey. A written set of questions designed to quickly accumulate information from a large number of respondents.

RACI Model. A common type of responsibility assignment matrix that uses responsible, accountable, consult, and inform statuses to define the involvement of stakeholders in project activities. Also known as a RACI chart.

Rational Reasoning. Using logic and reasoning to drive decision making.

Readiness Assessment. A determination of the ability and the interest of an organization to transition to the future state. The readiness assessment is used to identify any gaps in readiness that are considered risks to achieving the end state along with risk responses for addressing them. See also *transition plan*.

Real Options. A decision-making thought process that looks to reduce the number of decisions needing to be made in the short term and delays decision making until as late as is possible to reduce uncertainties.

Recommended Changes to Requirements and Other Product Information. The course of action that is proposed after analyzing all of the impacts associated to making a proposed change.

Recommended Solution Option. The solution choice determined the best approach for addressing the business need.

Refining the Backlog. See *backlog refinement*.

Regression Testing. Testing conducted to validate that new or enhanced functionality will not impact existing functionality.

Regulation. A requirement imposed by a governmental body. A requirement can establish a product, process, or service characteristic, including an applicable administrative provision that has government-mandated compliance.

Regulatory Standard. The criteria established by a governmental or industry or organizational body as to what constitutes compliance with rules and constraints. Regulatory standards can be imposed on products or on the procedures used to create or modify products.

Relationship Building. Social skills that enable one to develop partnerships and to operate as an effective member of a team or a group.

Relationships and Dependencies. The linkages established between objects, like components of product information, deliverables, and project work.

Relative Estimation. A technique for creating estimates that are derived from performing a comparison against a similar body of work rather than estimating based on absolute units of cost or time. See also *estimation poker*.

Release. One or more components of one or more products, which are intended to be put into production at the same time.

Release Decision. An agreement to either permit the release or partial release of the solution, delay it, or disapprove and prevent it. A release decision often includes a signoff.

Releasing Process Group. The business analysis process performed to determine whether all or part of a solution should be released and to obtain acceptance that all or part of a solution is ready to be transitioned to an operational team that will take ongoing responsibility for it.

Reliability. The capability of a product to operate error free, to maintain its level of performance under stated conditions, or for a stated period or percentage of time.

Report Table. A business analysis model that documents, in a tabular format, all of the requirements necessary to develop a single report.

Reporting and Analysis Tools. A category of tools used in business analysis for processing, analyzing, and reporting information at different levels of granularity.

Required Capabilities and Features. The list of net changes the organization will need to obtain in order to achieve the desired future state.

Requirement. A condition or capability that is necessary to be present in a product, service, or result to satisfy a business need.

Requirement State. An attribute of a requirement that identifies where the requirement falls within the requirements life cycle, for example, in-process, approved, deferred, or rejected.

Requirements and Other Product Information. See *product information*.

Requirements Architecture. Describes how requirements, models, and other product information or elements of those relate to each other.

Requirements Attribute. A property of a requirement used to store descriptive information about the requirement, such as last change date, author, source, etc.

Requirements Change Process. The process that defines how changes to requirements will be handled.

Requirements Definition. The process of specifying requirements and other types of product information at the appropriate level of detail, format, and level of formality.

Requirements Documentation. A record of product requirements and other product information, along with whatever is recorded to manage it. The degree of formality of requirements documentation depends upon the business analysis approach.

Requirements Elicitation. The activity of drawing out information from stakeholders and other sources for the purpose of further understanding the needs of the business, to address a problem or opportunity and the stakeholder's preferences and conditions for the solution that will address those needs.

Requirements Life Cycle. The flow or life of a requirement throughout a portfolio, program, or project. The requirement life cycle is managed by assigning an attribute or qualifier onto the requirement to depict the requirement state at a specified point in time.

Requirements Management Tool. A software product that allows for the capture and storage of requirements and other product information in a repository. Requirements management tools have features to assist in managing and maintaining requirements throughout the product life cycle.

Requirements Package. The culmination of a set of product information that is used to communicate information about the solution at a specific point in time (e.g., at the end of a phase or iteration). When using an adaptive delivery approach, the requirements package is often not composed of a formal set of documentation. Requirements packages can also be established in the requirements management tools.

Requirements Traceability Matrix. A grid that links product requirements from their origin to the deliverables that satisfy them.

Requirements Validation. The process of ensuring that the solution satisfies its intended use and anticipated value, ensuring the correct solution is delivered.

Research Skill. An ability to elicit useful information from relevant sources in a timely and effective manner.

Resourcefulness. Using alternative or creative means to elicit information and solve problems, especially when a clear or conventional solution is not available.

Retrospective. A type of meeting in which participants explore their work and results in order to improve both process and product. Retrospectives can occur on a regular basis (e.g., end of iteration or release), at the completion of a milestone, or after a special event (e.g., organizational change, accident).

Return on Investment (ROI). The percent return on an initial investment, calculated by taking the projected average of all net benefits and dividing them by the initial cost.

Risk Appetite. The degree of uncertainty an organization or individual is willing to accept in anticipation of a reward.

Risk Burndown Chart. On adaptive projects, risk burndown charts are used to show the status of risks across iterations. See *burndown chart.*

Risk Exposure. An aggregate measure of the potential impact of all risks at any given point in time in a project, program, or portfolio.

Risk Register. A repository in which outputs of risk management processes are recorded.

Risk Spike. A sprint or iteration specifically designated for research to address product risks. *See also spike.*

Role. In business analysis, a role represents a defined function to be performed by a product team member, such as research, analyze, model, specify, review, or update.

Rolling Wave Planning. An iterative planning technique in which the work to be accomplished in the near term is planned in detail, while the work in the future is planned at a higher level.

Root Cause Analysis. An analytical technique used to determine the basic underlying reason that causes a variance, a defect, or a risk. A root cause may underlie more than one variance, defect, or risk.

Rule Model. A model of concepts and behaviors that defines or constrains aspects of a business in order to enforce established business policies.

Scenario. A case of usage of a solution often manifested as a concrete example of a use case or user story or several functional requirements specified in the sequence in which they occur.

Schedule. See *project schedule*.

Scope. In business analysis, scope is defined as the boundary for the solution. In project management, scope is defined as the sum of the products, services, and results to be provided as a project. See also *project scope* and *product scope*.

Scope Creep. The uncontrolled expansion of a product or project scope without adjustments to time, cost, and resources.

Scope Model. A type of model that identifies the boundaries of the project, program, product, and/or system under analysis. A context diagram is one example of a scope model.

Scrum. A type of adaptive life cycle where a solution is built in small incremental portions and each cycle of development builds upon the last version of the product.

Segment. A portion of a product that is to be delivered in an iteration, a sprint, or a release.

Select and Approve Requirements. The process of facilitating discussions with stakeholders to negotiate and confirm which requirements should be incorporated within an iteration, release, or project.

Sequence Diagram. A modeling technique that describes how user or system processes interact with one another across any involved users or systems and the order in which the processes or steps are performed.

Self-Awareness. Being capable of identifying how one's actions are perceived by others. Self-awareness is also known as emotional intelligence.

Service. The performance of duties or work for another party. A service is a type of product. See also *product*.

Shared Product Information. Consists of the compilation of all the information discussed and shared across the product team during collaboration.

Simulated Production Testing. Testing a solution in a separate environment that is production-like, reduced in size, and contains small representative, cohesive samples of any data that are part of that environment. Simulated production testing is performed so that adverse interactions with other products can be observed and addressed before a solution is released to production.

Situation. A condition that may be an internal problem or external opportunity that forms the basis of a business need and might result in a portfolio component, program, or project to address the condition.

Situation Statement. An objective statement of a problem or opportunity that includes the statement itself, the situation's effect on the organization, and the ultimate impact.

Solution. Something that is produced to deliver measurable business value to meet the business need and expectations of stakeholders. It defines what a specific portfolio component, program, or project will deliver. A solution could be one or more new products, components of products, or enhancements or corrections to a product. See also *product*.

Solution Capability Matrix. A model that provides a simple, visual way to examine capabilities and solution components in one view.

Solution Design. Specifications and diagrams, typically based on business analysis findings, which describe how the solution will be implemented.

Solution Evaluation Knowledge Area. Includes the processes for validating a full solution, or a segment of a solution, that is about to be, or has already been implemented to determine how well a solution meets the business needs and delivers value to the organization.

Solution Evaluation Approach. Describes when and how a solution will be evaluated, the types of metrics that will support evaluation, the feasibility of collecting and communicating the actual performance data for these metrics, and who is responsible for conducting the evaluation and communicating results.

Solution Option. An approach for addressing a business need.

Solution Requirement. A requirement that describes the features, functions, and characteristics of a product, which will meet business and stakeholder requirements. Solution requirements are further grouped into functional and nonfunctional requirements.

Specialty Resource. An individual who plays a highly focused role within a portfolio, program, or project such as an architect or a release manager.

Speedboat. An elicitation technique that uses game play to elicit information about product features that stakeholders find problematic. See also *collaborative games*.

Spider Web. An elicitation technique that uses game play to discover unknown relationships between the product being analyzed and other products. See also *collaborative games*.

Spike. A short time interval within a project, usually of fixed length, during which a team conducts research or prototypes an aspect of a solution to prove its viability.

Sponsor. An individual or group that provides resources and support for the project, program, or portfolio and is accountable for enabling success.

Sprint. A short time interval within a project, usually of fixed length, during which a team commits to deliver a specified production-ready segment of a solution to its sponsors.

Stakeholder. An individual, group, or organization that may affect, be affected by, or perceive itself to be affected by a decision, activity, or outcome of a project, program, or portfolio.

Stakeholder Analysis. A technique of systematically gathering and analyzing quantitative and qualitative information to determine whose interests should be taken into account throughout an initiative.

Stakeholder Characteristics. The qualities and attributes of a stakeholder, which together determine aspects of how the stakeholder behaves.

Stakeholder Engagement and Communication Approach. Describes how best to effectively involve, interact, and communicate with stakeholders.

Stakeholder Engagement Knowledge Area. Includes the processes for identifying and analyzing those who have an interest in the outcome of the solution to determine how to collaborate and communicate with them.

Stakeholder Groups. A collection of stakeholders who have similar likes, interests, and characteristics. Stakeholder groups are used to manage large groups of stakeholders.

Stakeholder Identification. The process of determining the stakeholders impacted by a business problem or opportunity.

Stakeholder Map. A technique used to visually analyze stakeholders and their relationship to each other and to the problem or opportunity under analysis.

Stakeholder Matrix. A technique that uses a quadrant or matrix to analyze a set of stakeholders.

Stakeholder Register. A project document that includes the identification, assessment, and classification of project stakeholders.

Stakeholder Requirement. A requirement that describes the needs of a stakeholder or stakeholder group.

Standard. A document established by an authority, custom, or general consent as a model or example.

State Diagram. A data model used to show the valid states of an object and allowed transitions between them. Unlike state tables, which systematically consider and model all possible transitions, state diagrams model only the valid transitions of an object.

State Table. A data model used to show the valid states of an object and allowed transitions between them. All states are modeled as both a column and row in a table and systemic consideration is given to determine whether each potential state transition is permitted.

Storyboarding. A prototyping technique that shows sequence or navigation through a series of images or illustrations. See also *prototyping*.

Story Elaboration. The process by which user stories are supplemented with additional information from conversations with business stakeholders until they are sufficiently detailed for product development to begin work.

Story Mapping. A technique used to sequence user stories, based upon their business value and the order in which their users typically perform them, so that teams can arrive at a shared understanding of what will be built.

Story Points. A unit used to estimate the relative level of effort needed to implement a user story.

Story Slicing. A technique to split epics or user stories from a higher level to a lower level.

Subject Matter Expert (SME). A person who is considered an expert in a particular subject area.

Success Criteria. Measures that can be used to determine solution success.

Support Charter Development. The process of collaborating on charter development with the sponsoring entity and stakeholder resources using the business analysis knowledge, experience, and product information acquired during needs assessment and business case development efforts.

Supportability. The ease at which a solution can be maintained and managed by the organization over time, including the cost and level of effort.

Surveys. See *questionnaire and survey*.

SWOT Analysis. Analysis of strengths, weaknesses, opportunities, and threats of an organization, initiative, or option.

System. A collection of various components that together can produce results not obtainable by the individual components alone. See also *organizational system*.

System Interface Table. A model that depicts the requirements for the connections between interfacing systems, including how they are connected and what information flows between them.

Systems Thinking. The ability to analyze from both a holistic and detailed point of view. When applied at an organizational level, the organization is viewed as a system comprised of component parts made up of people, processes, and tools.

Tacit Knowledge. Personal knowledge that can be difficult to articulate and share such as beliefs, experience, and insights.

Team and Subject Matter Expert Knowledge. Knowledge that is usually not fully and formally documented but instead resides in the minds of individuals or groups.

Technical Debt. The accumulation of architectural and design and construction shortcuts during product development, which tend to make a product more difficult to maintain and enhance.

Technique. A defined systematic procedure employed by a human resource to perform an activity to produce a product or result or deliver a service, and that may employ one or more tools.

Technology Feasibility. An analysis to determine the extent to which a technology exists in an organization to support a potential solution and, if not present, how feasible it would be to acquire and operate the needed technology.

Templates. A partially completed document in a predefined format that provides a defined structure for collecting, organizing, and presenting information and data.

Test-Driven Development. A "test-first" approach that defines requirements in terms of test cases and then constructs a solution which can pass the tests. See also *behavior-driven development (BDD)*.

Time Feasibility. An analysis to determine how well a proposed solution can be delivered to meet the organization's needed timeframe.

Time-bound. Having a limit or constraint that is based on a point in time.

Timeboxing. An estimation or planning technique that can be used during prioritization by setting a strict time limit and prioritizing only the work the team can complete in that duration of time.

Time Management. The ability to stay organized, be productive, estimate and sequence work, and plan effectively.

Tool. Something tangible, such as a template or software program, used in performing an activity to produce a product or result.

Tool Knowledge. In business analysis, represents the collective knowledge a practitioner possesses about the toolset they utilize to perform their work.

Traceability. The ability to track information across the product life cycle by establishing linkages between objects.

Traceability and Monitoring Knowledge Area. Includes the processes for tracing, approving, and assessing changes to product information to manage it throughout the business analysis effort.

Traceability and Monitoring Approach. Defines how the traceability and change management activities will be performed throughout the portfolio, program, project, or product.

Traceability Matrix. See *requirements traceability matrix*.

Transition Plan. Defines the activities required to transition from the current to future state. Transition plans are developed from the results obtained from the readiness assessment and objectives as stated in the transition strategy. Encompasses actionable and testable transition requirements. See also *readiness assessment*.

Transition Requirement. A requirement that is a temporary capability, such as data conversion and training requirements, needed to transition from the current as-is state to the future state.

Transition Strategy. A guiding framework for conducting activities that are needed to transition from a current state to a future state.

Trigger. As an act or event, anything that serves as a stimulus and initiates or precipitates a reaction or series of reactions. Within the context of risk, a trigger is an event or situation that indicates that a risk is about to occur.

Trusted Advisor. A personal characteristic that signifies a person is trustworthy, competent, reliable, and held in high regard by others.

Unconfirmed Elicitation Result. The business analysis information obtained from completed elicitation activities. Elicitation results that are unconfirmed have not been agreed upon and validated for accuracy by the product team.

Use Case. An analysis model that describes a flow of actor-system interactions and boundaries for those interactions, including trigger, initiating and participating actors, and preconditions and post conditions.

Use Case Diagram. A business analysis model that shows all of the in-scope use cases for a solution and which actors have a part in those use cases.

User. A type of stakeholder or actor who will use the product.

User Class. A group of stakeholders who are users of a product and are grouped together due to the similarity in their requirements and use of the product.

User Experience Analyst. Also referred to as user interface analysts; individuals who are responsible for studying user behavior, preferences, and constraints to identify user interface and usability requirements for software applications and other products.

User Interface (UI). Anything that supports the interaction between a person and service that is provided to that person. Typically used to reference web pages, smartphone displays, and screen front-ends, but also applies more broadly to anything that is the intermediary between a person and whatever provides the service, such as the push buttons on a landline telephone or the cruise control buttons on a car steering wheel.

User Interface Analyst. See *user experience analyst*.

User Interface Design. The art and science of creating a user interface that meets users' interface requirements while exploiting the features of—and staying within the constraints of—overall organizational best practices related to how humans interact with the chosen type of interface.

User Interface Flow. A business analysis model that shows the specific pages or screens of an application and how a user can navigate between them.

User Story. A one or two sentence description written from the viewpoint of the actor that describes a function that is needed. A user story usually takes the form of "as an <actor>, I want to <function>, so that I can <benefit>."

Validate Requirements. The process of checking that the requirements meet business goals and objectives.

Validated Requirements and Other Product Information. Product information that the stakeholders agree meet the business goals and objectives. See also *product information*.

Validation. The assurance that a product, service, or result meets the needs of the customer and other identified stakeholders. Contrast with *verification*.

Valuation Technique. A technique used to quantify the return or value that an option will provide. Valuation techniques are utilized when conducting a cost-benefit analysis to establish criteria for objectively assessing a solution.

Value. A measure of the worth of a benefit.

Value Stream Map. A variation of process flows that can be used to locate delays, queues, or handoffs occurring in current processes. See also *process flow*.

Velocity. A measure of expected team productivity, typically expressed as the total story points expected to be delivered during an iteration or sprint.

Variance. A quantifiable deviation, departure, or divergence from a known baseline or expected value.

Variance Analysis. A technique for determining the cause and degree of difference between the baseline and actual performance.

Vendor Assessment. An evaluation of vendors and their products or services offered to understand the viability, strengths, weaknesses, and risks of each vendor solution.

Verification. The evaluation of whether or not a product, service, or result complies with a regulation, requirement, specification, or imposed condition. Contrast with *validation*.

Verified Requirements and Other Product Information. Product information that has been evaluated to assure it is free from errors and addresses the quality standards to which the information will be held. See also *product information*.

Verify Requirements. The process of checking that requirements are of sufficient quality.

Version Control. The process of maintaining a history of changes on software or documentation.

Version Control System (VCS). A system that is used to track the history of revisions, often but not always related to software.

Viable Design Option. A design option that has been reviewed by stakeholders and determined to be a feasible means for achieving the business goals and objectives.

Visual Communication Skill. The ability to communicate through the use of models and visual representations and knowing when best to use these representations over the spoken or written words.

Vision Statement. A summarized, high-level description about the expectations for a product such as target market, users, major benefits, and what differentiates the product from others in the market.

Walking Skeleton. A foundational part of a story map representing the full set of end-to-end functionality that the stakeholders require for the solution to be accepted or functional. This set of user stories is sometimes called the minimum marketable features. See also *story mapping* and *minimum marketable features (MMF)*.

Walkthrough. A technique used to review or share a set of information with stakeholders to obtain feedback or approval. Requirements walkthroughs are used to review requirements and to receive confirmation that the requirements as stated are valid.

Warranty Period. An agreed-upon interval during which a solution released to production is maintained by the team that developed it before it is turned over to the business operational area which owns it.

Waterfall Approach. An example of predictive project life cycle.

Weighted Criteria. Evaluation criteria that is adjusted by applying a multiplier to signify how important the criterion is to the decision-making process. Weighted criteria are used to evaluate the list of options participants are deciding upon when performing weighted ranking. See also *weighted ranking*.

Weighted Ranking. A technique to weight, rate, and score each criterion against a set of options used to add objectivity when formulating a decision or recommendation.

Weighted Ranking Matrix. A table used when performing the weighted ranking technique to weight, rate, and score each criteria against a set of options.

Weighted Shortest Job First (WSJF). A method used primarily in adaptive frameworks to rank user stories based on more dimensions than just business value and effort. WSJF= (business value + time criticality + (risk reduction/ opportunity enablement))/effort.

Wide-Band Delphi Technique. A variation of the Delphi technique which is sometimes used to bring convergence to widely differing estimates that have been developed separately for the same work item by a number of different individuals. For wide-band Delphi, those who created the highest and lowest estimates explain their rationale, following which everyone re-estimates. The process repeats until convergence is achieved. See also *Delphi*.

Wireframe. A diagram that represents a static blueprint or schematic of a user interface and is used to identify basic functionality. See also *prototyping*.

Work Breakdown Structure (WBS). A hierarchical decomposition of the total scope of work to be carried out by the project team to accomplish the project objectives and create the required deliverables.

Work Ethic. Being capable of completing tasks independently and being motivated and driven to do what needs to be done without being asked.

Work in Progress Limit. An agreed-upon maximum number of product backlog items that can be in a given state of the development workflow at the same time within the same project. Commonly referred to as WIP Limits.

Work Product. An output produced as a result of some completion of work.

INDEX

D

Data
  See also Business data object
  model, 393
  repositories, 38
  store, 393
Data dictionaries
  in Create and Analyze Models process, 187–188
  definition, 393
Data flow diagram, 188, 393
  for Assemble Business Case process, 97
  for Assess Business Analysis Performance process, 145
  for Assess Current State process, 64
  for Assess Product Design Options process, 245
  for Conduct Business Analysis Planning process, 128
  for Conduct Elicitation process, 164
  for Conduct Stakeholder Analysis process, 115
  for Confirm Elicitation Results process, 170
  for Create and Analyze Models process, 183
  for Define Acceptance Criteria process, 216–217
  for Define and Elaborate Requirements process, 208–209
  for Determine Analysis Approach process, 178
  for Determine Elicitation Approach process, 156
  for Determine Future State process, 75
  for Determine Solution Evaluation Approach process, 286
  for Determine Stakeholder Engagement and Communication Approach process, 123
  for Determine Traceability and Monitoring Approach process, 254
  for Determine Viable Options and Provide Recommendation process, 85
  for Evaluate Acceptance Results and Address Defects process, 291
  for Evaluate Solution Performance process, 280
  for Facilitate Product Roadmap Development process, 93
  for Identify and Analyze Product Risks process, 238
  for Identify Problem or Opportunity process, 58
  for Identify Stakeholders process, 111
  for Manage Changes to Requirements and Other Product Information process, 270
  for Manage Stakeholder Engagement and Communication process, 142
  for Obtain Solution Acceptance for Release process, 294–295
  for Prepare for Elicitation process, 160
  for Prepare for Transition to Future State process, 136
  for Prioritize Requirements and Other Product Information process, 230
  for Select and Approve Requirements process, 263
  for Support Charter Development process, 103
  for Validate Requirements process, 225–226
  for Verify Requirements process, 221
Day-in-the-life testing (DITL), 291, 393
Decision
  See also Autocratic decision making; Delphi
  by consensus, 393
  by sponsor, 393
  by weighted analysis, 393
Decision making, 368, 394
  group, 89, 139, 267, 273, 289, 298
  techniques, 89, 139, 267, 273, 289, 298
Decision tables, 394
  in Create and Analyze Models process, 189
  decision tree and, 189
Decision trees, 394
  in Create and Analyze Models process, 189–190
  decision table and, 189–190
Decomposition models
  for Conduct Business Analysis Planning process, 132
  definition, 394
DEEP. *See* Detailed appropriately, estimated, emergent, prioritized
Define Acceptance Criteria process, 175, 216–220, 337, 394
Define and Elaborate Requirements process, 25, 175, 208–216, 337, 394
Defining and Aligning Process Group, 21–22, 313, 314–317, 319–323, 394
Definition of done (DoD)
  in Define Acceptance Criteria process, 219
  definition, 394
Definition of ready, 394
  in Define and Elaborate Requirements process, 212
  in Select and Approve Requirements process, 265
Delighters, 80

Fishbone diagram
   See also Cause and effect diagram
   of Assess Current State process, 70, 71
   definition, 397
Five-Whys technique
   in Assess Current State process, 72
   definition, 398
Focus groups, 398
   in Assess Product Design Options process, 247
   in Conduct Elicitation process, 167
   in Evaluate Solution Performance process, 283
Force field analysis
   definition, 398
   in Select and Approve Requirements process, 266
Formality, 398
Forward traceability, 398
Foundational elements, 14–20
Functional managers, 50
Functional requirement, 10, 398
Future state, 398

G

Gap analysis
   definition, 398
   in Determine Future State process, 79
Geographic distribution, 34
Glossary, 398
   for Assemble Business Case process, 101
   for Assess Current State process, 69
   for Confirm Elicitation Results process, 172
   for Define and Elaborate Requirements process,
     212–213
   for Support Charter Development process, 106
Goal, 398
Goal model, 398
   business objectives model and, 194–195, 228, 233
   in Create and Analyze Models process, 194–195
   in Prioritize Requirements and Other Product
     Information process, 233
   in Validate Requirements process, 228
Good practice, 4
Governance, 34, 50
Government, 34, 50
Ground rule, 398

Group decision-making techniques, 89, 139, 267, 273,
   289, 298
Growth share matrix. *See* Product portfolio matrix
Guide, 305, 351–355
   audience for, 5
   BAs used by, 44
   Business Analysis for Practitioners: A Practice Guide
     used with, 8
   business analysis professional used by, 44
   components of, 20–30
   need for, 4–5
   overview, 3–4
   product information used by, 28
   purpose of, 3–4
A Guide to the Project Management Body of Knowledge
   (*PMBOK® Guide*) (PMI), 11, 112, 309

H

High fidelity, 199, 200, 207, 398
Human resources management policies and procedures, 35

I

Identify and Analyze Product Risks process, 175,
   237–244, 339, 398
Identify Problem or Opportunity process, 55, 57–63
Identify Stakeholders process, 109, 111–114, 323, 398
Impact analysis, 399
   of Establish Relationships and Dependencies process,
     258
   of Manage Changes to Requirements and Other
     Product Information: Tools and Techniques,
     273–274
Implementation dependency, 259
Independent, negotiable, valuable, estimable, small,
   testable (INVEST) characteristics
   definition, 399
   of Verify Requirements process, 223
Indifferent features, 80
Industry knowledge, 372
   BAs leveraging, 52
   definition, 399
Industry standards, 34
Influences, 31–33
Information technology (IT), 35, 44, 45

for Identify Problem or Opportunity Process, 61
for Identify Stakeholders process, 113
for Prepare for Elicitation process, 162
for Prepare for Transition to Future State process, 139
for Support Charter Development process, 106
Intuitive reasoning, 368, 399
INVEST characteristics. *See* Independent, negotiable, valuable, estimable, small, testable characteristics
IRR. *See* Internal rate of return
Ishikawa diagram. *See* Cause and effect diagram; Fishbone diagram
Issues
    of Define and Elaborate Requirements process, 210
    definition, 399
IT. *See* Information technology
Iteration, 315–316, 399
Iteration 0, 316, 399
Iteration backlog, 233, 274, 400
Iteration planning, 400
    for Prioritize Requirements and Other Product Information process, 233
    for Select and Approve Requirements process, 267
Iterative life cycles, 311, 400

J

Job analysis, 400
    of Conduct Stakeholder Analysis process, 117
    of Prepare for Transition to Future State process, 140

K

Kanban, 233, 311, 400
Kano analysis
    definition, 400
    in Determine Future State process, 79–80
KAs. *See* Knowledge Areas
Key performance indicators (KPIs)
    definition, 400
    of Determine Solution Evaluation Approach process, 287–288
Key stakeholder, 139, 327, 400
Knowledge areas (KAs), 22–25, 31, 131, 312–313, 400

Knowledge repositories, 38
KPIs. *See* Key performance indicators

L

Leadership, 54, 378–379, 400
Learner, 376, 400
Legal restrictions, 33
Lessons learned, 400
    of Assess Business Analysis Performance process, 149–150
    of Determine Analysis Approach process, 181
    of Determine Elicitation Approach process, 158
    of Determine Stakeholder Engagement and Communication Approach process, 126
    of Determine Traceability and Monitoring Approach process, 256
Life cycle knowledge, 39, 372, 400
Logical relationship, 240, 400
Logical system, 190, 400
Low fidelity, 199, 200, 207, 401
Low-fidelity prototype, 199, 200, 207, 401
Low-fidelity wireframe, 199, 200, 207, 401

M

Maintainability, 401
Majority, 267
Manage Changes to Requirements and Other Product Information process, 251, 269–275, 343, 401
Manage Stakeholder Engagement and Communication process, 109, 142–144, 342, 401
Managing risk, 7
Market analysis
    definition, 401
    of Identify Problem or Opportunity process, 61
Marketplace conditions, 33
Market research, 34
Maturity model, 86, 137, 141, 401
Measure, 287, 401
Measuring
    business value, 19
    project success, 20
Methodology, 26, 401

Risk
See also Spike
appetite, 33, 34, 410
exposure, 410
managing of, 7
Risk burndown chart
definition, 410
in Identify and Analyze Product Risks process, 242
Risk register
definition, 410
in Identify and Analyze Product Risks process, 243
Risk spike, 242, 244, 410
ROI. *See* Return on investment
Roles, 411
of BAs, 43–54, 308–309
boundaries, 7–8
governance, 50
Rolling wave planning
in Conduct Business Analysis Planning process, 134
definition, 411
Root cause analysis, 411
in Assess Business Analysis Performance process, 150
in Assess Current State process, 70–72
in Evaluate Acceptance Results and Address Defects process, 293
in Evaluate Solution Performance process, 284–285
in Identify and Analyze Product Risks process, 243
Rule model, 184, 189, 212, 411

S

Scenarios, 411
in Determine Viable Options and Provide Recommendation process, 89
in Facilitate Product Roadmap Development process, 93
Schedule. *See* Project schedule
Scope
See also Product scope; Project scope
creep, 411
definition, 411
Establish Relationships and Dependencies process managing, 258
model, 411
Scrum, 311, 411

Security, 35
Segment, 22, 137, 277, 312, 319, 345, 411
Select and Approve Requirements process, 251, 263–269, 340, 411
Self-awareness, 377, 411
Sequence diagram, 199, 411
Service, 9, 117, 306, 411
See also Product
Shared product information
definition, 411
of Support Charter Development process, 107
Simulated production testing, 291, 411
Situation, 411
analysis of, 98
Situation statement, 412
of Assemble Business Case process, 100
of Assess Current State process, 66
of Conduct Elicitation process, 165
of Conduct Stakeholder Analysis process, 117
of Determine Analysis Approach process, 180
of Determine Elicitation Approach process, 157
of Determine Future State process, 77
of Determine Solution Evaluation Approach process, 288
of Determine Stakeholder Engagement and Communication Approach process, 125
of Determine Viable Options and Provide Recommendation process, 88
of Identify Problem or Opportunity process, 62
of Identify Stakeholders process, 112
of Prepare for Elicitation process, 162
SMEs. *See* Subject matter experts
Social influences, 33
Social issues, 33
Solution
definition, 13, 412
option, 412
overview, 13
Solution capability matrix
definition, 412
in Determine Future State process, 82–83
Solution design
definition, 412
in Prepare for Transition to Future State process, 138–139

of Prioritize Requirements and Other Product
Information process, 235–236
of Select and Approve Requirements process, 268
Story points, 213, 413
Story slicing
for Define and Elaborate Requirements process, 214
for Establish Relationships and Dependencies
process, 261
Strengths, weaknesses, opportunities, threats (SWOT)
analysis, 414
in Assess Current State process, 72–73
in Identify and Analyze Product Risks process, 243
in Prepare for Transition to Future State process, 140
Structure, 34
Subject matter experts (SMEs), 14, 36, 39, 211, 234, 275
BAs working with, 51–52
definition, 413
review, 352
Subsets, 259
Success criteria, 20, 413
Supportability, 10, 86, 414
Support Charter Development process, 55, 103–107,
309, 325–326, 413
Surveys. *See* Questionnaires and surveys
SWOT analysis. *See* Strengths, weaknesses,
opportunities, threats analysis
System interface tables
in Create and Analyze Models process, 205–206
definition, 414
Systems, 414
See also Organizational system
thinking, 370

T

Tacit knowledge, 38, 414
Tailoring, 25–30, 46
adaptive, 62, 74, 84, 91–92, 96, 102, 107, 114, 122,
127, 135, 141, 144, 151, 159, 163, 169, 173, 182,
216, 220, 225, 229, 237, 244, 257, 262, 268, 275,
285, 290, 294, 298
of Assemble Business Case process, 102
of Assess Business Analysis Performance process,
151
of Assess Current State process, 74

of Assess Product Design Options process, 249
of business analysis plan, 311–312
of Conduct Business Analysis Planning process, 135
of Conduct Elicitation process, 169
of Conduct Stakeholder Analysis process, 122
of Confirm Elicitation Results process, 173
considerations, 62, 74, 84, 91–92, 96, 102, 107, 114,
122, 127, 135, 141, 144, 151, 159, 163, 169, 173,
182, 216, 220, 225, 237, 244, 249, 257, 262, 268,
275, 285, 290, 294, 298
of Create and Analyze Models process, 208
of Define Acceptance Criteria process, 220
of Define and Elaborate Requirements process, 216
of Determine Analysis Approach process, 182
of Determine Elicitation Approach process, 159
of Determine Future State process, 84
of Determine Solution Evaluation Approach process,
290
of Determine Stakeholder Engagement and
Communication Approach process, 127
of Determine Traceability and Monitoring Approach
process, 257
of Determine Viable Options and Provide
Recommendation process, 91–92
of Establish Relationships and Dependencies process,
262
of Evaluate Acceptance Results and Address Defects
process, 294
of Evaluate Solution Performance process, 285
of Facilitate Product Roadmap Development process,
96
of Identify and Analyze Product Risks process, 244
of Identify Problem or Opportunity process, 62
of Identify Stakeholders process, 114
of Manage Changes to Requirements and Other
Product Information process, 275
of Manage Stakeholder Engagement and
Communication process, 144
of Obtain Solution Acceptance for Release process,
298
predictive, 62, 74, 84, 91–92, 96, 102, 107, 114, 122,
127, 135, 141, 144, 151, 159, 163, 169, 173, 182,
216, 220, 225, 229, 237, 244, 257, 262, 268, 275,
285, 290, 294, 298
of Prepare for Elicitation process, 163

WIP limits. *See* Work in progress limits

Wireframes, 199–200

    See also Prototyping

    definition, 417

Work breakdown structure (WBS)

    for Conduct Business Analysis Planning process, 134

    definition, 417

Work ethic, 377, 417

Work in progress limits, 233, 417

Work products

    of Assess Business Analysis Performance process, 148

    definition, 417

WSJF. *See* Weighted shortest job first